Spinoza, the Epicurean

Spinoza Studies
Series editor: Filippo Del Lucchese, Brunel University London

Seminal works devoted to Spinoza that challenge mainstream scholarship

This series aims to broaden the understanding of Spinoza in the Anglophone world by making some of the most important work by continental scholars available in English translation for the first time. Some of Spinoza's most important themes – that right is coextensive with power, that every political order is based on the power of the multitude, the critique of superstition and the rejection of the idea of providence – are explored by these philosophers in detail and in ways that will open up new possibilities for reading and interpreting Spinoza.

Editorial Advisory board

Saverio Ansaldi, Étienne Balibar, Chiara Bottici, Laurent Bove, Mariana de Gainza, Moira Gatens, Thomas Hippler, Susan James, Chantal Jaquet, Mogens Laerke, Beth Lord, Pierre Macherey, Nicola Marcucci, Alexandre Matheron, Dave Mesing, Warren Montag, Pierre-François Moreau, Vittorio Morfino, Antonio Negri, Susan Ruddick, Martin Saar, Pascal Sévérac, Hasana Sharp, Diego Tatián, Dimitris Vardoulakis, Lorenzo Vinciguerra, Stefano Visentin, Manfred Walther, Caroline Williams.

Books available

Affects, Actions and Passions in Spinoza: The Unity of Body and Mind, Chantal Jaquet, translated by Tatiana Reznichenko

The Spinoza-Machiavelli Encounter: Time and Occasion, Vittorio Morfino, translated by Dave Mesing

Politics, Ontology and Ethics in Spinoza, Alexandre Matheron, translated and edited by Filippo Del Lucchese, David Maruzzella and Gil Morejón

Spinoza, the Epicurean: Authority and Utility in Materialism, Dimitris Vardoulakis

Forthcoming

Affirmation and Resistance in Spinoza: Strategy of the Conatus, Laurent Bove, translated and edited by Émilie Filion-Donato and Hasana Sharp

Experience and Eternity in Spinoza, Pierre-François Moreau, translated by Robert Boncardo

Spinoza's Political Philosophy, Ricardo Caporali, translated by Fabio Gironi

Spinoza and the Politics of Freedom, Daniel Taylor

Visit our website at www.edinburghuniversitypress.com/series/SPIN

Spinoza, the Epicurean
Authority and Utility in Materialism

Dimitris Vardoulakis

EDINBURGH
University Press

Edinburgh University Press is one of the leading university presses in the UK. We publish academic books and journals in our selected subject areas across the humanities and social sciences, combining cutting-edge scholarship with high editorial and production values to produce academic works of lasting importance. For more information visit our website: edinburghuniversitypress.com

© Dimitris Vardoulakis, 2020, 2022

Edinburgh University Press Ltd
The Tun – Holyrood Road, 12(2f) Jackson's Entry, Edinburgh EH8 8PJ

First published in hardback by Edinburgh University Press 2020

Typeset in 10/12 Goudy Old Style by
Servis Filmsetting Ltd, Stockport, Cheshire

A CIP record for this book is available from the British Library

ISBN 978 1 4744 7604 1 (hardback)
ISBN 978 4744 7605 8 (paperback)
ISBN 978 1 4744 7607 2 (webready PDF)
ISBN 978 1 4744 7606 5 (epub)

The right of Dimitris Vardoulakis to be identified as the author of this work has been asserted in accordance with the Copyright, Designs and Patents Act 1988, and the Copyright and Related Rights Regulations 2003 (SI No. 2498).

Contents

Reference Guide to Spinoza's Work	viii
Acknowledgements	ix

Preamble   1
1. Why Does it Matter to Read Spinoza as an Epicurean?   1
2. Authority and Utility: A Sketch   3
3. On Method   7

Introduction: Why is Spinoza an Epicurean?   10
1. 'The authority of Plato, Aristotle and Socrates carries little weight with me': Spinoza and Epicureanism   11
2. The Three Themes of Spinoza's Epicureanism: Authority, Monism and Judgement   23
3. The Dialectic of Authority and Utility: Spinoza's Promise   38

1. Freedom as Overcoming the Fear of Death: The Dialectic of Authority and Utility in the Preface   48
1. 'A free man thinks of nothing less than of death . . .': Fear and Freedom in Epicurus   50
2. Ante-secularism: The Construction of Authority and Human Nature in Lucretius   59
3. 'Fighting for their servitude as if for salvation': Monarchy versus Democracy   67

2. The Power of Error: Moses, the Prophets and the People (chapters 1, 2 and 3)   76
1. Moses: Prophecy as Communication   77

    2. 'God has no particular style of speech': The Error about God's Potentia   90
    3. Encountering the People: Causality and Instrumentality   97

3. Philonomianism: Law and the Origin of Finitude (chapter 4)   109
    1. *Ratio Vivendi*: Law and Living   111
    2. 'You cannot make a republic without killing people': The Tragedy of Legitimacy without Authority in Hannah Arendt   121
    3. On the Origins of Finitude: History as Tragedy or Comedy?   129

4. Political Monism: The Primacy of Utility over Authority (chapters 5 and 6)   141
    1. 'Society is advantageous': Utility and Social Formation   143
    2. Natural and Agonistic Democracy   152
    3. Political Monism: The Utility of Miracles   157

5. Love your Friend as Yourself: The Neighbour and the Politics of Biblical Hermeneutics (chapters 7 to 13)   172
    1. Monism and Interpretation: No Meaning Outside the Text   173
    2. Didactic Authority: The Universal as Communication   184
    3. Universality without Transcendence: Levinas contra 'Spinozism'   188

6. The Freedom to Philosophize: The Two Paths to Virtue (chapters 14 and 15)   203
    1. 'Finally'? The Politics of the Distinction between Faith and Reason   204
    2. The Necessary Rebel: The Transversal of Faith and Reason   212
    3. The Freedom to Philosophize: Freedom from Personal Authority and the Freedom to Transverse   223

7. Fear and Power: Natural Right and Authorization in Spinoza and Hobbes (chapter 16)   232
    1. Epicurean Communities: Fear and Utility   235
    2. The Robber in the Night: On the Promise   243
    3. The Right to Resist or the Fallibility of Judgement? On the Limits of Authorization   251

8. Theocracy: On the State of Authority (chapters 17 and 18)   263
    1. Josephus: The Anti-authoritarianism of Theocracy   264
    2. Between Tyranny and Revolution: The Limits of the State of Authority   270
    3. The Fragmentation of Authority: On the Reasons for the Destruction of the Hebrew State   283

9. The Authority to Abrogate: The Two Paths to Virtue and the Internal Enemy (chapters 19 and 20)   296
    1. The Path of the Emotions: Neighbourly Love as a Political Principle   297
    2. The Path of Reason: The Unendurable in Politics   306
    3. The Right to Abrogate: The Internal Enemy and Democracy   311

Conclusion: The Limitation of Spinoza's Epicureanism   322

Bibliography   328
Index   345

Reference Guide to Spinoza's Works

All references to Spinoza's *Theological Political Treatise* are to the translation by Samuel Shirley (Indianapolis: Hackett, 2001), cited parenthetically by page number. I have often altered the translation.

For the Latin, I have used the *Opera*, ed. Carl Gebhardt (Heidelberg: Carl Windters Universitätsbuchhandlung, 1924). The *Tractatus Theologico-Politicus* is contained in Volume 3. All page references to this edition follow after the English edition. If there is only one parenthetical page reference, then it is to the English edition of the *Theological Political Treatise*.

For the translations of all other works by Spinoza except the *Ethics*, I refer to his *Complete Works*, trans. Samuel Shirley (Indianapolis: Hackett, 2002).

I have used Edwin Curley's translation of the *Ethics* published by Princeton University Press as part of *The Collected Works of Spinoza*. I have used the following system in referring to the *Ethics*:

The Roman numeral in capital following E indicates the part of the *Ethics*. E.g., E I is *Ethics*, Part I, E II is *Ethics* Part II and so on. The following abbreviations are used:

A = Axiom
Ap. = Appendix
C = Corollary
D = Definition
L = Lemma
P = Proposition
Pr = Proof
Pref = Preface
S = Scholium

So, for instance, E II, P7 refer to *Ethics*, Part I, Proposition 7. And, E IV, P34S refers to *Ethics*, Parts IV, Scholium to Proposition 34.

Acknowledgements

There are a number of people who have contributed to this manuscript. First, I would like to thank my students, both at Western Sydney University and Columbia University, who have contributed invaluable thoughts in my seminars on Spinoza over the years. I also want to acknowledge the following colleagues: Gil Anidjar, Athena Athanasiou, Étienne Balibar, Charles Barbour, Andrew Benjamin, Brenna Bhandar, Omri Boehm, Chiara Bottici, Tim Campbell, Cesare Casarino, Jay Conway, Anna Cook, Thomas Corbin, Ingrid Diran, James Griffith, Lauren Guilmette, Erin Graff-Zivin, Peter Hallward, Joe Hughes, Nitzan Lebovic, Jacques Lezra, Marta Libertà De Bastiani, Filippo del Lucchese, Robyn Ferrell, Paul Fleming, Kyriakos Fytakis, Moira Gatens, Keith Green, Samir Haddad, Amanda Holmes, Gordon Hull, Jonathan Israel, Fiona Jenkins, Makis Kakolyris, Kiarina Kordela, Andrew LaZella, Richard Lee, Genevieve Lloyd, Gregg Lambert, James Martel, Yong Li, Zhi Li, James Martel, Yitzhak Melamed, Bahar Mirteymouri, Warren Montag, Vittorio Morfino, Knox Peden, Michael Polios, Janice Richardson, Jon Rubin, Martin Saar, Joseph Serano, Hasana Sharp, Aris Stylianou, Nicholas Tampio, Daniel Taylor, Spyros Tegos, Yannik Thiem, Anthony Uhlmann, Miguel Vatter, Joshua Visnjic, Daniela Voss, Chunming Wang, Zhang Yin and Gregg Yudin.

The idea of this book came about when I first taught the *Theological Political Treatise* in 2006. During the same semester, I met Amanda Third. Our relationship has changed just as much as the book in the past fourteen years but it has remained an indispensable part of my personal life as well as the life of the mind.

Peg Birmingham has been a trusted friend, colleague and confidant. She invited me to teach in her class at De Paul University, as a result of which I wrote Chapter 3 of *Spinoza, the Epicurean*. For her friendship and collegiality, the present book is dedicated to her.

for Peg Birmingham

Preamble

1. Why Does it Matter to Read Spinoza as an Epicurean?

Reading Spinoza's *Theological Political Treatise* as symptomatic of his epicureanism offers both a radical reconsideration of his work and suggests why he is still relevant to our contemporary political predicament. This double gesture – an historicization of Spinoza's argument so as to highlight his political relevance – is not uncommon. For instance, Gilles Deleuze in *Expressionism in Philosophy* reads Spinoza's materialism as a reversal of Platonism that leads to what he calls 'the plane of immanence', the basis of his own political philosophy. Or, Antonio Negri in *The Savage Anomaly* repositions Spinoza in a materialist tradition that privileges the idea of constituent power as a political force that is the linchpin of later writings such as *Empire*.

This historicized repositioning of Spinoza is in a certain sense prompted by the lack of work on the history of materialism. As Negri observes in a note to his *Savage Anomaly*, 'materialism has not been historicized!'[1] There are historical accounts of Platonism, Aristotelianism and Stoicism. There are historical accounts of medieval schools of philosophy such as nominalism. And there are historical accounts of all major schools of modern philosophy – the social contract tradition, idealism, Hegelianism, phenomenology and so on. But there is no authoritative account of materialism from antiquity to the present, with the exception of Friedrich Lange's book from 1864, which is both outdated and inaccessible today.[2]

---

[1] Negri, *The Savage Anomaly*, 268.
[2] Lange, *Geschichte des Materialismus und Kritik seiner Bedeutung in der Gegenwart*. Lange's book, which was first published in 1866, was well known in its day and exerted an important influence on the young Nietzsche. More recent accounts of materialism tend to be introductory and highly selective. See Bloch, *Le Matérialisme*; Wolfe, *Materialism: A*

This lack is both a hindrance and an advantage when writing on Spinoza. It is a hindrance in the sense that, to define the precise sense in which Spinoza is a materialist, we are forced to historicize our reading of Spinoza. As Lange establishes, the core idea of every form of materialism is the rejection of creation out of nothing, or the rejection of transcendence. But this can be understood in many different ways that lead to divergent positions. So scholars writing on Spinoza need to historicize their approach to determine the exact sense in which he is a materialist.

This can also be advantageous because it allows Spinoza's readers to position their reinterpretation of his materialism in such a way as to resonate with contemporary political issues. Materialism has always had an uncanny propensity to resonate with current political concerns. This may explain the flourishing of a number of materialist philosophies – such as affect theory, new materialism and post-humanism – all of which refer to Spinoza with an eye to contemporary issues.

The kind of materialism that I ascribe to Spinoza is epicureanism. Like all materialisms, epicureanism in Spinoza includes the rejection of creation *ex nihilo*. Specifically, in Spinoza this takes the form of the affirmation of a substance outside of which nothing exists, or his so-called monism. But there are two further epicurean themes that are crucial to Spinoza: authority and utility.

In describing Spinoza's epicureanism, I do not simply argue that we should pay attention to two concepts – authority and utility – that are marginal at best in the secondary literature on Spinoza. Moreover, I defend the stronger claim that Spinoza's materialism can be described only when the well-known function of monism in Spinoza is shown to be inextricable from the critique of authority and from the way in which we calculate our utility to decide on how to act. It is this parallel operation of monism, authority and utility that I understand as Spinoza's epicureanism.

Before outlining some key features of Spinoza's epicureanism, I need to plead with the reader to suspend their disbelief that such a quaint concept like authority can be of any contemporary relevance, and, more significantly, to leave aside their assumptions about the calculation of utility as an egotistical feature of human behaviour that is good for nothing other than promoting self-interested modes of conduct that contribute to neoliberalism. I am afraid not only that 'here, no doubt, my readers will come to a halt, and think of many things which will give them pause' (*E* II, P11S), but

Historico-Philosophical Introduction; and Brown and Ladyman, *Materialism: A Historical and Philosophical Inquiry*.

also that, annoyed by the insistence on authority and utility, they will not venture past this Preamble.

I have to confess that this danger has troubled me, and several colleagues have counselled me to find different names to refer to authority and, especially, utility. I tried this for some time, but decided against it for two reasons. First, it felt contrived. Authority and utility *are* the two terms Spinoza himself uses, and part of the exegetical enterprise is to highlight the function of these two terms in his texts. Second, it felt counterproductive. The most significant value of Spinoza's epicureanism is to question our prevalent assumptions about the outdated importance of authority and utility. This requires, of course, that the reader is prepared to put their presuppositions under scrutiny, which is not a small ask. I acknowledge that, and, appealing to Spinoza's authority, I ask the reader 'to continue on with me slowly, step by step, and to make no judgment on these matters until they have read through them all' (*E* II, P11S).

2. Authority and Utility: A Sketch

We have almost forgotten how important the concept of authority had been for close to two millennia. From the Roman republic onwards, authority is determined in a double sense that positions it at the centre of political considerations. First, one has authority when one is impervious to argumentation. For instance, the Pope had authority because his interpretation of the Bible could not be contested, according to Catholicism. The entire Reformation can be seen as challenging this Papal authority, or, which is the same thing, as an attempt to reformulate the concept of authority.

Second, authority always has a double origin, both theological and political. The obedience that is inextricable from authority is not just a pure political fact supported by power – it is not merely another way of saying that 'might is right'. Rather it is also to seek justification for one's actions in something transcendent, such as the glorious ancestors who founded Rome or in revelation according to the Judeo-Christian tradition.

For seventeenth-century philosophers, the paradigmatic figure who encapsulated these two meanings of authority was Moses. His authority derived both from revelation – receiving the Tablets directly from God – and from being the founder of the Hebrew state. We readily note that Moses is the protagonist of the *Theological Political Treatise*, but Spinoza never provides a clear definition of authority's double sense – its imperviousness to argumentation and its double origin in the theological and the political. Why is that?

I think there are two reasons why Spinoza does not give a clear definition of authority in the *Theological Political Treatise*. First, the discourse of authority is so prevalent in the seventeenth century – especially in a context where it is reanimated by the social contract theory, the understanding of the sovereign as one who is authorized to act on behalf of the people – that Spinoza does not feel the need to state the obvious. Second, the title itself succinctly captures authority. The treatise is 'theologico-political' because it is a treatise on authority. Spinoza could just as well have titled his work *Tractatus de auctoritate*.

Maybe Spinoza does not use the word authority in the title because the epicurean tradition he is working in approaches authority critically. This critical stance in early modernity comes from Lucretius's *On the Nature of Things*, which was published for the first time only in the mid-fifteenth century, but quickly had numerous republications throughout Europe gaining a wide readership. Lucretius opens his philosophical poem with a critique of authority. His example is the sacrifice of Iphigeneia. The priests and the head of the army conspire to sacrifice the young maiden to appease the gods. Lucretius sees in this joining of theological and political authorities nothing but superstition that arises from a misinformed fear of the gods.

I show in this book how a critique of authority that distinguishes its theological and political sides is one of the major threads that runs through Spinoza's *Theological Political Treatise*. In fact, we can identify three distinct parts of the *Treatise* by identifying the different ways in which authority is determined. Schematically, the three parts are as follows:

1. The first six chapters of the *Treatise* determine authority as the kind of power that one cannot argue with. This authority is presented primarily in terms of the personal authority of the prophets. The danger of personal authority is that it can morph into authoritarianism or despotism.
2. The concept of authority changes in chapters 7 to 15. Here the emphasis shifts to the apostles, whose authority is a *didactic* (139). This weakens authority, since the fact that it can be taught suggests that authority can be universalized and hence shared.
3. The final chapters describe a further transformation of authority. The focus now shifts to those who have the authority to question those whose power is legitimated by the state. Differently put, the focus shifts to those who have the 'authority to abrogate [*auctoritatem . . . abrogandi*]' (228/245).

The problematic that leads to the contemporary importance of authority is the following: The concept of authority organized so much of the political discourse for centuries. What is at stake when authority has all but disappeared from the contemporary political discourse? Part of the reason is that authority has been substituted by authoritarianism. Would it be of value today to examine our political predicament by asking again questions related to authority? I will return to some effects of this shift in section 3 of the Introduction.

Let us now turn to utility. The main reason that the concept of utility has such a bad name today is that it has been consistently used in the past half century or so to refer to the kind of selfishness or self-interest that is characteristic of neoliberalism. We have all but forgotten that instrumental reasoning was fundamental to the conception of the ethical in antiquity. For example, one of the most influential treatises on morality for centuries was Cicero's *De Finibus*. In the Middle Ages, for instance, this work was one of the main sources for understanding the ethical positions of the various ancient schools of philosophy. And as the title itself suggests, all these schools foreground the question of the ends of action.

The distinctive feature of epicureanism within this tradition is to determine instrumental reasoning in terms of *phronesis* or practical judgement. According to Epicurus, phronesis is the precondition of virtue and the good.[3] This instrumental character is conceived as fundamental to sociality. Or, to put it in a phrasing that will reoccur throughout the book, practical judgement understands one's utility in reciprocal terms with the utility of others. This is why the epicureans hold that one should love one's friends as oneself: the calculation of one's utility includes the other.

Spinoza embraces both the political and the ethical implications of this epicurean conception of phronesis or the calculation of utility. Thus, while discussing the Hebrew state, he refers to 'the calculation of utility [*ratio utilitatis*]' as 'the strength and life of all human action' (198/215–16). A well-functioning state requires this *ratio utilitatis*. At the same time, Spinoza translates the epicurean understanding of friendship into the discourse of neighbourly love. This becomes in the *Theological Political Treatise* the one and only fundamental principle of religion. It also explains why Levinas regards Spinoza as the great betrayer of Judaism. Whereas for Levinas, following Jewish tradition, the other or the neighbour is beyond calculation, Spinoza's politico-ethical reciprocity of utility entails that the other is always included in the practical calculations that we make.

---

[3] Diogenes Laertius, 'Epicurus', *Lives of Eminent Philosophers*, X.132. I discuss this passage in detail in the Introduction.

The instrumental character of phronesis is clear in the most detailed exposition of phronesis that has survived from antiquity, which is contained in Book VI of Aristotle's *Nicomachean Ethics*. Epicurus departs from Aristotle's position on phronesis in a fundamental way. According to the *Nicomachean Ethics*, episteme – the kind of knowledge that is concerned with universals – provides superior wisdom than phronesis. Epicurus reverses this relation. According to epicureanism, every kind of knowledge is inextricable from practical concerns – a point that we may put today by saying that knowledge is power. This point of view is shared by Spinoza. In the *Theological Political Treatise*, he describes the calculation of utility as expressing human nature, and the entire Part IV of the *Ethics* is structured around the initial definition according to which the good is that which is useful.

Why is it that utility gets a bad name? How is it transformed from a moral principle to a supposed justification for immoral conduct? I hold that these questions will remain unanswerable so long as we do not recognize the pivotal function of the calculation of utility in the materialist tradition from antiquity to modernity. For instance, the calculation of utility is pivotal to Marx's *Communist Manifesto*. The aporias about utility and the hesitations that we harbour against it are part of the lack of historicization that plagues the materialist tradition – as I noted at the beginning of this Preamble. In an accompanying volume to the present book, provisionally titled *Neoepicureanism*, I conduct a genealogy of the notion of the calculation of utility from antiquity to the present.[4] Spinoza occupies an important position in such a genealogy.

Let me conclude this sketch of authority and utility with the following observation: There is clearly a potential conflict between authority and utility. If authority exemplifies the stifling of argumentation and if phronesis indicates the propensity to form practical judgements about what actions lead to our utility, then they designate two different routes of human conduct: one through obedience and the other through rationality. The *Theological Political Treatise* fully explores and exploits the tensions between authority and utility.

Spinoza's unique approach to this tension is to hold that both paths – that of obedience and that of reason – can lead to the good and to virtue, so long as the conditions are in place to allow for transversals from one path to the other. I regard this as a unique position in the history of materialism or

---

[4] The complete working title is *Neoepicureanism: Materialism from Antiquity to Neoliberalism*. A summary presentation of the position I defend in that book can be found in Vardoulakis, 'Neoepicureanism'.

neoepicureanism, and I am not aware of any commentators on Spinoza who notice this move, with the exception of Étienne Balibar.

3. On Method

I am conducting in this book an immanent critique of the *Theological Political Treatise*. By this I mean that I endeavour to use the terms of the *Treatise* itself to tease out their implications. This explains why I conduct close readings of the *Treatise*, repeatedly turning to the Latin original and often changing the cited translations. It also explains why I avoid – as much as possible – attempting to resolve issues or problems with reference to the *Ethics* or other writings. I refer to other texts as little as possible, attempting instead to resolve the questions raised by the *Treatise* through the resources available in the *Treatise* itself.

I believe that an immanent critique of the *Theological Political Treatise* is the most expedient approach to the text because of a key trope that I call *the ruse of the obvious*. Spinoza presents most of his central arguments as self-evident: as if they are not controversial at all and everyone would agree if they only thought about the issue for a moment. Many a commentator has been seduced by this gesture, taking Spinoza's trope as a justification for not questioning their own presuppositions. Conversely, an immanent critique sidesteps the trope and seeks to highlight the implications of terms or arguments that may appear uncontroversial but are, in effect, unfamiliar and radical.

The conceptual framework of the book and its immanent critique are closely intertwined. One of its key contentions is that Spinoza's epicureanism can be understood as the interrelation of three key themes – the production of authority through fear and superstition; the political import of Spinoza's monism; and the function of utility in how he understands the human. The third in particular poses a significant challenge to today's reader, since the translations render 'utilitas' and its cognates variously as 'advantage', 'interest', 'benefit' and so on, thereby failing to underscore the technical use of the term. Consequently, my immanent critique of the *Theological Political Treatise* pays particular attention to the uses of utility by turning to the Latin original.

The overall neglect of the function of utility in Spinoza may be responsible for the lack of a systematic interpretation of Spinoza as an epicurean. Conversely, the recognition of the significance of Spinoza's concept of utility and the politics this entails ineluctably lead to the revision of a number of concepts that have pride of place in the exegetical history of the *Theological Political Treatise* – such as law, right and democracy. In other words, the emphasis on Spinoza's epicureanism leads to a revisionary exegesis of the *Treatise*.

To provide such an exegesis, I undertake a reading of the entire *Theological Political Treatise* from beginning to end. The aim is to show how Spinoza's epicureanism informs the text as a whole. The usual practice is that interpreters of the *Treatise* focus either on the first six chapters treating topics such as the prophets and miracles, or on the biblical hermeneutics of the middle part of the book, or on the politics of the last part. I am attempting to demonstrate the coherence of these topics and the continuities of the argument when the *Treatise* is read from the perspective of Spinoza's epicureanism. Thus, for instance, I am attempting to show that the treatment of the prophets in the first couple of chapters is important for Spinoza's insights on the Hebrew state in chapters 17 and 18.

At the same time, I want to enable the reader to delve into each chapter on its own. The only thing required is that the reader be aware of the three epicurean themes that I outline in the Introduction. These are used as heuristic principles to guide the reading of the *Treatise*. The aim is that a reader familiar with these three themes should be able to read each chapter independently.

Given that the mutual reliance of the three epicurean themes has not been noted before in readings of the *Theological Political Treatise*, I sought to avoid repeatedly noting this lacuna in the secondary literature. I do of course refer to important arguments or insights that influence my position, but to preserve the coherence of the story I am presenting I avoid interruptions merely for the sake of pointing out the lack of interpretations that accord with mine. Further, to present Spinoza's peculiar epicurean position, I stage a number of conversations or encounters with other thinkers – such as, for instance, Hannah Arendt, Leo Strauss and Emmanuel Levinas. This juxtaposition of Spinoza's position to other thinkers highlights its original features while positioning him in the context of current ideas.

In order to emphasize the connections between the three epicurean themes, and in particular the calculation of utility, as an indispensable part of action, I employ examples from recent political events throughout the book. This is not simply to draw attention to how Spinoza's thought can be relevant to contemporary matters. More significantly, it alludes to the genealogy of materialism that I referred to as 'neoepicureanism' in the previous section. Such a genealogy pays particular attention to how instrumental judgement runs through different conjectures of thought as well as historical configurations, even though instrumentality may not be recognized or may even be explicitly disavowed. I include these examples to draw attention to

Spinoza's pivotal position, both as the effect of a materialist tradition that goes back to ancient Greek thought and as prefiguring neoepicureanism in a way that pertains to our current predicament. Isn't genealogy, after all, not simply a reconstruction of the past, but a realignment within which past, present and future coalesce?

I bracket out the question of the development of Spinoza's epicureanism throughout this work so as to focus on the *Theological Political Treatise*. However, it is worth noting in passing the difference between the *Treatise* and earlier works, such as the *Treatise on the Emendation of the Intellect*. The Cartesianism of his early work is visible in the centrality of the question of method, while the question of utility is absent there. The opposite is the case in the *Theological Political Treatise*. Here method is discussed only in relation to biblical hermeneutics. The methodological function of doubt is no longer required when the emphasis shifts to utility that contains within itself the imperative to judge and hence to inquire and critique – as I explain in the Introduction.

One final clarification is required. I do not want to be perceived as if I am trying to defend Spinoza in my reading of the *Theological Political Treatise*. Instead, I am trying to outline a position – Spinoza's epicureanism – as it is constructed in the *Treatise*. The disadvantage is that readers who come with a certain discursive baggage in reading my book – for instance, if they are convinced that Spinoza is a liberal, or insist he should be read as a Jewish philosopher, or adopt the Deleuzian approach that essentially ignores as irrelevant a large part of Spinoza's work – are likely to remain unconvinced. The advantage of my approach is that it provides a new way of reading Spinoza that situates his work within a new way of conceiving the materialist tradition. This means that the present book does not provide final answers but rather invites further study of epicureanism as it is articulated both in Spinoza and in modernity more generally.

Introduction: Why is Spinoza an Epicurean?

Spinoza is pointedly silent about his philosophical allegiances. The only time he lets his guard down is in a letter to Boxel from September 1674 in which he positions himself in the epicurean camp (*Ep.* 56). Given this, it is surprising that in the multitude of Spinozas in the reception of his work an epicurean Spinoza is nowhere to be found – with a few exceptions that I discuss in the next section.[1]

I argue that Spinoza is an epicurean because he stages a dialectic between authority and utility. I do not mean a dialectics in the Hegelian sense, since it is not teleological. By dialectic I mean that the two terms, authority and utility, are in conflict but in such a way as to contribute to each other's determination, whereby it is impossible to thoroughly separate them. Like an old couple, they cannot stand each other even though they cannot do without each other.

The dialectic of authority and utility, specifically, stages the following conflict: Authority requires obedience whereas the drive to calculate our utility presupposes that we make our own practical judgements. Thus, under certain conditions, when authority takes over and suspends our judgements,

---

[1] The multitude of Spinozas that has been generated by the secondary literature shows both the vibrancy of Spinoza's reception and the fractious field. There is a liberal Spinoza and a communist Spinoza, who sit alongside the Jewish philosopher and the biblical hermeneuticist. The historical Spinoza engages in polemics with his contemporaries such as the Calvinists, and the rationalist Spinoza is the critic of Cartesianism. The Enlightenment Spinoza is, needless to say, incommensurable with the Romantic Spinoza, as is the Stoic with the Marxist ones, or the exoteric with the esoteric. And there are also the Spinozas who are relevant to all sorts of contemporary issues – the feminist, the environmentalist, the aesthetician and the critic of neoliberalism. For an overview of interpretative approaches to Spinoza, see Norris, 'Spinoza and the Conflict of Interpretations', in Vardoulakis (ed.), *Spinoza Now*, 3–37.

the result is political submission. But, also, under different conditions, we may calculate that it is to our utility to let someone else – for instance, someone with more knowledge or expertise – calculate our utility on our behalf. We can show the same interdependence by starting with utility: it is impossible to conceive of the human in terms of the calculation of utility without admitting that obedience, and hence authority, are necessary in certain circumstances. There is no such a thing as pure reason in human action. There is no human immune to obedience.

This dialectic is particularly prominent in the *Theological Political Treatise* – in fact, it structures the entire *Treatise*, as I argue in the present study. I am interested in this dialectic of authority and utility because it provides a new lens through which to read Spinoza. This dialectic allows me to conduct a philosophical reading of the politics of the entire *Treatise* – not only of some sections of it, as has been done in the past.

In addition, the dialectic of authority and utility provides us with a lens through which we can view our contemporary political predicament in unexpected ways.[2] In this Introduction, I situate Spinoza in the epicurean tradition and then show how authority and utility are intertwined in relation to what I call the three epicurean themes in Spinoza. Finally, I provide some insights into the relevance of Spinoza's epicureanism for the political today. I will start by showing how none of the three major approaches to epicureanism in the tradition – sensualist, physicalist and naturalist – square with Spinoza's epicureanism.

1. 'The authority of Plato, Aristotle and Socrates carries little weight with me': Spinoza and Epicureanism

Ancient epicureanism is a school of thought active for over half a millennium and highly influential in Rome just as much as Greece. It is, in fact, one of the four major philosophical schools in antiquity, alongside the Platonic, the Aristotelian and the Stoic schools.[3] The first thing that any student of epicureanism notices is the scant resources that have survived to-date, despite the influence of the epicurean school and the large number of epicurean books in antiquity. The reason is that, when Christian dogma is worked out in the fourth century, the Church fathers, turning to philosophical sources to seek conceptual legitimacy, quickly realize that they can mine ideas from

---

[2] The problematic of Spinoza's current relevance has exercised me at least since editing *Spinoza Now* (2011).
[3] For a synoptic presentation see Hadot, *What is Ancient Philosophy?*

the other philosophical schools, but that epicureanism is thoroughly incompatible with Christian metaphysics. Thereafter Christians not only take aim at epicureanism but also stop copying the epicurean manuscripts, leading to their eventual disappearance. As a result, for large periods of time, such as in the Middle Ages, the primary source of knowledge about epicureanism are summaries of epicurean positions, the most prominent of which are Cicero's philosophical dialogues *De Finibus* and *De Natura Deorum* that present epicurean positions in order to dismantle them.[4]

This spawns three basic approaches to epicureanism: the sensualist, the physicalist and the naturalist. It is instructive to note them: they may be reductive presentations of epicureanism, but they nonetheless prefigure some core epicurean positions in Spinoza.[5]

First, there is the interpretation of epicureanism as sensualism. This is the hedonistic interpretation, according to which epicureanism holds that the end of life is pleasure. The influence of this interpretation is enormous. Cicero certainly seems to espouse it in *De Finibus* and it becomes something of a commonplace later with the patristic fathers and medieval theologians who hurl it about without any substantiation from epicurean texts. The fact that it confuses the Cyrenaic position with the epicurean one did little to diminish the influence of this interpretation, and it is still prevalent today. An extension of the sensualist interpretation is the contrast between epicureanism and Stoicism. In the history of philosophy this is also a commonplace, repeated for instance in Hegel's *Lectures on the Philosophy of History*, where epicureanism is said to rely on the senses and pleasure whereas the basis of Stoic ethics is duty.[6]

A closer examination of epicurean texts leaves no doubt that the idea of living one's life guided by the pursuit of pleasure is much more complex than the hedonistic interpretation suggests. Let me quote a long passage from Epicurus's letter to Menoeceus that plays a crucial role in my interpretation of Spinoza's epicureanism:

> When we say, then, that pleasure is the end of action [ἡδονὴν τέλος ὑπάρχειν], we do not mean the pleasure of the prodigal or the pleasures of

---

[4] For an account of epicureanism in early Christianity and Medieval times, see Jones, *The Epicurean Tradition*.

[5] Usually these distorted positions are presented separately, although Catherine Wilson recently made a valiant attempt to synthesize them in *The Pleasure Principle: Epicureanism, A Philosophy for Modern Life*.

[6] Hegel, 'The Philosophy of the Epicureans', *Lectures on the History of Philosophy*, vol. 2, 276–311.

sensuality, as we are understood to do by some through ignorance, prejudice, or willful misrepresentation. By pleasure we mean the absence of pain in the body and of anxiety in the soul [τὸ μήτε ἀλγεῖν κατὰ σῶμα μήτε ταράττεσθαι κατὰ ψυχήν]. It is not an unbroken succession of drinking bouts and of revelry, not sexual love, not the enjoyment of the fish and other delicacies of a luxurious table, which produce a pleasant life [τὸν ἡδὺν γεννᾷ βίον]: it is sober reasoning [νήφων λογισμὸς] that calculates the causes of every judgment to do or avoid doing something good or harmful [τὰς αἰτίας ἐξερευνῶν πάσης αἱρέσεως καὶ φυγῆς], and banishing those beliefs through which the greatest tumults take possession of the soul. *Of all this the principle and the greatest good is phronesis [τούτων δὲ πάντων ἀρχὴ καὶ μέγιστον ἀγαθὸν φρόνησις].* Wherefore phronesis is more significant [τιμιώτερον] even than philosophy; *from it spring all the other virtues [ἐξ ἧς αἱ λοιπαὶ πεφύκασιν ἀρεταί]*, for it teaches that we cannot lead a life of pleasure [ἡδέως ζῆν] which is not also a life of usefulness, the good, and justice [φρονίμως καὶ καλῶς καὶ δικαίως]; nor lead a life of usefulness, the good, and justice, which is not also a life of pleasure. For the virtues have grown together with a pleasant life [συμπεφύκασι γὰρ αἱ ἀρεταὶ τῷ ζῆν ἡδέως], and a pleasant life is inseparable from them.[7]

This is not simply a passage that blatantly contradicts the interpretation of epicureanism as sensualism. Furthermore, the emphasis on phronesis, or what I also call in this book the calculation of utility, introduces a number of ideas that are crucial to Spinoza's epicureanism.

The first point to note is the startling predicate to pleasure that Epicurus provides, namely 'sober reasoning'. The word for reasoning here is *logismos* (λογισμός), not logos. If logos is what has come to be understood as Reason, *logismos* in the masculine or *to logistikon* in the neuter is instrumental reasoning – as, for instance, Aristotle makes clear in the opening of Book VI of the *Nicomachean Ethics*. The life of pleasure requires this kind of instrumental thinking that identifies means and ends.

A distinctive feature of this instrumental reasoning is that it posits the inseparability of mind and body – it is, as Epicurus says, the absence of pain in the body and of anxiety in the soul. This accords with the epicurean insistence that the end of action is the absence of anxiety, or *ataraxia*, as I will explain in more detail in Chapter 1. The point I want to stress here is that this instrumental reasoning coupled with the inseparability of mind

[7] Diogenes Laertius, 'Epicurus', in *Lives of Eminent Philosophers*, X.131–2 (emphasis added).

and body is translated into the following Proposition in Spinoza: 'From the guidance of reason, we pursue [ex rationis ductu sequemur] the greater of two goods or the lesser of two evils' (E IV, P65). Spinoza immediately explains that this calculative or instrumental reasoning is not confined to the present but also includes the future in its considerations (E IV, P66). In fact, Spinoza is not unique in expressing the combination of instrumentality with the inseparability of mind and body this way – the same articulation is often employed by other philosophers from the seventeenth century working in the materialist tradition (for instance, we will see in Chapter 7 how Hobbes uses an almost identical formulation). In any case, the point I am making is that this *logismos* is not abstract or theoretical reasoning but rather a practical kind of reasoning that entrains ends and considers action.

When Epicurus writes that this practical reasoning is more significant than philosophy, he is pointing to a reversal of Aristotle's position. According to the *Nicomachean Ethics*, theoretical reason leads to wisdom and virtue more than practical reason. I will return to the details of Aristotle's argument in Chapter 1. I only want to remind us here of the point that Heidegger makes when discussing the priority of theoretical over practical reason in the *Nicomachean Ethics*, namely, that this is the starting point of metaphysics and onto-theology.[8] We see Epicurus here evading that move. For him, the primary kind of knowledge is practical and it is articulated in the form of judgements that are calculations about utility – that is, calculations that combine ratiocination with considerations about the body.

Epicurus designates this practical, instrumental judgement as phronesis. This is the standard Greek name for this practical knowledge that he describes here. What is unusual in Epicurus is that he makes phronesis the precondition of both the good and of virtue. Such a move is indicative of his materialism – of the fact that knowledge is not abstract but rather articulated through its effects and how it impacts on the corporeal. It is the fact that – to use a contemporary formulation – knowledge is power. The suggestion that the good and virtue require phronesis is a bold one. Phronesis is a judgement that arises by assessing – or, calculating – one's given circumstances. Because it is a response to materiality, phronesis can never aspire to a thorough formalization. Materiality is contingent and hence unthematizable. Any calculation in relation to materiality is faced with its ineluctable unpredictability. Spinoza is fully cognizant of this point and he embraces its positive potential. As we will see, the notion of error is constitutive of his understanding of

---

[8] Heidegger, *Plato's Sophist*.

politics and of history.⁹ The seeming deficiency of phronesis – the fact that it has no steadfast rules to prove its validity or that it has to think 'without banisters' – is turned into a positive heuristic principle by Spinoza.

There is one final insight in this passage from Epicurus – an insight that plays a fundamental organizing role for the entire political discourse Spinoza develops in the *Theological Political Treatise*. I am referring to the circularity between phronesis and pleasure. The corresponding idea in Spinoza is that there are two paths to virtue and the good, the path of the emotions relying on obedience and the path of reason relying on the calculation of utility. As I will explain in Chapter 6, Étienne Balibar is the only reader of Spinoza who has really noticed this feature, in a series of writings starting with his exceptional analysis of Proposition 37 of Part IV of the *Ethics* and culminating in his conception of transindividuality.

If Negri's puzzlement about the lack of a historicization of materialism precipitated my historicization of Spinoza's argument resulting in the conception of his epicureanism, Balibar's analysis of the two paths to the good and virtue has been the critical idea that allowed me to discern a thorough argument – not without aporias but nonetheless programmatically pursued – about the political and democracy in the *Theological Political Treatise*. As I explain later, especially in Chapter 9, Spinoza's politics stands and falls with this idea of circularity between emotion and reason. Or, more precisely, the possibility of democracy hinges on how a transversal from one path to the other is possible. This can also be articulated in terms of the dialectic of authority and utility. If the path of the emotions is characterized by obedience as the key effect of authority and if the path of reason entails the calculation of utility, then their dialectic stages a chiasmus between the two paths. How does this chiasmus unfold? To answer that question, 'this is the task, this the toil [*hoc opus, hic labor*]' (187/203).

I have dwelled on this passage from the letter to Menoeceus because it contradicts the sensualist interpretation of epicureanism by bringing to the fore a number of ideas that are critical for Spinoza: the calculation of utility in conjunction with the inseparability of mind and body, the primacy of practical judgement despite the fact that it is fallible, and the two paths to virtue and the good. We will see in due course how these ideas are critical in Spinoza's philosophical program in the *Theological Political Treatise*, and I readily admit the pivotal role that this passage from the letter to Menoeceus has played in my own understanding of Spinoza's epicureanism.

The second significant way in which epicureanism is understood is through

---

⁹ See especially Chapters 2 and 3.

its physics. This is its corpuscularianism that was well-known in antiquity – the main source here is Cicero's *De Natura Deorum*. According to the physicalist doctrine of ancient epicureanism, there is nothing other than atoms and void. Atoms fall through the void – like drops of rain, Althusser writes in a moving essay that searches for the legacy of materialism within the history of philosophy. One question in particular creates difficulties for this doctrine: if all that exists are atoms that fall in straight lines in the void, then how can something be formed? To account for this, epicureans have recourse to the famous doctrine of the clinamen or the swerve: without reason, accidentally, atoms may decline from their straight lines, whereby they collide and create things. Or, differently put, nothing is created *ex nihilo* – there is no need to posit an external force, such as a god, to account for creation; instead, the process of creation is inherent in its own constituent elements. This rejection of creationism is common to Epicurus and the earlier atomists and is fundamental to the entire materialist tradition.[10]

The further implication of this materialism is that, as Lucretius describes it in Book 3 of *On the Nature of Things*, everything participates in a process of creation and destruction: 'one thing never ceases to arise from another, and no man possesses life in freehold – all as tenants'.[11] But then nothing is immortal. No spiritual soul can survive the demise of its body – or, put in positive terms: mind and body, the material and the spiritual, are inseparable. This is why there is no teleology. In the absence of some higher – spiritual – end, in the absence of any 'reason in history', actions can have specific ends as conceived through phronesis, but they lack any ultimate end. This lack of telos due to the interminable process of creation and destruction is also responsible for the irresolvability of the dialectic of authority and utility.

It is within the context of epicurean physicalism that we need to view Letter 56, in which Spinoza aligns himself with epicureanism. His correspondent, Hugo Boxel, is an educated Dutchman with progressive sympathies who remains nonetheless committed to certain superstitious beliefs including creationism. He writes to Spinoza to ask his opinion about ghosts and other supernatural phenomena such that cannot be admitted to exist according to the materialism espoused by the epicureans.[12] The brief corre-

---

[10] See Lange's *Geschichte des Materialismus und Kritik seiner Bedeutung in der Gegenwart* (1887), the most comprehensive study of the history of materialism that takes the rejection of creation *ex nihilo* as the starting point of materialism. Unfortunately, Lange has little to say about Spinoza.

[11] Lucretius, *On the Nature of Things*, 3.970–1.

[12] On Boxel, see Barbone, Rice and Adler, 'Introduction', in *Spinoza: The Letters*, 43.

spondence with Boxel includes six letters from September and October of 1674, three from each correspondent (*Ep.* 51–6).

Boxel writes to Spinoza to ask his opinion about the existence of ghosts, even though he knows very well that Spinoza's materialism does not admit of any supernatural phenomena. After the first, short letter, Boxel provokes Spinoza in his second letter. He offers a series of arguments why ghosts exist, holding that this 'reasoning will not convince those who perversely believe that the world was made by chance' (*Ep.* 53). Boxel is referring here to the idea of the swerve or clinamen, according to which atoms falling in a void can change direction without external influence – or, by chance. Effectively, Boxel asserts Spinoza's epicureanism. This poses a problem for Spinoza. Even though he shares the epicurean rejection of creation *ex nihilo* and of teleology, as well as the position about the inseparability of mind and body, still current advances in physics refute the epicurean position that there are only atoms and void. Further, Spinoza's own position – both in the *Ethics* and in the *Theological Political Treatise* – about the necessity of Nature is incompatible with the accidental nature of the clinamen. In his reply (*Ep.* 54), the first point Spinoza makes is to deny that the world is made by chance – that is, he denies the clinamen as exemplifying corpuscularianism.

Boxel presses on in a third letter by appealing to the authority of past philosophers (*Ep.* 55). In the final letter of the exchange (*Ep.* 56), Spinoza responds: 'The authority [*authoritas*] of Plato, Aristotle and Socrates carries little weight with me. I should have been surprised if you had produced Epicurus, Democritus, Lucretius.'[13] This is the moment Spinoza affirms his epicureanism as a response to the second provocation by Boxel. He clarifies that despite his rejection of epicurean corpuscularianism in his previous letter, he still holds onto the rejection of creationism as well as the inseparability of mind and body – whereby there are no spirits. The physics according to which only atoms and void exist, and the idea that nothing can be arbitrarily added to nature, can be separated, whereby modern epicureanism can reject the former but retain the latter. Further, the animosity toward Plato and Aristotle is not new. For instance, Spinoza writes in the Preface to the *Theological Political Treatise* that the Church supports 'mysteries' – meaning supernatural phenomena that suppose some kind of separation

---

[13] Democritus's influence on Epicurus's epistemology is well documented and explains the specific references in Spinoza's letter to Boxel. I am here leaving Democritus, and atomism in general, to one side as I am trying not to complicate the argument. Further, as will become clear later, the strong emphasis I place on phronesis is derived from Epicurus, not Democritus or the atomists.

between mind and body – with recourse to Aristotelianism and Platonism (5). Tellingly – for the argument I will put forward – Spinoza's allegiance to epicureanism of Letter 56 is staged as a gesture that is critical of authority.

Sensualism and physicalism dominate the way in which epicureanism is received in antiquity, and then from the consolidation of Christian dogma in the fourth century all the way through the Middle Ages and early modernity. Hedonism and corpuscularianism are used as terms of abuse by the Christians. The contrast between Christianity and epicureanism is telling. The early Church fathers were keen to incorporate elements of pagan philosophy into their teachings. But the idea of duty and suffering as the basis of morality that they appropriate from Stoicism is incompatible with hedonism. And the neo-Platonic metaphysics that relies on a hierarchy with God at the top is just as incompatible with epicureanism materialism – to say nothing of the epicurean insistence that the soul perishes with the body. Further, the medieval metaphysics that develops with the reintroduction of Aristotle through Islamic sources is incompatible with the stringent rejection of teleology that characterizes epicurean physics. It is true that some attempts are made to rehabilitate some epicurean ideas selectively, for instance by paying attention to how Seneca approvingly quotes moral epicurean maxims.[14] But such examples are the exception that prove the rule of unanimous condemnation of epicureanism. Symptomatic of this disapprobation is the tactic of labelling one's opponent an epicurean, as Luther does, for instance, in his debate with Erasmus.[15]

A third interpretation of epicureanism develops in early modernity – one that we can call the naturalist interpretation. This is implicated in the rise of the natural sciences. Catherine Wilson, who has written the most important book on this topic, goes so far as to argue that 'we are all, in a sense, Epicureans now'.[16] The sense she has in mind is distinct from sensualism and

---

[14] For Seneca's use of epicurean texts, see Fothergill-Payne, 'Seneca's Role in Popularizing Epicurus in the Sixteenth Century', in Olser (ed.), *Atoms, Pneuma, and Tranquility*, 115–33.

[15] For the Luther and Earsmus episode, see O'Rourke Boyle, *Christening Pagan Mysteries*, 63–95.

[16] Wilson, *Epicureanism at the Origins of Modernity*, 3. I should note the limited scope of Wilson's interpretation of Spinoza. She readily acknowledges his epicureanism in 'recognizing only physical causes' and in rejecting superstition. Nonetheless to account for other aspects of Spinoza's philosophy, such as his ethics, she simultaneously needs to argue that Spinoza has recourse to what she calls 'Plato's theory of the transcendence of mundane reality' (Wilson, *Epicureanism*, 125). Constraining epicureanism to scientific pursuits prevents Wilson from discerning how it influences Spinoza's ethics and politics. This is anything but unusual in the naturalist interpretations that seek to present Spinoza's epicureanism, as we will see shortly.

physicalism and it consists in the influence of epicureanism in the development of empiricism and its repercussions for the physical sciences. The influence is a double one. A different way of expressing the rejection of creation *ex nihilo* is by saying – to put it in Spinozan terms – that there is nothing outside nature. This means that – to put it in terms of natural science also employed by Spinoza – the laws of nature cannot be broken. Nature has no master and acts on its own, as Lucretius puts the same point.[17] This becomes the fundamental methodological foundation of modern science that allows it to conceive nature in mechanistic terms, or as a series of causes and effects, thereby overcoming the teleological epistemology of medieval philosophy. In addition, this methodological foundation from epicureanism is augmented by the also epicurean idea that knowledge can be derived from observation. Sense perception and experimentation can help us discover the chains of causes and effects that are regulated by natural laws. This approach is the foundation of empirical science.

The naturalist interpretation of epicureanism is crucial for the few attempts to read Spinoza as an epicurean – but also restrictive because it fails to account for the ethical and political motives of his philosophy.[18] In particular, it remains blind to the function of phronesis or the calculation of utility.

The only book-length study that examines Spinoza's epicureanism, Leo Strauss's *Spinoza's Critique of Religion*, is a reading of Spinoza as a stringent naturalist. Critical in this reading is Spinoza's naturalist position that the laws of nature cannot be broken, which leads to his refutation of miracles in chapter 6 of the *Theological Political Treatise*. Departing from this, Strauss presents Spinoza in the context of the great debate between religion and philosophy, or faith and reason, that torments modern thought since the rise of empiricism. Spinoza is an epicurean in the sense that he defends 'a fundamental cleavage between science and religion', write Strauss.[19]

Such a naturalist interpretation of Spinoza's epicureanism means that Strauss explicitly denies any political import to Spinoza's epicureanism. The bracketing out of ethical and political concerns is all the stranger, since

---

[17] Lucretius, *On the Nature of Things*, 2.1091–3
[18] It seems to me that naturalism is one of the very few areas where there seems to be a philosophical consensus between the so-called analytic and continental traditions. Post-war philosophy in both traditions veers toward naturalism in various ways. In this sense, Spinoza, who has been embraced by both traditions, may function as an important conduit of a rapprochement of the fractured philosophical landscape. But this will only ever be possible if naturalism is not confined to its epistemological dimension but rather embraces the materialist political tradition from which it arises.
[19] Strauss, *Spinoza's Critique of Religion*, 56.

Strauss relegates such concerns to Spinoza's averroist and machiavellian influences, which, on the one hand, he admits are intertwined with epicureanism in modernity, and, on the other, he insists on methodological grounds on their separation from Spinoza's epicureanism.[20] In this ambiguous – even strained – gesture, Strauss avows Spinoza's epicureanism by disavowing its materialist politics.

This allows Strauss to ascribe a political agenda to Spinoza that is thoroughly separated from materialism. The most explicit, even blunt, articulation of this move is recorded at the beginning of Strauss's 1959 lectures on Spinoza's *Theological Political Treatise*. Strauss mentions that Spinoza follows the epicurean tradition because of his naturalism. This leads to two inferences: first that, unlike Spinoza, the epicurean tradition was not political because it had no conception of power; second, as a consequence of not having to account for a materialist politics, Strauss is free to position Spinoza as 'the first philosopher of liberal democracy'.[21] As I will explain in Chapter 4 where I will look at Strauss's reading of Spinoza in detail, the premise of an apolitical naturalism – as if Spinoza's 'critique of religion' can be separated from his political materialism – is untenable.

Even though Gilles Deleuze does not explicitly tackle Spinoza's epicureanism but rather positions Spinoza within his naturalist reading of Lucretius, his approach opens up ways of addressing the deficiencies of Strauss's interpretation. Deleuze's essay 'Lucretius and Naturalism' was originally published in 1961 and then republished with changes in the appendix to *The Logic of Sense* in 1969 as 'Lucretius and the Simulacrum'.[22] Although Spinoza figures

---

[20] Strauss, *Spinoza's Critique of Religion*, 48–9. Strauss is following a long tradition that regards epicureanism as unconcerned with politics. This arises from Epicurus's own advice that the wise person should not indulge in public speaking and should avoid politics (see Diogenes Laertius, 'Epicurus', X.118 and X.119). Besides the fact that this is an oversimplification about *ancient* epicureanism that has been contested – see Brown, 'Politics and Society', in Warren (ed.), *The Cambridge Companion to Epicureanism*, 179–206 – more importantly, Strauss simply assumes that *modern* epicureanism is also apolitical. In fact, epicureanism's connection with averroism and machiavellianism prove precisely the opposite of what Strauss's wants to argue, namely, the *political* motivations of *modern* epicureanism. On this point, Strauss simply takes for granted the accepted dogma that epicureanism *tout court* is apolitical.

[21] Strauss, *Spinoza: Seminar on the Theological Political Treatise*, University of Chicago 1959, 2 and 1. Strauss repeats his position that Spinoza 'was the first philosopher who was both a democrat and a liberal. He was the philosopher who founded liberal democracy' in the 1962 Preface of his *Spinoza's Critique of Religion*, 16.

[22] There are, nonetheless, significant differences between the two versions and they are connected to the introduction of Spinoza in the second one, as Warren Montag

only fleetingly in the essay, if it is placed within the context of Deleuze's significant *Spinoza et la problème de l'expression* from 1968, then the affinities are clear. Lucretius's naturalism is situated within the project of 'reversing' Platonism, thus having a similar position to that of Spinoza in the book on expressionism. This suggests that materialism is an alternative philosophical tradition that leaves metaphysics behind: 'To distinguish in men what amounts to myth and what amounts to Nature, and in Nature itself, to distinguish what is truly infinite from what is not – such is the practical and speculative object of Naturalism. The first philosopher is a naturalist.'[23] And yet, when it comes to the quandary 'faith or reason', Deleuze ultimately does not venture much further than Strauss, as is indicated by the rejection of religion as superstition that the increase of one's power through the operation of reason is to overcome. Leaving aside the fact that Spinoza explicitly ascribes positive *political* functions to religion in the *Theological Political Treatise* – a book about which Deleuze has little to say – the political project that consists in the increase of power through the operation of reason simply restages the separation of faith and reason that Lucretian naturalism was supposed to have overcome.[24] As a result, Deleuze is laconic about Spinoza's politics. He cannot say much because the notion of phronesis or utility – the centre of Spinoza's epicurean politics – is absent from Deleuze, which is symptomatic of his highly selective reading of Spinoza.

Louis Althusser's late essay 'The Underground Current of the Materialism of the Encounter' is the most promising engagement with Spinoza's epicureanism because it connects naturalism with the political import of the materialist tradition. Althusser notes a materialist philosophical tradition in modernity that is affiliated with epicureanism. A key figure in this tradition is Spinoza – alongside others, such as Machiavelli, Hobbes, Rousseau and Marx. This materialism denies both origins and an end to actions, and hence any occurrence is contingent or aleatory, which has significant ramifications in how political action is to be conceived: 'One reasons here not in terms of the Necessity of the accomplished fact, but in terms of the contingency of the fact to be accomplished.'[25] In other words, what is, is not a fait accompli; rather, what is, is produced by the process of reasoning that inserts itself in a

---

explains in 'From Clinamen to Conatus: Deleuze, Lucretius, Spinoza', in Lezra and Blake (eds), *Lucretius and Modernity*, 163–72.
[23] Deleuze, *The Logic of Sense*, 278.
[24] Deleuze, *The Logic of Sense*, 279.
[25] Althusser, 'The Underground Current of the Materialism of the Encounter', *Philosophy of the Encounter*, 174.

network of calculation that determines how one exists by performing actions that aim toward something. This is not to say that being implies an ultimate end, but is rather to say that ends are posited in the process of reasoning – or, in Althusser's words, 'although there is no Meaning to history ... there can be meaning *in* history'.[26] Without realizing it, Althusser is describing here Epicurus's conception of the function of practical judgement as phronesis, which I outlined in the first interpretative approach to epicureanism. Althusser comes tantalizingly close to recognizing the political and ethical function of practical judgement as phronesis as central to the epicurean tradition. Unfortunately, the lack of thematization of this function is a missed encounter that we will never know how it could have resulted.

Althusser's reading of Spinoza as a materialist and naturalist profoundly shapes the readings of Spinoza in France, where a number of his students conduct significant research on Spinoza – I am thinking of scholars such as Balibar, Macherey and Moreau. This influence extends beyond France and has resulted in some publications that explicitly address Spinoza's epicureanism, such as works by Warren Montag in America and Vittorio Morfino in Italy.[27] The other significant work on Spinoza and materialism is Antonio Negri's *The Savage Anomaly*. Negri's central thesis of the two modernities is reminiscent of Althusser's thesis about the alternative or 'underground' current of materialism in philosophy, despite significant differences, and in fact predates Althusser's written work on the subject – *The Savage Anomaly* was first published in 1981.[28] Again, however, just like Althusser, the kinds of materialism that all these thinkers outline fail to thematize the function of phronesis.

The only interpretation of Spinoza as an epicurean that emphasizes phronesis can be found in Jean-Marie Guyau's largely forgotten *La morale d'Épicure* from 1878.[29] Guyau delineates a genealogy of epicureanism from

---

[26] Althusser, 'The Underground Current', 194.

[27] See in particular Montag, 'Lucretius Hebraizant: Spinoza's: Reading of Ecclesiastes', and Morfino, 'Tra Lucrezio e Spinoza: La "filosofia" di Machiavelli', in Visentin et al. (eds), *Machiavelli: immaginazione e contingenza*.

[28] Even though the essay is written around 1982, its main points are already contained in discussions between Althusser and his circle – exchanges that have Deleuze's essay on Lucretius as a point of reference. For instance, Montag describes how Macherey mobilizes Deleuze's essay on Lucretius in his correspondence with Althusser in 1965, to critique his teacher's notion of structure. See Montag, *Althusser and his Contemporaries*, 75–6.

[29] Guyau, *La Morale d'Épicure et ses rapports avec les doctrines contemporaines*. For a translation of the chapter on Spinoza as well as an introduction to Guyau's work, see Guyau, 'Spinoza: A Synthesis of Epicureanism and Stoicism'.

antiquity to the present, concentrating on the calculation of utility. This is the red thread that connects the thought of Epicurus and Lucretius with the ethical and political concerns of modern epicureanism.[30] Despite this significant insight, Guyau's account of Spinoza is surprisingly meagre. He presents Spinoza as caught up in the familiar contrast between epicureanism and Stoicism. This is the old opposition characteristic of the first interpretation of epicureanism (that is, sensualism vs duty) refashioned from the perspective of Guyau's ethical epicureanism as the alternative between utility and duty. Thus Spinoza is presented as caught in a double bind, and consequently of limited import.

How can we retain Guyau's insight about the centrality of the calculation of utility and develop it so as to demonstrate Spinoza's epicureanism?

2. The Three Themes of Spinoza's Epicureanism: Authority, Monism and Judgement

Of assistance to answer the above question is a book in which the name 'Spinoza' does not even appear. Alison Brown's recent *The Return of Lucretius to Renaissance Florence* traces the historical context in which epicureanism re-emerges in early modernity. She highlights the importance of the discovery of Lucretius's *On the Nature of Things* by Poggio Bracciolini in 1417 and Tavesari's Latin translation of Diogenes Laertius's *The Lives of Philosophers* – the book that contains the only extant texts from Epicurus.[31] Both were published in Florence within a few years of each other, or, as Brown puts it, 'Lucretius and Epicurus returned to Florence in the 1440s'.[32] Brown examines the writings of a number of Florentine humanists such as Bartolomeo Scala from the mid-fifteenth century to Marcello Adriani at the end of the century, culminating with Niccolò Machiavelli in the sixteenth century, to show how they are influenced by the newly published epicurean texts. Brown is concerned to show the initial impact in Florence of the publications of Epicurus's and Lucretius's writings, which is at the roots of modern epicureanism. She describes this alternative humanist discourse, which does not conform to the Platonism of the majority of the humanists. Eventually

---

[30] Guyau sees the endpoint of this development in nineteenth-century utilitarianism – as the sequel to the book on Epicurus's moral theory, *La morale anglaise contemporaine: Morale de l'utilité et de l'évolution* from 1879, shows. I discuss the differences between utilitarianism and Spinoza in the following section.
[31] Specifically, it contains three letters – to Herodotus, to Pythocles and to Menoeceus – as well as the so-called 'Principal Doctrines', a list of key Epicurean positions.
[32] Brown, *The Return of Lucretius to Renaissance Florence*, 16.

other humanists outside Florence are influenced by epicureanism, such as Pietro Pomponazzi in Padua and Bologna, leading all the way to Pierre Gassendi in France in the seventeenth century.

Brown argues that the initial return of epicureanism lacks a unified system, consisting instead in divergent ideas that she organizes into three thematic clusters.[33] First, there is the theme of fear and superstition. Religion exercises its grip by instilling fear of natural phenomena or fear of God. More generally, fear is the way in which a powerful individual can dominate the minds of his contemporaries so as to control them. This can lead both to repression and to the establishment of a secure sovereign reign. It is noteworthy that this theme is absent from the reception history of epicureanism that I outlined in the previous section. Second, there is the theme of naturalism or atomism. The epicureans reject creationism or creation *ex nihilo*. This also entails that mind and body are connected and that there is no remainder after one's death – which is why we should not fear punishment in some putative afterlife or why, as the epicurean motto goes, 'death is nothing to us'. This is the familiar doctrine of physicalism but not necessarily accompanied by strict adherence to the physics of atoms and the void – very much like the position Spinoza outlines in the correspondence with Boxel. Third, there is the theme that Brown calls primitivism and which can be traced to Book 5 of *On the Nature of Things*. Human action and interaction in *ante legem* and organized societies function according to the same logic because human nature is consistent through the ages – in particular, what is consistent is that humans act by calculating their utility. This provides a conception of the formation of society out of 'barbarism'. This theme returns to the importance of phronesis in Epicurus but now it is couched in modern terms as constitutive of the definition of the human – not just as the precondition of virtue. There are various subthemes, but these three themes remain the nodal points of Brown's account, despite the fact – and this is a significant point in Brown's book – that they do not form a systematic whole.[34]

My contention is that Spinoza synthesizes these three themes in a way that determines his epicureanism and marks his politics. More accurately, it is not each theme independently but the *interconnections* of the three themes that demarcate Spinoza's epicureanism. The interconnections operate due to the function of utility in Spinoza's thought. Such an understanding of

---

[33] Brown, *The Return of Lucretius*, 15.

[34] Alison Brown also summarizes these themes also in her 'Lucretian Naturalism and the Evolution of Machiavelli's Ethics', in del Lucchese, Frosini and Morfino (eds), *The Radical Machiavelli*, 105–27.

Spinoza's epicureanism not only positions his thought in relation to the reception history of epicureanism that I outlined above. In addition, it explains how his epicureanism develops a sharp political edge. Let me take the three themes in turn to show synoptically how they work – as the rest of the book consists in tracing these themes and their implications throughout the *Theological Political Treatise*.

First, there is the theme of authority arising out of superstition. This is the opening theme of Lucretius's *On the Nature of Things* and it is central to the *Theological Political Treatise*, introduced in the opening paragraph of the Preface.[35] Following the typical epicurean move, Spinoza highlights the function of fear in the spread of superstition. This account of superstition is concerned with the production of authority, understood as the structure of command and obedience. Fear and superstition precipitate the establishment of authority. Both Lucretius and Spinoza insist on the political *and* theological sources of authority.

It is somewhat deceptive to speak of authority in English in this context. The word 'authority' in English has such a broad range of signification that it can almost be a synonym of the word power – another word whose elusive range of signification makes it hard to determine. In the *Theological Political Treatise*, the determination of authority is more specific. *Auctoritas* relies on the Roman definition, according to which authority is impervious to argumentation. As Hannah Arendt puts it, authority 'is incompatible with persuasion, which presupposes equality and works through a process of argumentation. Where arguments are used, authority is left in abeyance.'[36] Or, in Alexandre Kojève's formulation, authority resides with someone whose 'action does not provoke a reaction'.[37] Spinoza has direct recourse to the same determination of authority when he asserts, for instance, that 'the authority of the prophets does not permit of argumentation [*prophetae auctoritas ratiocinari non patitur*]' (139/152).

It is easy to discern a tension between authority understood in this Roman sense and democracy. The more authority there is, which means the more one's opinions and actions are beyond dispute, the less democracy finds the right conditions to thrive. Where contestation is stifled because the position of whoever holds authority prevails unchallenged, there democracy is stifled too. Let me present some more details of authority that will also help us understand the anti-authoritarian impulse in Spinoza.

---

[35] I take this up in detail in Chapter 1.
[36] Arendt, 'Authority', in *Between Past and Future*, 93.
[37] Kojève, *The Notion of Authority (A Brief Presentation)*, 13.

Authority describes the model of command and obedience. Authority commands and the rest obey. As Paul Ricoeur observes, the command and obedience model of authority has a double source, both theological and political.[38] If authority comes from revelation or another religious source such as the veneration of the ancestors, then authority is theological. The political sense of authority is developed in Rome. According to Cicero's famous definition in *De Legibus*, 'supreme power [*potestas*] is granted to the people and actual authority [*auctoritas*] to the Senate'.[39] The people in the Roman republic have *potestas* in the sense that their power is instituted through the tribune. The authority of the senate, on the other hand, is derived from the foundations of the Roman republic, from a glorified past beyond reproach. Cicero's formulation is instructive also in showing the impossibility of separating the political from the theological. Even though Cicero is describing the senate's political authority, the fact that it is derived from the glorified ancestors entails a religious source too. In the seventeenth century, the most obvious figure representing this double origin of authority is Moses – which explains why, for instance, both Hobbes and Spinoza regard him as the most significant prophet.[40]

The theological and political aspects of authority cannot be separated. We know this from linguistics, since Émile Benveniste shows that the root *augeo* of *auctoritas* points to both the theological and the political realms.[41] Mythological accounts of authority also point to its double source, in theology and in politics, as the work of Georges Dumézil makes particularly clear.[42] This is widely recognized in early modernity. Thus, Machiavelli argues in the *Discourses* that, to establish his authority, a lawgiver or a law-reformer always has 'recourse to God . . . because without that they [i.e. the new laws] would not be accepted'.[43] From this perspective, we can see the title of the *Theological Political Treatise* as equivalent to *Treatise on Authority*. By contrast, the theological element recedes in the *Political Treatise* because the concept of *auctoritas* is absent. Instead, the *Political Treatise* is a more 'Greek' work in the sense that it relies on the theory of the three constitutions derived through Plato, Aristotle and Polybius.

So, who has authority? Let me provide some examples. The Pope had

---

[38] Ricoeur, 'The Paradox of Authority', in *Reflections on the Just*, 91–105.
[39] Cicero, *De Legibus*, 492.
[40] I examine Spinoza's treatment of Moses's theologico-political authority in section 1 of Chapter 2.
[41] Benveniste, *Le Vocabulaire des institutions indo-européennes II*.
[42] Dumézil, *Mitra-Varuna: An Essay on Two Indo-European Representations of Sovereignty*.
[43] Machiavelli, *Discourses on the First Decade of Titus Livius*, 225.

authority in the sense that his was the final judgement in any theological dispute. A judge has authority in the sense that his verdict is not subject to questioning in the court when it is delivered. A general has authority because his orders are not subject to contestation. A sovereign can also have authority to the extent that his political decisions are not subject to debate – an idea that informs Schmitt's famous definition that 'the sovereign is the one who decides on the exception', because a decision is not subject to debate.[44] Authority is also traditionally visually distinguished. The external mark of authority is usually the gown. The gown is nowadays substituted by modern equivalents. For instance, the modern sovereign may no longer have distinctive sartorial markers of authority, but still the head of the executive branch of government retains other external characteristics, such as a distinctive residence – for instance, the White House – or a designated position in the legislative council.

In general, Spinoza develops a position that seeks to undermine personal authority. The immediate *historical context* is important: Spinoza is writing in the aftermath of the Reformation, which influences his discourse. When Martin Luther posts his *Ninety-Five Theses* on the door of the church in Wittenberg on 31 October 1517, he is attacking the authority of the Pope. Protestantism sought to substitute the authority of the Pope with the authority of Scripture, thereby challenging the established sense of authority. At the same time, the *conceptual sources* of Spinoza's critique of authority are just as significant. Intimations of a conception of authority as beyond dispute are present in all ancient schools of philosophy with the notable exception of the epicureans. Its founder, Epicurus, famously admitted women and slaves at his garden – the symbolic centre of his school. Spinoza's epicureanism commits him to a position critical of authority.

Second, while the theme of monism is one of the most discussed topics in his work, it is rarely acknowledged that Spinoza's monism is also linked to his epicureanism – in fact, the only exception that springs to mind here is Strauss. The positing of a totality outside of which nothing exists, and which consequently does not admit of creation *ex nihilo*, has an atomist and epicurean provenance, and it is fully embraced by Spinoza. We learn, for instance, from the Scholium to Proposition 20 of Part IV of the *Ethics* that it is impossible for something to 'come out of nothing [*ex nihilio aliquid fiat*]'. Epicurus's letter to Herodotus, the most influential text on the epicurean theory of science and knowledge, opens with the idea that there is a totality outside of which nothing exists and explicitly rejects

---

[44] Schmitt, *Political Theology*, 5.

creationism.[45] Following upon this epicurean tradition, Spinoza's monism develops theological and political insights. It is incompatible with the idea of God as creator in both Christianity and Judaism, as well as with the idea of a divine will analogous to a mortal magistrate – a critique developed most famously in the Appendix to Part I of the *Ethics* but also raised explicitly in chapter 4 of the *Theological Political Treatise*.

Monism is also important for Spinoza's epistemology since it explains how the human is receptive to the world. The totality – regardless of whether it is called God, Nature, or substance – precedes any form of human knowledge. *Knowledge is possible on condition that there is a totality*. That knowledge presupposes a totality has been beyond dispute in Spinoza scholarship. This is the position described in Part I of the *Ethics*, according to which the substance precedes the two attributes of thought and extension. The debate in Spinoza scholarship concerns what this precedence or presupposition of the substance means and what it entails, not the presupposition itself, given how clearly it is stated in the opening of the *Ethics*. My point is that this opening move of the *Ethics* – which explicitly entails that there is nothing outside substance and hence the rejection of creation *ex nihilo* – is the same as the opening move of Epicurus's letter to Herodotus.[46]

Besides monism's importance for epistemology, there is also a significant anthropological implication of the positing of a totality outside of which nothing exists. This essentially means that mind and body are inseparable. This is a cardinal point that we find in both Epicurus and Lucretius, and subsequently in all materialist philosophies. Thus, epicureans hold that 'death is nothing to us' because in perishing there is no spirit or soul that survives the body, either in a heaven or a hell – the spirit perishes too because mind and body are inseparable.[47] According to epicureanism, then, there is no pure body completely severed from thought, there is no what Agamben calls 'bare life'.

Significantly, the inseparability of mind and body entails that there is both thought and emotion in any experience. This is why, for instance, Spinoza says in the first Definition of the Affects in Part III of the *Ethics* that desire (*cupiditas*) is the essence of the human insofar as desire is understood as affection accompanied by consciousness thereof. To put this in a monist terminology, it is not only that totality precedes knowledge; in addition, the human exercises at least a modicum of rationality every moment it is

---

[45] See Diogenes Laertius, 'Epicurus', X.38–9.
[46] I discuss this further in section 1 of Chapter 1.
[47] See Diogenes Laertius, 'Epicurus', X.126. See also Warren, *Facing Death*.

affected by its environment, that is, every moment it is part of the totality. The inseparability of mind and body means that there is always some reasoning in our experience.

This monist implication about the inseparability of mind and body is enormously significant for Gilles Deleuze's reading of Spinoza.[48] Deleuze's interpretation in its turn has had a profound impact on a number of exciting developments in theory in the past few decades, such as affect theory, new materialism and post-humanism. Deleuze articulates Spinoza's monism as the 'plane of immanence'. This essentially rejects the possibility of any kind of transcendence. The question then becomes what the criterion for human action is in such a plane of immanence. Deleuze's answer is compelling in its simplicity. There are no qualitative distinctions – Spinoza is 'beyond good and evil' – only quantitative fluctuations that indicate the co-implication of mind and body. The more certain actions increase one's power, the more they probe 'what a body can do', the better they are. Conversely, the more they decrease one's power, the worse they are. Further, it is reason, as the second kind of knowledge, as opposed to the imagination, that accomplishes the increase of power. Pointedly, Deleuze relies primarily on Part III of the *Ethics* to develop this interpretation of Spinoza's ethics – or, what Deleuze also calls 'ethology'.[49] This fluctuation of power that combines the mind and body has been central for affect theorists such as Brian Massumi, new materialists such as William Connolly, and post-humanists such as Rosi Braidotti.[50] Thus, it has opened up significant and influential new currents of thought.

The problem is that it is a lop-sided interpretation of Spinoza that ends up being distorting. There are two main reasons for this. First, the way that the quantitate increase of power through the operation of the mind is articulated relies solely on the distinction between imagination and the second kind of knowledge. But when we turn to Part IV of the *Ethics*, utility plays a pivotal role – as I will discuss in more detail later. And it is impossible to reconcile the calculation of utility with either the imagination or the second kind of

---

[48] Deleuze, *Expressionism in Philosophy: Spinoza*.
[49] Deleuze, 'On the Difference between the *Ethics* and a Morality', in *Spinoza: Practical Philosophy*, 17–29.
[50] See, for instance, Massumi's *What Animals Teach us about Politics* and the interviews in *Politics of Affect*, where Massumi admits that the 'way I use it [i.e., affect] comes primarily from Spinoza' (3); Connolly, *Neuropolitics: Thinking, Culture, Speed* and *A World of Becoming*; and Braidotti, *Transpositions*, 'The Ethics of Becoming Imperceptible', in Boundas (ed.), *Deleuze and Philosophy*, 133–59, and *The Posthuman*.

knowledge that relies on adequate ideas.[51] It is symptomatic of Deleuze's discomfort about utility that he has very little to say about Part IV. Any sense of utility or of the epicurean phronesis is totally absent in Deleuze and in the sub-disciplines that depart from his reading of Spinoza. Second, the conception of an ethology that consists in the increase and decrease of power and the subsequent kind of relational ontology that it spawns fails to adequately address the concept of authority.[52] This is why, again, neither Deleuze nor the other philosophers mentioned above have anything to say about the *Theological Political Treatise*. The effect of these readings is – I would not say a misinterpretation of Spinoza, since given their terms of reference all these philosophers provide astonishing insights into Spinoza's thought – rather, it is a missed encounter with the politics of the *Treatise*.

It is also the reason why none of these thinkers can arrive at a conception of Spinoza's epicureanism other than as a form of naturalism. For my determination of Spinoza's epicureanism, the third theme is also required, namely the calculation of utility or phronesis. Given that Spinoza refers to this as characteristic of human nature – for instance, in chapter 16 of the *Theological Political Treatise* – I sometimes refer to it as the anthropological principle. Let me start by showing how the second theme – monism – is related to the calculation of utility before I extrapolate further how this third theme of Spinoza's epicureanism is derived from Epicurus's conception of phronesis.

I mentioned above the epistemological insight derived from monism, namely, that knowledge presupposes a totality outside of which nothing exists. But this means that we can never have a complete knowledge of the totality – something that Spinoza recognizes as early as the *Treatise on the Emendation of the Intellect* (see paragraphs 100 to 102). This is a critical insight for the *Theological Political Treatise*: 'Universal consideration about fate and the interconnection of causes can be of no service to us in forming and ordering our thoughts concerning particular things. Furthermore, we are plainly ignorant of the actual co-ordination and interconnection of things ... so for our utility in living it is better [*ad usum vitae melius*], indeed, it is necessary, to consider things as possible' (48–9/58). Given the impossibility of knowing the totality that is characterized by absolute necessity, one necessarily knows first in relation to practical concerns and aims that pertain to what it is possible to do or achieve. If it is impossible to comprehend the

---

[51] I also take up this topic in Chapter 6.
[52] On this point, see the excellent article by Kujula and Regan, 'The Politics of Ethics: Spinoza and New Materialisms'.

interconnection of causes that constitutes the totality, that means that we need to position ourselves within that totality, something which is possible by focusing on our utility. This impossibility of complete knowledge *and* the necessity to draw on the resources that utility provides for us is constitutive of our human nature.

The fact that we cannot know God as such, or Nature in its totality – the fact that we are human – does not need to lead to a lament about our fallen state or our impotence. To the contrary, it places the onus on us to derive practical knowledge to assist our judgements about how to act in particular circumstances. The fact that we exist in a totality means that we exercise some kind of practical knowledge about how to act in the world. Let me put this point more emphatically. *According to the second theme of Spinoza's epicureanism, the totality is presupposed by knowledge; according to the third theme, the totality necessarily entails practical knowledge in the form of judging about how to act.* These practical judgements do not aspire to universality – they are not necessarily expressed as adequate ideas – they are fallible, precisely because knowledge of the totality as such is impossible.

The transition from the second to the third theme of Spinoza's epicureanism is signalled in a unique moment in Part II of the *Ethics*, when Spinoza makes a rare apostrophe to the reader: 'Here, no doubt, my readers will come to a halt, and think of many things which will give them pause. For this reason I ask them to continue on with me slowly, step by step, and to make no judgment on these matters until they have read through them all' (*E* II, P11S). What is so unfamiliar or potentially upsetting about Proposition 11 that Spinoza feels the need to appeal directly to the readers' patience? The proposition says: 'The first thing which constitutes the actual being of a human mind is nothing but the idea of a singular thing which actually exists [*Primum, quod actuale mentis humanae esse constituit, nihil aliud est quam idea rei alicujus singularis actu existentis*].' One could say that there isn't much that is contentious here. The primary constituent element of the mind is its being in the world. But if that is the case, then mind and body are connected. If anything universal is to be cognized, then we have to start with singularity. *Practical knowledge is more primary than knowledge of universals.*[53]

Spinoza does not stop at this interplay of singularity and universality in Proposition 11. He clarifies in the Corollary: 'From this it follows that the human mind is a part of the infinite intellect of God. Therefore, when we say that the human mind perceives this or that, we are saying nothing but

---

[53] We saw this move in Epicurus's letter to Menoeceus in the previous section, and I will return to it in the following chapter.

that God, not insofar as he is infinite, but insofar as he is explained through the nature of the human mind, *or* insofar as he constitutes the essence of the human mind, has this or that idea; and when we say that God has this or that idea, not only insofar as he constitutes the nature of the human mind, but insofar as he also has the idea of another thing together with the human mind, then we say that the human mind perceives the thing only partially, *or* inadequately.' The implication is clear: any kind of knowledge of both singularity and universality – all knowledge, both adequate and inadequate – presupposes God as a totality outside of which nothing exists. *The primacy of practical knowledge is a result of the rejection of creation.* The immediate reaction of his readers was – as Spinoza feared – devastating.

Pierre Bayle – whose long entry on Spinoza in his *Dictionary* was for over a century the primary source of knowledge on Spinoza – reflects dismissively on Proposition 11: 'in Spinoza's system all those who say, "The Germans have killed ten thousand Turks," speak incorrectly and falsely unless they mean, "God modified into Germans has killed God modified into ten thousand Turks," and the same with all the phrases by which what men do to one another are expressed.'[54] This is one of the most famous arguments against monism in the early reception of Spinoza's work. What Bayle does not understand – what Spinoza feared that his readers will not understand – is the connection between the second and the third themes of his epicureanism. Monism does not stand on its own, as the first significant response to Spinoza's philosophy assumes.[55] Monism implies the practical kind of knowledge that is imbued in the singular – the knowledge that responds to the given circumstances.

We can describe this practical knowledge in terms of judgement that is understood in instrumental terms or as the calculation of one's utility. This is consonant with one of the major preoccupations of modern epicureanism, namely, Epicurus's use of phronesis. Phronesis as a form of practical judgement that is concerned with action and hence with instrumental reasoning can be found in Book VI of Aristotle's *Nicomachean Ethics*. But there is a major difference from Epicurus's use.[56] Aristotle argues that there are three forms of knowledge: episteme, which is knowledge of the universal essence of things; poiesis, which is knowledge of how to make things; and phronesis, which is practical knowledge leading to judgements about how to act. Aristotle argues that episteme is superior to phronesis, thereby admitting the

---

[54] Bayle, *Historical and Critical Dictionary*, 312.
[55] I return to this early reception in Chapter 4.
[56] I explain this contrast in more detail in Chapter 1.

distinction between theoretical and practical knowledge. In his reading of Aristotle's Book VI of the *Nicomachean Ethics*, Heidegger notes this distinction as the starting point of metaphysics and onto-theology.[57] By contrast, because the totality in Epicurus's conception necessarily requires practical judgements – because the *primary* act of the mind pertains to singularity, as Proposition 11 puts it – epicureanism asserts the primacy of phronesis over episteme.[58]

Phronesis is a judgement relying on no predetermined criteria external to the circumstances that call for judgement. It is a judgement as a response to the situation that one finds oneself in. Phronesis is always for something – that is, it is an instrumental thinking that precipitates action. As Aristotle already recognizes in the *Nicomachean Ethics*, its instrumentality means that phronesis combines thinking and emotion. The inseparability of mind and body in the practical judgement of phronesis is further emphasized in the epicurean tradition. Spinoza expresses an epicurean sense of phronesis in the Scholium to Proposition 9 of Part III of the *Ethics*: 'we neither strive for, nor will, neither want, nor desire anything because we judge it to be good; on the contrary; we judge something to be good because we strive for it, will it, want it, and desire it'. Judgement does not rely on the good as an independent value functioning as the cause of our desires. Rather, a judgement – as phronesis or instrumental rationality – is inextricable from desires and from projected actions.[59]

There are two ways in which the reader can go astray in understanding phronesis or the calculation of utility: either to conflate it with the Kantian account of judgement that has dominated the thinking about judgement since the nineteenth century, or to reduce the calculation of utility into utilitarianism.

The Kantian conception of practical judgement has two distinct requirements: first, the separation of cognitive and aesthetic judgements; and, second, the separation of practical judgement from natural causality so as to identify – or strive to identify – universal moral precepts. An epicurean sense of phronesis is incompatible with both requirements. Phronesis cuts through both cognition and praxis – which explains why Spinoza's epistemology and

---

[57] Heidegger, *Plato's Sophist*.
[58] Cf. Diogenes Laertius, 'Epicurus', X.132, which I quote in the previous section.
[59] The most important work on Spinoza and judgement is Christopher Skeaff's *Becoming Political: Spinoza's Vital Republicanism and the Democratic Power of Judgment*. Skeaff also recognizes the importance of E III, P9S for a theory of judgement in Spinoza. Unfortunately, Skeaff's book was published after my present book was completed, so I could not give it the attention it deserves.

metaphysics are presented within a book on 'ethics'. And, phronesis takes into account one's emotional comportment toward the situation in which one makes a judgement, which entails that a separation between intellection and 'natural causality' is impossible. Differently put, mind and body are mutually determinative for Spinoza. I should note in this context the enormous Kantian influence on how we have come to understand judgement today – and I call upon the reader to be wary of this influence while considering Spinoza's epicurean sense of judgement.

The greatest misunderstandings can arise by confusing Spinoza's conception of the calculation of utility with the utilitarianism that develops in nineteenth-century England. There are two fundamental differences between them. First, the utilitarians seek to develop a way to measure utility. Consequently, the emphasis shifts away from a conception of practical judgement that arises within given contingent circumstances and toward an attempt to discover a *métier* to measure the utility of actions. There is no attempt in Epicurus or Spinoza to ground action on some *métier* determining the calculation of the utility. Thus, for Bentham utility indicates a kind of algorithm that measures how we arrive at felicity, while for the epicureans the calculation of utility is a process that has no secure criteria and whose failures are just as important as its successes – a point that I will return to in the next section. Another way to express the difference is to say that for utilitarianism the end of action is pleasure and the means to achieving it is the calculation of utility.[60] Conversely, for epicureanism, phronesis is not a means but a necessary precondition for any cognitive activity as well as for action, including the pursuit of happiness and virtue.

Second, as a result of the first point, the nineteenth-century utilitarians have to insist on a contrast between the individual and society. How the utility of the individual and the collective are measured are not necessarily the same, and in many cases they may in fact conflict. One example of this may be Mill's treatise on liberty, where freedom is defined from the perspective of the individual – both the one who acts freely and those affected by these actions. Mill holds that we are free to perform any actions so long as they do not harm others. But Mill has no particular interest in considering in his essay on liberty any social or communal setting within which the actions unfold. By contrast, in Spinoza not only does the measurement of one's actions take place within the interplay of the utility of others – in addition, for Spinoza utility is reciprocal, or, as Proposition 35 of Part IV of the *Ethics* puts it, 'there is no singular thing in nature that is more useful [*utilius*] to a

---

[60] See Guyau, *La morale d'Épicure*.

human being than another human being living according to the guidance of reason'. Thus there is no sustainable contrast between the individual and society in Spinoza. Instead, both sociality and the political field are informed by the calculation of utility. This is consistent with the epicurean tradition arising in modernity. Let me provide one example.[61] Spinoza, following a materialist and epicurean tradition that includes Machiavelli and La Boétie, notes that the sovereign's decisions are always conditioned by their reception by the people. Thus, even the sovereign, the personification of the body politic, is not able to draw practical judgements that are 'autonomous' – that are 'owned' by his individually. Every calculation of utility is conditioned by the material circumstances in which it is made and by how it is communicated.

After these clarifications, let me return to the historical context to explain why the modern epicureans translate the idea of phronesis as the *calculation of utility*. We can suppose that there two reasons for avoiding the common translation of 'phronesis' as 'prudentia', which was the standard Latin rendition. First it could have been confusing, given that prudentia has both Stoic and Christian overtones. Second, and more importantly, given that 'epicureanism' was a term of abuse, primarily because it was seen as inimical to Christianity, the modern epicureans sought a translation that would allow them to hide behind the Bible – and Christ's words in particular: The 'golden rule' from the Sermon on the Mount, which is usually paraphrased as 'don't do to others what you don't want them to do to you', was construed as an expression of the calculation of utility.[62] The modern epicureans' turned to the 'golden rule' to obscure the fact that judgement as a calculation of how one's actions lead to communal utility has its sources in epicureanism.[63]

In this context, Spinoza's own preoccupation with the Sermon on the Mount is symptomatic of his epicurean insistence on the calculation of utility. For instance, Matthew's Gospel is one of the most common New

---

[61] I derive this example from my book on *Neoepicureanism* that I mention in the Preface.
[62] See Brown, *The Return of Lucretius*, 28; and, Brown, 'Lucretian Naturalism', 112. This 'law' is rendered as follows in the King James translation: 'all things whatsoever ye would that men should do to you, do ye even so to them: for this is the law' (Matthew 7:12).
[63] This justification becomes a commonplace and persists well into the nineteenth century. For instance, John Stuart Mill repeats in his essay on utilitarianism: 'In the golden rule of Jesus of Nazareth, we read the complete spirit of the ethics of utility. To do as one would be done by, and to love one's neighbour as oneself, constitute the ideal perfection of utilitarian morality.' 'Utilitarianism', in *The Collected Works of John Stuart Mill*, vol. 10, 218. This is also a central insight in his book on liberty.

Testament references in the *Theological Political Treatise*; Spinoza explicitly says that the Sermon on the Mount contains the entire philosophical teaching of the Bible; and he also cites the golden rule as an expression of the love of one's neighbour. Thus, the calculation of utility is in Spinoza another way of expressing practical judgement or phronesis. In this Spinoza can be understood as following the modern epicurean tradition that translates Epicurus's phronesis into the calculation of utility. For this reason, I use the terms 'calculation of utility', 'phronesis' and 'instrumental rationality' interchangeably – their difference being only that they designate different routes, conceptual and historical, of arriving at the third theme of Spinoza's epicureanism.

The most sustained meditation on utility in the *Ethics* can be found in Part IV, which is not surprising if we recall that Spinoza completed Part IV after the *Theological Political Treatise*. Let me note some nodal points. The preoccupation with utility is evident already from Definition 1: 'By the good [*bonum*] I shall understand what is certainly known to be useful [*utile*] to us.' Further, Spinoza associates the calculation of utility with the drive for self-preservation, or the conatus. Proposition 19 insists that it is from the laws of nature that one needs to make judgements about what is good for one. And Proposition 20 links this judging capacity both with the calculation of one's utility and with the conatus. As the Scholium succinctly puts it, 'no one . . . neglects to seek their utility [*utile*] or to preserve their being'. The calculation of utility is part of human nature to the extent that it is conjoined with the conatus. This means that the calculation of utility is part of living, it is an active practice. This idea is expressed in terms of neighbourly love in the *Treatise*, becoming a crucial component of its political theory – as I explain in Chapters 5 and 6. Finally, the calculation of utility is situated in the immanence of one's being in the world – which means that it articulates one's power. Spinoza succinctly summarizes this idea in Proposition 65 when he uses the standard formulation of the calculation of utility in the seventeenth century, namely, that one chooses the best of two good alternatives or the least evil of two bad ones.

Before I close this outline of the three epicurean themes in Spinoza, I need to underscore how each of them has a variety of sources and influences other than epicureanism – from Maimonides to rationalism and from averroism to Tacitus, to name but a few here. It would be absurd to argue that each of the three themes on its own is solely epicurean – for instance, that Spinoza's monism is derived only from epicureanism. That is certainly not my contention. Rather, I hold that it is the *interactions* between these three themes that constitute Spinoza's epicureanism.

Thus, for instance, I do not see an incompatibility between Michael Della Rocca's insight on the importance of the principle of sufficient reason in Spinoza and my reading of his epicureanism.[64] However, I hold that Spinoza's rationalism in Della Rocca's account is unconcerned with another – large and important – part of his thought, namely, how the third theme of Spinoza's epicureanism necessitates practical knowledge and judgements that cannot be fitted into the principle of sufficient reason. The effect of Della Rocca's lack of concern with the calculation of utility is the repression of Spinoza's epicureanism. Conversely, in order to foreground Spinoza's epicureanism, I highlight the interconnections between the three themes.

It is important to note in this context that Spinoza himself often highlights these interconnections. For instance, I noted earlier in the present section the function of Proposition 11 from Part II of the *Ethics* in forging the connection between the themes. There are also entire positions that he constructs on the same basis; the rejection of miracles, for instance, is structured around the connection between the three themes.[65] Let me provide here a couple more examples of these interconnections.

They are so important for the *Theological Political Treatise* that they are already suggested in the epigram, which is a quotation from the First Epistle of John. The whole passage in the King James translation reads: 'No man hath seen God at any time. If we love one another, God dwelleth in us, and his love is perfected in us. Hereby know we that we dwell in him, and he in us, because he hath given us of his Spirit' (John, First Epistle, 4:12–13). Spinoza quotes this passage several times – including in a letter to Alfred Burgh (*Ep.* 76). The most detailed extrapolation can be found in chapter 14 of the *Treatise*. Spinoza insists there on the connection between God understood in monist terms and the practical import this has for us as humans: our love of God, says Spinoza, is expressed through our actions (160).[66] In particular, the love of our neighbour that expresses our connection to God is *simultaneously* of political import, since Spinoza argues that it is for the utility of the state if the citizens adhere to the fundamental principle of religion, namely, neighbourly love, irrespective of how this principle may be appropriated by holders of power to further their authority. Thus, the political dimension of the connection between monism and the calculation of utility as it is also linked to the critique of authority is foreshadowed at the beginning of the *Treatise*, even before the text proper.

---

[64] Della Rocca, *Spinoza*.
[65] I take this topic up in Chapter 4.
[66] I examine this passage in more detail in section 1 of Chapter 6.

The most striking way in which Spinoza talks about the relation between monism and the calculation of utility is by adopting what we may call the 'cosmic perspective' in chapter 16 of the *Theological Political Treatise*: 'Nature's bounds are not set by the laws of human reason which aim only at one's true utility and his preservation [*utile, et conservationem*], but by infinite other laws which have regard to the eternal order of the whole of nature [*totius naturae*], of which man is but a particle [*homo particula est*]' (174/190–1). We should note first that Spinoza repeats this in almost identical wording in the *Political Treatise* (2.8), as if he is reciting an important, memorized passage. This cosmic perspective makes us realize that we are insignificant in the large scale of things. Such recognition is possible on condition that there is a distinction between, on the one hand, the realm of utility or everything that pertains to our action and preservation, and, on the other hand, the totality of nature.[67] It is instructive to note how the argument proceeds after this distinction. Spinoza asserts that it is to our utility to use our reason in constructing political communities (175). And then he defines human nature in terms of the calculation of one's utility (175–6). Thus monism – the 'totality of nature' – and utility are intertwined in the argument that will soon lead to the determination of democracy as the most natural constitution.

So, the three epicurean themes do not suggest that we should read Spinoza's texts by creating a list of various themes. Rather, my suggestion is that we need to detect the dynamic connections between them, how they interact with and inform each other. No theme on its own is adequate to present Spinoza's position.

3. The Dialectic of Authority and Utility: Spinoza's Promise

What is the dialectic of authority and utility for? Or, which is the same question, what is Spinoza's epicureanism for? The dialectic performs various functions at the same time, which can be summarized under the following three categories: an account of social and political formation; giving us the basis to make judgements about events both in the past and in the present; and, conceiving democracy as a particular way of being with others. Let us take each one in turn.

First, the dialectic of authority and utility provides an account of the formation of society and the state. Using the dialectic, Spinoza explains how

---

[67] The connection between utility and the totality of nature distinguishes Spinoza's perspective from a Stoic conception of providence.

the state is formed in a way that is distinct from the standard contractarian account that we find for instance in Hobbes. I will provide details of this account later in the book.[68] I would like to note here only that as soon as the genesis of sociality and the state is located in an irresolvable dialectic, then Spinoza's politics rejects any normative certainty that could supposedly determine political action.

As I explained earlier, there is a dialectic of authority and utility because the two terms are in conflict – authority requires obedience whereas utility is the drive to form judgements about how to act in given circumstances. This conflict can also entail that in certain conditions it may be for the utility of the people to defer judgements to someone else, or to authorize the sovereign to act on their behalf. As Spinoza does not tire of reminding us, the multitude is 'fickle' and people miscalculate their utility because 'they see the better but do the worse'.[69] Given this, we can imagine that, for instance, in a security emergency it may beneficial for the citizens to defer to the authority of sovereignty that may have all the necessary information to respond to the situation. Spinoza's own most prominent example is the Hebrew state. In the desert, Moses finds himself leading an unruly people who are, moreover, accustomed to submission to political authority. His strong personal authority is beneficial for the establishment of the Hebrew state.

Spinoza outlines two ways in which this authority can be articulated within this dialectic. On the one hand, the collapse of the operation of phronesis and the spread of superstition contribute to the establishment of the personal authority of those who use fear to strengthen their power. Spinoza consistently castigates this sense of authority that he also calls despotism, and he is unwavering in his showing how it conflicts with utility. His anti-authoritarianism is directed toward authority's attempt to suppress the capacity of the people to calculate their utility. On the other hand, it is possible that obedience to a sovereign authority may contribute to the good of the community. This recognition ensures that Spinoza does not adopt an anti-statist position. The lack of an explicit demonstration of this other side of authority in Epicurus or Lucretius, much more than Epicurus's advice to avoid the political turmoil of the agora, may be responsible for the traditional understanding of epicureanism as apolitical. Modern epicureans such

---

[68] See especially Chapters 4 and 7.
[69] Spinoza repeats the proverbial 'to see the better and do the worse' several times in the *Ethics*, notably in *E* III, P2S2, in the introduction to *E* IV and in *E* IV, P17S. The saying comes from Medea's character in Ovid's *Metamorphosis* but, as Curley notes, it is a commonplace in seventeenth-century discussions of the free will.

as Machiavelli and Hobbes do not suffer from the same problem. Spinoza belongs with the modern epicureans in this regard.[70]

One may object at this point that there is a fine line between the negative and the positive senses of authority, compounded by the fact that Spinoza does not provide universal criteria to help us identify when it is necessary to authorize someone else to act on our behalf. I hold that Spinoza would not have viewed these objections as a negative critique. Spinoza is not a utopian thinker. His politics does not consist of a set of normative criteria for how to arrive at the good. Instead, as the Definition from Part IV says, the good is that which is perceived to be contributing to our utility. The only 'normative' criterion – although the meaning of the word 'normative' here is stretched – is the persistence of practical judgement or phronesis. But there are no certainties, no guarantees that the dialectic will have a happy outcome. The dialectic indicates the kind of work for the sake of the polity which needs to be undertaken each time anew, each time differently.

Differently put, Spinoza constructs his politics as a *promise* for the good. Just as a promise is liquidated the moment it is fulfilled, the dialectic persists as a promise because it can never be completely realized. Thus, the dialectic of authority and utility does not provide us with any secure guarantees. There are no normative criteria that can help us decide on the relation between authority and utility. Instead, Spinoza's politics places an inordinate emphasis on the exigency to calculate utility or to exercise practical judgement. Spinoza uses an idiosyncratic expression to describe this exigency, namely, the freedom to philosophize.[71] For the true materialist, philosophy or thought is inextricable from the freedom pursued in communal actions and decisions, and for the good epicurean, this pursuit is couched within an interminable, non-teleological dialectic of authority and utility.

Second, the dialectic of authority and utility becomes Spinoza's heuristic device to analyse the Hebrew state. Spinoza uses the dialectic to organize his historical account of the Hebrew state's creation and destruction. The most intriguing feature of this function of the dialectic of authority and utility is that it need not be confined to the analysis of the *Theological Political Treatise*. Spinoza's epicureanism can be used to interpret all sorts of historical, social and political phenomena. In fact, it seems to me that our

---

[70] I regard this distinction concerning authority that avoids anti-statism as fundamental to the history of materialism, and I discuss it further in my book *Neoepicureanism* that I am currently writing, as noted in the Preface.

[71] I explain at the beginning of the next chapter why Spinoza's use of the expression 'the freedom to philosophize' is idiosyncratic and how it is connected to phronesis.

INTRODUCTION: WHY IS SPINOZA AN EPICUREAN? 41

contemporary political analysis will be enriched by mobilizing this epicurean dialectic. Let me explain.

Authority had been one of *the* organizing political concepts for an exceedingly long period, from the Roman republic, through the Middle Ages and the Reformation, to the social contract tradition. It starts to wane with the French Revolution and the political philosophy that precedes it, but it was still not forgotten.[72] It is only in the twentieth century that authority is substituted by the discourses of totalitarianism and authoritarianism and thereby marginalized in political thought.

The gradual forgetting of authority is not due to the disappearance of authority in politics but rather due to a shift in the vocabulary of power toward its impersonal operation. Very influential in this regard is Max Weber's account of bureaucracy as a distinctively modern form of power.[73] Weber's recognition of the theological roots of this 'iron cage', as he calls it, still gestures toward authority that is, as I argued earlier, both theological and political.[74] But this is obscured by the fact that the term Weber uses is 'Herrschaft', which has in German a wider range of signification than the narrow command and obedience model traditionally defining *auctoritas*. The effect of Weber's shift of signification has been to narrow the use of the word 'authority' to refer only to political authority within an established state so as to function as a near synonym of sovereignty.[75] All work in the past quarter century I am aware of uses the term authority in this way, that is, as a synonym of sovereignty.[76] The rich, two-millennial tradition that determines authority as a figure that cannot be argued with and which is not commensurate with sovereign power has all but disappeared from view.

The push toward the discourse of totalitarianism was provided by Hannah Arendt.[77] This is an intriguing case, since Arendt in fact wrote the most stunning essay on authority in the twentieth century, an essay that predates

---

[72] See Marcuse, *A Study on Authority*, in *Studies in Critical Philosophy*, 49–155.
[73] See Weber, 'Politics as a Vocation', in *The Vocation Lectures*, 32–94; and *Economy and Society*.
[74] Weber, *The Protestant Ethic and the Spirit of Capitalism*, 123.
[75] As Sennett puts it, Weber 'identifies authority with legitimacy'. Sennett, *Authority*, 22.
[76] This is the only meaning of authority, for instance, in the most significant recent monograph on the subject: Michael Huemer's *The Problem of Political Authority: An Examination of the Right to Coerce and the Duty to Obey*; for the narrowing down of authority in political theory, see Wendt, 'Political Authority and the Minimal State'; and for legal studies, Raz, *The Authority of Law*; and, Edmundson, 'Political Authority, Moral Powers and the Intrinsic Value of Obedience'.
[77] See especially Arendt, *The Origins of Totalitarianism*.

her work on totalitarianism and informs it in complex ways – as I will examine in detail in Chapter 3. Nonetheless, the enormous literature that develops in response to her *Origins of Totalitarianism* does not draw a distinction between authority and totalitarianism. The explicit substitution of authority with authoritarianism as an object of study in political philosophy and theory takes place in the aftermath of the Second World War. Here the Frankfurt School is particularly important because of their monumental *The Authoritarian Personality*. The key influential insight contained there is that authoritarianism is not only not opposed to democracy, but in fact uses the population to prop itself up.[78] The concept of authority is largely – and hastily – absorbed within authoritarianism.

If the narrowing of the meaning of authority to refer to sovereignty has become the canonical and unquestioned use, the substitution of authority by totalitarianism and authoritarianism has positioned itself at centre stage of the political discourse since the rise of populism. Thus, since Trump's election, there has been a renewed interest in Arendt's work on totalitarianism and its contemporary relevance.[79] Or, the rise of populism as a threat to democracy that simultaneously leads to the rise of authoritarianism is customarily interpreted along the framework provided by the Frankfurt School, according to which authoritarianism is possible through the populist manipulation of the people.[80]

I hold that this trend has significant drawbacks that Spinoza's own account of two kinds of authority – a despotic one and one that can collaborate with utility – warns against. Let me provide one contemporary example of why this distinction is important. The chorus of voices who condemn Donald Trump for his authoritarianism fail to see a more interesting fact, namely, that he is a president without authority. I do not mean that he lost authority while being president. More emphatically, part of his electoral success has been the renunciation of personal authority. *Auctoritas* needs to retain a certain *gravitas* to remain impervious to argumentation. Trump's compulsive and transparent mendacity contradicts this feature of authority. As do also his antics, of which there is a plethora of examples, including for instance the video leaked shortly before the 2016 elections in which he expresses himself in crude sexist vocabulary and attitude. But I think the most stunning example of this is the way Trump was laughed at in the General Assembly of the United Nations on 25 September 2018 – and that

[78] Adorno et al., *The Authoritarian Personality*.
[79] Berkowitz, 'Why Arendt Matters: Revisiting *The Origins of Totalitarianism*'.
[80] Brown, Gordon and Pensky, *Authoritarianism: Three Inquiries in Critical Theory*.

he was not at all perturbed. As Hannah Arendt observes, authority cannot tolerate laughter, as it eradicates its capacity to avoid any contradiction. Laughter is the reaction that authority, by definition, ought to forestall. As Charlie Chaplin's *The Great Dictator* (1940) or the laughter at Trump in the UN show us, authoritarian leaders are often the subject of ridicule because there is an *inverse relation* between authority and authoritarianism. Increased authoritarianism invariably leads to a diminution of authority. It is because of this inverse relation that it is possible to have a laughable sovereign.[81]

A fruitful analysis of this question needs to start with its contextualization. First, as a person in a position of power, Trump may be the first president of the United States who lacks authority but he is certainly not the first instance of such a kind of sovereign without authority. Recall at this point the breath-taking analysis of the rise of Bonaparte to power in Marx's *Eighteenth Brumaire* – an analysis which can be summarized by saying that Bonaparte lacked authority. As I argue in *Sovereignty and its Other*, Marx's analysis constructs the figure of the sovereign that characterizes biopolitics. Biopolitics and authority appear at odds with each other. For instance, the employment of managerialism and regulation erodes the authority of figures such as the university professor who traditionally enjoyed authority. Symptomatic of this trajectory was the discourse, prevalent prior to 9/11, according to which the globalization characteristic of neoliberalism was taken to pose a threat to sovereignty, with some commentators even speculating about the end of sovereignty.

And yet, the head of the sovereign has not been cut yet – to paraphrase Foucault. What is eroded is authority, even though – significantly – it has not disappeared. Instead, what is stark in recent articulations of sovereignty, such as Donald Trump, is that authority operates through a system of tacit but discernible substitutions. The figure on the Trump executive who holds authority is the vice president, Mike Pence. This authority is not derived, at least primarily, through his political nous, but rather through his allegiances with the religious right. Pence's theological authority is further disseminated through a network of preachers and other leaders of the religious right as his avatars or substitutes – or, is Pence perhaps their avatar authority? This network of theological authority is happy to support Trump so long as his administration serves their interests – that is, their utility – by installing figures in the judiciary, such as Brett Kavanaugh, who may also lack authority, like Trump, but who can represent their positions on issues such as reproductive rights.

[81] See Vardoulakis, 'Was Donald Trump Elected Because He Is Laughable?'

Thus, the dialectic of authority and utility allows for an analysis of the system of substitution or the mechanism of exchange that characterizes the operation of authority in neoliberalism. Spinoza's thought can be useful in this task. For instance, his diagnosis of the reasons for the destruction of the Hebrew state points to one cause whose multiple effects eventually eroded that state, namely, the fractioning of theological and political authority. Is this what is happening in the United States now too? Maybe the *Theological Political Treatise* is much more relevant today than is usually admitted.

Third, Spinoza's conception of democracy arises through his epicureanism. The key here is the connection between phronesis or the calculation of utility and the political. Spinoza's idea of democracy as the most natural constitution in chapter 16 of the *Theological Political Treatise* is premised on the discussion in the same chapter that human nature consists in the propensity of humans to calculate their utility. Further, given the fact that judgement becomes central in his account, and that practical judgement lacks certainty or validity, Spinoza is driven to describe democracy in agonistic terms. These are major themes running through the book so I would like here to indicate briefly the significance of the calculation of utility for our present.

A large section of political philosophy and political theory is squarely opposed to instrumental thinking as a normative basis for the political. The roots of this attitude are surely in Kant's separation of instrumentality from practical reason. The moral attitude, upon which the political is founded according to Kant, is premised on treating others as ends in themselves, that is, irrespective of one's calculation of utility. But Kant's account still does not sufficiently undermine phronesis – or, more precisely, it is an account that is opposed to materialism and it would take a materialist account that is non-instrumental to subvert this entire tradition that goes back to Epicurus. That's Martin Heidegger's contribution.

Heidegger starts his fundamental ontology with the distinction between how we relate to objects, either as present ready for us to use for our projects, or as instituting an entire world or framework of reference for us so long as we do not reduce them to their instrumentality. The former, instrumental approach Heidegger castigates as the onto-theology that needs to be 'destroyed'. This inimical attitude toward instrumentality is first made clear in his interpretation of Aristotle's conception of phronesis in the first three seminars of his course on *Plato's Sophist*, and it culminates in his animosity toward *Machenschaft*.[82] From Heidegger onward, instrumentality is dismissed

---

[82] I take this topic up in detail in my forthcoming *The Ruse of Techne: Heidegger's Metaphysical Materialism*.

as obscuring the right path to ethics no less than to philosophy. We can see this influence in the entire hermeneutical and phenomenological tradition – in figures such as Gadamer, Blanchot and Derrida. Hannah Arendt's *On Violence* is part of the same trajectory: she draws there a distinction between a politics proper that has power without instrumentality and a politics of instrumentality that is mired in violence.

This rejection of instrumentality culminates in political theory's engagement with biopolitics and neoliberalism. Most significant here is Wendy Brown's *Undoing the Demos*, which presents instrumental rationality as the key feature of the 'homo economicus', the individual in the era of neoliberalism. The effect of this instrumentality, according to Brown, is to altogether lose the political import of action. The 'homo economicus' is no longer a 'homo politicus'.[83] Bonnie Honig attempts a more nuanced route in a series of publications including *Public Things: Democracy in Disrepair*. Honig contrasts the instrumentality of neoliberalism with the possibilities that a productive sense of the use of public things can offer. Such a revamped sense of use can reveal the public importance of objects in our environment. And yet, Honig shies away from analysing this use in terms of instrumentality.

There are two reasons why I find this trajectory unsatisfactory – and, I may add, it is this dissatisfaction that has prompted me to embark upon writing *Neoepicureanism*, a book that conducts a genealogy of phronesis or instrumental rationality from antiquity to the present.[84] First, I find it too defensive to abandon the entire conception of instrumentality in relation to practical judgement to neoliberalism. Effectively, this means that political philosophers and political theorists accept as correct Albert Hirschman's genealogy of self-interest as providing the conceptual foundation of neoliberalism.[85] Instead, it may be useful to consider this as the weak point of neoliberalism because – as Spinoza often repeats in the *Theological Political Treatise* – utility is reciprocal since there is no such thing as an autonomous individual. We do not own our practical judgements. Our judgements are formed in relation to the material reality that we find ourselves in, which includes others.

Second, it seems to me urgent to consider whether it is possible to conceptualize utility in such a way as to mobilize it *against* the very neoliberalism

---

[83] Brown, *Undoing the Demos*.
[84] The manuscript presently titled *Neoepicureanism: Materialism from Antiquity to Neoliberalism* is still unfinished. See discussion in the Preface.
[85] Hirschman, *The Passions and the Interests*. Hirschman's book was originally published in the 1970s.

that it is purported to support. Such a way of conceiving the calculation of utility appeared to me urgent in the wake of the financial crisis in Greece. The various political activists resisting the push of neoliberalism and the policies of austerity imposed on Greece were concerned with employing an instrumental thinking to promote their opposition. Examining Spinoza's thought on utility I became increasingly aware that political activists were well served by their lack of 'theoretical sophistication' or, more bluntly, their ignorance of the arguments against instrumentality. They were attempting to do what Spinoza proposes, namely, to use the calculation of utility in the service of a radical political agenda opposed to biopolitics.

I am not suggesting that Spinoza has all the answers or that he can tell us 'what is to be done'. I do believe, however, that the way he frames his political questions in relation to epicureanism allows us to see key ideas, such as power and democracy, in a different way. This is particularly pertinent in how we can conceive democracy today, in the wake of 'populism'. There are essentially two responses to the rise of populism. Some argue that it is necessary to develop a 'left populism'. The most prominent example of this has been Syriza in Greece, even if it is hard to conceive of Syriza as other than a failed experiment, given that it has been unable to implement the policies that characterized its left populism.

The liberal response to populism, and the one that seems to be prevalent in the United States, especially amongst political scientists, is to seek refuge in a perfectionist model of democracy. This is often referred to as a 'Jeffersonian' conception of democracy, according to which democracy requires cultivated citizens who make informed decisions that reflect their voting patterns. The more cultivated the citizens, the more informed their decisions, the better functioning is the democracy. I find this approach problematic on many counts. For instance, it suggests an elitist attitude toward those who voted for Trump in 2016, as if they were totally unable to calculate their utility. Further, I am dubious about the possibility of progress or perfection that is an ideal implicated in the 'dialectic of Enlightenment', whose destructive kind of instrumentality is memorably exposed by Adorno and Horkheimer.

The epicurean dialectic of authority and utility is not amenable to such a perfectionist conception of democracy. The reason is that phronesis, as a form of practical judgement that is a response to contingent circumstances without any steadfast external criteria, is a kind of judgement that is inherently fallible. The 'paradox of phronesis' is that it dictates our actions in the absence of any certainty, or, more emphatically, because it is paradoxical.⁸⁶ That's the reason why Spinoza is fascinated with how judgement fails. He diligently, and often humorously, records the mistakes that lead to the construction of authority, to the conception of human law, and to belief in miracles. I will repeatedly return to the fallibility of the calculation of utility in my reading of the *Theological Political Treatise*.

The fallibility of phronesis means that democracy for Spinoza has the structure of a promise – just like the political, as we saw earlier. There is no telos, no ideal that can or cannot be realized, no certainty of perfection. Instead, there is the commitment to ethically and politically relate to others by putting utility under scrutiny. This *promises* the good and virtue because – as we learn from Epicurus – phronesis is the precondition of good and virtue. But there is no guarantee that we will be successful. Spinoza understands democracy as this ethical and political exigency that is incommensurable with political institutions and yet inextricable from them. If individuals can be excluded from institutions – for instance, from the institution of citizenship – Spinoza's conception of democracy is more egalitarian since everyone can exercise their phronesis, and hence everyone can participate in the democratic ethico-political exigency, despite the limitations posed by institutions.

In the course of the book, I pause from time to time to reflect on how the dialectic of authority and utility informs our political condition today. But the most common way in which I try to demonstrate the current relevance of Spinoza's epicureanism is by bringing him into dialogue with significant figures who determine our thinking of the political. These may be figures who are opposed to Spinoza's epicureanism, such as Arendt, Strauss and Levinas. Or figures who are epicureans themselves but in ways that differ from Spinoza, such as Machiavelli and Hobbes. Or figures who seem to me to grasp the core of Spinoza's epicureanism even though they do not name it as such, like Balibar. I hope that these conversations will help the reader identify some of the uses of Spinoza's dialectic of authority and utility in the current academic conversation, but with a view to understanding it as a promise, that is, as an unfinished – and incompletable – project.

---

⁸⁶ The 'paradox of phronesis' is the central concept of my book on *Neoepicureanism*. For a synoptic view of my position as well as a discussion of the paradox of phronesis, see Vardoulakis, 'Neoepicureanism'.

1

Freedom as Overcoming the Fear of Death: The Dialectic of Authority and Utility in the Preface

The first part of the subtitle of the *Theological Political Treatise* may have been easily acceptable to Spinoza's contemporaries: the book shows that 'Freedom of Philosophizing can be allowed in Preserving Piety and the Peace of the Republic'. In the aftermath of the Reformation, this sentiment would not have been unfamiliar. The secular ideal of the separation of ecclesiastical from temporal authority requires that there is a division between the inner self that is subject to faith and receives the message of Scripture, and the external self that is subject to the authority of the sovereign and to the laws of the state. Mirroring this logic, philosophers and deists of various hues claim a private right to the freedom to philosophize – a right that is distinct from their public obligations to the state.[1]

Although the first sentence of the subtitle should have come as no surprise to the general educated reader in the seventeenth century, the sentence that follows would most likely have been unnerving. The book, indicates Spinoza, also wants to argue that 'it is not possible for such Freedom to be upheld except when accompanied by the Peace of the Republic and Piety Themselves'. Here, the freedom to philosophize acquires a public dimension. It is as if Spinoza is suggesting that the freedom to philosophize requires as a necessary precondition a well-functioning state and a pious Church.[2] It is as if, further, the external condition – the public dimension of life – cannot be separated from the internal life of the mind. Freedom to philosophize is

---

[1] At this point, I am only considering the subtitle on the title page of the *Theological Political Treatise*. I discussed the title in the Preamble and the Introduction. I also discuss the important epigram briefly in section 2 of the Introduction and in more detail in section 3 of Chapter 5 and in section 2 of Chapter 6.

[2] Pierre-François Moreau notes this tension in the subtitle in *Spinoza et le Spinozisme*, but he does not link it to epicureanism, nor to a discussion of freedom in Spinoza.

determined by the material conditions in which it unfolds. Such a materialism is not widely embraced by seventeenth-century readers.

The cumulative effect of the chiasmus of these two sentences of the subtitle suggests a radical position. It suggests that the absence of the freedom to philosophize would threaten the existence of a state and would make the Church impious. It is as if – to put it bluntly – the freedom to philosophize not only bridges the divide between private and public, but it also becomes the condition of the possibility of public liberty. Such a collapse of the distinction between the inside and the outside challenges authority, *both* the ecclesiastical authority that relies on internal faith, and the temporal authority that relies on the obedience to the law.[3]

I want to show that Spinoza's conception of freedom that does not rely on a division of an inside and an outside is intricately linked with the dialectic of authority and utility that characterizes his epicureanism. Let me sketch what I mean by this dialectic, as I presented it in the Introduction. Authority asserts the entity that is beyond dispute, or that is impervious to argumentation. One has authority when one cannot be challenged. The calculation of utility refers to the human propensity to make practical judgements in the course of acting. On the one hand, there is a conflict between authority that calls for obedience and the calculation of utility that one fulfils by judging for oneself. To do what you are told and to calculate what is the most advantageous action are two contradictory ways of acting. On the other hand, this does not establish an exclusion between authority and utility because it may be advantageous to obey. Differently put, one may calculate that one's utility is better served by suspending one's calculation and following someone else's lead.

The key in discerning the meaning of this 'freedom to philosophize' that Spinoza mentions in the subtitle is to note how the dialectic of utility is linked to the three themes of Spinoza's epicureanism – monism, practical judgement and authority. More emphatically, it is through the operation of these three themes that the dialectic of authority and utility is set in motion. Thus, our exploration of the freedom to philosophize will be simultaneously an investigation of how the three epicurean themes inform Spinoza's conception of freedom as it is presented in the Preface.

I underscore that the discussion here is not meant to be an exhaustive analysis of freedom in the *Theological Political Treatise* nor in Spinoza as a

---

[3] There is a significant body of work on Spinoza's 'alternative' modernity that is characterized, amongst other things, by the overcoming of the mind-body dualism. See, indicatively, Israel, *Radical Enlightenment*; and Mack, *Spinoza and the Specters of Modernity*.

whole. The present chapter highlights how epicureanism informs the presentation of freedom in the subtitle and the Preface of the *Treatise*.[4]

1. 'A free man thinks of nothing less than of death . . .': Fear and Freedom in Epicurus

The initial stumbling block in adumbrating the connection between freedom and the dialectic of authority and utility is that it is hard to identify a definition of freedom in Spinoza's works. Nowhere in the *Theological Political Treatise* can we find an explicit definition of freedom. If we turn to his other major work, the *Ethics*, the difficulties compound. Part V of the *Ethics* may be about human freedom, but freedom as such is not defined there.

The closest that Spinoza comes to a definition of freedom is Proposition 67 of Part IV: 'A free man thinks of nothing less than of death, and his wisdom is a meditation on life, not on death.' This is an unusual definition of freedom, one that does not provide us with a *prima facie* description of what we would have expected freedom to be. More damagingly, as soon as we start interpreting Proposition 67, we are quickly led to contradictions and paradoxes. If we interpret it in terms of one's personal overcoming of the fear of death, freedom's *political* aspect recedes into the background, reinstating the division between the inside and the outside – which is precisely what we thought the freedom to philosophize as presented in the subtitle overcomes. And as soon as the protection from death is delegated to a sovereign, Spinoza would require a strong sense of authority aligning his position with that of Thomas Hobbes.[5] How is it possible to understand Spinoza's conception of freedom without presupposing either individualism or authoritarianism?

It is notable that the opening of the *Theological Political Treatise* is concerned with fear, specifically with how people become 'prey to superstition [*superstitione*]' through fear (1/5). Spinoza observes that humans are under the sway of 'fortune's fickle favours', which makes them 'wretched victims of alternating hopes and fears [*spem metumque*]' (1/5). It is for this reason that fear 'engenders, preserves and fosters superstition' (2). Everybody is subject to fear and hence to superstition. If that is true for the common people –

---

[4] I further nuance Spinoza's conception of freedom later, especially in Chapter 6.

[5] Some of the most penetrating observations about the importance of the individual's fear of death in Hobbes's adumbration of the social contract can be found in Carl Schmitt's *The Leviathan in the State Theory of Thomas Hobbes*. I compare at length Spinoza's and Hobbes's uses of fear in Chapter 7.

Spinoza quotes Curtius saying that 'the multitude has no ruler more potent than superstition' – it is also true for exceptional and powerful individuals such as Alexander the Great, who, in hard times, turns to oracles – 'that mockery of human wisdom', according to Curtius, whom Spinoza quotes again (2). This is a significant example – the first one in the *Treatise*. It suggests the futility of a task to 'enlighten' ourselves as foolproof protection against superstition. If such a great individual as Alexander is prey to fear and superstition, we may be better served recognizing that we will always be subject to passions and that reason on its own will not liberate us. Is there perhaps, then, a link between the enslaving function of fear and the conception of freedom as overcoming the fear of death?

The above question allows us to turn to epicureanism. The importance of the overcoming of the fear of death is something of a commonplace in epicureanism. The famous '*tetrapharmakon*', or 'fourfold remedy', that summarizes the first four of Epicurus's principal doctrines devotes the first two to the overcoming of fear: 'Fear not the gods/ Fear not death.'[6] This entire discourse about overcoming fear culminates in the fear of dying, since death provokes the strongest emotional reaction. Fear overwhelms us with emotions and thereby curtails our capacity to make practical judgements that lead to freedom. It works in the opposite direction too: as Epicurus puts it, when we are 'altogether free from the fear of death', our actions can be free and not dependent on any authority ($\dot{\alpha}\delta\acute{\varepsilon}\sigma\pi o \tau o v$, X.133).[7]

The key to help us make sense of the definition of freedom in Proposition 67 of Part IV of the *Ethics* in conjunction with the discourse on fear in the *Theological Political Treatise* is the calculation of utility – the third epicurean theme. According to Epicurus, phronesis is the precondition of any virtue and any good (X.132). We will see here that freedom is understood as the operation of phronesis, where this operation also mobilizes the other two themes of Spinoza's epicureanism. Epicurus contributes to how we conceive the co-articulation of monism and phronesis, whereas Lucretius's contribution, as we will see in the next section, is to delineate the first epicurean theme – the construction of authority through fear – in relation to instrumental rationality.

---

[6] The so-called *tetrapharmakon* (meaning, literally, a fourfold *pharmakon* or medicine) is a summary of what Epicurus's students regarded as the four most important ideas of his teaching. The *tetrapharmakon* has been preserved in a Herculaneum papyrus by Philodemus.

[7] Diogenes Laertius, 'Epicurus', *Lives of Eminent Philosophers*. All references to Book X of the *Lives* are made parenthetically in the text. I have regularly modified the translations of this edition.

Phronesis in Epicurus is best grasped by noting first how he radicalizes Aristotle's position.[8] In Book VI of the *Nicomachean Ethics*, Aristotle distinguishes between scientific knowledge or episteme and practical knowledge or phronesis.[9] The main characteristic of scientific knowledge is that its causes are necessary because it refers to unchanging things (1139a–b). To put this point differently, scientific knowledge is universal. By contrast, practical knowledge is concerned with contingent things. As such, it relies on rational calculation (τὸ λογιστικόν, 1139a). Phronesis in particular is concerned with calculating or judging how one can achieve a good life (τὸ εὖ ζῆν, 1139b). This is why Aristotle describes phronesis as concerned with calculating means and ends relations and as the kind of knowledge that pertains to the political.[10]

Aristotle summarizes his separation between scientific knowledge and instrumental rationality as follows: 'Phronesis is concerned with the affairs of men, and with things that can be the object of deliberation. . . . But no one deliberates about things that cannot vary, nor yet about things that are not a means to some end' (1141b). The lack of deliberation and instrumentality characterizes the one who practises scientific knowledge, the one who will be described later in the history of thought as a removed, disinterested observer. The reason is simple: 'Thought by itself moves nothing' (1139a). Thought does not lead to action – it is not practical – unless it is accompanied by emotion or desire. Significantly, for Aristotle this relation between thought and action in the operation of phronesis is not a hierarchical one. It can be either a thought coupled with desire or desire accompanied by thought (1139b). The starting point can be either, but *for phronesis to aspire*

---

[8] I am summarizing here a detailed discussion of phronesis in Aristotle and Epicurus that is contained in chapter 1 of *The Ruse of Techne: Heidegger's Metaphysical Materialism* (forthcoming). I also note there the influence of Heidegger's course on the *Sophist* in repressing the importance of instrumentality in Aristotle's extrapolation of phronesis. The course on the *Sophist* was particularly significant for Heidegger's development as it was delivered just before the writing of *Being and Time* and was attended by a number of students – such as Gadamer, Arendt, Marcuse and Jonas – who, in their own ways, followed Heidegger's lead to have an aversion to instrumentality when it comes to practical knowledge.

[9] Aristotle, *Nicomachean Ethics*. All references to this edition are made parenthetically in the text. I have often amended the translations. Also, I note that the distinction is more complicated. Aristotle is also concerned with technical or artistic knowledge – the knowledge about how to create things. I am presenting here the Aristotelian theory only insofar as it has a bearing on the epicurean discussion of phronesis.

[10] I explain in the Introduction why I am using phronesis, calculation of utility and instrumental rationality interchangeably.

to truth there must be a balance between the two – emotion cannot overwhelm thought, nor vice versa. This is an important point never questioned by Epicurus who otherwise significantly departs from Aristotle.

The contingency characteristic of phronesis comes at a price. At the end of Book VI of the *Nicomachean Ethics*, Aristotle raises the question of whether sophia (as the highest form of theoretical knowledge) or phronesis (as the highest form of practical knowledge) is superior. Noting that phronesis cannot arrive at universal truths because its reliance on contingency makes it fallible, Aristotle accords supremacy to theoretical knowledge.

When Epicurus writes that phronesis is the precondition of the ends of human life and is 'the beginning and rule of everything [πάντων ἀρχὴ] and the greatest good [τὸ μέγιστον ἀγαθὸν]' as well as 'the cause of all virtues [ἐξ ἧς αἱ λοιπαὶ πᾶσαι πεφύκασιν ἀρεταί]' and hence 'more significant [τιμιώτερον] even than philosophy' (X.132), he effectively rejects the separation of theory and praxis and thereby turns Aristotle's hierarchy of knowledge on its head. Suddenly phronesis emerges as the primary form of knowledge. Let us turn to Epicurus's letter to Herodotus, his most detailed account of a theory of knowledge, to see why Epicurus places so much emphasis on phronesis.

Epicurus begins by stressing what knowledge of nature is *for*, specifically, for a peaceful and calm life (X.37). He explains at this point that there are two sources of knowledge, either directly through perceptions, or indirectly through words that communicate experiences. But for this empirical conception of knowledge to be possible, Epicurus asserts that it is required to assume regularity in nature. He summarizes this position by saying that 'nothing is created out of nothing' (X.38). The rejection of the possibility of creation *ex nihilo* was prevalent amongst the 'physiologists' who tried to explain nature in material terms.[11] For instance, the same view was held by Democritus, the atomist who greatly influenced Epicurus.[12] Significantly, Epicurus recognizes that the rejection of creation *ex nihilo* can be expressed in terms of totality: 'There is nothing outside the totality [τὸ πᾶν] – nothing that can enter the totality in order to change it' (X.39).[13] The recognition that the rejection of creation *ex nihilo* entails a totality outside of which nothing exists essentially asserts that knowledge is possible on condition

---

[11] Aristotle, *Metaphysics*, 986b. For an account of prevalence of the position that 'nothing comes out of nothing' as well as the role that the totality or *to pan* plays in this position, see Furley, *The Greek Cosmologists*.
[12] Diogenes Laertius, 'Democritus', *Lives of Eminent Philosophers*, IX.44.
[13] I could have translated τὸ πᾶν as substance using the Spinozan expression from Part I of the *Ethics*.

that there are no divine interventions that change the laws of nature.[14] Or, knowledge presupposes a complete or unchanging totality that requires the regularity of natural laws.

The affinities with Spinoza's monism are significant. The opening of the *Ethics* consists in a repetition and defence of this epicurean insight about totality. Substance, Spinoza's word for this totality, 'cannot be produced by anything else' is how Proposition 6 of Part I of the *Ethics* puts it. The totality of substance or God is also a key position of the *Theological Political Treatise*. For instance, the rejection of miracles in chapter 6 is indebted to this epicurean idea: if nothing comes out of nothing, no event can be precipitated by a deity intervening into the natural course of things. The fact that the totality of nature has no outside means that natural laws cannot be broken. Or, more broadly, ontologically speaking, there is no transcendence. We can readily see how this monist principle – that the totality can admit of nothing outside it – is incompatible with the Judeo-Christian metaphysics that requires both creation and transcendence.[15]

As I explained in the Introduction, the presupposition of a totality for knowledge to be possible leads to the primacy of practical judgement – the third theme of Spinoza's epicureanism. As soon as we impute a totality of being, a complete theoretical knowledge of that totality appears impossible. Thus, knowledge always begins with a practical purpose. Knowledge always has certain ends. Epicurus designates the ultimate end as tranquillity. The word that he uses at the beginning of the letter to Herodotus is γαληνισμός, which is more commonly expressed in his writings as ἀταραξία (ataraxia) and its cognates signifying the serenity and blessedness characteristic of the wise person who has phronesis (see e.g. X.83, 85 and 124–5). The letter to Menoeceus says that such a disposition makes the wise person live 'like a god amongst humans' (X.135). *Ataraxia* means literally the absence or negation of 'anxiety' (τάραχος) – and fear of death is singled out as the most detrimental anxiety in our pursuit of blessedness (X.81–2).

The mutual support between phronesis and *ataraxia* is central in Epicurus and it explains why *ataraxia* is the ultimate end. If phronesis signifies the balanced relation between thought and emotion in the process of making

---

[14] This is the reason, as Frederick Lange explains in his monumental history of materialism, that the idea of the rejection of the creation *ex nihilo* played such a decisive role in the development of modern empiricism. See Lange, *Geschichte des Materialismus und Kritik seiner Bedeutung in der Gegenwart*. This is also why epicureanism is important for the scientific revolution. See Wilson, *Epicureanism at the Origins of Modernity*.

[15] Leo Strauss makes this point very clearly in *Spinoza's Critique of Religion*. I discuss Strauss in detail in Chapter 4.

judgements about how to act, then *ataraxia* is the state of mind and body that results from the balanced exercise of thought and emotion characteristic of phronesis (X.132 and X.140). This means that *ataraxia* is not an end that we can reach once and for all. Rather, it is a form of practice, one in which we can comport ourselves in the world. Further, *ataraxia* is not a pleasure in the sense that it allows the desire toward an external object. Rather, it is a pleasure in the 'middle voice', to speak, or it is a 'static pleasure', as Cicero puts it.[16] Differently put, *ataraxia* is the state in which we are *free from* the dominance of emotions such as fear of death that curtail our calculative capacity, *as well as* free from the illusion that the mind or the spirit can predominate over the body.

The epicurean refusal of the separation of mind and body combines the materialism of monism – no transcendence and no creation – with the inseparability of thought and emotion characteristic of phronesis. The interconnection of thought and emotion entails that no body is created out of nothing and that no mind contains a transcendent quality. When the body dies, the mind dies with it – there is no immortal soul or spirit that outlives the body. This means that – as Epicurus puts it in a phrase that was perhaps his best known in antiquity – 'death . . . is nothing to us' (X.126). The reason is that, while we are alive, we should concern ourselves with living – as Spinoza puts it in Proposition 67, one is free when one's activity 'is a meditation on life' – and when we are dead, we feel nothing and hence death can no longer affect us. The fear of death, then, is a state in which our knowledge starts from false premises and as such derails our judgement by overwhelming our emotions. In other words, it destabilizes the balance in phronesis of thought and emotion that *ataraxia* requires.

This balance between thought and emotion provides a basic conception of free action. Phronesis cannot accommodate the hierarchical division between spirit and body – the division that is the metaphysical foundation of the conception of the free will. Another way of expressing this idea is to say that instrumental rationality conceives of *freedom as being free from the free will*.[17] This is a fundamental idea in Spinoza that Moira Gatens and Genevieve Lloyd express by saying that in Spinoza 'freedom fundamentally is the emergence from the illusion of freedom – that is, from the illusion of

---

[16] Cicero, *De Finibus Bonorum et Malorum*, 2.10, 2.31–2 and 2.75. Cicero reports the difference between static and kinetic pleasure as if it were a well-known epicurean distinction.

[17] See Vardoulakis, *Freedom from the Free Will: On Kafka's Laughter*.

free will'.[18] It is also noteworthy at this point that the Latin translation of *ataraxia* is 'beatitudo', usually rendered in English as 'blessedness', a word that plays a significant role in Part V of the *Ethics*, which is concerned, as its title discloses, with 'human freedom'.

Following Epicurus, we could say that beatitudo as understood by Spinoza is the state that arises when one acts without being overwhelmed with the fear of death, but rather by exercising judgements that pertain to living – that is, when one acts freely, according to Proposition 67 of Part IV of the *Ethics*. That Spinoza adopts the epicurean position of linking phronesis and *ataraxia* in terms of overcoming the fear of death is also supported by the fact that Proposition 67 is preceded by two propositions that essentially summarize the calculation of utility: Proposition 65 holds that 'from the guidance of reason, we shall follow the greater of two goods or the lesser of two evils'. And Proposition 66 explains that this calculating applies not only to the present but also to the future.[19]

We see then how the parallel operation of the themes of monism and practical judgement lead to a conception of freedom. But a difficulty arises at this point. If monism designates a totality outside of which nothing exists, does not this entail determinism?

Even if Epicurus does not tackle this problem explicitly, his letter to Pythocles may be used to respond to the charge of determinism by working out a distinction between causality and instrumentality.[20] This letter discusses celestial or 'meteorological' phenomena (X.83), such as thunder, lighting and eclipses. These are natural phenomena that may generate fear in us, which is why people have attributed them to the interference of gods. Epicurus approaches the discussion of these phenomena by saying that they may admit of a multiplicity of causes, none of which contradicts the senses (X.86). From a modern scientific perspective, it is inadmissible to impute

---

[18] Gatens and Lloyd, *Collective Imaginings*, 51.

[19] Propositions 65 and 66 are summarized at a pivotal moment of the argumentation in chapter 16 of the *Theological Political Treatise* (175). I have already mentioned that moment in terms of the 'cosmic perspective' in the Introduction.

[20] A central argument of my book *The Ruse of Techne* is that, on the one hand, the distinction between instrumentality and causality is critical for materialism, and, on the other, that the metaphysical tradition systematically represses this distinction. Thus, the stakes are high in relation to this distinction that has hardly been noticed in the secondary literature. I cannot expand in detail on these high stakes here, except to say that the repression of the distinction is a critical component of the rejection of the priority of practical knowledge or phronesis, and hence of the privileging of theory over practice.

multiple causes to the same natural occurrence.[21] And if for Epicurus the senses were indeed the only way in which existence is experienced, as Hegel accuses him of in his lectures on the history of philosophy, then such an admission of multiple causes would have constituted an empiricism on a weak foundation.[22]

Hegel's accusation presupposes a separation of theory and practice, which is precisely what Epicurus seeks to deny through the primacy of practical knowledge. But for the inseparability of theory and praxis, Epicurus requires the distinction between causality and instrumentality. Epicurus admits of multiple causes to defend the idea of a substance outside of which nothing exists and to reject creation *ex nihilo* as a way of arguing for the primacy of phronesis. There may or may not be multiple causes for thunderbolts, writes Epicurus almost nonchalantly, but – and this is the point – 'the only thing that really matters is not to lapse into myth' while providing an explanation (X.104). In other words, if we cannot find the single cause of a phenomenon, we can experiment with different causes based on sense-experience, but we must avoid at all cost concocting divine interventions in the totality of nature, which only ever precipitates fear. The end of instrumentality – expressed here as avoiding the fear generated by meteorological phenomena – is distinct from the causes that precipitate those phenomena.

The multiplicity of causes is not a theoretical point about epistemology but a point about how to avoid emotional surges that overwhelm us and lead to fanciful ideas about gods. In other words, the discourse on multiple causes points to the primacy of practical knowledge, that is, phronesis or instrumental rationality. This is not to reject theoretical knowledge or to devalue it in any way. It is, rather, to recognize that theory is founded on practice and inseparable from it. Another way to put this is by saying that Epicurus draws a distinction between instrumentality and causality. This is what I call the primacy of practical knowledge.

We can put the same point starting with the second theme of epicureanism as it leads to the third one: the totality that includes everything is, by virtue of the fact that it includes everything, impossible to know completely. On certain occasions we may even be allowed to impute multiple causes to a natural phenomenon so as to avoid being trapped in the fear of this phenomenon. Instrumental rationality in this construal is the form of knowledge that does not simply have an epistemic function but that is the

---

[21] See also Bakker, *Epicurean Meteorology*.
[22] Hegel, 'The Philosophy of the Epicureans', *Lectures on the History of Philosophy*, vol. 2, 276–311.

necessary outcome of the substance and that organizes all the various ways of being in the world. Ontology necessarily entails that actions take place within contingency, requiring the human to make practical judgements – to exercise phronesis – so as to act in the world. Differently put, the operation of phronesis breaks the hold of determinism.

The priority of phronesis indicates that the epicurean question is not 'what is truth?' Rather, the question is about how we arrive at falsities. How is it that we err? This is an epistemological question – it asks how we can avoid errors. It is simultaneously an ethical question – it asks about the effects of our capacity to know, especially as they pertain to our well-being. And, finally, it is a political question that address the motivation for action – either because we are influenced by certain desires that drive us to error, or because falsities motivate us to act so as to rectify them. Note how congenial this line of thought is to Spinoza's understanding of the imagination in the *Theological Political Treatise*. The imagination does *not* lead to truth – which is why it is about action and therefore, as we learn in chapter 2 of the *Treatise*, the imagination 'is beyond the limits of intellect [*multa extra intellectus limites percipere*]' (20/28). And that's why it is also related to freedom: A universal truth does not demand any action, whereas the possibility of error requires action, it calls for it as a way of presenting or amending the error. Thus error contains within it the possibility of political freedom.[23]

The discussion of the multiple causes of celestial phenomena indicates also that epicureanism is not naturalism if by naturalism we understand that any natural explanation is referred to science.[24] Phronesis precedes scientific explanation. But this is not humanism either, because phronesis is an effect of materiality. There is an hylocentricism operating here – as opposed to anthropocentrism. The imputation of multiple causes is, in fact, not uncommon in the materialist tradition. For instance, Machiavelli often draws attention to how the same actions do not necessarily lead to the same outcome.[25] Machiavelli is also cognizant of the distinction between causality and instrumentality.

Overcoming the fear of death, then, suggests a theory of freedom that is irreducible to the free will, because it understands the mind and the body,

---

[23] I expand upon the issues raised in this paragraph in detail in Chapter 2.

[24] See, e.g., Wolfe, *Materialism: A Historico-Philosophical Introduction*; and Brown and Ladyman, *Materialism: A Historical and Philosophical Inquiry*.

[25] For an excellent discussion of multiple causes in Machiavelli, see Morfino, 'The Five Theses of Machiavelli's "Philosophy"', in del Lucchese et al. (eds), *The Radical Machiavelli*, 145–73.

emotion and thought, as inseparable. The calculation of utility or phronesis is the kind of practical comportment to the world that makes such a materialist sense of freedom possible because phronesis relies on the parallel operation of desire and rationality. Thus, the overcoming of the fear of death emerges as a way of expressing *freedom as the exercise of phronesis*.

2. Ante-secularism: The Construction of Authority and Human Nature in Lucretius

In Epicurus, freedom as overcoming the fear of death shows how monism – the second epicurean theme in Spinoza – and the calculation of utility – the third theme – work together for the good life of the human. For this to be possible, practical knowledge or phronesis needs to take priority. Knowledge is never disinterested or, as we might express it today, 'knowledge is power'.

It is here that the shortcoming of Epicurus arises. Despite certain incidental intimations, Epicurus never develops a theory of power, stopping instead at the designation of *ataraxia* as the end of action.[26] This is a significant deficiency for two reasons. First, authority – the first epicurean theme – is an underdeveloped concept in Epicurus; and, second, the historical dimension of the dialectic of authority and utility is lacking. Lucretius may claim that his *On the Nature of Things* adds nothing new to his philosophical master and it is merely an attempt to popularize his view in Rome (5.336–7).[27] But in fact it is more than that, as it addresses the two shortcomings we identify in Epicurus. Let me take these two innovations by Lucretius in turn.

At the beginning of his poem, immediately after the opening hymn to Aphrodite, Lucretius turns to 'religio'. This is also addressed by Epicurus, namely, when he describes how we assume gods or mysterious entities to be the efficient causes of natural phenomena that cause us fear or anxiety. Consequently, we are 'oppressed beneath the weight of *religio* [*oppressa gravi sub religione*]' (1.63). But this oppression is no longer *solely* an effect of the phenomena themselves. Rather, it is produced by those who interpret the phenomena in such a way as to gather power for themselves by making others

---

[26] More accurately, no theory of power is discernible in the small fraction of writings by Epicurus that have survived.

[27] Lucretius, *On the Nature of Things*. Hereafter cited parenthetically by book and verse number. On occasion, I have modified the translation. On the discovery of Lucretius's manuscript, see Greenblatt, *The Swerve*. For an overview of different approaches to Lucretius's reception and impact in modernity, see the collection edited by Lezra and Blake, *Lucretius and Modernity*.

obey them – that is, by positioning themselves as figures of authority.[28] Let me put this differently: according to Epicurus, ontologically there is nothing transcendent, since there is nothing outside the totality. Fear of nature creates transcendent ideas – what Epicurus calls 'myths'. With Lucretius, transcendence is not produced solely, or even primarily, by natural phenomena as such. Rather, it is produced through the interpretation of natural phenomena by the proponents of religion. Essentially this means that the practitioners of *religio* actively counter the operation of phronesis through fear. *Religio* appropriates instrumental rationality for itself and for its own ends, that is, to perpetuate its own power. Or, more succinctly, *religio* stifles freedom. This is a significant shift because it allows for a thinking of authority.

That Lucretius has *auctoritas* in mind when he writes *religio* – or that, at least, we can substitute one term for the other – is also shown by the fact that he indicates both a theological and a political source to *religio*, just as authority's origins are theologico-political. The example Lucretius puts forward for the 'evil' of *religio* (1.101) is the sacrifice of Iphigeneia (1.80 ff.). Her father, Agamemnon, does not sacrifice her only because he is ill-advised about the reasons why the winds won't carry his Greek army to Troy. In addition, he draws his justification for the sacrifice from the matrix of beliefs and practices instituted as religion. Thus, in *religio*, as this example demonstrates, collude those who derive their authority through theological and through political means.

Note that authority signifies a kind of power that is constructed and that is not shared – a power that is confined to priests and kings. Such an artificial power that is not common to all is what Spinoza calls 'potestas' or constituted power. As Negri has demonstrated, Spinoza stages a conflict between potestas and the kind of power that is shared by everyone and which is creative – as opposed to created.[29] This is the kind of power that Spinoza calls 'potentia'. Let us see how Lucretius stages the conflict between potestas and potentia as a way of presenting the dialectic of authority and utility.

Lucretius writes that Epicurus took a stand against (*obsistere contra*, 1.67) religion and the misery it brought to the world.[30] This consists in questioning the myths (*fama*, 1.68) about Gods as well as searching for the causes of the natural phenomena that provoke fear.

---

[28] As Thomas Nail also observes, *religio* in Lucretius does not mean religion in a narrow sense, but rather signifies restriction, for instance, the restriction that obedience requires, which is why it functions as a near synonym of *auctoritas* here. See Nail, *Lucretius I: An Ontology of Motion*, 59.

[29] Negri, *The Savage Anomaly*.

[30] For the distinction between taking a stand and taking sides, see Vardoulakis, 'Stasis: Notes Toward Agonist Democracy'.

FREEDOM AS OVERCOMING THE FEAR OF DEATH

Therefore the lively power of his mind [*vivida vis animi*] prevailed, and forth he marched far beyond the flaming walls of the world, as he traversed the immeasurable universe in thought and imagination; whence victorious he returns bearing his prize, the knowledge what can come into being, what cannot, in a word, how each thing has its powers limited [*finita potestas*] and its deep-set boundary mark. (1.72–7)

This is a complex passage. The main metaphor presents Epicurus as a powerful adversary who conquers *religio*. In parallel, there are two further metaphors presenting monism. First are the fiery walls that signify the end of the world, and the second is about the boundary mark that indicates the laws of nature that we as humans cannot overcome – for instance, the fact that we will all die.

It is important to note that the two parallel metaphorics – about the overcoming of *religio* and about monism – are possible on condition that a conception of power other than constituted power is presupposed. Specifically, the power (*vis*) that Epicurus has to take a stand against the oppressions of *religio* is not premised on any instituted form of power. Rather, the source of his power is that he has 'marched' to the end of the world, or, to put the same point in the vocabulary of the letter to Herodotus, he has grasped the totality (τὸ πᾶν). This power that Epicurus employs is finite (*finita potestas*). It is a power that comes from his thought that, as finite, pertains to the particular circumstances that allow for the emergence of that power. We can understand this power as phronesis, that is, as the power exercised through practical judgement and which is opposed to the power of authority that operates by employing fear. Thus, here the potestas of authority is pitted against the potentia of Epicurus's phronesis.

From this vantage point, we may be able to explain why the expression 'freedom to philosophize' from the subtitle is absent from the Preface – and in fact it is not used again until chapter 14 of the *Treatise*. It is substituted by the idea of the freedom to judge, repeated three times in the Preface. The first use suggests that preventing people from making judgements freely erodes their political freedom: 'To invest with prejudice or in any way coerce each person's free judgment [*liberum uniuscuiusque judicium*] is altogether incompatible with public freedom [*communi libertati*]' (3/7). The freedom to judge is opposed to constituted power that derives its authority from 'prejudices'. The second takes the same point further, accusing priests who 'distort the true function of the Church' from 'inhibiting everyone from judging freely [*unusquisque libero suo judicio*]' (4/8). This point could have come from Lucretius. The final use asserts that 'everyone should be allowed freedom of judgment [*unicuique sui judicii libertatem*]' (6/11) – because this freedom to judge is distinctive of human nature and of potentia, the kind of power that everyone has access to. We see here how Lucretius's first innovation helps organize the dialectic of authority and utility in terms of power in the Preface.

The second innovation that we find in Lucretius consists in highlighting the historical import of phronesis. If phronesis is constitutive of human nature, its operation cannot be confined to the here and now. It also operated in the past. Not only does this allow for the employment of history in the pursuit of 'free philosophizing', it also solves a problem about the connection between instrumentality and teleology. It is in Book 5 of *On the Nature of Things* where Lucretius introduces this second innovation.

Lucretius's theory of the stages of social formation requires an initial step, namely, the denial of any anthropomorphic conception of the divine as well as the denial of creationism: 'the world was certainly not made for us by divine power' (5.198–9). This leads to a conclusion that is familiar to readers of the Appendix to Part I of the *Ethics*. As Spinoza puts it there, 'Nature has no end set before it, and ... all final causes are nothing but human fictions'. Consequently, the 'sanctuary of ignorance' is the belief that God has a will. The epicureans express this also by saying that the gods do not care about us – they are unconcerned with human affairs.

Following upon the denial of the divine creation of the world 'for us', in Book 5 Lucretius spends close to two hundred lines on the interconnection between creation and destruction. Nothing created is exempt from destruction, 'even stones [of the gods' temples] are conquered by time' (5.306). This mutual dependence of birth and death ought to be placed within the argument about the mutual dependence of forces of power that Lucretius developed in Book 3: 'one thing never ceases to arise from another, and no man possesses life in freehold – all as tenants' (3.970–1). One exists by virtue of the fact that one is inserted in a network of power relations.[31] No one is absolutely free. Everybody depends upon the relations of power – both of potestas and of potentia – that unfold within the specific context one finds oneself in. Differently put, the totality consists of power relations that are responsible for the continuous, incessant unfolding of genesis and destruction, birth and death – and there is no end or meaning to this process. The rejection of creation *ex nihilo* or monism and the rejection of teleology go hand in hand.

---

[31] We will see the importance of this insight for Spinoza's conception of the relation between faith and philosophy as well as for Balibar's extrapolation of transindividuality in Chapter 6.

The discussion of the formation of society is premised on the realization that, even though there is no ultimate end in this matrix of power relations, still we can identify particular ends that regulate behaviour. Instrumental rationality or phronesis has no need for final causes at a metaphysical level, which is what allows for the operation of particular ends in history. Or, in another formulation employing vocabulary from Book 1 of *On the Nature of Things*, we strive for particular ends as opposed to an ultimate end because our power is finite. We can find the same move in Spinoza, who rejects ultimate ends in the Appendix to Part I of the *Ethics* but admits of instrumental reasoning – the kind of reasoning that relies on means and ends as a way of calculating utility – in Part IV of the *Ethics*.[32] And we also saw the same point earlier in Epicurus's distinction between causality and instrumentality when he discusses how we can overcome the fear generated by meteorological phenomena.

Lucretius employs the principle that human action is premised on the finite, instrumental ends pursued by phronesis to delineate three stages of social and political formation. Every epoch in the three stages of society is adumbrated by stipulating how humans use their instrumental rationality to respond to specific material conditions.[33] An historical analysis has recourse to phronesis to describe power relations that articulate the finite or particular ends – as opposed to final ends – of action. Thus Lucretius uses phronesis to distinguish between the three stages of society.

In the first stage of social formation life is nomadic, based on hunting, but humans lack a conception of the common good and do not have laws (5.925–69). Being close to nature, they do not fear natural phenomena and hence have no use of religion, but they fear the wild beasts. In the second stage, humans start living in settlements. At this point, Lucretius provides his account of the creation of language in terms of the utility (*utilitas*, 5.1029 and 1047) of communication. Here Lucretius also stipulates that property

---

[32] As Julia Annas argues, ancient moral theories take for granted that their starting point is the investigation of the ends of action that lead to happiness and virtue. See *The Morality of Happiness*, 9 and passim. Such a moral end is very different from the teleology relying on the presence of a divine law-giver, which Spinoza attacks in the Appendix to Part I of the *Ethics* and elsewhere. It is prevalent amongst Spinoza's commentators to infer from the rejection of an ultimate end (in the Appendix to Part I) that Spinoza rejects that action is directed toward ends. I have found no textual evidence that supports this inference, nor does it make sense within Spinoza's framework.

[33] Lucretius is here a long distance from Hesiod's mixing of myth and stories about gods to describe the various stages of humankind in *Works and Days*. See Hesiod, *Theogony; Works and Days; Testimonia*, lines 109–201.

and wealth start developing, but with that also comes ambition (5.1132), leading to the slaying of kings and general warfare – resembling what Hobbes calls a war of all against all. The feature that inaugurates the third stage is the creation of laws (5.1143–4), whose purpose is to arrest the violence characterizing the previous stage. The humans in this stage overcome the fear of violence but now they fear punishment from the law instead (5.1151).[34]

Two features of this schema are notable. First, Lucretius extrapolates how instrumental rationality is based on material conditions (see, e.g., the account of the development of metallurgy, 5.1241 ff.). Any articulation of phronesis is thus historical – which is to say, finite. Second, the drive toward the preservation of life or *conatus* accounts for the transition from one stage to the next – and fear is the dominant emotion. Thus in the first stage humans fear for their life from wild animals, in the second they fear for their life through the ambitions leading to generalized violence, and in the third stage they fear punishment from the law. Consequently, the main features of each stage are thoroughly determined by the exercise of instrumental rationality that responds to material circumstances with the aim to preserve life. What characterizes humans by virtue of being humans, all the way from a state of barbarism to the development of complex political structures, is the fear for their lives and the drive for self-preservation.[35] This constant feature affords Lucretius a method to think about the evolution of society. To put this differently, history shows us that human nature consists in how we exercise our phronesis to overcome fear. Or, that human nature consists in the unfolding of the dialectic of authority and utility – where authority is understood as the power produced through fear.

When Spinoza links conatus to the calculation of utility (for instance in E IV, P20S), he makes available to himself the historical methodology that we find in Book 5 of *On the Nature of Things*.[36] Thus, he can employ the example of the founding of the Hebrew state through the contribution of Moses's authority not simply as an historical analogy, as is common in the newly founded Dutch republic.[37] Moreover, as soon as history is founded on phronesis as a distinctive feature of human nature, the lessons about the dialectic of authority and utility derived from the analysis of the Hebrew state become

---

[34] This transformation of fear is fundamental to Hobbes – see Chapter 7.
[35] The similarities with Hobbes's state of nature are stark and the Englishman's debt to Lucretius still remains to be fully explored.
[36] I have learned a lot on this point from Joshua Visnic's MA thesis *Conatus and Practical Judgment in Spinoza*, Western Sydney University, 2019.
[37] See Schama, *The Embarrassment of Riches*, chapter 2.

relevant to the present. Spinoza can reconstruct an instrumental logic that leads to the foundation of the Hebrew state by identifying the means and ends relations that were at play in conjunction with the various forms of power – but, crucially, *without* recourse to ultimate ends, or to transcendent entities that miraculously intervene to support a supposedly 'elect' people (as Spinoza argues in chapter 3 of the *Theological Political Treatise*).[38]

A significant implication arises from Lucretius's analysis of authority in conjunction with its historical articulation, one pertaining to the inseparability of the two sources of authority, the theological and the political. In a move that today would seem counter-intuitive, Lucretius locates the emergence of *religio* in the third stage of human progress (5.1161 ff.). As soon as society is politically organized by providing laws to protect the state and to lead to order, peace and stability, humans realize that they are still subject to sudden death: 'when cities are shaken and fall or threaten to fall, what wonder if the sons of men feel contempt for themselves, and acknowledge the great potency and wondrous might of gods in the world, to govern all things?' (5.1237–40). The fear of punishment distinctive of the third stage is transfigured into a fear of gods as the punishers *par excellence*.[39] This creates the theological support for the structure of command and obedience that political authority relies on. Differently put, it is not religious practice as such that is produced in the third stage; rather, what is produced is the *theologico-political* authority.

This entails that the political and the religious are inextricable in any organized polity. But this is not the kind of post-secularism that has become prevalent the past few years, for instance through the work of Charles Taylor or Jürgen Habermas. The main characteristic of the recent 'return to religion' presupposes that a separation was forged between Church and state and that contemporary sensibilities transverse this secular moment.[40] Their aim is for post-secularism to point toward a pluralism sustained through reason. As opposed to this, Lucretius locates the genesis of *religio* in the creation of the political community through obedience to laws. The demand to *obey the laws* is psychologically distorted to create the illusion that we also need to *obey the*

---

[38] There are significant similarities between what I describe here as the historiographical attempt to reconstruct the instrumental logic of action and R. G. Collingwood's conception of re-enactment. See his *The Idea of History*.

[39] It may be worth comparing Lucretius's argument to that of the second essay of Nietzsche's *Genealogy of Morals*. For both, religion is intricately linked to how punishment is conceived.

[40] For a critique of this conception of secularism as well as an adumbration of secularism from a radical democratic perspective, see Gourgouris, *Lessons in Secular Criticism*.

divine. This recognition of the theologico-political roots of authority cannot be used to defend pluralism as it is simply a fact of historical development. Differently put, it indicates a historical or finite dimension of phronesis that explains the creation of law and that lacks any normative traction dictating what the law ought to legislate. Since it describes how a distinction between religious and state law is possible, we can talk of Lucretius's *ante*-secularism.

Instead of a normative dimension, ante-secularism fuels the dialectic of authority and utility. On the one hand, the production of authority as the theologico-political conjunction is positive. This is the reason why Lucretius locates *religio* at the advanced stage of society. In the move characteristic of epicureanism, the calculation of utility leads to commonality and the political structures that result from this can contribute to the utility of the community. The calculation of utility is thus necessary for the political.[41] Further, the fact that the citizens obey the law is necessary for the law to function and reach the third stage of development in Lucretius's schema. The structure of command and obedience is here positive.

On the other hand, the theologico-political authority can lead to negative consequences for the community when the calculation of utility is co-opted by those in authority to further their own purposes. Such a theologico-political authority can be concentrated in one person – Spinoza's example in the Preface is Alexander. Or it can be split between Church and state. But this 'secular' separation of powers is immaterial compared to the fact that the production of authority reunites within itself politics and religion. Obedience in a community relies on both political and religious motivations that may promote the ends of those who hold authority against the utility of the community. The negative articulation of authority contains within it a strong anti-authoritarian impulse.

This double movement of authority – both required under certain conditions to protect the utility of the people and under other conditions detrimental to them – is characteristic of the dialectic of authority and utility. And such a dialectic operates *irrespective* of a constitutional separation of Church and state, which is why Spinoza is ante-secular. Such an ante-secularism arises in Lucretius through the mobilization of the first epicurean

---

[41] The correlation of utility and commonality is a feature of phronesis at least since Aristotle, but it is most clearly presented in Spinoza. As I argue in *Neoepicureanism*, the rupture between utility and commonality mirrors the rupture between thought and emotion in the adumbration of instrumental rationality, for instance, in the way Adam Smith describes self-interest in the *Wealth of Nations*. This rupture is fully effected in neoliberalism, such as in Kenneth Arrow's *Social Choice and Individual Value*. As such, Spinoza can be seen to respond to neoliberalism.

theme – the production of authority through fear – in conjunction with the third epicurean theme – the operation of phronesis. This ante-secularism, then, complements Epicurus's analysis of the interactions and interconnections between the second and the third epicurean themes.

3. 'Fighting for their servitude as if for salvation': Monarchy versus Democracy

The most forceful and paradoxical co-articulation of freedom and the dialectic of authority and utility in the Preface occurs soon after the discussion about fear and superstition:

> Granted, then, that the supreme mystery [*arcanum*] of monarchism [*monarchici*], its prop and stay, is to keep people [*homines*] in a state of deception, and with the specious title of religion to cloak the fear by which they must be held in check, so that they will fight for their servitude as if for salvation [*pro servitio, tanquam pro salute pungent*], and count it no shame, but the highest honour, to spend their blood and their lives for the glorification of one man. Yet no more disastrous policy can be devised or attempted in a free state [*in libera republica*]. To invest with prejudice or in any way coerce each person's free judgment [*liberum uniuscuiusque judicium*] is altogether incompatible with public freedom [*communi libertati*]. (3/7)

The most 'mysterious' feature of the dialectic of authority and utility is that in certain political settings, the dialectic seems to suspend itself. The people stop calculating their utility and thereby lose their freedom. The regime of power that results is monarchy. Monarchy should be taken literary – as the authority that incorporates both political and religious obedience. Monarchy is despotism – not just authority but authoritarianism.[42]

At the same time Spinoza entertains the possibility of an opposed regime of power, namely, the free republic or democracy. Spinoza notes only one characteristic of a democratic regime – as if a regime is democratic if and only if it has this characteristic – namely, the capacity to judge freely. In other words, the exercise of phronesis that we have already seen as

---

[42] We will see later, especially as Spinoza starts developing a positive conception of authority in the second part of the *Theological Political Treatise* (chapters 7 to 15), the importance of the distinction between authority and authoritarianism. I take this distinction up at various places – e.g. in section 1 of Chapter 5.

synonymous with freedom in the epicurean tradition here becomes the necessary condition for democracy. With this move, the dialectic of authority and utility is transformed into the conflict between two regimes of power, monarchy and democracy. Let us explore some of the context of this move, before examining Spinoza's answer to the threat to freedom posed by voluntary servitude – what the *Treatise* designates as 'people fighting for their servitude as if for salvation'.

Spinoza's insight is that even in the most abject and total state of obedience, the possibility persists of a re-inscription of utility. He shares this insight with Étienne de La Boétie who, a century and a half before the *Theological Political Treatise*, frames the issue of voluntary servitude as follows: 'how it happens that so many men, so many towns, so many cities, so many nations at times tolerate a single tyrant who has no other power than what they grant him, who has no other ability to harm them than inasmuch as they are willing to tolerate it, who could do ill to them only insofar as they would rather suffer it than oppose him. It is certainly quite something.' In other words, 'it is the people who enslave themselves'.[43] Voluntary servitude presupposes democracy in the sense that the people have more power than any other entity within the polity. This power consists in the capacity to calculate their interest – that is, it consists in the exercise of instrumental rationality. The suspension of this power produces tyrannical authority but its re-energizing – always a possibility – describes a robust anti-authoritarian impulse that shook a lot of La Boétie's contemporaries, including his good friend Montaigne, who thought it prudent to leave the *Discourse on Voluntary Servitude* unpublished.

Let me express this another way: La Boétie realizes that authority does not rely on command but on obedience. Command on its own is useless – as anyone who has encountered the 'no' of a young child easily realizes. Command is effective only so long as it is obeyed. Thus, the power of the sovereign relies on the continuous submission to obedience. But – and this is La Boétie's significant insight – the people actually have the capacity to calculate their utility, which may lead them to the conclusion that they need not obey. To put it in a phrase that I will explain in Chapter 3, disobedience is the precondition of obedience. This means that the people have more power than the one who relies on their obedience. The critical insight is about the calculation of utility: power can only be mobilized against authority through the actualization of instrumental rationality, that is, through phronesis.

---

[43] La Boétie, *The Discourse of Voluntary Servitude*, 2 and 6.

The articulation of voluntary servitude in the *Theological Political Treatise* relies on instrumental rationality to grasp the function of obedience. This often remains unrecognized. At a strategic moment in *Anti-Oedipus*, Deleuze and Guattari refer to Spinoza's phrase that people 'fight for their servitude as if it is their salvation' to support the pivotal claim of their work, namely, that the forms of production and reproduction leading to a capitalist society rely on desire. They invoke Spinoza to show the paradoxical nature of desire, which consists in willingly striving for something that is against one's interests.[44] And yet, *pace* Deleuze and Guattari, Spinoza's insight is not just that every rational calculation is determined by desire. It also moves in the opposite direction: every desire is also equally determined by rational calculation. There is a reciprocal movement between desire and practical judgement. I won't indulge here in all the medieval debates as to what comes first, emotions or intellect. Aristotle is fully aware that this is the wrong question when he asserts that either is possible because phronesis 'may be called either thought related to desire or desire related to thought; and man as an originator of action is a union of desire and intellect'.[45] This co-operation of thought and emotion characterizes phronesis specifically, according to Aristotle. We have already seen how epicureanism radicalizes the Aristotelian notion of phronesis and how Spinoza appropriates this radicalization. In their extrapolation of Spinoza's conception of voluntary servitude, Deleuze and Guattari pay scant attention to the operation of phronesis in how obedience is constructed in the *Treatise*, and thereby miss the dialectic of authority and utility.

Deleuze and Guattari's blindness to that dialectic is in fact the norm in the secondary literature. Even Frédéric Lordon, who in *Willing Slaves of Capital* makes Spinoza's voluntary servitude resonate with the twenty-first century, only points to the dialectic to envisage its suspension.[46] In an analysis full of insightful observations, Lordon shows how obedience can be mobilized in all sorts of seemingly irrational ways so as to precipitate submission to capitalist and neoliberal forms of production and reproduction. Toward the end of the book, Lordon asks how it is possible to evade voluntary servitude. He points to Spinoza's argument from the *Political Treatise*, according to which the indignation of the multitude is the motivating factor in resisting power when it acts against their interests.[47] Indignation implies recognition of one's

---

[44] Deleuze and Guattari, *Anti-Oedipus*, 29.
[45] Aristotle, *Nicomachean Ethics*, 1139b.
[46] Lordon, *Willing Slaves of Capital*.
[47] I return to the important notion of indignation in Chapter 9.

predicament and a drive to change. There is, then, here, an intimation of the dialectic of authority and utility. But what does this change amount to? To the multitude regaining control of government in what would amount to 'a second coming of sovereignty', writes Lordon at the very end of the book. This solution erases the dialectic of authority and utility. Utility will triumph over superstition but then democracy will be completely absorbed within sovereignty. Besides the danger that the dialectic here may contain a telos, I primarily fear that the abandonment of the agonistic framework – the conflict of authority and utility – at this critical juncture of the argument contains the danger of resurrecting a revamped sense of voluntary servitude, one in which we are slaves by exercising our power (potestas). We are slaves by being rulers – not as a master and slave dialectic but as a coincidence of master and slave. At this point utopia becomes indistinguishable from dystopia. The exercise of pure utility supposedly freed from obedience is just as, if not more, disturbing than the surrendering of utility in the act of blind obedience – because voluntary servitude at least retains the prospect of resistance.

Both Deleuze and Guattari's and Lordon's positions stumble when the question arises about how to overcome voluntary servitude. The problem is that neither desire on its own nor the elimination of obedience seem adequate. So what is Spinoza's position? His solution is unexpected. He grants that – quoting Curtius – '"the multitude has no ruler more potent than superstition"' (2). But he avoids the usual move, whereby democracy is defined by arguing that the people or the multitude should rise from their servitude by perfecting themselves through education, a better political system, and so on. Instead, he accentuates the conflict between the two regimes of power, monarchy and democracy.[48] This accentuation of the conflict in the dialectic of authority and utility is at the heart of what I take to be Spinoza's conception of agonistic democracy.[49]

Let us see how Spinoza signals such a move. I am citing here the passage that immediately follows the one in which Spinoza determined voluntary servitude while distinguishing between monarchy and the free state:

---

[48] I have described this move in my own work by saying that democracy does not need to be defined by starting with the definition of the demos and then inquiring how the demos can rule. Instead, we can start with the second noun of the compound *democracy*, namely, the word *kratos* that means both constituted power as well as conflict, disagreement and overpowering. See Vardoulakis, 'Stasis: Notes Toward Agonist Democracy'.

[49] I provide here only the general framework of Spinoza's agonistic democracy. I discuss it further at various other places in the book, in particular, in Chapters 4 and 9.

Alleged seditions [*Et quod ad seditiones attinet*] that are pursued under the cloak of religion, they surely have their only source in this, that law intrudes into the realm of speculative thought [*leges de rebus speculativis conduntur*], and that opinions are put on trial and condemned as crimes. The adherents and followers of these opinions are sacrificed, not to the public health/salvation [*publicae saluti*], but to the hatred and savagery of their opponents. If under state law [*ex jure imperii*] 'only deeds were arraigned, and words were not punished', seditions of this kind would be divested of any appearance of legality [*nulla juris specie similes seditiones ornari possent*], and controversies would not turn into seditions [*controversiae in seditiones verterentur*]. (3/7)

This is a complex passage, not least because of Spinoza's propensity to present something as self-evident, whereas in fact it may deviate from our preconceptions – what I call the 'ruse of the obvious'. So let us read the passage attentively.

This first point to note is that the word 'seditio' is repeated three times. Seditio enters forcefully the vocabulary of political philosophy through Hobbes's translation of Thucydides *Histories of the Peloponnesian War*. Hobbes translates as 'seditio' the word 'stasis'.[50] It is well-known that stasis as civil war, or internal unrest, or conflict within the city denotes a negative political experience. For instance, Plato contrasts the glory and virtue that arises through *polemos*, the war against external enemies, with the *stasis*, the internal war that he describes as the greatest ill of the polity.[51] From ancient times onward, stasis is described as the greatest disease of the polis.[52] This assessment is still pivotal in Carl Schmitt's distinction between the enemy and the foe – who is the internal enemy. Schmitt defines the political as the identification of the enemy, whereas the foe is explicitly excluded from this definition.[53] Significantly, the identification of the internal enemy, *pace* Schmitt, is also a way of strengthening sovereign power, as the flourishing of sedition laws in the aftermath of 9/11 demonstrates.

Sedition or stasis is never accomplished by a single individual or a group of people. There may be an orchestrator of an internal unrest, but for that to be a threat to the state, the participation of the people is also required. For instance, Locke strongly advocates for the toleration of any opposing view,

---

[50] See Vardoulakis, 'Stasis: Beyond Political Theology?'
[51] Plato, *Republic*, 470a–471c.
[52] Cf. Kalimtzis, *Aristotle on Political Enmity and Disease*.
[53] Schmitt, *The Concept of the Political*, 28–30 and passim.

but with one exception, namely, when opinions that can be detrimental to the state start appealing to a large number of people.[54] The 'fickle multitude' that is swayed this way and that by the enemies of the state is indispensable for sedition to be actualized. Thus, 'seditio' signifies the worst that a state or polity can encounter and which consists in the people, the *vulgus*, inciting conflict with established authority. So, the word 'seditio' is loaded with over two millennia of unanimity as to its pernicious influence on the state, a unanimity that is accompanied by the fear of the multitude.[55]

Within the historical and conceptual context that I describe above, Spinoza's discussion of 'seditio' is extraordinary. He completely reverses the entire structure of the concept. Instead of the people precipitating sedition against authority, Spinoza presents authority as being seditious when it is using the law to suppress the free exercise of judgement. He starts by introducing not real but false seditions. These alleged seditions are perpetrated 'under the cloak of religion' to the extent that religion is a vehicle of superstition advancing authority. Religion, as we will learn soon and as Spinoza will tirelessly repeat throughout the *Theological Political Treatise*, has a positive function that consists in instilling obedience as a precondition of legality (6). Authority – to repeat – is not bad per se. But obedience, when promulgated through superstition, is counterpoised to the freedom to judge (4). Alleged seditions are the intrusion of law (and hence obedience whose negative side is superstition) into our freedom to judge and to calculate our utility. The effect of this is that alleged seditions will lead to prosecution. Differently put, authority seeks to substitute instrumental rationality, a move which is against the *salus* of the people or against the multitude's utility.

The tension between authority and utility comes to a climax around the word *salus*. Meaning both health and salvation, it repeats the word used in the expression about the people fighting for their servitude as if for their salvation (*pro salute*). So there is certainly an echo of this phrase here. At the same time, the medical metaphorics of the term stasis are unmistakable. As I mentioned above, since Plato stasis has been consistently designated as the greatest disease of the political. Spinoza is aware of this tradition, to which he responds to by totally subverting it. Here, the loss of health is attributed to those who seek to exercise authority despotically.

This reversal of the traditional understanding of stasis allows Spinoza to dramatize the dialectic of authority and utility leading to an understanding of democracy as agonistic practice. The idea of stasis, from Plato and

---

[54] Locke, 'An Essay on Toleration', in *Political Essays*, 134–59.
[55] See Montag, 'Who's Afraid of the Multitude? Between the Individual and the State'.

Aristotle all the way to the seventeenth century, was uniformly attributed to the 'fickle multitude', whereas here it is attributed to those who hold political authority and invoke the law against those who want to exercise phronesis.[56] Seditio is, according to Spinoza, an effect of seeking to consolidate authority by eliminating instrumental rationality in the name of the law. The accusation is directed primarily against authority – both religious and political – as is stated unambiguously a bit later: 'Church and Court are breeding bitter factions [dissidia] which readily turn people to sedition [seditiones]' (5/9). This claim is repeated in chapter 7 and further amplified in chapter 14 of the Treatise – as we will see in detail later. The seditious role of what Lucretius calls 'religio' is presented in political terms that mirror the distinction between monarchy and democracy: sedition is the prosecuting – exercised in the service of monarchy – of the freedom to judge that characterizes democracy. In this sense, sedition here stages the conflict between monarchy and democracy.

The argument concludes that if we recognize this seditious activity of monarchical authority, then controversies will no longer be thought of as seditions. In other words, democracy here is not defined through the people achieving rule. Such a rule is always liable to voluntary servitude when the people miscalculate their utility. Instead, the starting point of Spinoza's democratic thinking is the controversies and conflicts (another word in Greek for this could actually be stasis) allowed to unfold within the polity.[57] Thus, democracy is only possible if the dialectic of authority and utility is operative.[58]

The subversion of stasis performed by Spinoza is not unprecedented. The word 'seditio' has another equally, if not more, important side. As I argue my book *Democracy and Violence*, an alternative tradition about the function of stasis does exist.[59] For instance, Nicole Loraux discovers the foundation of the political in ancient Athens precisely in stasis.[60] And centuries

---

[56] La Boétie also makes this point in *Discourse on Voluntary Servitude*, 7.
[57] See on this point again Vardoulakis, 'Stasis'.
[58] And, can the dialectic of authority and utility ever be thoroughly suspended? If, following Spinoza, we assert that that's not possible, then we can grasp why Spinoza calls democracy the absolute form of government in the final chapter of the *Political Treatise*. I return to this at various points in the book, such as in the discussion of natural democracy in Chapter 4.
[59] The book *Democracy and Violence* is still in draft form. A lot of the ideas from that book have informed the present study. Also, *Democracy and Violence* contains an analysis of Spinoza's *Political Treatise* that I eschew in the present book for reason of space.
[60] See Loraux, *The Divided City*.

later Machiavelli – one of the major, if never named, conversants in the *Theological Political Treatise* – rehabilitates stasis by arguing in the *Discourses* that the greatness of the Roman republic was due to the instituted conflict between the senate and the people – that is, between authority and potestas.[61] The position I defend in *Democracy and Violence* is that such an alternative tradition is crucial for an understanding of democracy. Within such a genealogy of stasis, the passage we are dealing with here is of singular significance.

Differently put, Spinoza engages in this paragraph with a long tradition that sees stasis or sedition as the bane of the political – as the greatest fear of any state. As opposed to this tradition, Spinoza inscribes free judgement or phronesis at the centre of the regime of power that is democratic. This means that internal controversies are indispensable for democracy to be possible. And yet, that possibility is not envisaged as an ultimate outcome that would put an end to the conflict with authority – that is Lordon's deficient move. Instead, free judgement is counterpoised to sedition as the attempt by authority to repress judgement so as to institute voluntary servitude.

Nothing in Spinoza's passage indicates that this conflict characteristic of the dialectic of authority and utility can end. It does suggest, however – and this is fundamental in Spinoza's conception of democracy – that monarchy cannot exclude that conflict and therefore that the democratic is always presupposed, even when it is seditiously repressed. If freedom as the overcoming of death consists in nothing else than the exercise of phronesis, then the political regime embodying this freedom is democracy, even though – or, perhaps, because – the threat of authority and voluntary servitude can never be eliminated.

* * *

The subtitle suggest that freedom will be a central topic of the *Theological Political Treatise*. But the expression 'freedom to philosophize' is used in the subtitle in an unusual way, and it is also not regularly used in the *Treatise*. Further, nowhere in the *Treatise* can we discover a definition of freedom. To resolve these difficulties, we can start with the closest Spinoza comes to a definition of freedom, Proposition 67 of Part IV of the *Ethics* that associates freedom with a thinking of life, not of death. This accords with the epicurean conception that fear of death curtails our capacity to make practical

---

[61] Machiavelli, *Discourses on the First Decade of Titus Livius*, 200–1. For the designation of the senate as representing *auctoritas* and the people representing *potestas* in the Roman Republic, see Cicero, *De Legibus*, 492.

judgements. This further links to the other two epicurean themes: monism as the rejection of transcendence, which also implies that no part of the self can survive the demise of the body or that mind and body are connected; and authority as being reliant on the suppression of the capacity to judge.

Three important inferences follow if we read the subtitle and the Preface with recourse to this epicurean tradition. First, freedom can be understood as the exercise of phronesis. Second, this further requires that the three epicurean themes work in parallel – they rely on each other, and are impossible to separate. Third, the conception of freedom and the parallel operation of the three themes has significant political implications, especially for how democracy is determined agonistically. This suggests that already from the subtitle and the Preface Spinoza presents an epicurean framework to his *Treatise* that is critical for his conception of democracy as it is presented in the final part of the work.

2

The Power of Error: Moses, the Prophets and the People (chapters 1, 2 and 3)

I have been arguing thus far that the *Theological Political Treatise* is organized according to the dialectic of authority and utility. A problem emerges when we consider that a practical judgement about utility arises as a response to given circumstances, and if the circumstances are so manifold and unpredictable that they cannot be organized under steadfast rules, then practical judgement or phronesis can never aspire to either certainty or truth. It is, as Hannah Arendt puts it, a judging 'without banisters'. Any particular calculation of utility – be it at a personal or communal level – can never know for sure that its inferences are correct, since it needs to extract the criteria for judging from the unpredictable and uncodifiable situation it assesses.

Spinoza turns this feature of the calculation of utility into a mechanism that allows him to trace the operation of the dialectic of authority and utility. This is possible because the dialectic is not concerned with the truth or falsity of judgements that pertain to action. Instead, it concerns the effects of action. And such effects are registered when mistakes are made just as much – if not more – than when the correct decisions are taken. The first two chapters of the *Theological Political Treatise* suggest that the effects of these mistakes can be productive – and what they produce is authority. Subsequently, these mistakes are carried out in the definition of the people as described in the third chapter of the *Treatise*.

To discern these productive mistakes, we need to recall Lucretius's distinction between potestas – the kind of power that is artificial and that is instituted, as well as the kind of power that authority enjoys – from potentia – the ontological or 'natural' power that indicates the potentiality or capability of entities. All three mistakes – about the production of authority in the first two chapters and the production of the people in the third chapter – consist in misunderstandings about potentia, and thereby affect the interplay of potentia and potestas, which produces significant effects for the dialectic of authority and utility.

Schematically, the errors are as follows: The first error is made by the people. They mistake revelation as a kind of special knowledge that is superior to the natural knowledge shared by all. Thus they erroneously attribute a superior potentia to the prophets, which creates their authority. The second error is made by the prophets themselves, who fail to understand the nature of God, in particular monism, which entails that God has no potestas. They anthropomorphize God by mistakenly assuming that God has authority, thereby reinforcing their own authority. The third mistake is initiated by Moses and it consists in how he conceives of the special position of the Jews in relation to other nations. This leads to the false belief that the Jews are elected because of their potentia, whereas in fact it is only their contingent circumstances that articulate into their political institutions – or, potestas – that are unique. The unfolding of these three errors traces the unfolding of the dialectic of authority and utility in the first three chapters. Let us take them in turn to see how Spinoza presents them.

1. Moses: Prophecy as Communication

Is it the figure of authority that produces the matrix of command and obedience? Or is it, conversely, the fact of obedience that precipitates the establishment of authority? This circularity at the origins of authority points to its theologico-political roots.[1] If obedience comes from the figure of authority, then it is derived from a transcendent source characteristic of the theological. If authority is grounded on the immanent basis of the fact of obedience, then it is political.

The figure of Moses represents the question of the theologico-political origins of authority. He is both a prophet, whose authority is derived from revelation, and a statesman, whose authority is derived from the law. This is noted by Spinoza, who makes Moses the 'protagonist' of his *Theological Political Treatise*. Spinoza is following a long tradition going back at least to Machiavelli, who notes and praises the theologico-political power of Moses. Others, such as Hobbes, insist on the superiority of Moses over the rest of the prophets. In the iconography of the time, Moses becomes the figure *par excellence* to present the double origin of authority, both theological and

---

[1] See section 2 of the Introduction for more details on the definition of *auctoritas* as both theological and political. See also Paul Ricoeur, who describe this circularity as a paradox in 'The Paradox of Authority', in *Reflections on the Just*.

political. Turning to this iconography later will help us discern the originality of Spinoza's solution.

Spinoza addresses the double origin of authority by displacing it into the issue of communication. Moses is superior to other prophets because of how he communicates with God. More precisely, Christ is the highest prophet because 'Christ communed with God mind to mind [*de mente ad mentem*]' (14/21). Then comes Moses, since he is the only human who 'spoke with God face to face [*de facie ad faciem*]' (14/21).[2] Finally come the rest of the prophets who receive God's message through images. With the figure of communication Spinoza also signals his own original appropriation of the double origin of authority.

Communication is introduced from the beginning. Spinoza opens chapter 1 of the *Theological Political Treatise* with a definition of prophecy that, at first blush, may appear entirely uncontroversial. This is indicative of Spinoza's ruse of the obvious, as the definition contains a slight deviation from the norm, creating a cascading effect with multiple consequences:

> Prophecy, or revelation, is the certain knowledge [*certa cognition*] of some matter revealed by God to humans. A prophet is one who interprets God's revelations to those who cannot attain to certain knowledge of the matters revealed, and can therefore be convinced of them only by simple faith. (9/15)

Prophecy is identified as revealed knowledge. Prophecy is a cognition that is certain in the sense that it is beyond contestation. As Spinoza puts it in chapter 2, signs enshrine the prophecy's certainty that, consequently, is distinct from the 'mathematical certainty' (23) attainable through reason. Reason allows for contestation and improvement. Revealed knowledge does not. Thus revelation enshrines authority whose definition – as I noted earlier – is precisely that it is impervious to argumentation. Nothing controversial here. Spinoza presents himself as adhering to the doctrine of revealed religion.

And yet, there is a minor but significant dimple in this otherwise straight definition of prophecy. Prophecy is described as establishing a communica-

---

[2] In chapter 2 (p. 28), Spinoza will designate Adam as a prophet. Spinoza needs to do so, as he will extrapolate the Fall as a repetition of the same misunderstanding that characterizes the other prophets with the exception of Christ, namely, the misunderstanding about God's omnipotence. However, this creates a difficulty here, as Adam also communicated with god '*de facie ad faciem*'.

tion between God and humans. It is, specifically, a one-way communication from God to humans. This one-way direction of revelation accounts for the authority of the prophets, as only they can interpret the message of God, the others being convinced 'only by simple faith'. But if revealed communication requires interpretation, then revelation never discloses its content immediately. The prophetic mediation establishes prophetic authority in relation to the divine but it also simultaneously weakens it, since as an interpretation on the part of the prophets it is a self-constructed authority. Prophetic authority is theological because of the human capabilities or powers of the prophets. Moses is higher than the rest of the prophets due to his communicative capabilities – as we saw above – which means that he is not chosen by God in any special sense. He simply has better 'communication skills' – as we might say today. Displacing the origin of authority onto communication means that *authority is always mediated.*

This slight change is Spinoza's way of linking the theological provenance of authority to its political roots. As Étienne Balibar insists, 'Spinoza's philosophy is, in a strong sense of the term, a philosophy of *communication* – or, even better, of *modes of communication* – in which the theory of knowledge and the theory of sociability are closely intertwined.'[3] Communication's function is social and political. In Spinoza knowledge and power are intertwined. There is a practical and political element in the communication of prophecy because it is indissoluble from utility. The prophets interpret the divine message *for* the benefit or utility of those they communicate the message to.

To highlight the radicality of Spinoza's position, we can juxtapose it to the rich iconography of Moses. Depictions of Moses become prevalent in the Reformation and they are consistently concerned with the presentation of his authority. Examining such depictions will help us see the uniqueness of Spinoza's presentation of Moses's authority. In particular, it will help us see the answer that is traditionally given as to the double origin of authority, and Spinoza's deviation from that tradition.

I start with an earlier depiction from the late Renaissance. Cosimo Rosselli's *Moses and the Tables of the Law* is inextricable from the issue of authority, not only because of its subject-matter but also due to its placing. It can be seen at the Sistine Chapel in the Vatican. It was painted around 1481–82. The place and the date are important. Rosselli paints at the centre of power of the Catholic Church. One of the first viewers of the painting would have been none other than the Pope himself, Sixus IV, who

---

[3] Balibar, *Spinoza and Politics*, 101.

Cosimo Rosselli, *Moses and the Tables of the Law*, Sistine Chapel, the Vatican, 1481–82, image © Frederico Zeri Foundation

commissioned the Sistine Chapel. This is as close as one can get to the Pope, the apogee of religious authority at the time – four decades before the Reformation.

Rosselli divides the canvas into distinct sections each depicting one part of the story. This compartmentalization helps him depict the events with minimum interpretation. For instance, he does not choose to depict one privileged moment in Moses's contribution to the exodus from Egypt but rather seeks to depict all important moments. In addition, this evasion of interpretation pertains to the depiction of Moses as well, who is visually distinct from all the Hebrews. He is bigger and wears a distinctive golden gown that immediately distinguishes him in the heavily populated scenes – a figure of authority has external markers, as I indicated in the Introduction. The only significant intervention by the painter is a complicating of the direction in which the scenes are read. The earlier scenes are on the right and the later episodes on the left – for instance, the establishment of the Temple. The same right to left direction is followed in the central triangle, which shows the smashing of the tablets in front of the Golden Calf after the first descent from Mount Sinai and on the left the second descent from Mount Sinai. The handing of the tablets on the top of Mount Sinai is depicted only once, but it is placed higher than any other scene, conveying Moses's communication with God.

Why does Rosselli reverse the standard direction of reading? I want to suggest that this is his way of rendering the traditional interpretation of the theologico-political origins of authority. Alexandre Kojève captures this traditional conception when he insists on the 'spontaneous' genesis of authority – on the fact that authority is *sui generis*.[4] The vertical axis of the painting depicts the theological origins of authority by placing Moses higher than everybody else, whereas the horizontal axis depicts the path to the political origins as the trajectory to the establishment of the Hebrew state. The direction of the horizontal narrative is reversed so as to depict the inscription of the theological origins of authority in the political origins. It is as if to say that the end of political authority is at the beginning just as the glory of God is the Alpha and Omega. Or, differently put, as if the horizontal axis revolves around the vertical one, making the latter the stable one that organizes the rotation.

Spinoza's shift to communication cannot square with this depiction. The comparison with Rosselli's depiction shows in stark relief the position on authority that is rejected in the opening couple of sentences from chapter 1 of the *Theological Political Treatise*. The authority of Moses is either *sui generis*, as Rosselli suggests following a long tradition, or it is artificial, as Spinoza insists following a baroque tradition – as we will soon see by turning to a couple of depictions of Moses contemporary to Spinoza's *Treatise*. Let me put this more clearly: Spinoza's radical refashioning of *auctoritas* consists in that its origins are – as is the case in the tradition – theologico-political but – unlike the tradition – the reason for this double origin is its artificiality, since authority arises out of an interpretative activity that is a human construct. Spinoza establishes the incontestability of authority in such a way as to provide the possibility that it can, in fact, be contested, specifically when the interpretation performed by the prophets may no longer contribute to the utility of the people. The epicurean dialectic between authority and utility is a necessary consequence of the artificiality of prophetic authority. It is precisely this possibility that cannot be entertained in Rosselli's depiction because of the *sui generis* conception of the origins of authority.

To delve deeper into this artificial communication that determines the authority of the prophets and the superiority of Moses, we need to examine its link to knowledge. As Balibar correctly observes, Spinoza's understanding of knowledge and sociality are conjoined – and, as I added, Spinoza refers authority to this conjunction. So, what is the kind of knowledge conveyed through prophecy? In chapter 1 it is clearly stated that 'prophets perceived

---

[4] Kojève, *The Notion of Authority*, 31–8.

God's revelations with the aid of the imaginative faculty alone' (19). In Part II of the *Ethics*, Spinoza appears to construct an epistemic hierarchy. There, he identifies three kinds of knowledge: imagination, reason and intuition. It appears as if the imagination is the lowest form of cognition, since only reason and intuition, not the imagination, 'teach us to distinguish the true from the false' (*E* II, P42). If this epistemic inferiority of the imagination were all that Spinoza meant, then his philosophy would only be a 'critique of religion' in the Enlightenment tradition.[5] In other words, Spinoza would have simply been asserting the superiority of philosophical and scientific knowledge over revealed knowledge.

Contrary to such an impression, in chapter 1 of the *Theological Political Treatise*, Spinoza compares the imagination favourably to reason: 'Since, then, the prophets perceived the revelations of God with the aid of the imaginative faculty, they may doubtless have perceived much that is beyond the limits of intellect [*multa extra intellectus limites percipere*]. For many more ideas can be constructed from words and images than merely from the principles and axioms on which our entire natural knowledge is based' (20/28). Spinoza is not making the Kantian point, according to which moving beyond the limits of the intellect would be nothing but metaphysical fancy without a foothold in reality. According to the Kantian architectonic, the epistemic and the practical need to be clearly demarcated. Spinoza is making an epicurean point that – as I have shown in the Introduction and in Chapter 1 – asserts the primacy of practical knowledge and the calculation of utility over other forms of knowledge.

This allows Spinoza to highlight the political import of the imagination by showing how it combines concerns about knowledge and power.[6] A discourse of truth forecloses action. A universal truth cannot function as an impetus to act. No scientific genius has ever been a successful politician because of his scientific ingenuity. The epicurean sense of practical knowledge does not start with the question of truth, but rather with the question of error. The Scholium to *Ethics* II, Proposition 17 notes that the distinctive feature of imagination is that it is not concerned with truth or falsity. An image may lead to ideas that are false (cf. *E* II, P41) but an image in itself cannot be questioned as to its veracity.[7] Instead, practical knowledge in the epicurean tradition relies on phronesis or the calculation of utility and

---

[5] See respectively Strauss, *Spinoza's Critique of Religion*, and Israel, *Radical Enlightenment*.
[6] Cf. Gatens and Lloyd, *Collective Imaginings: Spinoza, Past and Present*.
[7] With regard to the image, see Chiara Bottici's important work, *Imaginal Politics*, which is inspired by Spinoza even when Spinoza is not a direct point of reference.

sets out from the recognition that the good is what is known as useful (E IV, D1). The authority of the prophets relies on imaginative knowledge, which contributes to social and political utility by conveying revelation to the people – and whether that knowledge is true or false is irrelevant insofar as its effects and its utility are concerned.

The imagination is *beyond* the limits of the intellect because it is *beyond* the distinction between true and false. That's why it is connected to phronesis that is concerned with practical knowledge, and that's why it is political. The imagination opens up a field that is larger than reason understood as the pursuit of knowledge through adequate ideas. In the political realm, we have no universal truth. Instead, we encounter the 'effective truth of materiality', as Machiavelli puts in chapter 15 of *The Prince* – a point that Spinoza is highly attuned to.[8] Politics can be cognized through its effects.

This epistemic perspective about the effectivity of the imagination also explains the theological origins of prophecy. As an interpretation, prophecy is *fallible*. The fallibility of the imagination stages the dialectic of authority and utility through prophecy. The fact that the effects of prophecy are neither true nor false is what allows the prophets to be beyond contestation, establishing their authority *and* also potentially subjecting them to contestation when they fail in the practical aim of making prophetic knowledge useful. Differently put, the test of authority pertains to its utility, not to the veracity of revelation.

From this vantage point, the question about the theologico-political roots of authority returns with a vengeance. Let me put this in terms of Moses. According to Spinoza, the *power* of Moses is constructed through the imagination that allows him to communicate with God in a way unparalleled by any other mortal. If authority as artificial can no longer be *sui generis*, then it is no longer possible to account simultaneously for both its theological and its political origins.

Spinoza does not directly tackle how the artificiality of authority configures its double origin. We need to reconstruct his answer. For this it is useful to turn to the baroque iconography of Moses that also grapples with the artificiality of authority in relation to its double origin. Unlike in Renaissance

---

[8] For instance, the opening two paragraphs of the *Political Treatise* rely heavily on chapter 15 of *The Prince* – but that's a topic for another occasion. For an insightful analysis of the presence of Machiavelli in the *Theological Political Treatise* – a book in which Machiavelli is not mentioned by name – see Morfino, 'Memory, Chance and Conflict: Machiavelli in the *Theologico-Political Treatise*', in Kordela and Vardoulakis (eds), *Spinoza's Authority Volume 2*, 7–26.

depictions such as Rosselli's, Moses's authority is no longer presented as *sui generis*. The figure of Moses in baroque painting addresses precisely the problem of the possibility of accounting for the theological and political origins of authority when they can no longer be posited as created spontaneously at the same time.

The double origin of authority is structured through establishing a hierarchy between the most high and the most low.[9] This contrast between the most high and the most low has significant political and cultural implications for modernity, as Walter Benjamin points out. The paradigmatic figure of this idea in theatre, according to Benjamin, is Hamlet, whose all-powerfulness – the fact that he is the heir to the throne and as such potentially the highest power in Denmark – also renders him incapable of action – it renders him the lowest of humans or 'creaturely life' as he cannot decide how to act.[10] This hierarchy also mirrors the secular separation of Church and state. In modernity, the two need to be kept apart.

In painting, Moses represents the double origin of authority through the use of the same hierarchy between the most high and the most low. The question of authority and the question of hierarchy are intertwined through the attempt to separate the theological and the political origins of Moses's authority. Let me demonstrate this with reference to two paintings from the Dutch republic around the time of the *Theological Political Treatise*.

Ferdinand Bol's *Moses Descends from Mount Sinai with the Ten Commandments* from 1664 hangs at the Royal Palace of Amsterdam.[11] Unlike Rosselli, Bol depicts the complexity of the narrative without dividing the painting into distinct parts. Instead, he relies on an extreme spatiotemporal condensation. The entire story is retold in a single temporal instant, the moment Moses descends from Mount Sinai a second time. This moment also includes references to the past through the man in blue dress,

---

[9] We can understand the hierarchies of baroque painting as effects of its artifice. For instance, as art historians note, the baroque abandons the Renaissance attempt to depict the world as we see it – a move signalled by the abandonment of geometrical perspective or by the extreme use of perspective. E. H. Gombrich is particularly important in describing this transformation (see his *Art and Illusion*). This artificiality has been part of the appeal of the 'neo-baroque'. See Lambert, *On the (New) Baroque*, and Calabrese, *Neo-Baroque*.

[10] Benjamin, *The Origin of German Tragic Drama*. For a detailed analysis of the issue of the hierarchy of power in *Hamlet*, see Vardoulakis, *Sovereignty and its Other*, 99–109.

[11] Michael Rosenthal provides some significant contextual information and draws some insightful parallels between this painting and the *Theological Political Treatise*. See his 'Why Spinoza Chose the Hebrews', in Ravven and Goodman (eds), *Jewish Themes in Spinoza's Philosophy*, 225–60.

Ferdinand Bol, *Moses Descends from Mount Sinai with the Ten Commandments*, Royal Palace Amsterdam, 1664, image © Stichting Koninklijk Paleis Amsterdam, photo: Tom Haartsen

averting his gaze in shame from Moses. He is Aaron, Moses's brother, who was responsible for the veneration of the Golden Calf. Simultaneously, there is a spatial condensation collapsing the distance between sky and earth. The starkest depiction here is along the diagonal axis that connects the tablet in Moses's hands to the child in red kneeling at the feet of Aaron. The child's head is not turned up to look at Moses, as if distracted by something on the ground. The innocence of the child touching the earth is contrasted with the prophet who has just communicated with God 'face to face' in the heavens. The contrast condenses the distance between the most high and the most low, the divine and the innocent, 'creaturely life' – to use Walter Benjamin's expression.

Bol's solution to the problem of the double origin of authority utilizes this double condensation. The temporal condensation refers to the episode that results in the acceptance of the law by the Hebrews and hence of Moses's political authority. The spatial axis refers to Moses's reception of that law from God. This spatial axis organizes the entire composition. The temporal dimension is incorporated within the pregnant moment depicted by Bol and which is organized on the spatial axis. Thus, the political origin of Moses's authority is absorbed into the theological one. Moses has authority over his people, who obey him due to the divine origins of his authority. His legitimacy is conferred through *transcendent* means; that is, through his proximity to heaven. His authority is primarily theological.

We see the opposite move in Rembrandt's *Moses Breaking the Tablets of the Law* from 1659.[12] Unlike in Bol's painting, here Moses's legitimacy is grounded on immanence through his extreme exercise of violence. Rembrandt depicts the moment when Moses is about to smash the tablets before the unleashing of an extreme violence.[13] According to Exodus 32:26–8, when Moses descends from Mount Sinai the first time and sees the Israelites venerating the Golden Calf, he smashes the tablets and immediately orders the massacre of those who lapsed into idolatry. Rembrandt captures that moment between the breaking of the tablets and the exercise of the most distinctive mark of sovereignty – the exercise of the right over life and death. The picture is like a memento mori – it prefigures the death

---

[12] For a discussion of Spinoza and Rembrandt, see Bal and Vardoulakis, 'An Inter-Action: Rembrandt and Spinoza', in Vardoulakis (ed.), *Spinoza Now*, 277–303.

[13] Some interpretations have contested the title of the painting according to which Moses is breaking the tablets. Christopher Brown argues that 'Rembrandt may well have attended a Jewish religious service where he would have seen the scroll of the Torah . . . being raised up. . . . This action could have suggested Moses's pose to him.' Brown et al., *Rembrandt: The Master and His Workshop*, vol. 1, 274. I do not find this interpretation credible as it makes a number of circumstantial assumptions about Rembrandt, for instance that he would have been to the Synagogue. More to the point, the standard iconographic practice is to portray the tablets raised over Moses's head when he is about to break them, whereas when he holds them, as when he descends from Mount Sinai the second time, they are held at his waist – for instance, see how Rosselli depicts both of these moments. I have not seen a good explanation as to why Rembrandt would have gone against standard iconographic practice, and hence I do not believe that a change of the title is warranted.

Rembrandt, *Moses Breaking the Tablets of the Law*, Gemäldegalerie, Staatliche Museen zu Berlin, 1659, image © Gemäldegalerie, SMB, Christoph Schmidt

resulting from Moses exercising the sovereign prerogative to take the life of his subjects.

Graham Hammill argues that Rembrandt's painting involves the spectator, who becomes a participant in the story. For this reason, Hammill discovers a democratic drive in Rembrandt's rendition, and hence argues it is akin to Spinoza.[14] But, it seems to me, the spectators are facing the cold fury of Moses. His face is expressionless but determined to assert his power. The only vestige of emotion is conveyed through the use of chiaroscuro, with only his right cheek and forehead in bright light, indicating the turmoil in his mind.[15] There is a spatiotemporal condensation here too, just as in Bol's

[14] Hammill, *The Mosaic Constitution*, 11–16.
[15] For a detailed analysis of the inscriptions on the tablets, see Sabar, 'Between Calvinists and Jews', in Merback (ed.), *Beyond the Yellow Badge*, 371–404.

painting, but with different effects vis-à-vis authority. The spectator is put in the position of the Jews who are about to incur the sovereign punishment because of the adoration of the 'graven image', that is, an 'idol' – and a painting such as Rembrandt's is understood by the iconoclasts precisely as an idol. Thus, the spatiotemporal condensation links the Jews and the spectators as facing the anticipated explosion of violence that is a mark of sovereignty. It is as if Rembrandt is reminding the spectators of their mortality when confronted with the immanence of the authority controlling the prerogative of life and death. The anticipation of violence shows that authority is here primarily political.

We see, then, that as soon as the origin of authority is not assumed as *sui generis*, one has to privilege either the theological or the political origin. The iconography of Moses – the paradigmatic figure of theologico-political authority – is faced with this conundrum in seventeenth-century painting. Some, like Bol, privilege the theological origin, others, like Rembrandt, the political. In either case, the fracturing of the origin of authority only ever enhances its power.

So, what is Spinoza's answer? It is instructive that he never explicitly mentions Exodus 32:26–8, that is, Moses's command for the capital punishment of those who venerated the Golden Calf. This is despite the importance that he will accord to the incident with the Golden Calf in his account of the Hebrew state in chapters 17 and 18, and despite how much discussed in political philosophy this episode is – for instance, Machiavelli is fascinated by Moses's exercise of violence.[16] Spinoza is not seduced by the idea of a founding violence for the political.[17] The authority of Moses does not have a primarily political foundation. Negri is correct in saying that Spinoza deviates from the standard baroque expectations because he insists that 'the impossibility of a linear and spontaneous mediation of this polarity [that is, between the most high and the most low] . . . consists precisely of the crisis of the constitutive force'.[18] The crisis of 'constitutive force' – that is, the rejection of violence as the origin of sovereign authority – is responsible for Spinoza's silence over Exodus 36:26–8.

This lack of mediation between the most high and the most low also under-

---

[16] See Machiavelli, *Discourses on the First Decade of Titus Livius*, 26 and 496, which refer to Exodus 36:26–8.
[17] Even though Spinoza never explicitly mentions Moses's order for the massacre, the episode of the Golden Calf is presented later as the cause of the splitting of authority into its theological and political parts, which contributed to destruction of the Hebrew state. See section 3 of Chapter 8.
[18] Negri, *The Savage Anomaly*, 77.

cuts the privileging of the theological origins of authority. As we saw, Spinoza defined prophecy as a one-directional communication from God, through the prophets, to the rest of the people. This establishes a hierarchy with God at the top and the people at the bottom. No sooner has Spinoza established the hierarchy of prophecy than he disturbs it by noting that prophecy is a species of natural knowledge since it 'depends solely on the knowledge of God' (9). And he immediately adds: 'natural knowledge is common to all humans [*omnibus hominibus communis*]' (9/15). The hierarchy of prophecy is challenged by the commonality of natural knowledge. The authority of the prophets is grounded on revelation that is *no* exceptional knowledge falling outside the cognitive capacities of the human. Without such an exceptional status for prophecy, Moses's authority cannot be primarily theological.

So how are we to understand Spinoza's conception of the authority of Moses and the prophets? If it is neither *sui generis*, nor primarily political, nor primarily theological, then what is its origin, according to Spinoza? His answer is that it is predicated on error: Given that natural knowledge is common to everybody, 'it is not so highly prized by the multitude who are ever eager for what is strange and foreign to their own nature, despising their natural gifts. Therefore, prophetic knowledge is usually taken to exclude natural knowledge' (9). The multitude are eager to subject themselves to the prophets. They do so by positing that there is a special kind of knowledge exceeding the natural knowledge that is common to all. Revelation cannot be shared and hence it is beyond dispute, whence its authority. The people mistake the potentia of the prophets as a kind of power that grants them special knowledge that is superior to natural knowledge – which is impossible because natural knowledge is knowledge of nature outside of which nothing exists. The error about the exceptional potentia of the prophets is the origin of their authority.

We saw a similar misapprehension in Lucretius's extrapolation of religion, according to which the errors about the power of nature spread by *religio* establish forms of constituted power. False fears create superstitions that establish authority. Spinoza appropriates this point. Prophetic authority is about power guaranteed by error – that's the epicurean insight.

Instead of focusing on the problem of having to distinguish the theological and the political origins of authority, Spinoza displaces the issue to power. The authority of the prophets is a matter of power. At the same time, power is split into potentia and potestas. Now it can no longer be an issue of a theological and a political side to power. Potentia, just as natural knowledge, is common to all. Everyone – Spinoza will also say in chapter 16, every*thing* – has potentia.

Spinoza understands the origin of authority as the erroneous interplay between potentia and potestas. Let me provide one example: Spinoza says that 'there is nothing to prevent God from communicating by other means to man' (10). There is nothing outside God, hence communication with God can take all sorts of forms. Everybody has the capacity (potentia) to communicate with God. In fact, however, prophecy is 'the only means of communication between God and man that I find in the Bible' (13). It is because of this unique *circumstantial* or *accidental* fact that the potentia of the prophets appears to endow them with special powers. This perception that accounts for their authority presupposes an erroneous understanding of the interplay of potentia and potestas, namely, that their potentia is superior to natural knowledge. That's what makes the people believe that the prophets' interpretations – and Moses's in particular – are beyond contestation. The authority of the prophets requires this error about the potentia of the prophets on the part of the people – there is no need for privileging either a theological or a political origin. The effectivity or utility of authority that I mentioned earlier is supported by the cognitive errors made by those who perceive that authority.

Spinoza, then, rejects the classical answer about the spontaneous origin of authority in both the theological and the political. Moses – the paradigmatic figure of the theologico-political – requires communication and interpretation to establish his authority, which means that authority is mediated and constructed. Spinoza also rejects the baroque solution that fractures the origins of authority privileging either the theological or the political – and always with the same result of strengthening authority's potestas. Instead, the origin of authority is located in the interplay of potentia and potestas, which however presupposes a fundamental error by the people, namely, the mistake about the superiority of revelation over natural knowledge. This error makes people believe that the potentia of Moses is superior to everyone else's. Given the irreverence of the Jews, this is a useful error as it adumbrates the theologico-political authority of Moses, assisting him in establishing the Hebrew state. At the same time, every error contains the possibility of its rectification. Spinoza's anti-authoritarianism is inscribed in this possibility at the origins of authority as the error in the interplay of potentia and potestas.

2. 'God has no particular style of speech': The Error about God's Potentia

The people's mistake about revelation as a kind of knowledge that cannot be shared produces the prophets' authority. The prophets, on their side, accentuate and perpetuate authority by committing a new error, namely, they misunderstand the potentia of God as a kind of potestas that legitimates their own interpretations of revelations.

What does the potentia of God consist in? As Deleuze notes, Spinoza denies 'that God has any power (*potestas*) analogous to that of a tyrant, or even an enlightened prince'.[19] There is no interplay between potentia and potestas in God. God's power has no outside, and hence no artificiality – God is nature. Spinoza expresses the universality of God's potentia in terms of language: 'God has no particular style of speech [*Deum nullum habere stylum peculiarem dicendi*]' (25/34). God's potentia entails that he has an infinite linguistic capability.

This insight is important if the relations of authority established between the prophets and the people rely on communication. The prophets need to interpret the divine communication for the people. Thus, Spinoza stresses repeatedly that the communication of the prophets relies on the linguistic and expressive capabilities of the prophets, which are in turn contingent upon the capacity of those they are addressing to receive the message communicated. As I put it earlier, prophecy as interpretation is mediated – which also means, it is always idiomatic. By contrast, God's speech is not idiomatic. The prophetic potestas, then, arises at the moment there is idiom.

But idiom is not a sufficient condition for the establishment of potestas. The reason is that idiomatic language as the language of the imagination is 'fleeting [*vaga*] and inconstant [*inconstans*]' (20/29). So, how can the imagination that 'does not of its own nature carry certainty with it' (21) institute the authority of the prophets? To compensate for this lack of certainty, the images of revelation are accompanied by signs 'to assure them of certainty' (22). The sign infuses the idiom with certainty. The signs that the prophets receive are beyond dispute. For instance, no Israelite could argue with the content of the Tablets; that is, with the sign that Moses received. The sign infuses the bearer of the sign with a personal authority that consolidates his potestas.

Spinoza underscores the utility of prophetic authority: the prophets only had 'moral' authority because they were concerned 'exclusively with what was right and good [*aequum, et bonum*]' (23/31). Provided we recall the determination of the good (*bonum*) as that which is useful (*utile*) in Definition 1 of Part IV of the *Ethics*, we see Spinoza here contending that the authority of the prophets can contribute to social utility. The people receive the sign as indisputable only so long as the sign has moral certainty, which means,

---

[19] Deleuze, *Spinoza: Practical Philosophy*, 97.

only so long as it benefits them *as a community*. The potestas of the prophets is effected by the dialectic of authority and utility.

This puts the prophets in a precarious position. The onus is on them not only to find the proper linguistic idiom for successful communication. In addition, the expression of their message must also establish their authority by contributing to the utility of the people. To avoid this conundrum, the prophets misunderstand God's potentia. Thus, the interplay of potentia and potestas is the origin of authority only because of a double error about potentia – on the part of the people who misunderstand the potentia of the prophets and on the part of the prophets who misunderstand the potentia of God. Let us see more clearly what the error of the prophets consists in.

The prophetic error goes back to the first human: 'Adam, to whom God was first revealed, did not know that God is omnipresent and omniscient' (28). Adam is not Spinoza's focus – not yet. Moses 'similarly did not sufficiently [*satis etiam*] comprehend' (28/38) God's omniscience and omnipresence. Moses's understanding is confused. For instance, he understands, according to the biblical evidence cited by Spinoza, that God 'has always existed, exists, and will always exist' (29), but at the same time Moses believed that God 'gave authority' (29) to others in nations other than the Hebrews. So Moses makes an error about God's omnipresence – and soon Spinoza describes a second error: 'He furthermore taught that this Being had reduced our visible world from chaos to order . . . and had given Nature its seeds. He therefore possesses supreme right and power [*omnia summum jus et summam potentiam*] over things, and . . . in virtue of [*pro hoc*] this supreme right and power he had chosen the Hebrew nation for himself alone, together with a certain territory . . . leaving other nations and lands to the care of other Gods standing in his place' (29/39). Moses then ascribes omnipotence to God because he created the universe – God produced 'order' thereby demonstrating his 'supreme right and power'. God does not have *summa potestas*, like a sovereign. Rather, he has *summa potentia*, absolute capability or omnipotence. But then Moses also thought that God exercised this supreme power in order to (*pro hoc*) create a select state, the Hebrew state. This is the point where Moses misunderstands omnipotence. He thinks there is no other nation subject to God's *summa potentia*.

Moses's errors about divine potentia produce some amusing results – 'Moses even climbed the mountain to speak with God, which he certainly need not have done if he could just as well have imagined God as being everywhere' (31), writes Spinoza in his distinctive playfulness. But there is a serious side as well. The error about God's potentia means that the prophets misunderstand monism – the second epicurean theme in Spinoza. Monism rejects creation *ex nihilo* by the positing of a totality – what Epicurus calls *to pan* and Spinoza calls substance, God or nature – outside of which nothing exists. God is simply that totality, and as such God does not intervene in human affairs and cannot be conceived as a lawgiver.

I hasten to add that Spinoza does not lament such a misconception of divine power. Instead, he emphatically underscores the effects of error that are beneficial because they strengthen the authority of the prophets. The most important of these is to enable Moses to teach the Hebrews 'a moral code ... as a lawgiver, compelling people to live good lives by command of law' (31). Command and obedience – the entire machine of prophetic authority requires that error about God's power. Moses can be a lawgiver and a state founder because he can spread this misunderstanding that the law is derived from a divine lawgiver, which enables him to demand obedience of those who are admitted in the newly formed Hebrew state. In other words, there is no inherent sanction of the law – there is no divine intervention or originary act of violence to legitimate authority. The constitution of a state – its potestas – is premised on a misconception of divine potentia. A misconception that is, for that very reason, incredibly expedient as it contributes to the good and the utility of the state. Their error here too is effective.

We can put the same point in terms of Spinoza's epicureanism: the error of the prophets enshrines their authority because it is mediated by utility. The way that the interplay between potentia and potestas is erroneously understood effects the operation of the dialectic of authority and utility.

Let me add a brief remark here about Gilles Deleuze's typology of the sign. Deleuze identifies three kinds of sign. First, the indicative sign is characterized by the arbitrariness of meaning in language. Second, the imperative sign is produced by revelation and propagates obedience. And, third, the interpretative sign requires the prophet as an external guarantee to authenticate, or authorize, the sign.[20] Deleuze concludes his typology of signs as follows: 'The unity of all signs consists in this: they form an essentially equivocal language of imagination which stands *in contrast* to the natural language of philosophy, composed of univocal expression.'[21] The problem with this position is that Deleuze fails to notice the link between signs, the errors they generate, and the authority produced by these errors as well as the utility the errors make possible.[22] If we take the typology not as indicating different

---

[20] Deleuze, *Spinoza*, 105–7.
[21] Deleuze, *Spinoza*, 107, emphasis added.
[22] Cf. Lambert, 'Spinoza and Signs', in Kordela and Vardoulakis (eds), *Spinoza's Authority Volume 2*, 153–66, and, Malabou, 'Before and Above: Spinoza and Symbolic Necessity'.

signs, but rather as identifying different *effects* of the sign that forge different ways in which the calculation of utility is articulated, then Deleuze's typology appears in a totally different light. Instead of imagination being 'in contrast' to natural knowledge, they will always be in a relation that amplifies the tension between authority and utility. The advantage of such a reading consists in that the prophet is no longer presented in contrast to the philosopher. Instead, now philosophy achieves a political function that consists in challenging the errors that produce authority, while also recognizing the utility of authority. Philosophy also participates in the dialectic of authority and utility.

The prophetic error about God's potentia is connected with the error about the prophets' potentia generated by the people. This marks the contemporary significance of Spinoza's *Theological Political Treatise*. In a significant letter from 1665, Spinoza informs Henry Oldenburg that he has started working on the *Treatise* because he wants to make an intervention that is contemporary (*Ep.* 30). But at the same time, he indicates from the very beginning that 'there are no longer any prophets amongst us today' (10). Spinoza explains the contemporary relevance in the second note to chapter 2 where he explicitly addresses the issue of the authority of prophets and sovereigns.

We should recall first that Spinoza started adding the notes to the *Treatise* after its publication in 1770, while he was considering a revised edition. That edition was never completed and the notes were first published in the posthumous edition of his works. The notes are sometimes minor clarifications, and sometimes moments of self-reflection. This note is of the latter category.

This is a note to the assertion in the *Treatise* that the professors of natural knowledge cannot be considered as prophets, 'that is, interpreters of God. For an interpreter of God is one who has a revelation of God's decrees which he interprets to others who have not had this revelation, and who accept it solely in reliance on the prophet's authority [*sola prophetae autoritate*] and the confidence he enjoys' (231/251). The erroneous understanding of the potentia of the prophets gives a certain authority to their interpretation making them beyond dispute. This is analogous to the sovereigns: 'Similarly [sic], sovereign powers [*summae potestates*] are the interpreters of their own laws [*juris*], since the laws that they enact are upheld only by their own sole sovereign authority [*sola ipsarum summarum potestatum autoritate*], and are supported only by their sole testimony [*solo testimonio*]' (231/251). Similarly, the authority of the sovereign rests on interpretation. In this case, it is the interpretation of the law that secures sovereign authority by virtue of the fact that it is not contested. What remains constant between the two senses of authority is the interplay between the capacity or potentia to interpret and the potestas that the authority of interpretation entails. The origin of authority is this contingent and unpredictable interplay presupposing an error about the capacity to interpret either revelation or the law.

Wedged between the designation of the authorities of the prophets and the sovereigns is a significant observation: 'Now if those who listen [*audiunt*] to prophets were themselves to become prophets, just as [*sicut*] those who study [*audiunt*] with philosophers become philosophers, the prophet would not be an interpreter of divine decrees; for his hearers/students [*auditores*] would rely not on the testimony and authority [*autoritate*] of the prophet but on the divine revelation itself and on their own inward testimony, just as the prophet does' (231/251). This is a complex sentence because it says two things at once. It says first that not everyone could be a prophet because that would then have had a profound impact on the interplay between potentia and potestas. If everybody had the capacity to prophesize, then the authority vested in prophecy would disappear altogether. At the same time, authority is approached from another side. There is another potentia that is cultivated by philosophy that undermines the personal authority of the prophet. Those who receive the communication from the prophets and the philosophers are different – even though the same substantive in Latin applies to them. Whereas in the case of prophecy they will always remain listeners (*auditores*) who have to accept passively the message communicated to them – whence their error – in the case of philosophy they will be students (*auditores*) who will process the message of their teacher based on their own capability or potentia – whence their striving to overcome error.

This sentence inserted between the prophetic and sovereign authority makes two moves at once. First, through the linguistic play on the two senses of *auditor*, both listener and student, Spinoza introduces the sense of *didactic* authority that will prove so important later for the transition from a sense of personal authority that is idiomatic to a sense of authority that is universally communicable. This is a significant transformation of authority, as I will argue in Chapter 5.[23] Second, this sentence also indicates the way in which authority can be undermined, namely, through philosophy. Philosophy seeks to avoid the two errors determining the interplay of potentia and potestas so as to produce authority. A philosopher questions interpretation instead of accepting it passively, avoiding the error of the

---

[23] It is also a significant transformation of authority for the structure of the *Theological Political Treatise*, as I argued in section 3 of the Introduction.

people. And, a philosopher seeks to comprehend monism and thus does not fall into the error of the prophets. Philosophy also introduces the role utility plays in resisting authority. Thus, when authority does not strive for the utility of the community, then reason necessarily rebels, as Spinoza notes in chapter 14 and later again in chapter 20. Through the complex grammatical structure of the middle sentence of note 2, Spinoza suggests, but does not yet spell out, the challenge to authority that is possible through the freedom to philosophize.

This capacity to philosophize is not in itself without its dangers, which Spinoza presents through the figure of Solomon. At the beginning of chapter 2, Spinoza notes that Solomon may surpass all others in the second kind of knowledge, but 'not in the gift of prophecy' (21). As a result of his wisdom, Solomon 'considered himself above the law' and he even 'plainly violated these laws' (31). This arrogance led him to behave in a manner 'unworthy of a philosopher' (31). Spinoza is not simply making an anti-Platonic point against the idea of the philosopher-king. Because of his wisdom, Solomon personifies the two traditional sources of authority. He functions as the primary example of a benevolent sovereign in the Middle Ages, defined as *legibus solutus* or standing above the law; and he also metonymically stands for the figure of the Pope, who had claimed for himself the ultimate authority to interpret the Bible. The Reformation's undermining of the authority of the Pope also precipitates a shift from Solomon as the wise-king to Moses as the founder of a new state. Moses is the one who rises against the old authority, the Egyptians, in order to found a new state based on a new interpretation of faith – akin to the Protestant rise against Catholicism.

Spinoza's privileging of Moses over Solomon can be viewed within the historical context of the Reformation. Still, as note 2 reminds us, Solomon and Moses operate through the same interplay of potentia and potestas – an interplay that is premised on the fallibility of their interpretations. Thus, Spinoza is making here the same point about Solomon that he makes about the authority of the prophets: wisdom in the political realm can only be articulated as the calculation of utility and, to the extent that it produces political authority, it articulates as the dialectical relation between authority and utility.

To conclude the discussion of chapter 2 of the *Theological Political Treatise*, we could see that the error the prophets make about the power of God is helpful in solidifying their authority. God is presented as a law-maker and the prophets, especially Moses, as his mouthpiece. But the error of the prophets also undercuts their interpretation of revelations from the very beginning. This interpretation rests on the contingent interplay of potentia and potestas and the erroneous starting point about divine potentia builds prophetic authority on shaky foundations.

3. Encountering the People: Causality and Instrumentality

The argument against the election of the Hebrews in chapter 3 of the *Theological Political Treatise* applies the same logic of the error about potentia, this time employed in the construction of the notion of the people. Spinoza argues that the Hebrews, the people given a state by Moses, have nothing peculiar in comparison to other peoples other than what is related to the formation of their state, that is, other than their history. Their peculiarity pertains only to potestas. But this is nothing exceptional since every polity is unique by virtue of the historically specific external causes that give rise to the state and preserve its existence. Conferring a special status on the Hebrews makes the error of supposing that they have been granted a divine potentia, which is denied by Spinoza. Spinoza shows instead that the origin of the people – just as the origin of authority – derives from the interplay of potentia and potestas, an interplay that is unique to each distinct people. Further, such an interplay describes an origin that is plural as it rests on differential power, which means that it is an origin without a determinate source nor with a predetermined end.

If we examine the contextual use of the Hebrews in the sixteenth and seventeenth centuries, we can see that Spinoza's argument is not exclusively – maybe even not primarily – about the Hebrews as such.[24] Spinoza's argument can be understood as being about the origin of peoples in general. It is about the differential origins of any instituted community. The historical context is informative: as Simon Schama demonstrates, the Mosaic narrative was utilized at the time as a metaphor for the creation of the Dutch state, formed at the end of the sixteenth century.[25] There is not only an identification of the Dutch state, newly formed by liberating itself from Spanish imperial rule just as the Hebrews liberated themselves from Egyptian rule; the story of the exodus can also be used as a critical reference. Thus, when Spinoza points to the mistakes of the Hebrews, he could be understood as pointing to faults of his contemporaries. This is a significant tactic, since Spinoza could not have referred to his contemporary politics explicitly for fear of persecution and prosecution.

---

[24] Others have made similar arguments about the use of the Hebrews in the *Theological Political Treatise*. See, for instance, Bottici, *A Philosophy of Political Myth*, 170–1 and 175.

[25] Schama, *The Embarrassment of Riches*, chapter 2.

Spinoza's argument about the rejection of the election of the Jews has been one of the – if not *the* – main point of reference for those accusing Spinoza of anti-Semitism. This argument was forcefully put forward by Herman Cohen at the turn of the century.[26] Levinas further develops it after the Second World War,[27] and in recent years, this attack on Spinoza based on the supposed anti-Semitism of chapter 3 of the *Theological Political Treatise* has been carried out by Jean-Claude Milner.[28] I will refrain from engaging in this debate. The reason is not merely that Ivan Segré has provided an excellent reply.[29] In addition, the accusation appears misplaced if we recognize that the main point of the chapter is not an historical one about the Hebrews but a philosophical one about the origins of a notion of a people – such as the Dutch – through the interplay of potentia and potestas; or, which is the same thing, how it is possible to develop a notion of a people without falling into the error of ascribing a special potentia to the people as its origin. If the argument is put in this philosophical framework, then we can see Spinoza staging a series of intriguing polemics – with Calvinism, contractarianism, Machiavelli and European colonialism – around the differential origins of community. It is these encounters that I would like to explore here.

The most immediate contemporary target of the chapter on the 'vocation of the Hebrews' is the Calvinist doctrine of predestination.[30] The polemic with the Calvinists could not be conducted openly so it is displaced to the discussion of the Hebrews as an elect people.[31] Spinoza introduces already in the Preface the distinction between deeds and words. The freedom to philosophize (words) is distinguished from the actions of the individuals in relation to human law (deeds). There is a similar separation in the Calvinist doctrine of grace and predestination, according to which it is impossible to erase the original sin merely through acts. Salvation is only possible through

---

[26] Cohen, *Spinoza on State and Religion, Judaism and Christianity*. Leo Strauss was influenced by this volume and returned to it half a century later in the well-known preface to the English edition of his *Spinoza's Critique of Religion*.

[27] Emmanuel Levinas's rejection of Spinoza has its origins in such accusations of anti-Semitism. See the texts on Spinoza contained in his *Beyond the Verse* and in *Difficult Freedom*. I return to Levinas in detail in Chapter 5.

[28] See, for instance, Milner, *Le sage trompeur*.

[29] Segré, *Spinoza: The Ethics of an Outlaw*. For a recent, significant reading of Milner's intervention, one that has a different approach than Segré, see Stetter, 'Spinoza and Judaism in the French Context'.

[30] Susan James describes in unparalleled detail and clarity the confrontation between Spinoza and Calvinism in *Spinoza on Philosophy, Religion, and Politics*.

[31] See again Schama on the specifically Calvinist use of the Mosaic narrative in the Dutch Republic, *The Embarrassment of Riches*, chapter 2.

God bestowing grace on certain individuals to fulfil the Word of Scripture. Even though both Spinoza and the Calvinists distinguish between words and actions, the important difference is that Spinoza is vehemently opposed to the idea that any people or peoples are ever elected by, or have the grace of, God to fulfil His Word. No people have a special potentia that separates them from other peoples. No one is elected by God.

This difference is important if we regard it from the perspective of the genesis of potestas. There is potestas so long as there is idiom – as we saw in the previous section. Society and the polity are premised on the idiomatic appropriation of forms of constituted power. Given that nobody can speak a pure, unidiomatic divine language, one is always under the law – a Spinozan position that I will describe as philonomianism in the following chapter. In other words, one's language is never pure, unaffected by contingent circumstances, given that we are all liable to superstition, and hence the various forms of communication always place the human in relations of potestas. The separation of words and actions in Spinoza indicates this idiomatic aspect of communication as linked to constituted power.

Conversely, the immediate reunification of words and actions through divine grace and the doctrine of predestination leads to the suspicion that select individuals can stand above the law. The Reformed Church never manages to renounce the possibility of antinomianism. The details of the various controversies already from the early sixteenth century are well documented. For our reading, it is important to note that antinomianism can be defined in terms of the interplay between potentia and potestas as follows: Antinomianism consists in the supposition that certain individuals through the grace of God have a special potentia that exempts them from obedience to summa potestas or that they have a special potentia that exempts them from the law. Understood this way, antinomianism can only occupy a negative position in Spinoza's argument. Those endowed with grace seek a certain authority that stands above state law. When Spinoza writes that 'a state cannot subsist [*subsistere potest*] unless the laws [*nisi legibus*] are binding on everybody [*unusquisque*]' (38/48), we can discern his opposition to any form of antinomianism. A community loses it potentia to exist as soon as its laws are no longer observed leading to the evaporation of its potestas.

At this juncture we can also discern the second target of chapter 3, namely, the contractarian conceptions of the polity and the people. A contractarian understanding of the formation of the people in the seventeenth century relies on the distinction between three forms of human interaction. There is the level of the state of nature that consists, as Hobbes memorably puts it, of a war 'of every man, against every man'.[32] In order to step out of this predicament, wherein life is 'solitary, poore, nasty, brutish, and short', the individual has to renounce their natural right and submit to the rule of law that is guaranteed, or authorized, by the sovereign.[33] This renunciation of natural right is what forms the society of the people and the political field within which the sovereign is the ultimate arbiter. In other words, the utility derived from escaping the state of nature is accomplished by renouncing the right to make decisions about political utility and transferring that right to the sovereign. This transference consists in the submission of the individual to the authority of the sovereign. Thus, Hobbes follows Lucretius's account of the formation of the state as based on the calculation of one's utility but he deviates to the extent that the sovereign assumes the responsibility to calculate the utility on behalf of the citizens who transfer their right to the state. He is a materialist and an authoritarian at the same time.[34]

Spinoza justifies why everybody should obey the laws of the state by insisting that the calculating of one's utility cannot be transferred. I cite the sentences before and after the assertion that the state exists only so long as its laws are obeyed: 'the purpose of every society and state [*finis universae societatis, et imperii*] is to achieve security and ease. Now a state can subsist only if the laws are binding on all individuals. If all the members of one society choose to disregard the laws, by that very fact they will dissolve that society and destroy the state' (38/48). *The utility of the state is coextensive with its existence.* Obeying the laws is an effect of authority. But the origin of authority in the interplay of potentia and potestas is plural and it can take many forms. Hence there is no one form that the legal code ought to assume. There can be different laws and they are functional so long as they are directed toward the purpose of societies and states, namely, security. When that purpose is absent, then the society and the state no longer exist.

Spinoza does not make a normative argument against the dissolution of the state. In fact, the suggestion here is that the purpose of the community is no longer served when the laws are not obeyed and maybe then it is better to dissolve the community. Spinoza points squarely at instrumental rationality as responsible for the preservation of the state. This is precisely the argument about the function of the law that we find in Epicurus's 'Principal Doctrines': The moment the law is no longer obeyed, it ceases to be useful.

---

[32] Hobbes, *Leviathan*, 88.

[33] Hobbes, *Leviathan*, 89.

[34] I underscore how Hobbes's materialism coupled with authoritarianism poses a significant challenge to epicureanism in Chapter 7, where I discuss this issue in detail.

The law and the state rely on their utility.³⁵ The full force this argument is realized in the distinction between divine and human law, as we will see in Chapter 3.

The contractarian tradition argues that the utility of the people can be safeguarded in the political field by the sovereign. Spinoza responds that utility is the constitutive feature of both society and state. No one can renounce or transfer their instrumental rationality. As such, everyone who is part of the society retains their right to calculate their utility. In other words, *the people are constituted as a people by sharing a common sense of utility*. This is an important point. Spinoza avoids any fetishization of the people. The people are not defined through a supposed identity or unity. This move avoids the error of understanding the origin of the people in a unique and unifying potentia – the error characterizing the vocation of the Hebrews.

The understanding of the people through the operation of the calculation of utility goes much further than the narrow issue of the election of the Hebrews. Negri has written insightfully on Spinoza's distinction between the people as defined through an essential identity that confers unity on them as opposed to the differential identity of the multitude.³⁶ The unified sense of the people rejected by Spinoza is constitutive, as Negri shows elsewhere, not only of contractarianism but also of colonialism, nationalism and biopolitics – or, what he calls 'empire'.³⁷ Further, from the perspective of Spinoza's epicureanism, we start seeing here the social and political implications of utility. The only thing that can possibly unify the multitude is a shared sense of the calculation of utility. Spinoza will formalize later, through the figure of neighbourly love, how utility provides a plural and differential origin to society. All this is not to say that Spinoza rejects the notion of the contract; rather, his notion of the contract is based solely on the calculation of utility.³⁸

The various encounters in chapter 3 are mediated by a critical – in both senses of the word – interaction with Machiavelli. Arguably, this is the most significant encounter with far-reaching implications. The Florentine philosopher and politician is only mentioned in the *Political Treatise*, but

---

³⁵ Diogenes Laertius, 'Epicurus', *Lives of Eminent Philosophers*, X.152 (§38 of the 'Principal Doctrines').

³⁶ Negri, *The Savage Anomaly*, see esp. chapters 5 and 8.

³⁷ Negri returns to the distinction between the people and the multitude often in his later work, usually without direct reference to Spinoza, even though the Spinozan background is obvious to someone who has read the *Savage Anomaly*. See, e.g., Hardt and Negri's *Empire* and *Multitude*.

³⁸ I develop this argument in detail in Chapter 7.

his presence in the *Theological Political Treatise* is indisputable, and nowhere more so than in chapter 3.[39]

In chapter 6 of *The Prince* Machiavelli singles out Moses as one of the paradigmatic lawgivers who attain power through virtue.[40] The important point about virtue is that it is artificial – it is constructed through human actions. Virtue does not indicate adherence to a certain transcendent quality, but rather the exercising of one's power – just as Spinoza asserts that virtue is power (*E* IV, D8). Virtue is inextricable from fortune. Machiavelli argues that virtuous persons find it harder to become leaders than those favoured by fortune, but when they do take control of a princedom, their reign tends to be longer and most successful. In chapter 25 of *The Prince*, Machiavelli uses the metaphor of the river to describe the relation between virtue and fortune: When the river swells, it is unstoppable and fortune has brought disaster to us. But this does not mean that we cannot 'take precautions by means of dykes and dams' to pre-empt its ferocity. Thus our actions are determined half by fortune and half by virtue.[41] Virtue indicates the use of instrumental rationality by those who hold authority in order to attain the utility of the community within the contingent circumstances indicated by fortune.[42]

Spinoza both adopts Machiavelli's reasoning and also modifies it in one significant respect.[43] In the context of rejecting the vocation of the Hebrews, Spinoza analyses what he means by God's aid or selection. He makes the following distinction: 'whatever human nature can effect solely by its own power [*ex sola sua potentia*] to preserve its own being can rightly be called God's internal help [*Dei auxilium internum*], and whatever falls to one's utility [*utile*] from the power [*ex potentia*] of external causes can rightly be called God's external help [*Dei auxilium externum*]' (36/46). Spinoza describes here how divine *potentia* affects humans. There is both an internal and an external causality operating. I argued in the Introduction that Spinoza is clear in

---

[39] For a penetrating study on the relation between Spinoza and Machiavelli, see del Lucchese, *Conflict, Power, and Multitude in Machiavelli and Spinoza*. For an argument specifically about the presence of Machiavelli in the *Theological Political Treatise*, see Morfino 'Memory, Chance and Conflict'.
[40] The other three are Cyrus, Romulus and Theseus. See Machiavelli, *The Prince*, 20. Machiavelli consistently uses these four figures as paradigmatic state founders and law-givers, not only in the *Prince* but also in the *Discourses*.
[41] Machiavelli, *The Prince*, 85.
[42] On fortune as contingency, see Pocock, *The Machiavellian Moment*, 31–48.
[43] I am indebted to Vittorio Morfino who draws the comparison between Spinoza's thought and virtue and fortune in *The Spinoza-Machiavelli Encounter*.

Part IV of the *Ethics* that conatus, or the striving for self-preservation, can be understood in terms of the calculation of utility. It is in one's utility to continue living. Here, we see that both aspects of what Spinoza calls 'God's help' are mediated by the notion of utility – the third epicurean theme in Spinoza. What is the function of the distinction between internal and external divine help here?

The internal help is divided between the understanding and virtue, while external help is described as 'the gift of fortune' or as providing a life 'in security and good health' (37). The entire argument against the election of the Hebrews rests on this distinction. Spinoza explains that understanding and virtue 'lie within the bounds of human nature itself, so that their acquisition chiefly depends on human power alone [*a sola nostra potentia*]; i.e. solely on the laws of human nature. For this reason it is obvious that these gifts are not peculiar to any nation [*haec dona nulli nationi peculiaria*] but have always been common to all humans [*toti humano generi communia*]' (37/46–7). In other words, potentia is common to all. Conversely, 'the means that serve for the attainment of security and physical wellbeing lie principally in external circumstances' (37). The Hebrews were unique only because of how their fortune inflected their potestas, which is never universal but always contingent, accidental, aleatory: 'the Hebrews surpassed other nations in this alone, that they were successful in achieving security for themselves and overcame great dangers, and this chiefly by God's external help alone' (38). To clarify this distinction between the universalizable potentia and the particular potestas, Spinoza also specifies that 'it was not in respect of their understanding that they were chosen by God before others. Nor yet in respect of virtue' (38). So Spinoza adopts Machiavelli's distinction between virtue and fortune to talk about an instrumental unfolding of power.

Let me put this in another way that underscores Machiavelli's significance for the intersection of metaphysics and politics in Spinoza. God is defined in Part I of the *Ethics* in terms of causality. Thus, for instance, the first thing one reads, Definition 1, says: 'By cause of itself I understand that whose essence involves existence.' This is the definition of God as an immanent cause. The two attributes are also distinct because the causality of extension is separate from the causality of thought (E I, P10). And, finally, the modes too are described in terms of their infinite causal interconnection (E I, P28).[44]

---

[44] The starting point is important. Hegel criticizes Spinoza as an 'acomist', that is, on the grounds that the only real thing is the substance and that everything else is illusory. See, e.g., *Lectures on Logic, Berlin, 1831*, 49. But Hegel's starting point for the critique of Spinoza is always his own idealist question about knowledge, and specifically, under

Thus, the entire ontological plain is outlined in terms of causality. But this ontological description in terms of causality poses a significant problem if we are to understand Spinoza as a materialist and an epicurean. Specifically, the distinction of the attributes requires that the causalities of thought and extension have to be separate. From one point of view, Spinoza is saying something uncontroversial: that which causes the pen to be on my desk and my thought that I want to lift the pen belong to different causalities – my thought alone cannot lift the pen. But from another perspective, this creates a serious problem because mind and body are inseparable according to epicureanism. In addition, if all causes can be attributed either solely to thought or solely to extension, then it is hard to see how Spinoza can evade the accusation of determinism.

The present distinction between the two senses of 'God's help' in conjunction with the inseparability of virtue and fortune from Machiavelli can help us find a solution – one that Spinoza never spells out but that is readily available in his argument. Specifically, the level of causality is what Spinoza refers to as 'God's external help'. Here there is only divine potentia and any particular potestas can be understood as its effect. In fact – and this is Spinoza's argument about the Hebrew state – every potestas is unique by virtue of the distinctive causality that produces it. This is what Machiavelli calls fortune, and it is the level that a human has no hope of mastering, either in terms of cognizing the totality of causes or in terms of controlling causality. This level is responsible for the presupposition of a totality for the generation of knowledge, as I put it in the Introduction. The discourse of causality is suited to describe monism.

This level of causality is distinct from, but intersects with, the level of instrumentality, or what Spinoza calls 'God's internal help'.[45] This is what Machiavelli calls virtue. It describes the field where the human can calculate utility. This level depends on the previous one but is not identical with it. As I put it in the Introduction, the totality in Spinoza necessarily leads to practical knowledge or the third theme of Spinoza's epicureanism. Further, at this level only can we talk of the interplay of potentia and potestas, as it is at this level that contingency is inscribed. This also aligns with the

---

what conditions it is possible to know the absolute. This is not Spinoza's starting point, for whom the question of knowledge does not arise until Part II of the *Ethics*. For the most perspicacious analysis of Hegel's reception of Spinoza, see Macherey, *Hegel or Spinoza*. See also more recently Moder, *Hegel and Spinoza: Substance and Negativity*.

[45] I noted the centrality of the distinction between instrumentality and causality, both for Spinoza and the materialist/epicurean tradition more generally, in sections 1 and 2 of Chapter 1.

epicurean definition of freedom as the exercise of phronesis, as we saw in Chapter 1. Finally, without this level that is distinct but inseparable from the previous one, epicureanism as the intersection of the three themes would be untenable: instrumentality or the calculation of utility (the third theme) and causality (which belongs to monism or the second theme) conflict, but in such a way as to let the other arise and make itself visible.

Without this distinction between causality and instrumentality there is no politics in Machiavelli. For instance, Machiavelli is fascinated by how the distinct virtue of political actors does not necessarily lead to the same outcomes even if they undertake the same actions. The best example of this is Machiavelli's analysis of Cesare Borgia in *The Prince*.[46] Machiavelli argues that Cesare Borgia's political virtue was excellent as he calculated his utility with a cold rationality that maximized his chances of success. However, fortune intervened – in particular, the premature death of his father, Pope Alexander, at a time that Cesare Borgia happened to be ill – giving his enemies the chance to destroy him. The causes of history are distinct from the instrumental rationality that determines the virtue of the political actors. From this perspective, Machiavelli's thought on virtue and fortune is the palimpsest of Spinoza's discussion in chapter 3 as well as for the crucial distinction between causality and instrumentality.

The divergences from Machiavelli are just as instructive. The first obvious difference is one of degree: Spinoza develops a much more elaborate metaphysics than Machiavelli. This allows his thought greater flexibility. As a result, Spinoza does not confine the dialectic of virtue and fortune to the state founders and lawgivers. For Machiavelli, ultimately it is the state founders and sovereigns who are fascinating insofar as the intersection of causality and instrumentality is concerned. Spinoza broadens the perspective on this intersection, including both those in authority as well as the people. This is possible because Spinoza employs the broader dialectic of authority and utility.

The interplay between potentia and potestas has been presented thus far as starting with the contingency of potestas. For instance, the prophets are presented as starting with their idiomatic forms of communication that underwrite their personal authority. And the Hebrews are defined as a people due to their fortune, that is, due to the external circumstances that secure their state. However, parallel to this approach there is another one, starting from the opposite direction, that of universality. This argument looks at the interplay of potentia and potestas by examining that which is

---

[46] See Machiavelli, *The Prince*, especially chapter 7.

common to all, namely, potentia. Spinoza turns to this approach at the end of chapter 3.

This argument can be presented as yet another polemic contained in Spinoza's text. Specifically, the rejection of the vocation of the Hebrews has repercussions on the colonialist project underlying the flourishing of capitalism in the Netherlands and the expansionist projects of the entire Western European Christendom. Spinoza argues that 'all nations possessed prophets' (40) and that 'by his miracles God made himself known to other nations more so than to the Jews of that time . . . and that the Gentiles possessed rites and ceremonies by which they were acceptable to God' (39). When the argument against the election of the Jews is further expanded, then, the upshot is a stringently anti-colonial position: 'in respect of understanding and true virtue there is no distinction between one nation and another and in regard to these matters God has not chosen one nation before another' (47). If potestas is accidental but potentia is something that all people and peoples share in common, this ultimately means that no potestas is superior to any other potestas. In a single move, the justification of colonization is undermined. For instance, if every nation can possess prophets, that is, if every nation can have revelations, even if they have never heard of the Bible or even if they have not even developed a system of writing, then this precludes the justification of colonization on the grounds that it will precipitate the spread of the word of God and hence the salvation of the colonized.

This shift of perspective to the universal aspect of power provides an additional element that is key in the architectonic of the entire book. The universality of potentia refers to the power of God, which can only ever be potentia, never potestas – as I explained earlier. The idea that God is not a sovereign whose will can intervene in human affairs, or that God only has potentia but no potestas, provides us with significant insights into the hierarchy established at the opening of the *Theological Political Treatise* – whereby revelation as communication relies on a message from God to humans via the mediation of the prophets. The differential power between God and the prophets is solely in relation to potentia, whereas the differential power between the prophets and the rest of humanity establishes relations of both potestas and potentia. The special gift (potentia) to communicate with God places the prophets in specific positions of potestas.

But this does not give them an absolute licence because their potentia qua prophecy is only interpretative. As Spinoza puts it, 'the gift of prophecy did not render the prophets more learned, but left them with the beliefs they had previously held, and therefore we are in no way bound to believe them in matters of purely philosophic speculation [*res mere speculativas*]' (26/35).

This does not preclude the possibility that those who have the potentia to philosophize may in fact be more useful to the community or even have a more comprehensive understanding of God's potentia and hence transplant the authority of the prophets. We see clear anti-authoritarian implications here.

This anti-authoritarian vantage point afforded by the effects of the errors in the interplay of potentia and potestas can assist us in thinking through significant concepts in political philosophy. For instance, we can consider equality from this perspective.

Let me start from the side of potestas. Authority entails the operation of an inequality of power within the social and political field. But the inequality is artificial as it relies on potestas. No one is intrinsically endowed with more potestas and hence one has to work to achieve it – for instance, the prophets have to interpret and communicate their imaginations. This entails that potentially anyone could achieve authority – which also means, of course, that anyone can lose their authority or their position in the hierarchy of power. At the vanishing point, we can posit a community that dissolves the distinction between potestas and authority. From the perspective of institution, then, everyone could be equal. Communism, as an ideal, is premised on this.

Let us now consider equality from the side of potentia. All beings are equal to the extent that they all partake of potentia and hence they are singular. But each singularity is different. This differential power entails an ineliminable inequality of power.[47] An absolute equality is impossible from the perspective of potentia. Everyone may *partake* of the potentia, but no one *has* the same potentia as anyone else. This is to insist on the differential and relational aspect of potentia. If potentia indicates one's capabilities, then to posit a radical equality where everyone has equal potentia or where everyone can do the same thing would be to posit a community of robots made from an identical mould. Potentia is distinct from potestas in that it indicates differential power, that is, the power that is responsible for each being's singularity. The hierarchy of power is derived from potestas, whereas potentia sets in motion differential relations of power.

The interplay of potentia and potestas provides Spinoza's dialectic of authority and utility in the *Theological Political Treatise* with an agonistic edge. It is this interplay that resists any secure identification of authority or of the way in which authority is conferred – through the interpretation of

---

[47] See Vardoulakis, 'Equality and Power', in Kordela and Vardoulakis (eds), *Spinoza's Authority, Volume 1*, 11–31.

revelation or the law – or of the community produced by such identifications. Instead of identity, its formulation of differential power is inherently incompatible with – indeed, *oppositional to* – any sense of the incontestable required by authority. The various errors that strive for authority by misconstruing potentia can be countered in a political field determined by power, that is, determined by the differential and agonistic relations between potentia and potestas. Spinoza's agonistic politics is presented in chapter 3 through various polemical encounters implicit in his text. Thus, there is not only a confluence of metaphysics and politics in the *Treatise*. In addition, the rhetoric of the text stages this confluence.

* * *

Let me close with a final comment about the use of error – a comment that pre-empts some of the discussion in the next chapter. It is instructive to note that Spinoza does not lament the various errors he describes. Thus he does not perform the usual move in the history of philosophy, whereby, when an error is identified, this leads to either the imperative to rectify the error through enlightenment or to indulge in mourning for the fallen state of humanity that suffers under its unavoidable errancy. Instead, Spinoza reads errors as effects of his dialectic of authority and utility – moreover, effects that help us understand power relations. We can express this difference in terms of genre, too. Whereas the tragic genre views error as that which precipitates disaster, the comic genre views error as instigating joy and merriment. An epicurean who is concerned with the pleasures in living ought to be predisposed to the comic genre, and Spinoza will not disappoint us on this count.

3
Philonomianism:
Law and the Origin of Finitude (chapter 4)

The title of chapter 4 announces that it is concerned with 'divine law'. The opening couple of sentences draw a distinction between divine and human law:

> The word law, taken in its absolute sense [*legis nomen absolute*], means that according to which each individual thing – either all in general or those of the same kind – acts in one and the same fixed and determinate manner, this manner depending either on Nature's necessity or on human will. A law which depends on Nature's necessity is one which necessarily follows from the very nature of the thing, that is, its definition; a law which depends on human will, and which could more properly be termed a statute [*jus*], is one which men ordain for themselves and for others with a view to making life more secure and more convenient [*ad tutius, et commodius vivendum*]. (48/57)

It is striking what is elided in this distinction. Specifically, it does not say that the source or origin of divine law is revelation and that of human law is legitimacy or the sovereign as the one who has the authority to legislate. Further, the definition does not define the law in terms of command and obedience.

The reason for these omissions is that these traditional avenues of approaching the law are not open to Spinoza. Revelation, according to chapter 1, is a communication with God that is mediated through the prophets' interpretation, which makes it a human construct. And the command and obedience model cannot account for divine law, since God or nature is understood in strictly impersonal terms by Spinoza. Instead of the traditional routes of approaching legality, Spinoza has recourse to a qualitative distinction between the absolute necessity of divine or natural law, and the dependence of human law on the will of a polity to preserve itself.

No sooner has Spinoza solved one problem than another arises. The qualitative distinction between necessity and will may be challenged on the grounds that human will cannot be separated in reality from the necessity of nature. What we will and do forms part of the concatenation of causes and effects that constitute the totality of nature. To bypass this further problem, Spinoza concedes that it appears as if we are using the word 'law' as it applies to nature '*per translationem*', as a figure of speech or as a translation, of what is commonly understood by law, namely, human law (49/58). The suggestion is that a more rigorous (*particularius*) definition of the law is required, which Spinoza promptly supplies:

> law should be defined . . . as a logic of living that one prescribes to oneself or to others for some end [*finem*]. (49/58)

The most notable feature of this definition is the supposition of the use of instrumental reasoning as a defining feature of the law. The law concerns a certain rationality in how we conduct our lives, which is concerned with calculating the ends of our actions. In other words, by refusing, on the one hand, to identify the origin of the law theologically through revelation or politically through command, whereby he refuses to reduce the obedience that the law demands to the obedience characterizing authority; and, on the other hand, by underscoring the function of phronesis or the calculation of utility, Spinoza sets in motion the dialectic of authority and utility. Differently put, Spinoza defines the law in epicurean terms.

Ivan Sergé notes that Spinoza's conception of the law is incompatible with Jewish, Aristotelian, Platonic and Stoic conceptions of legality.[1] I agree, but would like to add that this is because the definition of the law in terms of its use and utility is distinctively epicurean. The connection between utility, law and justice is best described in Epicurus's 'Principal Doctrines', a collection of forty maxims or articles describing the key ideas of epicureanism, which are preserved in Diogenes Laertius. Articles 31 to 38 define legality in terms of utility.[2] Thus, article 33 says: 'There is no absolute justice [καθ' ἑαυτὸ δικαιοσύνη] but only a reciprocal agreement in specific places and times to prevent inflicting or suffering harm.'[3] No justice is absolute, and hence no laws are inviolable, because justice consists in calculating within specific circumstances what is good and what is bad. In article 36

---

[1] Sergé, *Spinoza: The Ethics of an Outlaw*.
[2] Diogenes Laertius, 'Epicurus', *Lives of Eminent Philosophers*, X.150–3.
[3] Diogenes Laertius, 'Epicurus', X.150.

Epicurus articulates the same idea in positive terms: 'justice is common to all [κοινὸν πᾶσιν] and it consists in calculating the utility [συμφέρον] that contributes to sociality [πρὸς ἀλλήλους κοινωνία]; thus, depending on particular conditions, justice articulates itself differently'.[4] This notion of justice entails that the law is not defined in terms of command and obedience. According to article 38, 'the laws are just so long as they contribute to the utility of those living in a political community [τῶν συμπολιτευομένων], and when they cease to be expedient they are consequently not just'.[5] Instead of relying on obedience, the law is defined through its utility.

Now, this epicurean understanding of the law immediately faces another hurdle. If the law is understood in terms of the operation of the calculation of utility that is constitutive of human nature – I called it the anthropological principle in the Introduction – then this would suggest that there is nothing outside the law: if we posit an ante-legal or extra-legal space, it would entail positing something outside human nature, which is impossible. This is a productive conundrum for Spinoza. I call it philonomianism and I argue in this chapter that it is indispensable in understanding his conception of the law, as well as of history and finitude. To put into relief the originality of Spinoza's position, I compare it to Hannah Arendt's own rejection of an ante-legal or extra-legal space but for reasons very different, namely, as an attempt to ground legality not on phronesis but on legitimacy and authority.

1. *Ratio Vivendi*: Law and Living

There is one term that is unusual in Spinoza's definition of the law: 'law should be defined ... as a logic of living [*ratio vivendi*] that one prescribes to oneself or to others for some end' (49/58)'. The term is *ratio vivendi*. This expression is not uncommon in the *Theological Political Treatise* – for instance, we find it in the title of chapter 13. But its critical use in the definition of the law is unusual.[6] There are three distinct meanings of *ratio*: 1) it can be rationality or logic, as a translation of the Greek *logos*; 2) *ratio* can

---

[4] Diogenes Laertius, 'Epicurus', X.151.
[5] Diogenes Laertius, 'Epicurus', X.153.
[6] It is perhaps the polysemy of 'ratio' that forces all translators to render the expression 'ratio vivendi' in various different ways throughout the *Theological Political Treatise*. I will not trace here all the uses of *ratio vivendi* in the *Treatise* or its translations, not because this would be an arduous or tedious exercise, but rather because the most crucial and most ambiguous use is in chapter 4 where it is used as the predicate of the law that is, in its turn, linked to authority by virtue of the fact that they both refer to obedience.

also mean proportion, just as the English ratio; and, 3) it can mean rule or regulation. In fact, the second and third meanings are derivative of the first one: proportion is a kind of mathematical logic and rule is the application of rationality.[7]

It is instructive to peruse how the expression *ratio vivendi* is translated in the major English editions: Shirley translates *ratio vivendi* as 'a rule of life'. Curley translates it as 'a principle of living'.[8] And Israel's edition renders it as 'a rule for living'.[9] These translations, even if they seem similar, in fact suggest significantly different meanings to the predicate of the law. Shirley's translation suggests that *ratio* refers to some externally imposed prescription. Curley's that it denotes a universal principle. And Israel's that *ratio* is more like an instruction for the conduct of one's life. Thus, all these renditions of *ratio vivendi* translate it in such a way as to make it amenable only to human, not to divine law – even though Spinoza provides a second definition that is meant to cover both.

The reason that these translations fail to include divine law in the second definition is that none of them entertains the possibility that *ratio* refers here to rationality or phronesis, which are established meanings of *ratio* – and which is precisely the meaning I am trying to convey with my translation as 'logic of living'. The effect of not rendering *ratio vivendi* in such a way as to capture the idea that there is a logic to living, or that thought and life – mind and body – are intertwined, is to obscure an idea that is critical for Spinoza, namely, that there is nothing outside the law. If the law is a *ratio vivendi* indicating that there is no life without thought, then *ratio vivendi* is a property not only of the law but also of human nature. This impossibility of stepping outside the law I call philonomianism. I return to the term philonomianism after I investigate the meaning of *ratio vivendi*.

If we look for other uses of *ratio vivendi* in chapter 4, we note that the term and its cognates appears no less than nine times in the three opening pages of chapter 4, from 58 to 60 in the Gebhardt edition. Let us examine them in sequence:

1) The first use of the term occurs at the beginning where Spinoza extrapolates the distinction between divine and human law. Spinoza highlights the necessity of divine or natural law. Humans have no capacity to break or

---

[7] The edited volume by Beth Lord, *Spinoza's Philosophy of Ratio*, has contributed a lot in identifying the first and second meanings of *ratio* that I identify above, but the third meaning is strangely repressed.
[8] Spinoza, *Theological-Political Treatise*, in *The Collected Works of Spinoza*, vol. 2, 127.
[9] Spinoza, *Theological-Political Treatise*, ed. Israel, 58.

disobey divine law – nor do they have a say in how it operates. This is not the case with human law. 'The fact that people give up, or are compelled to give up, their natural right and bind themselves to live under certain *rationi vivendi*, depends on human will' (48/58). *Ratio vivendi* refers specifically to human law or specific statutes – notice the plural. It signifies the living arrangements that allow for the operation of the law.

Spinoza immediately qualifies this distinction by noting that 'in an absolute sense, all things are determined by the universal laws of Nature' (48), whereby it may appear that a distinction between divine and human law is impossible. And yet, Spinoza insists on this distinction based on the transition from the second to the third theme of his epicureanism, namely, from the monism contained in the idea that there is nothing outside the necessity of nature to the primacy of practical judgement. Spinoza outlines this move in two steps. First, he argues that human law 'depends especially on the power of the human mind in the following respect, that the human mind, insofar as it is concerned with the perception of truth and falsity', has a capacity which 'can be quite clearly conceived without these man-made laws, whereas it cannot be conceived without Nature's necessary law' (48). As I put this point in the Introduction, any form of knowledge presupposes what Epicurus calls the totality or Spinoza calls substance. Second, given that there is no usefulness in tracing every thought or every action back to its original causes, 'in terms of usefulness to life [*ad usum vitae*] it is better, indeed, it is necessary, to consider things as possible [*possibiles*]' (49/58). In other words, the impossibility of knowing the totality requires that we make practical judgements.

So, the first use of *ratio vivendi* refers to human law insofar as it requires the operation of practical judgement as a result of the recognition of nothing existing outside nature or God. We already see that the standard translation of *ratio* as rule in the definition of the law is limited and it would not allow for the parallel operation of the second and the third epicurean themes in the first use of *ratio vivendi* in chapter 4.

2) The second use is in the definition of the law we saw already as the *ratio vivendi* prescribed toward certain ends. I will return to this definition after examining all the remaining uses of *ratio vivendi*.

3) Immediately after the definition of the law, Spinoza qualifies it by observing that such a conception of the law is obvious only to a minority whereas most people fail to perceive it since they 'nihil minus quam ex ratione vivunt' (49/59). Instead of the participle 'vivendi', Spinoza uses here the indicative of the verb 'vivere', to live. Ratio is also in a prepositional phrase with 'ex' meaning according to. Here, then, Spinoza is referring to

people who live with nothing like (*nihil minus*) rationality. Or, more simply, most people live without the capacity to make good practical judgements. In the sentence immediately after the definition, then, *ratio* clearly has the meaning of rationality – not that of rule.

4) Spinoza further explicates what it means for the law when people fail to exercise their *ratio* properly. He argues that since the majority do not understand the real meaning of the law, the legislators devised an expedient measure, namely, rewards for those following the law and punishments for those who do not. Due to this expediency, most people have a wrong understanding of the law as a *ratio vivendi* that is prescribed (*praescribitur*) by a sovereignty exterior to themselves (*ex aliorum imperio*) (49/59). Thus the logic of living of the law comes to be associated with the 'fear of the gallows', that is, with the sovereign prerogative of life and death. This, however, does not make one a 'just [*justus*]' person (49/59) because this conception of the law on the model of command and obedience is nothing but a trick or deception on the part of those who have power. Note that Spinoza does not outright reject this model, since it is still associated with *ratio vivendi*, that is, with a certain rationality concerned with the utility of the community. In other words, Spinoza is not an anti-statist, nor an anarchist. Rather, his position is that political power (*imperium* or *summa potestas*) cannot possibly be the precondition of how the law operates. *Ratio vivendi* precedes legitimacy – not the other way round.

5 and 6) All uses up to now seem to suggest that *ratio vivendi* refers to human law. The fifth and sixth uses dispel this impression. Here Spinoza repeats the definition of the law (use 5) as a *ratio vivendi* used for a specific end, but now specifies that this applies both to human and divine law. It is only the end of this *ratio vivendi* that changes. For human law, it is the protection of life and the state (*rempublicam*), whereas for divine law it is the knowledge of God as the only supreme good (*solum summum bonum*) for the human (49/59). If the definition of the law above (in use 2) is consistent with the use here, then we cannot possibly translate *ratio* as rule, since no human rule can lead to the supreme good of Spinoza's divine law.

In other words, if both human and divine law are to be defined on a common basis that refers to instrumentality or utility, then *ratio vivendi* cannot refer to a restriction or a compulsion of living according to specified rules. Rather, for the human and divine law to have a common basis, *ratio* here must refer to rationality concerned with ends, which is what I call the calculation of utility. Such a calculation may be linked to specific rules, but only to the extent that they are useful, that is, as effects of calculation. This means that those who do not understand the real meaning of the law, *ratio* may be usefully misunderstood according to the command and obedience model – as we saw above in the fourth use. In other words, the misunderstanding of the law that confines it to a model applicable only to human law and that relies on command and obedience can still perform a positive function in society – for instance, so as to lead people to obey the law. But this misunderstanding is only an expedient and not definitional of the law. Prior to legitimacy, we have *ratio* as the calculation of utility. Prior to authority there is phronesis.

This priority of phronesis points to the dialectic of authority and utility. It shows that judgements about the utility of a community precede obedience, in which case no authority has legitimacy from the fact that it has potestas or sovereignty – no constituted power is ipso facto legitimate. This allows for the mobilization of utility to contest any notion of authority. It also shows that authority is grounded on how it justifies itself – that is, it uses instrumental rationality to justify its actions so as to construct its legitimacy. In short, *justification precedes legitimation*.[10]

7, 8 and 9) Immediately after specifying that the *ratio vivendi* applies both to human and to divine law, Spinoza goes on to explain in what sense the divine law can be useful. This consists in the perfection of our intelligence (*intellectus*) as the means to secure our utility (*utile*), a process identified as the supreme good (49–50/59). The supreme good consists in recognizing 'firstly, that without God nothing can be or be conceived, and secondly, that everything can be called into doubt as long as we have no clear and distinct idea of God' (50). In other words, the supreme good consist in the recognition that there is nothing outside God (or monism), which is the precondition for avoiding the distracting and distressing idea that there are deities who can intervene in the course of nature to punish or reward us. Recognition of monism, then, leads to the overcoming of fear and anxiety – it leads to blessedness (*beatitudo* or *ataraxia*).

Spinoza summarizes his discussion of the supreme good as follows:

> the *ratio vivendi* that has regard to this end [*hunc finem*] [i.e. to the supreme good] can fitly be called the Divine Law. An enquiry as to what these means [*haec media*] are, and what *ratio vivendi* is required for this end [*hic finis*], and how the fundamental principles of an optimal commonwealth and the *ratio vivendi* of human relations [*inter homines*] follow from it, belongs to a general treatise on Ethics. (50/60)

---

[10] This precedence of justification is described in detail in my book *Sovereignty and its Other*.

Here, the supreme good achieved by following the divine law is described in instrumental terms. The means and ends are provided by the *ratio vivendi* that is also responsible for good relations – social, political and ethical – amongst human beings. The supreme good has a *ratio vivendi* understood in terms of instrumentality. It is a living that rationalizes conduct according to certain means and ends relations. *Ratio vivendi* as the predicate of both divine and human law can be translated as living under the guidance of phronesis.

Spinoza concludes the discussion of the supreme good that can be derived from the *ratio vivendi* by saying that its proper exposition belongs to a treatise on ethics, that is, the *Ethics* whose writing Spinoza suspends in 1665 to compose the *Theological Political Treatise*. If we turn briefly to the discussion of the supreme good in the *Ethics*, we will discover more about its indissoluble relation to phronesis.

In Part IV of the *Ethics* – that is, the Part written immediately after the completion the *Treatise* – Spinoza defines the supreme good (*summum bonum*) in Proposition 36 as follows: 'The greatest good of those who seek virtue is common to all, and can be enjoyed by all equally.' The Demonstration explains that virtue is to 'act according to the guidance of reason', which Spinoza supports with reference to Proposition 24 of Part IV: 'Acting absolutely from virtue is nothing else in us but acting, living, and preserving our being [*agere, vivere, suum esse conservare*] (these three signify the same thing) by the guidance of reason [*ex ductu rationis*], from the foundation of seeking one's own utility [*utile*].' From Propositions 36 and 24, then, we can say that the supreme good is to act, live and preserve oneself through the use of reason or rationality (*ratio*) insofar as *ratio* signifies both the virtue and the utility of human conduct. There is a coupling, then, of rationality and living, but the rationality here is not directed toward adequate ideas that are universally true but toward practical knowledge and the calculation of one's utility.[11] In other words, *ratio* here signifies phronesis or instrumental rationality.

But why is this calculation of one's utility 'enjoyed by all equally'? Why does phronesis contribute to sociality? Spinoza addresses this in Proposition 35: 'Only insofar as men live according to the guidance of reason [*ex ductu rationis vivunt*], must they always agree in nature.' The demonstration relies on the principle that what advances the utility of one person contributes to the utility of others given that rationality is common is to all. Consequently,

---

[11] For the incompatibility between the calculation of utility and the second kind of knowledge, see section 2 of Chapter 6.

as the second Corollary puts it, 'when each one most seeks one's utility for oneself, then everyone contributes the most to everyone else's utility'. Or, as the Scholium puts it more succinctly, 'man is God to man'.[12] The exercise of phronesis or the calculation of one's utility is not the same as egoistic self-interest. Rather, a proper exercise of phronesis is a precondition of sociality. We share common ends because the process whereby we arrive at those ends – that is, *ratio* or phronesis – is common to all. Phronesis as a guide to living is common to all. Nobody is excluded from *ratio vivendi*. And this also means – given that *ratio vivendi* is the predicate of the law – nobody is excluded from the law.

If we return now to the definition of the law, how can we understand *ratio vivendi* so as to encompass all the meanings we discovered? We can say that law is a 'logic of living that one prescribes to oneself or to others for some end'. Such a logic of living is a means toward the prosperity of both the individual and the community. This can take two forms that are not mutually exclusive. It can be either the blessedness that arises from monism, or the preservation of individual life and the life of the community that arises from human law. *Ratio vivendi* is, then, irreducible to the logic of authority that appeals to legitimacy so as to demand obedience. This does not mean that it may not be expedient to use authority, but authority relies on something prior to it, namely, this *ratio vivendi*, that can be understood as phronesis, which in the epicurean tradition is the highest good for humans and the cause of all virtues – in Epicurus's formulation, as we saw in the Introduction.[13]

Spinoza's adherence to the epicurean insight of defining the law in terms of the calculation of utility can be articulated as three interconnected ideas. First, Spinoza defines the law without recourse to a model of command and obedience, that is, the model that links legality with authority and legitimacy. Instead, he defines the law in terms of the calculation of utility. Second, it entails that everyone is subject to the law, since everyone has the capacity to calculate their utility. This capacity is enough to place one within legality. In other words, Spinoza rejects the possibility that one can find oneself outside the law. Third, if everyone is subject to the law, the account of the genesis of the law no longer requires an ante-legal or extra-legal origin, either in revelation or in some founding violence – that is, it does not require a political theological authority.

---

[12] There is a long literature examining Spinoza's idea of the mutual utility of the humans. For an astute account, see Sharp, *Spinoza and the Politics of Renaturalization*, chapter 3.
[13] Diogenes Laertius, 'Epicurus', X.132.

What I call Spinoza's *philonomianism* is the confluence and co-presence of these three ideas – the rejection of the command and obedience model as definitive of legality, the recognition that no one can be outside the law, and the anti-authoritarian thrust of the previous two positions. Philonomianism registers the operation of the dialectic of authority and utility in the law and legality.

More generally, I use the term philonomianism to distinguish a philosophical and political position from other positions that we can call antinomian.[14] By antinomian I refer to positions that define the political with recourse to something that is outside the law. This may be something like the state of nature in Hobbes and other contractarian thinkers. According to this tradition, the state of nature precedes the political in such a way as to legitimize the formation of the state. It may also refer to theories of the exception, such as Carl Schmitt's, which determine sovereignty through its transcendence from the law.[15] Finally, it may refer to biopolitical theories such as Agamben's, which requires the positing of a separation between political life and 'bare' life in order to account for the production of sovereignty.[16]

Antinomianism has recourse to a founding act of violence to ground not only political authority – as we saw in the previous chapter – but also political legitimacy. As Spinoza puts it, it is through the 'fear of the gallows' (49), that is, through the sovereign prerogative of life and death, that legitimacy is grounded in an authority that commands. The safeguarding of obedience inevitably inscribes within the law the possibility of violence. Thus, in Hobbes, it is the violence of a 'war of all against all' that justifies the sovereign gathering in his power the exercise of violent punishment as soon as the commonwealth is formed. For Schmitt, the political is defined as the identification of the enemy, that is, as the exercise of violence within a legal framework.[17] For Agamben, too, bare life is distinguished by a special kind of violence, one that can kill the body but cannot sacrifice it.[18]

---

[14] See Vardoulakis, *Freedom from the Free Will*, chapter 4.

[15] See Schmitt, *Political Theology*; cf. Vardoulakis, 'Spinoza's Empty Law', in Lord (ed.), *Spinoza Beyond Philosophy*, 135–48.

[16] To the examples offered above we can add the antinomianism of the Reformation, especially Calvinism. I do not want to be side-tracked here in a discussion of the roots of antinomianism. I should only note that Spinoza's polemic with the Calvinists can be framed in terms of their antinomianism. For the most detailed and far-reaching account of Spinoza's interaction with Calvinism, see James, *Spinoza on Philosophy, Religion, and Politics*.

[17] Schmitt, *The Concept of the Political*.

[18] Agamben, *Homo Sacer*, 8; cf. Agamben, *Remnants of Auschwitz*.

Spinoza's philonomianism has no recourse to legitimacy as the grounding of the political, and hence he bypasses the antinomian position that requires a founding violence. Instead, the law is defined through the operation of phronesis. The calculation of utility contained in *ratio* is about living or the *vivendi* of human being. Thus, it is about the preservation of life for the individual and the community. It other words, in the *ratio vivendi* of human law, the calculation of utility encounters the conatus. Spinoza's law is about living.

It is noteworthy that Giorgio Agamben in *The Highest Poverty* identifies a tradition that interrogates the law in terms of its use. This is the tradition of communal use in the Franciscan tradition. There is a key difference, however, from the epicurean tradition that I have designated as the source of Spinoza's philonomianism. For the epicureans, the calculation of utility or use in life is definitional of the law. For Agamben, by contrast, the Franciscan conception of use delineates an extra-legal space. For instance, he writes that 'the juridical argumentation is here [i.e., in the context of referring to use] bent on opening a space outside the law'.[19] Whereas, according to Agamben, use pertains to jurisprudence through its exclusion from the law, according to epicureanism and Spinoza use pertains to jurisprudence because it is internal to the law by indicating the limits of legality.[20] Despite this contrast, Agamben's starting principle that 'Western philosophy lacks even the most elementary principles' of what he terms 'a theory of use' is nonetheless sound.[21] We can demonstrate this by comparing two dominant ways in which the law has been conceived in the Western tradition to contrast them briefly with philonomianism.

First, we can identify legal positivism. I do not want to be distracted here in the various views expressed within this school of jurisprudence, starting with John Austin in the nineteenth century before being further developed by Hans Kelsen in Austria and H. L. A. Hart in England in the following century. I just want to point out one key feature of this tradition, namely, that law needs to be understood as a system that is closed. Thus, Hart in his *The Concept of Law*, which is a sustained attempt to define the law, rejects any view that conflates legal with moral norms, or that does not draw a clear line of separation from social factors. Such a conception of the law

---

[19] Agamben, *The Highest Poverty*, 125.
[20] For a critique of Agamben's conception of something that is outside the law, see Vardoulakis, *Freedom from the Free Will*, where I discuss a similar argument in Agamben's reading of Kafka's 'Before the Law'.
[21] Agamben, *The Highest Poverty*, xiii.

as a closed system is incompatible with any definition of the law in terms of living, as in Spinoza's definition in chapter 4 of the *Theological Political Treatise*.

Second, one of the major critics of legal positivism – more precisely, of Kelsen's legal positivism – in the twentieth century was Carl Schmitt, whose influence in political philosophy has been powerful, especially in the last couple of decades. Unlike the positivists, Schmitt holds that the system of law can never be self-sufficient. Thus, he famously defines the sovereign as the one who decides on the exception. The law, according to Schmitt, lacks legitimacy in itself. Instead, the law requires the presence of a sovereign who has the capacity to transcend the law within specific circumstances of emergency.[22] Contra Schmitt, the epicurean conception of law as philonomianism rejects any notion of transcendence and it is decidedly anti-authoritarian in requiring no recourse to a strong notion of sovereignty.

I have noted legal positivism and decisionism because they seem to form the antinomy upon which current political philosophy thinks the law, namely, either as a closed system or as something that requires a strong personal political authority. This antinomy is not so much mediated as entirely evaded by the epicurean definition of the law as *ratio vivendi*. If the law is a logic of living, then the law is positioned prior to any codification, irrespective of whether that codification is understood as complete or incomplete.

Further, the philonomian position that I describe here can be mobilized in productive political ways that challenge established forms of power – something that Spinoza is well aware of in his recounting of the Fall, as I argue in section 3 of the present chapter. Thus, scholars have noted the function of use in jurisprudence, even if this has not been explicitly thematized. For instance, this is the case in the way that property has been defined in the colonial project. One of the key concepts that justified colonization was the legal principle of *terra nullius*. The idea is that uncultivated lands, that is, lands that are in 'disuse', are not legally owned and hence they can be claimed by colonial power.[23] As Brenna Bhandar argues in *Colonial Lives of Property*, the concept of use was mobilized by colonialism to justify legal definitions of property that were both racially tinted and justifications of the appropriation of native land. This shows the danger of a principle of use:

[22] See Schmitt, *Political Theology*.
[23] For a concise account of the history of this legal term, see Fitzmaurice, 'The Genealogy of *Terra Nullius*'.

it can be moulded in such a way as to suit established power – it can be a weapon in the service of 'the right of the strongest'.

At the same time, as Bhandar further argues, the 'fundamental paradox' of use is that many indigenous land claims also rely on the concept of use.[24] For a native title claim to succeed in a court of law, indigenous people need to demonstrate a use of land. The notion of use may be adapted from its native conception to that of the jurisdiction of the court that is designed to defend ownership and the use of land in settler society, but in any case the key term is 'use'. The most famous example of this in Australia is the Mabo ruling that upheld the claim of native title.[25] Significant work has also been done to challenge colonial understandings of the use of land. For instance, Bruce Pascoe's *Dark Emu* shows that, far from being 'uncultivated', Australian aboriginal peoples had sedentary communities that had developed sophisticated systems of agriculture. Again, the challenge to colonialism here consists in employing the concept of use.

Thus, even though epicureanism and its philonomian position have never had an impact on the official story about the development of the law and of jurisprudence, in fact the concept of phronesis in how the law is used can be traced in varied historical moments. This can function both as a heuristic principle for a revisionist history and as a means to challenge established laws and to effect political change that asserts the rights of the repressed.

2. 'You cannot make a republic without killing people': The Tragedy of Legitimacy without Authority in Hannah Arendt

Hannah Arendt offers an instructive counterpoint to Spinoza's philonomianism. Philonomianism at its barest is the notion that there is nothing outside the law. Spinoza adopts this position because of his epicurean understanding of the law, according to which legality springs from the human propensity to calculate one's utility. There is nothing outside the intermingling of the authority of the law and the process of calculating utility. Arendt also rejects the possibility of an outside to the law in a political community. However, as we will see, she is also fiercely critical of instrumental rationality. Her supposition that there is nothing outside the law consists instead in

---

[24] Bhandar, *Colonial Lives of Property*, 65.
[25] For a Spinozan account of the Mabo case, see Gatens and Lloyd, *Collective Imaginings*, chapter 6.

the insistence that the laying of legal foundations is an activity essential to the political. So long as one is part of the political community, one is connected to that foundation – there is no outside to this foundational activity. In other words, Arendt substitutes the calculation of utility with the activity of founding. I will present Arendt's argument here, before I turn to a comparison with Spinoza in the next section.

Arendt's essay 'Authority' provides a genealogical account of the political conception of laying foundations.[26] Authority is 'one, if not the decisive, factor in human communities' (A 104) because of the laying of foundations. This is accompanied by the assertion on the very first page of her essay that 'authority has vanished from the modern world' (A 91). Spinoza also holds that the authority of the prophets has disappeared today (10). This similarity is, however, only a symptom of a profound disagreement between Arendt and Spinoza. In order to fill the vacuum of authority, Arendt argues that political communities have recourse to instrumentality. At the same time, Arendt sharply opposes the political and instrumentality on the grounds that the calculation of utility entails violence. Thus, Arendt denies the notion at the heart of Spinoza's philonomianism, namely, the dialectic of authority and utility. Utility operates in the absence of authority and as the threat of violence to the political proper, according to Arendt. Let us examine how Arendt constructs her argument.

The issue of violence is foregrounded from the beginning in Arendt's collection of essays *Between Past and Future*, which contains 'Authority'. The key distinction is between tradition and violence. The concept of tradition and its central role in the development of the argument is made explicit in the 'Preface'.[27] The clash between tradition and violence emerges in the first essay, 'Tradition and the Modern Age'. In a discussion of Marx that rehearses some of the key moves of the rest of the book – as well as several other works by Arendt, as I will show later – she writes: 'That violence is the midwife of history means that the hidden forces of development of human productivity, insofar as they depend upon free and conscious human action, come to light only through the violence of wars and revolutions.'[28] Arendt is referring here to Marx's famous assertion in chapter 31 of *Capital*, volume 1, that violence is the midwife of every old society giving birth to a new one. Arendt is correct to point out that in this sense revolutionary violence is

---

[26] Arendt, 'Authority', in *Between Past and Future*, 91–141; hereafter cited as A parenthetically in the text.
[27] See, e.g., Arendt, *Between Past and Future*, 15.
[28] Arendt, *Between Past and Future*, 22.

crucial for Marx – a point also affirmed by Engels in *Anti-Dühring* and which becomes subsequently a crucial issue of contention for Marxism.

Arendt further elaborates: 'the challenge to tradition is clear. Violence is traditionally the *ultima ratio* in relationships between nations and the most disgraceful of domestic actions, being always considered the outstanding characteristic of tyranny. . . . To Marx, on the contrary, violence or rather the possession of the means of violence is the constituent element of all forms of government.'[29] Arendt critiques Marx here on his conception of constituent power. Arendt's critique, if viewed in the light of a standard understanding of constituent power, is problematic. According to a standard account, constituent power precedes constituted power.[30] This leads, paradoxically, to two incompatible alternatives: Does this mean that constituent power can legitimately upturn and eliminate the current constituted power? If that were the case, then violence does indeed appear as the productive force of history, as Marx recognizes, given that no constituted power will abdicate without a fight. Or does it mean, conversely, that constituent power can do no more that reform constituted power. If that were the case, it is difficult to see how constituent power can bring something new to the political – something that was not already inchoate within the pre-existing power structure.[31] We can rephrase the two alternatives from the perspectives of violence and the new: either constituent power creates something new, in which case violence cannot be precluded; or constituent power merely transforms already existing power structures, in which case violence is eliminated and along with it also disappears the novelty of the founding activity that is so important for Arendt.[32] So how can Arendt reconcile her critique of Marx's conception of violence in history with her own insistence on the importance of the new foundation for the political?

Her critique of Marx may be explained by looking at the context of Arendt's work just before she embarks on writing *Between Past and Future*. Arendt has just completed *The Origins of Totalitarianism*. When she writes about violence as 'the most disgraceful of domestic actions', we can hear

---

[29] Arendt, *Between Past and Future*, 22.
[30] As Sieyès put it in 1788, 'a constitution is not the work of a constituted power but a constituent power. No type of delegated power can modify the conditions of its delegation.' Sieyès, 'What is the Third Estate?', in *Political Writings*, 136.
[31] The paradox of constituent power is well-known and expressed in various different ways. For one intelligent account, see del Lucchese, 'Machiavelli and Constituent Power'.
[32] See Vardoulakis, *Stasis Before the State*, thesis 1, for a more detailed account of this argument.

echoes of her description of totalitarianism as a regime generalizing internal violence in order to spread its power to the entirety of society. Arendt does not quite collapse Marx's position to totalitarianism, but she rather emphasizes the proximity of a politics that is instrumental – a politics that holds that 'the possession of the means of violence is the constituent element of all forms of government' – and the kind of violence characteristic of a totalitarian society. Thus, even if Marx himself may not have lapsed into totalitarianism, still his link of history and violence inevitably leads his successors down the totalitarian path. This seems inevitable to Arendt if constituent power is configured through the mediation of violence.[33]

It is within the context of such a bleak diagnosis about the present that we can read Arendt's opening assertion in 'Authority' regarding the vanishing of authority from the present. In addition, and significantly from the perspective of the paradox of constituent power, 'Authority' also constructs a genealogy that explains how authority is essential for the establishment of foundations without reliance on violence. In other words, *the concept of authority is Arendt's attempt to sidestep the paradox of constituent power*, according to which either one insists on political novelty thereby having to accept violence, or one is a reformist so as to defend a nonviolent politics devoid of novelty.

The opening distinction of the essay directly refers to violence: 'Since authority always demands obedience, it is commonly mistaken for some form of power or violence. Yet authority precludes the use of external means of coercion; where force is used, authority itself has failed' (A 92–3). Obedience as a definitive feature of authority precludes violence, according to Arendt. Obedience is not so much about the fact of obeying as about precluding any means of disobedience. Differently put, the command-obedience model and the evasion of violence are linked in Arendt's account of authority. Obedience and nonviolence are the obverse sides of authority. Or, to put it in yet another formulation: so long as the act of founding relies on obedience – as a hallmark of authority – then the founding activity can be performed in a nonviolent way. In Arendt's construal, then, authority can provide an account of the new – in particular, of new political foundations – without lapsing into the paradox of constituent power.

This argument is of immense importance for Arendt, but before

---

[33] The story is more complex of course, since *The Human Condition*, as we know from Arendt's notes, was originally conceived as a book on Marx. These notes have recently been published as the first volume of the critical edition of Arendt's work, *The Modern Challenge to Tradition: Fragmente eines Buchs*.

proceeding I want to add one further observation. The passage above continues: 'Authority, on the other hand, is incompatible with persuasion, which presupposes equality and works through a process of argumentation. Where arguments are used, authority is left in abeyance' (A 93). Authority is in an uneasy relation with the democratic – as I also point out in the Introduction. How can one pursue a democratic politics without placing argumentation, persuasion and disputation at the centre of politics? Arendt is taking a notable risk with her emphasis on authority and obedience in order to tackle the paradox of constituent power – a risk that may explain why Arendt is not a proponent of democracy, turning to republicanism instead.

In 'Authority', Arendt constructs authority's conceptual genealogy. This genealogy is inextricable from her philonomianism. As I mentioned, the starting principle of the essay is the loss of authority in modernity. This loss undermines all the links to the past that had provided human societies with a sense of security for centuries. She concludes this line of thought by observing: 'But the loss of worldly permanence and reliability – which politically is identical with the loss of authority – does not entail, at least not necessarily, the loss of the human capacity for building, preserving, and caring for a world that can survive us and remain a place fit to live in for those who come after us' (A 95). This possibility of creating within the political realm relies on the presence of political foundations.

The rest of the essay sketches the way in which authority and the presence of foundations figures in Greek, Roman, Medieval and Modern politics. Thus, authority becomes for Arendt the cypher for interpreting historical development. This is not the idea of progress so central to Enlightenment reasoning, nor is it a dialectical understanding, as if authority discloses a kind of reason operating within history. Rather, it is the striving for a concept of authority, as it is related to the 'human capacity for building, preserving, and caring for a world', that is, as it is related to the founding activity of authority, which becomes the heuristic principle for forging distinctions between historical periods. Let us see how this works.

According to Arendt's analysis, 'the concept of authority ... is exclusively Roman' (A 106). Ancient Greek politics lacks this concept. This is not for want of recognizing the need for a concept of authority. The decisive event for this recognition is, according to Arendt, the death of Socrates: 'It was after Socrates' death that Plato began to discount persuasion as insufficient for the guidance of men and to seek for something liable to compel them without using external means of violence' (A 107). The act of violence against his teacher forces Plato to search for a political concept that is nonviolent and yet does not rely on persuasion. To this end, he turns to the conception of the philosopher-king that most approximates the concept of authority in the Greek polis (A 107). The solution proposed by Plato, like subsequent attempts, fails because 'in the realm of Greek political life there was no awareness of authority based on immediate political experience. Hence all prototypes by which subsequent generations understood the content of authority were drawn from specifically unpolitical experiences' (A 119), such as that of artistic creation or by analogy to the private realm of the household (A 120).[34]

The word and the concept 'authority' are 'Roman in origin' (A 104) because the Romans found a specifically political function for authority, arising from that which is 'at the heart of Roman politics', namely, 'the conviction of the sacredness of foundations' (A 120). The decisive feature of the concept of the foundation is that it derives its authority from the past – and hence it is connected to tradition and religion – and it is forward looking in the sense that it determines political action in the now with a view to future developments (A 121–2). At the same time, authority finds representation in a specific institution, the senate. As Arendt puts it, the 'most conspicuous characteristic of those in authority is that they do not have power' (A 122). On this, Arendt relies on Cicero's distinction between *auctoritas* and *potestas* from *De Legibus*: 'supreme power [*potestas*] is granted to the people and actual authority [*auctoritas*] to the Senate'.[35] What characterizes the Roman world, then, is that authority gives rise to legitimation. The founding generates a realm of legality that leads to the construction of institutions and processes of legitimating political bodies, but in such a way as to rely on obedience instead of violence.

What fascinates Arendt is the 'miracle of permanence' that characterizes the political when it is founded on the legitimacy of authority (A 127). She speaks with admiration of the thousand years of successful rule based on authority that the Roman empires enjoyed followed by Christendom: 'Thanks to the fact that the foundation of the city of Rome was repeated in the foundation of the Catholic Church, though, of course, with a radically different content, the Roman trinity of religion, authority, and tradition could be taken over by the Christian era' (A 126). Arendt continues to

---

[34] In a sense, Arendt is right that the Greek polis does not privilege authority, and it is worth remembering that *auctoritas* does not have an equivalent term in ancient Greek. But in another sense, Arendt is profoundly mistaken to think that the Greeks were unaware of authority, given their institution of *ostracism*, that is, the expulsion from the city of anyone who gained too much obedience. See Nietzsche's discussion of this point in 'Homer Contest', in *On the Genealogy of Morality and Other Writings*, 174–81.

[35] Cicero, *De Legibus*, 492.

specify more precisely the political import of authority as it extends into the Christian era: 'The most conspicuous sign of this continuity is perhaps that the Church, when she embarked upon her great political career in the fifth century, at once adopted the Roman distinction between authority and power, claiming for herself the old authority of the Senate and leaving the power – which in the Roman Empire was no longer in the hands of the people but had been monopolized by the imperial household – to the princes of the world' (A 126). The content of the relation between power and authority changes when the Church 'embarks on its political career' and yet the structure remains essentially unchanged. We are still dealing with a politics that relies on foundations based on the past while looking forward to the future. More precisely, it is a politics that is reliant on the link between authority and legitimation, even though the producer no less than the product of this legitimatory process is the Church.

The decisive turn in Arendt's historical narrative is secularization: 'The separation of church and state . . . far from signifying unequivocally a secularization of the political realm and, hence, its rise to the dignity of the classical period, actually implied that the political had now, for the first time since the Romans, lost its authority and with it that element which, at least in Western history, had endowed political structures with durability, continuity, and permanence' (A 127). In medieval times, the Church retains for itself the founding moment. When in modernity the political seeks its independence from the Church, it loses the prerogative of foundation, and with it also the legitimacy of authority. Secularism is nothing but the loss of authority in the modern world. As Arendt also puts it, even though most of the characteristics of authority are of Greek origin, 'the one political experience which brought authority as word, concept, and reality into our history – the Roman experience of foundation – seems to have been entirely lost and forgotten' (A 136). What is lost with authority is the legitimacy of foundation.

The effect of this loss is the *tragic* search for legitimacy in modernity. The cause of the tragedy is the modern ineptitude in laying foundations. More specifically, the secular turn of modernity is faced with the prospect of laying foundations without authority, and that's the reason it turns to violence instead. The paradox of constituent power is an effect of this loss of authority, according to Arendt. After the loss of authority, 'you cannot make a republic without killing people' (A 139). Arendt singles out Machiavelli and Robespierre as the two figures who want to retain the notion of the foundation, but now without authority. As a result, they understand the act of foundation as a making and creation, separated from tradition. Consequently, they have to rely on a logic of instrumentality, on a logic of means-and-ends. However, the decoupling of political authority and the act of foundation leads to the mobilization of violence: 'they felt that for this supreme "end" all "means," and chiefly the means of violence, were justified' (A 139). The calculation of utility leads to justification, instead of legitimacy, for the foundation of the political. This is the founding violence of Moses's political authority that we saw represented in Rembrandt's painting in the previous chapter. This move, 'which was to become so fateful for the history of revolutions', means that 'Machiavelli and Robespierre were not Romans' (A 139). And the 'legitimate' end that they sought could only be actually accomplished through force – the force that they precisely sought to justify. We have entered the tragedy of *realpolitik* – the tragedy of legitimacy without authority.

There is an additional dimension to the historical tragedy of revolutions, namely their futile attempt to restore authority: 'if . . . the famous "decline of the West" consists primarily in the decline of the Roman trinity of religion, tradition, and authority, with the concomitant undermining of the specifically Roman foundations of the political realm, then the revolutions of the modern age appear like gigantic attempts to repair these foundations, to renew the broken thread of tradition, and to restore, through founding new political bodies, what for so many centuries had endowed the affairs of men with some measure of dignity and greatness' (A 140). The 'decline of the West' and the loss of greatness coincide with the modern notion of the revolution that seeks justification in means-and-ends relations instead of a legitimation through authority. The history of revolutions is tragic because revolutions resort to a logic of utility and are inherently violent, according to Arendt, as violence is the only source of legitimation that they can discover. And the 'fact that . . . all revolutions since the French have gone wrong, ending in either restoration or tyranny, seems to indicate that even these last means of salvation provided by tradition have become inadequate. Authority as we once knew it . . . has nowhere been re-established' (A 141). The outcome of revolutions is either restoration or tyranny. In other words, the outcome of the use of instrumental rationality in the political is either the perpetuation of the same kind of government or the institution of an even more repressive regime. Legitimacy without authority, which is to say, legitimacy resting on the justification of violence, is a project of illegitimate foundation, as its only certain outcome is violence. That is Arendt's vision of the tragic fate of the Occident after the loss of authority.

This tragic vision is premised on the impossibility of establishing a dialectic of authority and utility. Their relation is one of exclusion: there is either authority or utility – and, tragically for Arendt, utility and instrumentality have prevailed in modernity.

3. On the Origins of Finitude: History as Tragedy or Comedy?

Despite the tragic loss of authority aptly described at the end of her essay, 'Authority' does not end without a glimmer hope. Arendt avers that 'to live in a political realm [without] authority . . . means to be confronted anew . . . by the elementary problems of human living-together' (A 141). We can read Arendt's trajectory as an attempt both to define what this 'living-together' would consist in, and to work out how to conceptualize the political form it can assume from a philonomian perspective. The key in such an undertaking would be to see how her philonomianism can be asserted, that is, how legitimacy can rise above utility, and in such a way that authority can lead to a republican and anti-totalitarian politics.

One of the significant pieces of writing that Arendt embarks upon after *Between Past and Future* is adding a new final chapter to the second edition of *The Origins of Totalitarianism*. This addition is prompted by the Hungarian Revolution of 1956. Writing in 1958, Arendt opens the preface to the second edition with what may appear as a cautious move: 'At this moment, hardly two years after the uprising, no one can tell whether this was only the last and most desperate flare-up of a spirit which, since 1789, has manifested itself in the series of European revolutions, or if it contains the germ of something new which will have consequences of its own.'[36] The new chapter itself, added as an 'Epilogue', belies this caution. Here, the Hungarian Revolution is described as a 'spontaneous revolution' that 'had no leaders'.[37] Further, Arendt notes the 'amazing thing' about the Hungarian Revolution, namely, the lack of violence and of civil war.[38] This is not in small measure due to the lack of ideology, which translates politically into the establishment of a council system that is thoroughly nonpartisan. Instead, the councils consist of 'a body of trusted men'.[39] The description of those elected to the councils brings to mind features of the Roman senators. For instance, these are 'trusted and trustworthy men'.[40] In this context, the reason for Arendt's assessment of the Hungarian Revolution – its 'flaming light . . . is

---

[36] Arendt, *Origins*, xi.
[37] Arendt, *Origins*, 482.
[38] Arendt, *Origins*, 496.
[39] Arendt, *Origins*, 499.
[40] Arendt, *Origins*, 500.

the only authentic light we have' – may be due to the fact that, unlike all other revolutions after the French Revolution, the council system restores a sense of authority. Even though Arendt does not make this explicit claim, it is implied within the context of her earlier essay 'Authority'. The council rekindles authority and thereby reanimates the republican spirit.

This rediscovered optimism stemming from a renewed sense of authority appears to have been short-lived. The other major project Arendt is working on in the 1950s and published around the same time is *The Human Condition*. Even though the notion of authority itself has receded into the background to such an extent that it is barely visible, the emphasis placed on founding bears the marks of Arendt's earlier solution to the paradox of constituent power through the figure of authority.[41] The absence of authority as a key concept in *The Human Condition* means that Arendt has to expand the function of founding. It is in this expanded notion of the foundation – given the name 'natality' – that Arendt now places her hopes: 'The miracle that saves the world, the realm of human affairs, from its normal, "natural" ruin is ultimately the fact of natality, in which the faculty of action is ontologically rooted. It is, in other words, the birth of new men and the new beginning, the action they are capable of by virtue of being born. Only the full experience of this capacity can bestow upon human affairs faith and hope.'[42] The effect of this move is to give an ontological grounding to the political process of legitimation.

Arendt must not have been quite happy with the solution through the concept of natality, since she returns to the notion of the political foundation in her book *On Revolution*, published five years after the 'Epilogue' to the second edition of *The Origins of Totalitarianism*. Where the second edition of the *Origins* positions the Hungarian Revolution of 1956 as the only exception to all revolutions since the French Revolution that were doomed to recycle tyrannical forms of government, *On Revolution* reserves a special position for the American Revolution. There are two reasons for this: the founding gesture of the Constitution as well as the founding activity of the council system. Both of these are missing, according to Arendt, from the French Revolution. If the further theorization of the council system expands upon the discussion of the Hungarian experience, the regular references to

---

[41] There are various interesting connections to 'Authority' that I cannot take up in any detail here. For instance, it seems that the notion of the *homo faber* developed in *The Human Condition* is precisely the notion of authority grounded on making that characterizes the Platonic tradition, according to 'Authority'.

[42] Arendt, *The Human Condition*, 247.

authority throughout *On Revolution* presuppose, as opposed to advance, the discussion from the earlier essay 'Authority'. In any case, Arendt revives the attempt to conceive a republican politics through the council system defined in relation to authority.

From the perspective of Arendt's rejection of political activity outside the founding of the law, the most important development is her 1970 book *On Violence*. Violence is defined by Arendt as instrumental. It is a means-and-ends relation. This entails that 'violence always needs justification'.[43] Or, as she further explains a bit later: 'Violence, being instrumental by nature, is rational to the extent that it is effective in reaching the end that must justify it.'[44] The means-and-end relations contain an element of rationality. Consequently, violence is always linked to a rationalized instrumentalism. Conversely, the link between foundation and authority entails that the foundational moment is not subject to the means-and-ends relation. As such it does not require justification. It is, instead, a matter of legitimacy. The impossibility of a dialectic of authority and utility is here presented in its starkest, purest form. I quote a long, important passage:

> Power needs no justification, being inherent in the very existence of political communities; what it does need is legitimacy. . . . Power springs up whenever people get together and act in concert, but it derives its legitimacy from the initial getting together rather than from any action that then may follow. Legitimacy, when challenged, bases itself on an appeal to the past, while justification relates to an end that lies in the future. Violence can be justifiable, but it never will be legitimate. Its justification loses in plausibility the farther its intended end recedes into the future. No one questions the use of violence in self-defense, because the danger is not only clear but also present, and the end justifying the means is immediate. Power and violence, though they are distinct phenomena, usually appear together. Wherever they are combined, power, we have found, is the primary and predominant factor.[45]

This is a complex passage to which I cannot possibly do justice here. I only want to point out a double move that forms the core of Arendt's rejection of antinomianism. The first step is the separation of justification and legitimacy as a way of separating violence from power or the political. And the second

---

[43] Arendt, *On Violence*, 77.
[44] Arendt, *On Violence*, 79.
[45] Arendt, *On Violence*, 52.

is the privileging of legitimation over justification whenever they occur together – such as in cases of self-defence. Succinctly put, *authority and utility are separated, and authority is privileged over utility*. The explicit thematization of this double move in *On Violence* points to the core of Arendt's conception of legality.

Both moves characterizing Arendt's conception are problematic. Let me take them in turn. How can politics be clearly separated from violence, or legitimacy from justification, especially in a present in which authority has vanished? It is telling that Arendt recognizes the force of this question, and her celebration, for instance, of the Hungarian and the American Revolutions are attempts to provide examples of such a separation. Further, the concept of authority, as it is constructed in *Between Past and Future* and later redeployed in various modified forms, is critical in this undertaking, as it points to a nonviolent foundation of the political. And yet, Arendt is unable to provide a successful example of such a separation to illustrate her point with a historical reference. Even if – *concesso non dato* – the Hungarian and the American Revolutions can be illustrations of the recuperation of authority in modernity, still they are at best fleeting revivals of a concept that seems alien to a world that, as Arendt never tires pointing out, has lost its links to tradition and religion. Thus Arendt's argument seems to suggest a distinction between authority and utility. But such a distinction is not yet the separation Arendt is striving for, since a distinction still implies an implication between the two terms – it implies a dialectic – which is precisely what Arendt wants to deny.

The privileging of legitimacy over justification – Arendt's second step in the argument above – betrays what I call the ruse of sovereignty.[46] If rational calculation is resolved in legitimacy, then what criterion can we have at our disposal to judge forms of legitimacy themselves, other than their very perpetuation? When legitimacy is primary, then there does not seem to be a criterion that allows for political change, other than the transformation of the existing forms of legitimacy. Arendt is fully aware of that – which after all is her own critique of every revolution since the French Revolution always resulting in the restitution of the old regime or in the constitution of an even more repressive one. But her privileging of legitimacy over justification does not leave any room for any other 'midwife' of history other than the founding activities of authority – or natality – which is precisely what needs to be addressed for an account of historical change. Hence, her tragic narrative about the inscription of violence in revolutions in the aftermath

---

[46] See Vardoulakis, *Stasis Before the State*. See also the next chapter.

of the loss of authority can be viewed as a lament for losing the capacity to think of political change in modernity.

We discover here another vantage point from which to describe the tragic in Arendt. It is the tragedy of the impossibility to realize in history her conception of nonviolent founding – that is, the separation of authority and utility as well as the privileging of authority. Legitimation always lags behind the historical movement. The conceptual ideal of legitimation may be actualized, but it fails to be separated from justification, with the result that violence determines all futile attempts at political change. From this perspective, the tragedy consists in history's inability to live up to legitimation and authority. Such a sense of the tragic permeates historical time – or, more emphatically, time since modernity is the tragic inability to separate authority from utility. Time is – Arendt suggests – the tragedy that we are trapped in the dialectic of authority and utility.

Spinozan philonomianism is differently positioned because of the different way in which the relation between justification and legitimacy is construed due to his epicurean definition of the law in terms of utility. Spinoza uses the parable of the Fall to describe the genesis of the calculation of utility as the basis of the law – which also means, the Fall is Spinoza's way of describing the creation of contingency, and hence the creation of history. Unlike in Arendt, the narrative that results from Spinoza's account of history originating in the Fall is not a tragic one. Spinoza mobilizes error – the kind of error we saw in the previous chapter – in his presentation of the origin of history and finitude. There is a veritable paroxysm of error here, whose genre appears to be comic rather than tragic.

Error is introduced through a series of questions that Spinoza poses in the aftermath of the definition of the law as a logic of living that has two distinct ends, that is, after the distinction between divine and human law. Spinoza asks whether 'by the natural light of reason we can conceive God as a law giver or ruler, ordaining laws for men' (52). Spinoza outright rejects the idea that God is a lawgiver and hence analogous to a sovereign on the grounds that 'God's will and God's intellect in themselves are in reality one and the same thing' (52).[47] As we saw in the previous chapter, God has no *potestas*. In other words, God has absolute *potentia* – there is nothing outside God. He

---

[47] This is a direct reference to *E* II, P49: 'The will and the intellect are one and the same' (*E* II, P49C). I will only note here how concerned he is in this Proposition of the *Ethics* to link error to the conception of the free will, and how he lapses into a kind of humour himself to prove this point with reference to Buridan's ass – who in fact is the Cartesian subject. See Clemens, 'Spinoza's Ass', in Vardoulakis (ed.), *Spinoza Now*, 65–95.

is not a lawgiver since he could not invent any new laws because that would imply something outside his power, it would imply creation *ex nihilo*. And he is not a ruler or sovereign since his laws are absolutely necessary and hence they are subject neither to obedience nor to disobedience. To think of God as a lawgiver and a ruler is mere anthropomorphizing. It would be, in the wording of the Appendix to Part I of the *Ethics*, the 'sanctuary of ignorance'. The prophets' misunderstanding of God's potentia – as we saw in the previous chapter – is responsible, as Spinoza explains to Blyenbergh, for their 'depicting God as king and lawgiver' (*Ep.* 19). Spinoza turns at this point in chapter 4 to Adam to show how the prophets' error in ascribing potestas to God is responsible for the origin of the dialectic of authority and utility.

Spinoza's account of the Fall starts by pointing a logical contradiction: 'So if, for example, God said to Adam that he willed that Adam should not eat of the tree of knowledge of good and evil, it would have been a contradiction in terms [*contradictionem implicaret*] for Adam to be able to eat of that tree. And so it would have been impossible [*impossibile*] for Adam to eat of it, because that divine decree must have involved eternal necessity and truth [*aeternam necessitatem et veritatem debuisset involvere*]' (53/63). In Spinoza's monism, the fact that the will and the intellect of God are one and the same, as he puts it in chapter 4, implies that God's will cannot be violable. There is nothing outside the divine law, just as there is nothing outside God and divine potentia.

The inviolability of the divine will is a question that has traditionally been asked in relation to the Fall. This conundrum is particularly acute in the fourth century, just as Christianity emerges as the official religion of the empire. One of the major points of contention dividing Christianity as it urgently needs to organize its dogma is the question of evil. How can there be evil if God is omniscient, omnipresent and omnipotent? Augustine's answer prevails partly because of its simplicity: evil is not a property of the divine, but rather of the human. It consists in the human choice, through the exercise of the free will, to do either good or evil. Augustine uses the story of the Fall as the prime example to support his account of the creation of evil through the exercise of the free will.[48]

Even if the starting point is similar to Augustine's – that is, the positing of a divine entity that is inviolable – still Spinoza takes the story in a totally dif-

---

[48] Augustine's account of the Fall can be found in various of his works. See, e.g., *The City of God Against the Pagans*, Books XXII and XXIII; and, *On the Free Choice of the Will*, *on Grace and Free Choice*. See also Arendt's insightful analysis of Augustine's role in the invention of the free will in 'What is Freedom?' in *Between Past and Future*, 143–71. Finally, see Connolly, *Identity / Difference*.

ferent direction, making it a parable not about the creation of evil through the free will but about the genesis of utility and human law. Spinoza resolves the contradiction as follows: 'However, since Scripture tells us that God did so instruct [*praecepisse*] Adam, and that Adam did nevertheless eat of the tree, it must be accepted that God revealed to Adam only the bad consequences he must necessarily incur [*malum tantum revelavisse, quod eum necessario sequeretur*] if he should eat of that tree, while the necessary entailment of these bad consequences [*at non necessitatem consecutionis illius mali*] was not revealed' (53/63). The first thing to note here is that Adam is treated as a prophet since God 'revealed' something to him. God revealed to Adam only what was going to happen if he ate the fruit, namely, the expulsion from the Garden of Eden. But he did not reveal to Adam this was a necessary consequence of divine law. This necessity is consequently implied in the nature of divine potentia, but as a prophet (28) Adam misunderstands the power of God. In other words, Adam repeats the error of the prophets that we saw in the previous chapter, mistaking God's potentia that is characterized by absolute necessity for a certain potestas that can potentially be disobeyed.

Adam's error about God's instruction is responsible for the genesis of human law: 'Consequently, Adam perceived this revelation not as an eternal and necessary truth but as a law [*revelationem non ut aeternam et necessariam veritatem perceperit, sed ut legem*], that is to say, an enactment from which good or ill consequence would ensue not from the necessity and nature of the deed [*non ex necessitate et natura actionis*] performed but from the sole will and absolute sovereignty of some ruler [*ex solo libitu et absolute imperio alicujus Principis*]' (53/63). Adam failed to understand that he was confronted with a divine – that is, an eternal and necessary – law. He thus broke the link between the act and the application of the law. His error led to the rupture of the symmetry between will and intellect, creating instead the structure of law's legitimacy, whereby the sovereign authority who controls the law also controls the punishments administered to the law-breakers. In other words, Adam's error created the idea of human law by conceiving the idea that a law can be disobeyed.

Let me pause to highlight the idiosyncrasy of Spinoza's position. The key feature that traditionally connects authority and human law is obedience. What makes obedience possible in Spinoza's narrative of the Fall? Well, it is nothing other than disobedience! Adam is presented with an absolute necessity – he is presented with a divine law. And what his actions produce is not obedience, but rather the idea that the law can be broken. The error about the nature of divine law – which cannot be broken because it is absolute – creates the idea of human law, which is contingently necessary and hence breakable. The error about the divine law is an act of disobedience – not to the divine law, as this is by definition impossible – but to the human law that did not exist before and is thus created by Adam's act of miscognition-cum-disobedience. Or, more succinctly, disobedience is the condition of the possibility of obedience. Disobedience is the origin of legality.

Spinoza's account should not be confused with the Augustinian one that focuses on the creation of evil. In his reading of Spinoza's reconstruction of the Fall, Gilles Deleuze concentrates on the correspondence with Blyenbergh, who privileges questions about the existence of evil, thus adhering to the Augustinian interpretation. The effect of this is that Adam's error that establishes the law in disobedience is elided in Deleuze's interpretation.[49] This has had a profound influence in reading this passage from the *Theological Political Treatise* in terms of Deleuze's distinction between ethics and morality.[50] And even though there are other interpretations that do not bear Deleuze's mark as heavily, still none of them aspires to a reading of this passage that concentrates on the lawgiving capacity of the prophetic error. For instance, Hasana Sharp concentrates on the relation between Adam and Eve, while Nancy Levene reads this in the context of biblical interpretation, for example Maimonides's account of the Fall.[51] But the connection between disobedience and legality is not addressed.

Spinoza's subversion of the 'original sin' consists in the thesis that, so long as there is authority, there is disobedience. Disobeying is the condition of obeying and it is responsible for the creation of human law. Despite trying to identify similarities between Augustine and Spinoza, Milad Doueihi concludes that the difference between them ultimately has to do with their attitude toward authority.[52] The difference is discernible in how disobedience is conceived. One disobeys by making a calculation that it will be in one's utility to break the law. Disobedience presupposes the calculation of utility. All this is to argue that the use of rationality toward calculating one's utility – that is, the use of phronesis – is 'in absolute agreement with' divine law. Not only does Spinoza have no use for Augustine's doctrine of grace, but in fact he suggests that revealed knowledge of the law is only good so long as it is accompanied by the operation of phronesis. If grace suggests that revealed

---

[49] See Deleuze, *Expressionism in Philosophy*, 247–8. See also Deleuze, *Spinoza: Practical Philosophy*, 2 and 30–43.

[50] For the influence of Deleuze's interpretation, see, for instance, Albiac, 'The Empty Synagogue', in Montag and Stolze (eds), *The New Spinoza*, 108–43.

[51] Sharp, *Spinoza and the Politics of Renaturalization*, 208–9; and Levene, *Spinoza's Revelation: Religion, Democracy and Reason*, 38 ff.

[52] Doueihi, *Augustine and Spinoza*.

law is to be obeyed for the attainment of salvation, Spinoza responds that this is the mark of a slave and that true freedom consists in continuously interrogating the law's utility.

The Spinozan narrative about human finitude, his narrative about the Fall, suggests that disobedience is the condition of the possibility of obedience and legality because disobedience mobilizes the calculation of utility. Thus Spinoza arrives at the same conclusion in the account of the Fall that he arrived at earlier through the definition of the law as *ratio vivendi*, except that Adam's story adds one thing, namely, that the genesis of the law coincides with the genesis of the calculation of utility. This is not to suggest that the calculation of utility is something uniform or that the origin of utility has any kind of unity. To the contrary, it is to suggest that the adamic disobedience is the first act of phronesis. Adam's error in the narrative of the Fall points to the origin of origin, since with the calculation of utility in Adam's disobedience the human law is created, which has an origin, unlike the divine law. The Fall explains the invention of the dialectic of authority and utility as the material expression of the logic of finitude (*ratio vivendi*) which arises from Adam's error.

Augustine also describes the Fall as the starting point of history. But for Augustine the Fall is a tragedy. The expulsion from paradise not only leads to finitude, but also burdens the human with the original sin. The Fall is the tragedy of the creation of sin as the defining characteristic of human history. Subsequently, the Fall is always presented as a tragedy, regardless of whether the tragic element strictly conforms to Augustine's narrative.[53] Contrary to this entire tradition, Spinoza's narrative presents the Fall as a comedy of errors. The various errors – about authority, potestas and the people – described in the previous chapters of the *Treatise* reach a crescendo in Spinoza's recounting of the Fall. There is an error of communication between God and Adam, resembling the failures of communication that lead to all sorts of comical happenings in theatre.

If God represents the identity of the will and intellect, which is to say, the inseparability of materiality and 'spirituality' because God is a totality outside of which nothing exists, then the first human error and the first moment of history represent a cognitive dissonance about this identity and about God. The narrative of the Fall is about this miscognition of divine law, which in turn creates the idea of human law. Potestas and authority are possible

---

[53] For the narration of the Fall as a tragedy that attributes melancholia to humankind, see the analysis of St Hildegard in Klibansky, Panofsky and Saxl, *Saturn and Melancholy*, 78–80.

because of this first cognitive error, which is also an error about power. God is not a lawgiver because he can be neither obeyed nor disobeyed. The moment there is disobedience, at that very moment contingency is created and historical time comes into effect. This first disobedience is nothing but the miscalculation – and yet a first calculation nonetheless – of authority. It is a miscalculation that brings with it authority, lawgiving, legitimacy as well as the opening up of historical time. The Fall and the comedy of errors Spinoza describes are not an isolated episode confined to an obscure past, but rather the necessary condition for the creation of contingency and practical knowledge – the creation of phronesis. As such, the Fall shows how the calculation of utility is at the basis of legality, potestas and authority.

This can be understood as an anthropological principle delineating our finitude: we are all little Adams, and this is not a sin from which we need to be purified, but rather the reality of living in historical time. The fact that we are all little Adams points to the fact that we are continuously repeating in the now the error about the divine law in the form of disobedience, which entails that we are caught in the dialectic of authority and utility. To conceive of a position exterior to human law would amount to a yearning for a return to Eden prior to the first calculation of utility through the act of disobedience. Spinoza does not entertain such utopian phantasies. Spinoza's philonomianism entails instead that the now exists only so long as human law is being created by us, that is, only so long as we continuously exercise our instrumental rationality even if our shortcomings mean that we also need authority.

This idiosyncratic construal of the Fall has far-reaching political consequences. It suggests that *auctoritas* is beyond disputation not because her judgements are inviolable but rather because her judgements presuppose an error: the error that it is possible to disobey divine potentia and divine law. This is a profoundly anti-authoritarian insight. It is not anti-authoritarian in the sense that Spinoza advances a utopian position – which is to say, a position outside history and contingency – where authority will disappear. It is rather anti-authoritarian in the sense that the notion of authority is not dependent on legality and obedience and hence it is not matter of determination, but it is reliant on the calculation of utility and hence subject to contestation.

Let me be more precise: Spinoza never denies the necessity of authority for the community. However, if the basis of authority is utility, and if everyone has the *right* to calculate their utility, then authority is immanently contestable. In other words, there is a conflict – a *dialectic* – between authority and utility that is the obverse side of understanding historical time as the first comedy of errors in the protoplasts' story. This conflict is articulated as Adam's laughable error – an error that we as humans are bound to repeat in historical time.[54]

In Spinoza's philonomianism the persistence with the dialectic of authority and utility signals, on the one hand, the epicurean conception of the law, according to which justification is more primary than legitimacy. This allows Spinoza to adopt an anti-authoritarian stance, as any form of political justification of authority can potentially be dejustified through the operation of phronesis.[55] On the other hand, philonomianism is also responsible for a sense of historicity as it interrogates the origins of finitude and the dialectic of authority and utility determining human action. Human finitude is introduced by the error about God's potentia that makes God into a lawgiver. The anti-authoritarian impulse is registered here too in Spinoza's emphasis on the comedy of errors that characterizes the history of this error.

Arendt's attempt to bypass the dialectic of authority and utility leads to a tragic conception of temporality. Spinoza's laughter offers a more materialist outlook: not a lament about our political predicament but the recognition that the impossibility of stepping outside the dialectic of authority and utility leads to an agonistic politics that places an exigency upon us to fight for our freedom. This is a fight, suggests Spinoza, that we should take up with a smile on our face, no matter how terrible the effects of power and authority as a result of our errors might be. We need this smile so as to recognize the errors as errors, that is, so as to recognize that we are all little Adams.

* * *

This varied complex of ideas that I designate as philonomianism appears easily graspable if we trace it onto the three epicurean themes that, as I argue, determine Spinoza's epicureanism. The important point I have underscored is that the three themes are not independent of each other, but rather work in tandem to produce Spinoza's epicureanism.

The distinction between divine and human law can be understood as the way in which the law is inscribed in the relation between monism and the calculation of utility. The limited understanding of the law, according to which law is determining actions, fails because it cannot account for this

---

[54] Laughter, as Nietzsche and Kafka very well knew, and as Arendt herself admits, is a significant means to the dialectic of conflict with authority since 'the surest way to undermine it [i.e. authority] is laughter'. Arendt, *On Violence*, 45. See also Vardoulakis, *Freedom from the Free Will*.

[55] On dejustification, see Vardoulakis, *Sovereignty and its Other*.

relation. Conversely, this is precisely what the definition of the law as *ratio vivendi* achieves. Human law is defined through the operation of practical judgement that strives to calculate what is the utility of the community. And divine law strives for the supreme good that Spinoza identifies with the knowledge of God, that is, with knowledge of the monist idea that there is a totality outside of which nothing exists. The two are connected because they describe utility in different ways that show how the human lives in an organized community while also being cognizant of the lack of transcendence and creation *ex nihilo*.

The question whether God is a lawgiver or ruler introduces the third theme, namely, authority. Spinoza rejects any anthropomorphization of the divine. God is the totality outside of which nothing exists, which also means that it is the same as nature. At the same time, the erroneous idea that God is a ruler is responsible for the production of obedience, that is, for the generation of authority. Significantly, Spinoza's retelling of the story of the Fall indicates that disobedience is the precondition of obedience. This suggests that there is no absolute authority. Authority can be challenged.

This convergence of the three epicurean themes in philonomianism has another implication. As Spinoza explains in the *Political Treatise*, the outcome of the Adamic story shows that 'it was not in the power of the first man to use reason aright' (2.6). The error about God as lawgiver leads to the miscalculation according to which one transfers one's right to calculate – this is the spectre of voluntary servitude that haunts the dialectic of authority and utility. Servitude is the prospect that the error is so overwhelming that one becomes a voluntary slave, that is, gives up one's right to calculate one's utility. The slave, then, threatens the dissolution of the dialectic of authority and utility – a threat pivotal to the argument of the *Theological Political Treatise*, as we will see.[56] Thus, philonomianism conceives of the law in such a way as to make possible positive political change while remaining attuned to the threats facing the political community and as such adopting a pragmatic, anti-utopian position. What remains for Spinoza to address is a genetic account of such a conception of the political – a task that he fulfils in the following couple of chapters.

---

[56] See section 3 of Chapter 7.

4

Political Monism: The Primacy of Utility over Authority (chapters 5 and 6)

What is the relation of priority between authority and utility, the two terms of the epicurean dialectic? Does authority cause utility or is it the other way round? What comes first, authority or utility? Spinoza's conception of democracy stands or falls with this problematic. If authority means that which is impervious to argumentation and if democracy requires the freedom to decide about collective actions, then the priority of authority would suggest that democracy is merely a consequence of authority. It is not easy to reverse the relation, since what does it mean to have democracy before the instituted kind of power modelled on authority's structure of command and obedience? That is, how can we conceive of democracy before written law?

The relation between authority and utility may seem to mirror one of the major issues in the interpretation of the *Theological Political Treatise*, namely, whether the prosperity and well-being of the community and the state are ensured by obedience or reason. The vast majority of commentators on Spinoza's *Treatise* feel compelled to take either side. As I suggested in the Introduction, I present the relation of authority and utility as a dialectic to bypass the disjunction of – or, differently put, to overcome the false binary of – either obedience or reason. Nonetheless, the dialectical relation cannot evade the problematic of what comes first, authority or utility.

Let me highlight some of the complexities of this problematic via Michel Foucault. He develops a theory of power understood as something constructed, as potestas, which in Foucault's terms includes what we call authority here. It is fundamental to this theory that there is no power as such, but it is rather always accompanied by resistance. His approach consists, as he puts it in his essay 'The Subject and Power', in

> taking the forms of resistance against different forms of power as a starting point . . . using this resistance as a chemical catalyst so as to bring to light

power relations, locate their position, find out their point of application and the methods used. Rather than analyzing power from the point of view of its internal rationality, it consists of analyzing power relations through the antagonism of strategies. For example, to find out what our society means by sanity, perhaps we should investigate what is happening in the field of insanity. And what we mean by legality in the field of illegality.[1]

Foucault's notion of power requires resistance, which registers all those areas and activities that are incommensurable with power. Foucault's conception of resistance has clear affinities with the epicurean approach to power adopted by Spinoza: there is no power that is outside materiality, there is no utopian conception of a 'revolution' that completely transforms material relations, and there is no absolute authority beyond contestation. Rather, power or *potestas* as well as authority are determined through their effects, which are most visible at the points of strain – what I called 'errors' earlier or what Foucault calls resistance.

Foucault further clarifies his conception of the relation between power and resistance in Volume 1 of the *History of Sexuality*, when he insists that resistances 'are inscribed in [power] as an irreducible opposite'.[2] With this clarification we discern the limit of Foucault's approach, as well as the difference from epicureanism. If resistance is inscribed within power, this means that power is presupposed. In Foucault's framework, resistance is conceived as arising from, or as caused by, power. There is no resistance in the absence of power. This move essentially consists in the primacy of authority over utility – to put it in terms of the dialectic I have been describing in this book.

Foucault faces two significant shortcomings in his conception of the relation between power and resistance. First, it means that power can adapt itself to appear as counter-resistance or disguise itself as if it accepts that which resists it.[3] For instance, it may be in the name of the care and welfare of indigenous populations that a government may justify new and draconian controls and regulations of that population.[4] Second, it traps us in what I

---

[1] Foucault, 'The Subject and Power', 211.
[2] Foucault, *The Will to Power*, 96.
[3] Caygill, *On Resistance: A Philosophy of Defiance*.
[4] I am thinking here specifically of the so-called Northern Territory intervention. The intervention was prompted by the 2007 report titled *'Little Children are Sacred': Report of the Northern Territory Board of Inquiry into the Protection of Aboriginal Children from Sexual Abuse*, available at <http://www.inquirysaac.nt.gov.au/pdf/bipacsa_final_report.pdf>. For an informed and critical perspective on the intervention on its tenth anni-

call elsewhere 'the ruse of sovereignty'.[5] If power is the cause of resistance, and if there is no utopian conception of something outside power, then the most that resistance can achieve is to tactically intervene against particular articulations of power. The problem is not so much that this means we have not yet cut off the head of the king.[6] It rather means that – to continue Foucault's metaphor – the king's head can never be cut off if resistance is to persist. Resistance requires the 'king', or authority, for its continuous existence. It is symptomatic of this predicament that Foucault has nothing to say about democracy in his works. Democracy is simply understood as another form that power as a regime of government can take, qualitatively indistinguishable from any other regime.

To summarize the problematic, Foucault presents a materialist relation between power and resistance, but the terms of this relation are still dictated by power. The question I am posing here is: Can the dialectic of authority and utility restructure this relation? Can utility be conceived in such a way as to be primary in relation to power? And how can this possibility inform a conception of democracy? I will pursue this problematic by examining first how Spinoza outlines the origin of society. Then I will present two key terms of his conception of democracy, namely, its naturalism and its agonism. And, third, I will show how Spinoza's monism is political through and through, which entails the importance of practical judgement for politics. Cumulatively, these three points show the primacy of utility over authority in Spinoza.

1. 'Society is advantageous': Utility and Social Formation

We can explore how Spinoza reformulates Foucault's problematic of the relation between power and resistance into the problematic of the relation between authority and utility by turning to his privileged example in the *Theological Political Treatise*, the Hebrew state. This reformulation occurs in chapter 5 in the course of Spinoza's discussion of the constitution of the Hebrew state through instituted ceremonies.

The Jews live under Egyptian law for generations. When Moses leads them to a flight through the desert they are 'no longer bound by the laws of any state' (64), until they receive the Tablets of the Law and they establish

---

versary, see Perche, 'Ten years on, it's time we learned the lessons from the failed Northern Territory Intervention'.
[5] See Vardoulakis, *Stasis Before the State*.
[6] Foucault, *Will to Power*, 89.

their own state. This new state relies on numerous ceremonial practices that are the ostensible object of Spinoza's inquiry at the beginning of chapter 5. Spinoza insists that ceremonies are human laws since they 'are good only by convention, not by nature [*ex solo instituto, et non ex natura*]' (60/70), adding that 'ceremonial observances contribute nothing to blessedness' (65), meaning that ceremonies are distinct from divine law. Spinoza concentrates on the utility of ceremonies for the preservation of the Hebrew community. Thus, he notes the 'practical value' (59) of ceremonies, and he explains throughout the chapter the 'promise' of ceremonies (60, 61, 62 and 64) as contributing to the prosperity of the community. Following Epicurus's point that the law is functional so long as it is useful, Spinoza asserts that the Jews are not bound by their laws after the disappearance of their state, since their utility disappears at that point.[7] To illustrate his point, Spinoza observes that when the Jews lived in Egypt 'they were bound by no law other than the natural law [*nisi naturali jure*], and doubtless the law of the state [*jure reipublicae*] in which they dwelt' (62/72). Spinoza appears to take his understanding of the law as utility to its logical conclusion by asserting that there is no political authority to obey when the Jewish state is dissolved, whereby their ceremonies are no longer useful.

Immediately after asserting that the Jews were bound to Egyptian law, Spinoza qualifies this assertion by saying that they are required to observe the laws of the Egyptians 'insofar as [*quatenus*] that was not opposed [*non repugnabat*] to natural divine law [*legi divinae naturali*]' (62/72). This appears close to Foucault's position about resistance. State law is not determined independently but rather in relation, even in opposition, to whatever it cannot accommodate. And yet, there is a significant difference from Foucault. The fact that resistance is heterogeneous to power, in Foucault's terms, entails that power is the source of resistance, as there can be no resistance to nothing – resistance needs power to direct its force against. The distinction between human and divine law is different in Spinoza. As we saw in the previous chapter, law, both human and divine, is defined as a logic of living directed toward certain ends. This means that both human and divine law rely on the calculation of utility. The distinction between them pertains to the kind of utility they pursue. Divine law aims toward the supreme good, such as blessedness, whereas human law aims toward self-preservation for both the individual and the community. It is the ends of the instrumental relations entailed in divine and human law that differ, not the fact that they are both instrumental.

[7] Diogenes Laertius, 'Epicurus', *Lives of Eminent Philosophers*, X.150–3. See the extensive discussion of this point in section 1 of Chapter 3.

This difference from Foucault may open the way toward sidestepping the problems that I outlined at the beginning – counter-resistance and the ruse of sovereignty. The notable feature is that the problem has now been reconfigured in a new matrix of concepts, namely, in terms of the relation of authority and utility. To really respond to the conundrum that Foucault's resistance as responsive to a pre-existing power poses, we need to show how utility precedes authority in this re-articulation of the problem.

This is not an easy task, not least because the Hebrew state is used by contractarianism in the seventeenth century to stage the relation between authority and utility in the course of explaining the origin of the political. The most prominent example is Hobbes, who uses the Hebrew state in the *Leviathan* to show the three stages of the formation of the political.[8] The wandering in the desert corresponds to the lawless state of nature. The social sphere is formed when the Jews decide to obey the laws. And the political community is formed when the Jews receive the laws. In the wording of the *Leviathan*, 'the Kingdome of God is a Civill Kingdome; which consisted, *first* in the obligation of the people of Israel to those Laws, which Moses should bring unto them from Mount Sinai'.[9] There is 'first' a political community when the people submit themselves to the command and obedience model, that is, to political authority, in this case, to Moses. The earlier stages are pre-political, the state of nature because it signifies an interminable enmity between humans, and the social because it still lacks the law to enforce the command and obedience model. Differently put, the social formation model propagated by Hobbes and adhered to by contractarians posits a pre-legal or ante-legal position that is insufficient for community formation. There is a political community only in the presence of authority. As soon as there is authority, the subjects of that authority are in a position to use their rationality to calculate their self-preservation, including how to avoid capital punishment from the law that they have vowed to obey. Differently put, the narrative of the formation of the Hebrew state is used in the contractarian tradition to explain the primacy of authority over utility.

After insisting that the law of the state is to be obeyed only 'insofar as' it does not contradict divine law, Spinoza makes a methodological apostrophe to the reader. He explains that his discourse on the Hebrew state has proceeded thus far through 'Scriptural authority [*Scripturae authoritate*]' (62/73). He signals that he now wants to demonstrate the origin of society 'through

---

[8] I return in more detail to the issue of the social contract in Hobbes and Spinoza in Chapter 7.
[9] Hobbes, *Leviathan*, 284, emphasis added.

a universal basis [*ex universalibus fundamentis ostendam*]' (62/73). It is crucial that Spinoza's argumentation proceeds through a double route, both through the piety and obedience distilled by 'Scriptural authority', and through the employment of reason. I noted earlier how Spinoza employs the same double argumentative strategy in chapter 3 of the *Theological Political Treatise* (see section 3 of Chapter 2). I note this strategy here again to underscore its importance, as it represents two argumentative strategies that privilege either of the two terms of the dialectic, authority and utility. It is important to recognize that by employing both strategies, Spinoza suggests that he does not privilege either. This is a critical point for Spinoza's conception of faith and reason, as we will see in Chapter 6. I will also argue in the final chapter of the book that this double strategy is indispensable for understanding the conception of democracy in chapters 19 and 20 of the *Treatise*.

The shift to arguing about the origin of human law from the perspective of reason leads to a discussion that corresponds roughly to two pages in the Gebhardt edition – a discussion that is astonishing in the density and clarity with which it approaches the question of the origins of society. I find these pages the most succinct presentation of Spinoza's overall political project. Surprisingly, as far as I know, these couple of pages have not been the subject of a systematic analysis in the secondary literature. Given their importance, I want to read them carefully and slowly – here and in the following section.

To present his account of how utility precedes authority, Spinoza needs nothing less than a complete reconstruction of the account of the origins of the political according to the three stages outlined by Hobbes – namely, the state of nature, the social and the political. Immediately after asserting that he will proceed on a 'universal basis', Spinoza turns to the question of the origins of the political community by emphasizing utility: 'A society is advantageous [*perutilis*], even absolutely necessary [*necessaria*], not merely for security against enemies but for its expedient accomplishment [*compendium faciendum*] of a variety of things' (62–3/73). The utility of society is not merely a negative one, consisting in the protection from enemies. It also has the positive function of providing utility to the life of each person. This utility, however, requires one condition: 'If humans were not willing to work for each other [*invicem operam mutuam dare velint*], they would lack both the skill and the time to support and preserve themselves to the greatest possible extent' (63/73). The condition for the utility of social formation is articulated in the pleonasm between the adverb *invicem* and the adjective *mutuus*. The utility Spinoza has in mind is reciprocal and mutual. It consists in doing things, in working, not only for oneself but for others too. Differently put, *the origin of society is located at the point that we recognize that our utility is never a strictly personal matter. Our utility is implicated in the utility of the other.*[10]

Spinoza demonstrates the reciprocity of utility with the following example:

> Not everyone is equally suited to all activities, and no single person would be capable of supplying all his own needs. Each would find strength and time fail him if he alone had to plough, sow, reap, grind, cook, weave, stitch and perform all the other numerous tasks to support life, not to mention the arts and sciences which are also indispensable for the perfection of human nature and its blessedness. (63)

This passage may bring to mind Adam Smith's description of division of labour in terms of self-interest in the *Wealth of Nations*:

> It is not from the benevolence of the butcher, the brewer, or the baker, that we expect our dinner, but from their regard to their own interest. We address ourselves, not to their humanity but to their self-love, and never talk to them of our own necessities but of their advantages.[11]

There is, however, a fundamental difference. Smith describes this natural propensity to calculate one's interest and the interest of the other as occurring only after an organized society with laws and a sovereign authority are established. The 'natural' operation of the economy still presupposes, according to Smith, the 'nation state' of a constructed political authority.[12]

This is not the case with Spinoza, whose point is that the formation of society through the reciprocity of utility does not require an established legal or political authority. No written laws are presupposed for his 'working for each other' so as to achieve utility. This is made explicit in what he says immediately after the passage about the division of labour within society: 'We see that those who live barbarously without a commonwealth [*barbare sine politia*] lead a wretched and almost brutish [*paene brutalem*] existence, and even so their few poor and crude [*impolita*] resources are not acquired without some degree of mutual labor [*sine mutua opera*]' (63/73). There are people who are barbarous in the sense that they live in a polity with scant

---

[10] The full import of this point will be analysed in the following chapter.
[11] Smith, *An Inquiry into the Nature and Causes of the Wealth of Nations*, I.ii (26–7).
[12] This argument in the *Wealth of Nations* is complicated by Adam Smith's conception of 'conjectural history' in his lectures on rhetoric. I take up this point in my book on materialism provisionally titled *Neoepicureanism* (see Preface).

resources. Notice that Spinoza emphasizes this by using the Greek word *politia* instead of a variety of Latin words that he has at his disposal, such as *imperium*. The lack of material resources (*impolita*) is related to their lack of a state with written laws (*sine politia*). In this 'barbarous' state they lack the command and obedience model that characterizes a commonwealth. And yet, they still have arrangements for reciprocal utility by sharing resources. For Hobbes and the contractarian tradition life in a state of nature without laws is 'nasty, brutish, and short', which necessitates the establishment of authority for any utility to be achieved.[13] Conversely, life in a lawless society is brutish for Spinoza because of the limited resources, but this does not lead to violence but rather to the mutual labour characterizing social utility.

Thus, *pace* Hobbes, the formation of society is not the transition from lack of laws to legitimate rule supported by written laws. Rather, so long as there is more than one individual, there is shared utility that binds individuals together. Or, more emphatically, Spinoza rejects the idea of what Marx disparages as 'Robinsonade', that is, that society is merely the aggregate of autonomous individuals each pursuing their self-interest.[14] Instead of individuals, Spinoza's account of social formation requires what Étienne Balibar refers to as 'transindividuals'.[15] One's individual identity is given in relation to others. Being is being with. From this perspective, what every society has in common with every other society, including the 'barbarous' ones that have no written laws, is the fact that social relations are determined by the calculation of utility, that is, through the operation of the epicurean notion of phronesis. Where they differ is that this calculation is contingent and it allows for variation – whereby it is differently articulated in a 'barbarous' polity and in a state with institutions grounded on statute. Utility is common to all but it is articulated in a multiplicity of ways that differ depending on the conditions. Thus, the origin of society can be located at the point that phronesis operates – not at the point that authority is formed. Utility is more primary than authority.

Let me provide two clarifications. First, the provenance of the idea that the origins of society can be found in the human's capacity to calculate its utility is epicurean. I have already referred to this idea. In the Introduction, I noted how Alison Brown's *The Return of Lucretius to Renaissance Florence* describes this move as primitivism and notes that it is inspired by Book 5 of Lucretius's *On the Nature of Things*. In a subsequent article addressing

---

[13] Hobbes, *Leviathan*, 89.
[14] See Marx, *Grundrisse*, 17. Cf. Marx, *Capital, Volume 1*, in *Collected Works*, 87–8.
[15] Balibar, *Spinoza: From Individuality to Transindividuality*.

Machiavelli's epicureanism, Brown describes 'Lucretian primitivism' as the idea that all sentient beings – animals, 'barbarous' humans as well as those living in an organized polity – retain the natural virtue of prudence.[16] This means that phronesis is inscribed in all the different forms of society. Further, in Chapter 1 I described Lucretius's presentation of the 'stages' of society in Book 5 of *On the Nature of Things* to show how it makes possible a conception of history that is organized according to the principle of utility. Even if there are no final ends in human action, still action presupposes the conception of some end, no matter how provisional or misguided. This is an end that is always grounded on one's material existence and as such indicative of one's instrumental rationality as the *sine qua non* of community.

Second, one schooled in contractarianism and the subsequent conceptions of liberal democracy may still regard Spinoza's account of social formation with incredulity: how is it possible to have a society without established laws? To lend some credence to Spinoza's position, let us turn to the political anthropologist Pierre Clastres, and in particular his work *Society Against the State*. The key point of agreement between Clastres and Spinoza is that social formation does not require written laws based on the command and obedience model. Rather, the social arises through the calculation of utility. Clastres describes primitive technics in terms of a social praxis or task that does not aim at a complete mastery of nature, but at the use of the environment only to the extent that it fulfils the human's needs – whereby the measure of technics becomes the 'power of invention and efficiency'.[17] Clastres could just as well have said that technics are articulated as phronesis. Studying tribes in South America such as the Guayaki, Clastres can then contend that there is social formation even in the absence of the command and obedience model. Social being is regulated even in the absence of written laws.[18] The principle of efficiency – that is, the principle of the calculation of utility – forms a sufficient basis for the formation of society.

---

[16] Brown, 'Lucretian Naturalism and the Evolution of Machiavelli's Ethics', in del Lucchese, Frosini and Morfino (eds), *The Radical Machiavelli*, 115.

[17] Clastres, *Society Against the State*, 191.

[18] Clastres's position as I describe it here does not necessarily contradict his alleged anarchism, as described by, amongst others, Lefort or Abensour. Rather, the important point is that the absence of written laws does not preclude the possibility of social organization. Stathis Gourgouris provides some powerful reflections on Clastres – for instance, an intriguing comparison between ancient democratic Athens and Clastres's description of the primitive or stateless society – that accord with my point. See Gourgouris, *The Perils of the One*, ch. 2.

I will return to Clastres in the following section – I just want to indicate here that the notion of a social formation that places the primacy on utility as opposed to the obedience and command model is not simply a philosophical concept, but can also be supported by research in anthropology.

After these two clarifications, let us return to Spinoza's text. We have seen that he argues for the primacy of utility over authority. But he has still not shown how the three-step contractarian account of the formation of society – from state of nature, to society, to the commonwealth – is reformulated in his own account. That is the next topic of his argument. He develops a position in three steps. The first is the logical conclusion of the priority of utility: 'Now if people were so constituted by nature as to desire nothing but what is prescribed by true reason [vera ratio], society would stand in no need of any laws. Nothing would be required but to teach them true ethical examples [vera documenta moralia], and they would then act to their true utility [vere utile] of their own accord, wholeheartedly and freely' (63/73). If society included members who all calculated their utility according to the operation of reason, without being overwhelmed by emotions such as fear, then there would be no need for statutory law. The entire social function would then consist in the coordination between reason and utility, and no authority would be required to instruct humans what is the right conduct, nor written laws to institute a command and obedience model. The repetition of verus three times – true calculation, true ethics and true utility – structures this movement of thought. The primacy of utility leads to the conception of society without authority.

Such a conception is immediately qualified with a disjunction introduced with verum, the adverbial form of verus meaning 'however': 'However [verum] human nature is far differently constituted' (63/73). Humans consistently miscalculate their utility. They misuse their instrumental rationality, and hence they focus only on their personal advantage (suum utile, 73). As a result, 'no society can subsist without government [imperio] and coercion [vi], and consequently without laws [legibus]' (63/74). If the exercise of a vera ratio, an accomplished phronesis, does not accord with human nature – not least because of the fallibility of practical judgement, as I have been arguing since the Introduction – then a different social organization is needed that does not rely on the calculation of utility but rather on the force (vis) of the command and obedience model. It is because of the inherent limitation of humans to 'see the better and do the worse' that authority is a necessity. Written laws help us overcome the shortcomings of the errors we commit and which threaten our utility both as individuals and as a community. Thus, authority is an outcome or aftereffect of utility. Authority is produced because it is useful due to the inherent fallibility of the calculation of utility – a conclusion consistent with the account of error in the previous four chapters of the *Theological Political Treatise* and with the explanation of the genesis of human law and historicity in chapter 4.

At this point Spinoza introduces a second disjunction: 'Yet [*tamen*] human nature does not allow itself be forced absolutely [*patitur absolute se cogi*]' (63/74). Spinoza supports this view with a quotation from Seneca: 'a state based on violence is never long-lasting [*violenta imperia nemo continuit diu*]' (63/74). The reason is revealing: 'For as long as humans act only from fear [*ex solo metu agunt*], they are doing what they are most opposed to doing, without calculating the utility and the necessity of their actions [*rationem utilitatis et necessitates rei agendae tenent*], concerned only not to incur capital or other punishment' (63/74). The problem with human law based on the command and obedience model and with the authority arising from fear is that they seek to eliminate instrumental rationality. This is the definition of voluntary servitude that we found in the Preface; namely, the repression of phronesis. However, phronesis is impossible to eliminate completely. Whenever law and authority are too repressive, then there is the possibility that people will calculate that resistance is preferable to their present state of obedience. It is a small step from here for the citizens to resent their rulers and to rise against them – and Spinoza here is not far from Machiavelli who also argues in *The Prince* that hatred and resentment lead to the uprising of the people. Differently put, no authority is absolute. The authority of human law presupposes the possibility of disobedience because it can never eliminate the calculation of utility.

We see then that Spinoza follows a tripartite structure to delineate an account of social formation – just like contractarianism. But his account is very different. According to Hobbes, lawlessness and its violence (the state of nature) lead to the recognition that for self-preservation people need to renounce their right to do as they wish (social stage) and authorize a sovereign to regulate the law on their behalf through reward and punishment (the political sphere). By contrast, in Spinoza we find, first, the possibility of social interaction in terms of the reciprocity of utility; second, the construction of authority as a means to address the fallibility of the calculation of utility; and, third, the ineliminability of utility when the command and obedience model comes into effect, whereby authority is never absolute but always limited by its usefulness to the community. For Hobbes, authority is presupposed for the calculation of utility in the political sphere. For Spinoza, political interaction can take place even in the absence of authority, whereby utility is the primary term of the relation.

2. Natural and Agonistic Democracy

Spinoza starts the account of the origin of society with a standard contractarian example, the Hebrew state. But his presentation of that example turns the conclusion of contractarianism on its head. Perhaps we should not be surprised since we saw a similar tactic in Spinoza's narration of the Fall in the previous chapter, where the Fall is used to argue for a position that contradicts the standard account from Augustine. The Hebrew state is, by comparison, a more significant example in the *Theological Political Treatise*. Spinoza will devote two whole chapters to its analysis in the final, 'political' part of the *Treatise* – chapters 17 and 18. Given its importance for his account of social formation, Spinoza draws three inferences that he develops further later.

The first inference from the priority of utility over authority states that 'the entire community, if possible, should hold government in common [*collegialiter imperium tenere*], so that all are thus servants to themselves and no one to his equal [*sic omnes sibi, et nemo suo aequali servire teneatur*]' (63/74). The key feature of this political formation is that each member of the society renders obedience to themselves. One serves the laws of the society freely, without compulsion or command. The regime Spinoza has in mind is democratic in the sense that participation is required for the function of the political. This requires freedom – or serving oneself – as the calculation of utility to determine action at the individual and collective level; it requires, in other words, the reciprocity of phronesis that Spinoza identified already in the 'barbarous' society. I want to call this political regime 'natural democracy'. There are two reasons for this. First, because it relies on human nature or the anthropological principle, namely, the calculation of utility; and, second, because this kind of political formation is called democracy as the most natural regime of power in chapter 16 of the *Theological Political Treatise* (179).

Spinoza continues his first inference with a conjunction: 'or [*vel*], if sovereignty [*imperium*] is invested in a few men or in one alone he should have extraordinary virtue [*summis viribus*], or at least attempt to persuade the masses [*vulgo*] of this' (63/74). The 'or' introduces an alternative kind of regime of power, one that relies on authority. If the political regime is an aristocracy or monarchy, it requires the holders of power to be extraordinary individuals – like Moses – or at least individuals who are perceived to be so. This will strengthen their authority, whereby their actions will not provoke a reaction. Spinoza presents a government relying on authority as a *bona fide* alternative to natural democracy. This is consistent with the dialectic of authority and utility, according to which authority can be useful for society when the people find that their utility is better served by authorizing someone else – the sovereign – to decide on their behalf.

Let me return to Clastres to highlight the originality of Spinoza's position. After Clastres describes the possibility of a 'society without a state', that is, a social formation based on the calculation of utility, he further argues that 'history affords us in fact only two types of society utterly irreducible to one another. . . . On the one hand, there are primitive societies, or societies without a State; on the other hand, there are societies with a State.'[19] There are two key differentiations between these two societies, according to Clastres. First, there is a political difference. The 'advanced' societies that rely on the state utilize the command and obedience model. By contrast, Clastres insists, the function of the chief in the primitive societies he studies is not to issue commands since the entire community partakes in decision making, and the chief's role is merely to facilitate that process. The effect is that a society with a state must justify violence for its self-preservation, whereas the chief has no access to any justification of violence. Second, the economic structure is different. In the primitive societies, the economic principle is 'the refusal of useless excess'.[20] Conversely, in societies with a state the 'political relation of power precedes and founds the economic relation of exploitation. Alienation is political before it is economic.'[21] This requires excess – or what Marx calls surplus value – to operate.

We see clear parallels between Clastres and Spinoza. They both identify the origins of community in utility and they both distinguish between a political community where people render obedience to themselves and a community where authority relies on a command and obedience model. And yet, at the same time, there is an instructive difference between Spinoza and Clastres. According to *Society Against the State*, the two kinds of society are – as we saw above – 'utterly irreducible to one another'. This is both an historical assertion – there are no societies that are both primitive and with a state – and a conceptual one, alluding to the incommensurability of the two social models. This creates a problem for Clastres, namely, how to account for the transition from primitive to state societies. On this issue, Clastres equivocates. At certain points, he insists that it is impossible to know what causes this transformation.[22] He also hints at two other explanations. One

---

[19] Clastres, *Society Against the State*, 200.
[20] Clastres, *Society Against the State*, 195.
[21] Clastres, *Society Against the State*, 198.
[22] Clastres, *Society Against the State*, 204–5.

is an external eruption of violence that subjugates the members of the primitive society.[23] The other is the internal development of what he calls 'prophets', that is, religious leaders who sow the seeds for the development of the structure of command and obedience.[24] Nonetheless, these are provisional answers that fail to satisfy.[25]

Conversely, Spinoza never asserts that these two forms of society are separated. In fact, his entire political project hinges – as I have already said and as we will see later, especially in the last chapter of the book – on how the two are related. It is because of this conflictual relation that I have been talking about the *dialectic* of authority and utility. In other words, the distinction between natural democracy and a state of authority does not designate constitutional formations such as monarchy, aristocracy and democracy – that is the task of Spinoza's later book, the *Political Treatise*. Rather, it describes the form of any constitution in terms of the two ways in which the dialectic of authority and utility can be articulated.[26] The following two inferences that Spinoza draws from the priority of utility over authority as the form of constitution expand upon this ineliminable relation between natural democracy and a state of authority.

According to the second inference, 'in every sovereignty [*imperio*] laws should be so instituted that the people may be influenced not so much by fear as by hope of some good that they urgently desire; for in this way each will be eager to do his duty [*officium*]' (63–4/74). This is an unusual definition of duty – one that can conform neither to Cicero's nor to Kant's conceptions of duty, both of which require a sense of authority. Here, imperium refers to both societies Spinoza has just identified – natural democracy and a society of authority. Thus, duty is understood as that which is allowed to take place in any organized political society (*imperium*) when people are not restricted by fear. Already from the Preface, Spinoza describes fear as the emotion that leads to superstition and to voluntary servitude; that is, fear is the kind of emotion that overwhelms humans so as to deprive them of their ability to draw practical judgements. Spinoza is suggesting, then, that in every regime of power – either in a natural democracy or in a state based on authority – laws should facilitate the exercise of judgement or phronesis. Differently put, if the calculation of utility is the starting point of the account of the origin of the political, its oper-

---

[23] Clastres, *Society Against the State*, 203.
[24] Clastres, *Society Against the State*, 218.
[25] Deleuze and Guattari criticize Clastres precisely on this point. See their *A Thousand Plateaus*, 357–61.
[26] Cf. Vardoulakis, *Stasis Before the State*.

ation continues in any political formation. As such, the calculation of utility, or practical judgement, becomes the common ground, and thereby enables the relation, between the two regimes of power – and more broadly, it facilitates the operation of the dialectic of authority and utility: neither obedience without rationality nor reason purified of structures of command.

The third inference elaborates on the relation between the two regimes of power, natural democracy and a regime of authority. Spinoza observes initially that 'since obedience consists in carrying out a command simply by reason of the authority of sovereignty [*mandata ex sola imperantis authoritate*], it follows that obedience has no place [*nullum locum habere*] in a community where sovereignty belongs to everybody [*imperium penes omnes*], and laws are sanctioned by common consent [*leges ex communi consensu*]' (64/74). This is the kind of natural democracy where the people 'remain equally free' (64) regardless of how many laws there are, because actions 'are not dictated by an external authority [*non ex authoritate alterius*] but from the people's own consent' (64/74). This is not a normative argument. Spinoza is not listing a number of conditions for how such freedom can be accomplished. In fact, that is impossible if such freedom requires the exercise of phronesis that relies on the assessment of specific material conditions. Given the contingency of material circumstances, Spinoza cannot be prescriptive. Rather, freedom simply consists here in a community that is not structured according to the command and obedience model.

Spinoza immediately adds: 'But the opposite is the case [*at contra*] when sovereignty [*imperium*] is vested in one person only; for all do the state's bidding following a single authority [*ex sola authoritate*]' (64/74). The other possibility consists in vesting the power of judgement in one person. This is what Spinoza describes in the Preface as voluntary servitude. He concedes that under certain conditions, this is a possible outcome, such as when 'the people have been trained from the beginning [*ab initio educati*] to hang upon the lips of authority [*ab ore imperantis pendeant*]' (64/74). He uses the Jewish state as an example of this regime of power. Since the Jews were accustomed to 'hang upon the lips of authority [*ab ore imperantis penderet*]' (65/75), Moses instituted ceremonies to regulate every facet of their lives. The objective of these ceremonies was that the Jews should do nothing freely (65), which is it to say, that they should unquestioningly follow authority.[27] There is

---

[27] Spinoza will return to this point in chapters 17 and 18, where he will designate this utter obedience as a theocracy, and where he will also demonstrate how the defining characteristic of theocracy – namely, complete obedience – contained *in nuce* the undoing of the Hebrew state.

an important difference here between the state of authority described earlier – which still allows for the operation of utility – and a state in which the sovereign becomes a mouthpiece of the people, or a state in which the people become voluntary slaves. We can call the latter authoritarianism or, using the vocabulary of the Preface, monarchism We will see in the following chapter that this distinction plays a critical role in the development of Spinoza's concept of authority – so I defer further discussion until then.

The question suggested when the distinction is drawn between the free state and monarchy as a form of despotism is the following: What happens when people start exercising their judgement and thereby cease to be docile subjects? The implication is clear: the people feel indignation and they resist the commands of the ruler. They no longer 'hang upon the lips' of sovereignty to hear what their utility is, but they use their own rationality to determine it. I described this relation between democracy and monarchy as conflictual in Chapter 1. I would like to call it 'agonistic democracy'. There are various reasons for this.

First, the term agon seems to me to capture what Spinoza has in mind. Agon does not simply signify conflict, but a kind of competition that requires that one takes a stand against an opposing position.[28] Thus, for instance, in Greek tragedy the dialogue between two leading characters espousing opposing positions is called an agon – such as the dialogue between Zeus and Prometheus, or Creon and Antigone. So agon is not just any kind of conflict, but the confrontation between opposing forces, such as between natural democracy and authoritarianism.

Second, this confrontation is democratic in the sense that its basis is the same as that which characterizes natural democracy, namely, the operation of the calculation of utility. This insight realizes its potential in the *Political Treatise*, where democracy is described as an absolute regime.[29] I do not want to deviate here into a lengthy analysis of the *Political Treatise*, I just want to draw attention to the argument there that every constitutional form presupposes natural democracy in the sense of the calculation of utility. For instance, Spinoza argues that even in a monarchy, the most powerful entity is the multitude, and from that perspective a monarchy contains within itself natural democracy (see, e.g., 7.31). And then he applies the same argument to aristocracy (e.g. 8.12). The reason is that in both regimes those in power draw judgements determined by what the people think – that is, they depend on the people's calculation of utility.

[28] See Vardoulakis, 'Stasis: Notes Toward Agonist Democracy'.
[29] See Negri, 'Democracy and Eternity in Spinoza', in *Subversive Spinoza*, 101–12.

Third, what I call agonistic democracy here is not a normative condition, nor a constitutional form that can be solidified in positive law. *Pace* Clastres, Spinoza suggests that natural democracy and monarchy cannot be separated. They are part of the same dialectic of authority and utility, a dialectic that is incessant. In fact, these two political regimes can be better understood as impulses that – as we will see at the end of the book when considering chapters 19 and 20 of the *Theological Political Treatise* – are intertwined. Thus agonistic democracy does not describe a particular regime of power but rather the conflict or agon inherent in the dialectic of authority and utility that is present in any regime of power because of the operative presence of the calculation of utility.

These points show that the primacy of utility over authority is not simply a genetic argument about the progression of society from a barbarous, pre-legal state to a more advanced society organized by laws. Rather, the primacy of utility over authority describes the condition that pertains in society conceived in terms of the dialectic of authority and utility. The primacy of utility in this sense describes not only a past condition that causes the present one, but also the conflicts and paradoxes of the present as they inform the future. Agonistic democracy signifies, then, the vicissitudes in time of the dialectic of authority and utility.

I have spent so much time on these couple of pages from chapter 5 because they appear to me to present Spinoza's political outlook in a uniquely condensed form. This is not simply the earliest point in Spinoza's oeuvre when the conception of democracy occurs. It also outlines all the key points, concerning the primacy of utility over authority, that are developed in detail later in the *Theological Political Treatise* and even further in the *Political Treatise*. Thus, these couple of pages are programmatic, which makes them obscure if the programme itself is not in sight. But if they are placed within the programme that frames the dialectic of authority and utility, then they assume a clarity and simplicity of message that Spinoza achieves in the very best pages of his philosophy.

3. Political Monism: The Utility of Miracles

The argument of chapter 6 may appear deceptively simple, presented in the disjunction: either monism or miracles – which is essentially the disjunction that organizes Leo Strauss's reading of Spinoza as an epicurean, as we will see. But there is more to this simple disjunction. Monism is not simply an ontological doctrine for Spinoza. Rather, following Epicurus's insight, monism is *both* an epistemological matter – the fact that knowledge needs to presuppose a totality outside of which nothing exists – *and* also a political one – namely, the primacy of practical judgement. Thus monism in Spinoza has a distinctly political flavour, one that is inseparable from the priority of utility over authority.

Spinoza argues for monism in two distinct ways, namely, using arguments from reason and from Scriptural authority.[30] The latter relies on the book of Ecclesiastes, which states, in Spinoza's paraphrase, that 'Nature observes a fixed and immutable order, that God has been the same throughout all ages that are known or unknown to us, that the laws of Nature are so perfect and fruitful that nothing can be added or taken away from them' (84). It is worth remembering, as Warren Montag reminds us, that this doctrine from Ecclesiastes was regarded as heretical in the Jewish tradition, and moreover that the word 'heretical' is the same as the word 'epicurean' in Hebrew.[31] The inference from the monism of Ecclesiastes Spinoza draws is that 'miracles seem something strange only because of human ignorance [*propter hominum ignorantiam*]' (84/95).[32] If the laws of God and nature are the same and immutable, then miracles, understood as the suspension of natural law, are impossible.

The same argument is pursued also from reason. Thus, Spinoza argues that if the laws of nature are the same as divine laws, then it is impossible to interrupt them: 'if anyone were to maintain that God performs some act contrary to the laws of Nature, he would at the same time have to maintain that God acts contrary to his own nature – of which nothing could be more absurd [*quo nihil absurdius*]' (72/83). Spinoza further holds that to imagine that God made nature imperfect so that he has to intervene to rectify its faults 'I consider to be utterly divorced from reason [*ratione alienissimum*]' (73/83). And, echoing the Appendix to Part I of the *Ethics*, he says that 'recourse to the will of God . . . is no more than a ridiculous way of avowing one's ignorance [*ridiculus sane modus ignorantiam profitendi*]' (75/86). Spinoza then infers that to suppose that there is creation *ex nihilo* making miracles possible, far from proving God's existence, is on the contrary a way to 'cast doubt on it' (74). Differently put, the perfection of nature on the grounds that its laws are the

---

[30] This is the case with ceremonies, as I have shown in section 1, and is also the case with Scripture as a historical narrative, as I show later in the present section.

[31] Montag, 'Lucretius Hebraizant: Spinoza's Reading of Ecclesiastes'.

[32] Leo Strauss draws attention to Ecclesiastes, according to which 'nature maintains a fixed and unalterable order, and hence that there are no miracles', to construct the either/or that structures his book: either epicurean monism or miracles and religion. See Strauss, *Spinoza's Critique of Religion*, 121. I discuss Strauss's book at length later in this section.

same as divine law cannot accommodate any events such as miracles that suggest a rupture in the completeness of God or nature.

It is worth recalling at this point that chapter 6 is the only chapter of the *Theological Political Treatise* that proceeds by arguing from monism. In all other chapters of the *Treatise*, it is either the first epicurean theme – the production of authority through fear and superstition – or the third theme – the human propensity to calculate one's utility before acting – that structure the argument. Chapter 6 is the only one whose argument starts from the second theme – monism. Nonetheless, the early reception of Spinoza concentrates on this topic, often at the exclusion of the other two epicurean themes. This produces a significant distortion, namely, that monism lacks a politics or that monism is essentially apolitical.

The most significant example of the early reception of Spinoza that presents itself as a critique of his monism can be found in Pierre Bayle's entry on 'Spinoza' in his *Historical and Critical Dictionary* from the late seventeenth century (1693–96). I draw attention to Bayle because this entry is *the* main source on Spinoza's thought until the Paulus edition of Spinoza's work is prepared in Jena in the first years of the nineteenth century. Thus, for almost a century and a half, Bayle's entry functions as the *de facto* substitute for Spinoza's own texts, with philosophers such as Hume certainly and Kant almost certainly having relied exclusively on Bayle.[33] Thus, Bayle's interpretation is determinative for how philosophers read Spinoza for over a century – they literally read Bayle instead of Spinoza.

Bayle's entire discussion aims to present the absurd implications of the position that God is immutable and that no modifications can be made to God or nature – that is, monism. The core of Bayle's critique is that if God and nature are one and immutable, then 'they [i.e. the Spinozists] would have to claim that there has not been, and there never will be, any change in the universe, and that all change, the very greatest or the very smallest, is impossible'.[34] Monism is, in this interpretation, the loss of contingency and hence the loss of the possibility of human action, or of praxis, which is not amenable to universal laws of nature.

From this central critique advanced by Bayle, several implications follow. The most important are the following three, all explicitly rejecting the possibility of the political. First, the one who comprehends divine necessity lacks any motivation for action: 'A man like Spinoza would sit absolutely still if

---

[33] On Bayle's rationalist reading of Spinoza, see Ryan, *Pierre Bayle's Cartesian Metaphysics*, esp. ch. 6.
[34] Bayle, *Historical and Critical Dictionary*, 327.

he reasoned logically. "If it is possible," he would say, "that such a doctrine might be established, the necessity of nature would establish it without my book. If it is not possible, all of my writings would accomplish nothing."[35] There is no politics in monism – there is no desire to act, there is only passivity. Another way to put this is to say that there is no freedom in monism.

Second, political history becomes an absurdity. As Bayle puts it in his unique rhetoric, 'in Spinoza's system all those who say, "The Germans have killed ten thousand Turks," speak incorrectly and falsely unless they mean, "God modified into Germans has killed God modified into ten thousand Turks," and the same with all the phrases by which what men do to one another are expressed.'[36] Monism eradicates any basis for differentiation. Thus, there is no history because there is no vicissitude, since ultimately everything refers back to the single, immutable substance. Note the rhetoric of this example, which was to become famous: the eradication of history is also the eradication of the difference between believers and unbelievers. Consequently, monism is not simply a tenuous metaphysical credo, but moreover a deeply, even offensively atheist one.

And, third, monist indifference entails the eradication of singularity: 'even when a man is burned alive, no change happens to him'.[37] Whatever we suffer as well as the effects of our sufferings are ultimately irrelevant from the perspective of the one, all-encompassing substance. All this amounts to saying that Spinoza's monism eradicates particularity and hence politics. Again, this is a loaded example: in Spinozistic monism, there is no heaven or hell, there is no redemption or damnation.

This critique of monism due to the purported lack of historical specificity becomes the dominant trope of the critique of Spinoza, who is viewed as the arch-villain espousing this position. The critique culminates in Hegel's reading of Spinoza as denying reality to anything but the substance: 'In Spinoza's system, God alone is. What is other than God is a being that at once is not a being, and so is show. Thus it cannot be said that Spinozism is atheism. It is rather the exact contrary of atheism, namely, *acosmism*. The world is no true being, there is no world. Rather, God and God alone is.'[38] This rejection

---

[35] Bayle, *Historical and Critical Dictionary*, 314.
[36] Bayle, *Historical and Critical Dictionary*, 312.
[37] Bayle, *Historical and Critical Dictionary*, 328.
[38] Hegel, *Lectures on Logic, Berlin, 1831*, 49. The influence of this idea can be seen by noting that Emmanuel Levinas repeats the accusation of acosmism (in *Alterity and Transcendence*, 69–70) even though Levinas's own reading of Spinoza consists in accusing him of constructing a crude sense of immanence, which is the very opposite of acosmism. (I turn to Levinas in detail in section 3 of the following chapter.)

of monism on the grounds that it entails that only the substance is real and the rest is just 'show' – a view referred to as 'acosmism' – is articulated more famously as Hegel's accusation that Spinoza lacks determinate negation.[39] History is robbed of its dialectical grounding. The human is trapped within that omniscient and omnipresent substance. Macherey provides an exhaustive analysis of Hegel's critique of Spinoza, but at the same time it is useful to remember that Hegel's critique follows a tradition that stretches back to the initial reception of Spinoza's monism in the seventeenth century.[40]

Leo Strauss's significant contribution in this reception history is to illustrate the epicurean provenance of Spinoza's monism, even if in Strauss the predominant idea of this reception history from Bayle onward remains unaltered, namely, that Spinozan metaphysics is incommensurable with any politics. In fact, as we will see, Strauss goes one step further by separating Spinoza's epicurean monism from a politics that relies on authority.

Monism as epicureanism is the pivot of Strauss's book *Die Religionskritik Spinozas als Grundlage seiner Bibelwissenschaft: Untersuchungen zu Spinozas Theologisch-politischem Traktat* from 1930. The influence of Strauss's interpretation of the *Theological Political Treatise* extends beyond his book, translated as *Spinoza's Critique of Religion* in 1965.[41] His seminars on Spinoza at Chicago University influenced generations of scholars.[42] In both the book and the classroom, his attack on Spinoza's monism is ferocious and it is not inconceivable that it played a role in dissuading subsequent scholars from further exploring Spinoza's epicureanism.

The entire argument of *Spinoza's Critique of Religion* is framed as a mortal combat between two metaphysical ideas, namely, the epicurean insistence that nothing comes out of nothing and the opposing idea that God can create something *ex nihilo*, which Strauss links to Jewish metaphysics and biblical faith. The central metaphysical conflict that organizes Strauss's discourse is profoundly indebted to Jacobi, on whose epistemology Strauss had completed his doctorate under Ernst Cassirer's supervision in 1922. Jacobi's epistemology is most famously expressed in the two notorious controversies

---

[39] For a forceful refutation of the accusation that Spinoza espouses acosmism, see Melamed, 'Acosmism or Weak Individuals? Hegel, Spinoza, and the Reality of the Finite'; and Melamed, 'Why Spinoza is not an Eleatic Monist (Or Why Diversity Exists)'.

[40] Macherey, *Hegel or Spinoza*.

[41] Hereafter cited parenthetically in the text as *CR*.

[42] A typescript of his 1959 seminar on the *Theological Political Treatise* titled *Spinoza: Seminar on the Theological Political Treatise* is available at <https://issuu.com/bouvard6/docs/leo_strauss_-_spinoza_1959>.

that he conducts, first with Mendelssohn and then with Fichte. Spinoza is at the centre of both of these controversies.[43] Let us look at this background before turning to Strauss's book.

Both controversies about Spinoza present monism in terms of reason – which is to be expected as the targets of the polemics were first the Enlightenment and then transcendental idealism. Thus, whereas epicurean monism holds that there is nothing outside being, the monism Jacobi describes questions whether there is anything outside reason. Jacobi presents two possibilities. The first is that there is nothing outside rationality, and hence that the absolute can be conceived through the mind and its epistemic capacity. The second is to uphold faith in God as that which cannot be reduced to or conceived by one's mental abilities. The former is the predicament of Enlightenment and transcendental idealism – Jacobi coins the term nihilism to refer to this absoluteness of reason – the latter is that of the faithful.[44] The problem with the preponderance of rationality, according to Jacobi, is that it rests on a *petitio principii*. It needs to presuppose the mind's mental capacities to conceive of the absolute, which can only be done from within rationality itself. The mind needs to presuppose its own capacity in order to achieve epistemic certainty.[45] This circularity, Jacobi suggests, entails that the absoluteness of rationality rests on an act of faith in the mind's mental capacities.[46] Or, reason cannot renounce faith without relying on a faith in its own capacity to know.

There is only one reference to Jacobi in *Spinoza's Critique of Religion*, but it is telling: 'on the basis of unbelieving science one could not but arrive at Spinoza's results'. These results include the identity of God and nature – that is, monism. Strauss continues: 'But would this basis itself thus be justified?' In other words, can the mind on its own accord, without support in something external that is not rational, and which thereby inscribes a certain faith in the process, justify this presupposition? Strauss does not explicitly answer

---

[43] For a perspicacious account of the controversies, see Beiser, *The Fate of Reason*.
[44] The common philosophical use of the term terms relies on Nietzsche, for whom 'nihilism' means the opposite. For Jacobi, nihilism is the atheist attitude that understands being as material thereby denying transcendence. Conversely, nihilism for Nietzsche is the attitude – moral no less than metaphysical, but always a pathological renunciation of the world – that arises from the supposition of a transcendent beyond.
[45] *Mutatis mutandi*, the same argument has come to be called the naturalist paradox.
[46] For Jacobi's position, see the texts contained in Jacobi, *The Main Philosophical Writings and the Novel Allwill*, especially the correspondence with Mendelssohn, as well as the open letter to Fichte. See also his account of the meeting with Lessing that contains the famous reference to the *salto mortale*.

this question, saying instead that it 'was Friedrich Heinrich Jacobi who posed this question, and by so doing lifted the interpretation of Spinoza – or what amounts to the same thing, the critique of Spinoza – on to its proper plane' (CR 204).

Following Jacobi, Strauss insists that Spinoza and other epicurean atheists have failed to show that reason succeeds in undermining faith. 'The orthodox premise [i.e., belief in God, revelation etc.] cannot be refuted by experience or by recourse to the principle of contradiction' (CR 29). He expands: 'The last word and the ultimate justification of Spinoza's critique is the atheism from intellectual probity. . . . Yet this claim . . . can not deceive one about the fact that its basis is an act of will, of belief, and, being based on belief, is fatal to any philosophy' (CR 30). Strauss's pivotal argument in his engagement with epicureanism is that monism relies, on the one hand, on the capacity of reason to refute revelation through a complete scientific explanation, but, on the other, epicureanism cannot do so without surreptitiously introducing belief in the capacity of reason. This is *mutatis mutandi* Jacobi's argument, which amounts to saying that the naturalism entailed by monism rests on a *petitio principii*.[47]

Strauss draws a further conclusion: 'Philosophy, the quest for evident and necessary knowledge, rests itself on an unevident decision, on an act of the will, just as faith does. Hence the antagonism between Spinoza and Judaism, between unbelief and belief, is ultimately not theoretical but moral' (CR 29). Despite appearances, the monism that Strauss ascribes to Spinoza is not primarily 'theoretical', that is, confined to epistemology, but 'moral', that is, it pertains to an attitude toward the world. Thus, monism as an attitude is first atheist – and hence 'moral' – and secondarily theoretical. Strauss defines this practical or 'moral' attitude of monism as epicurean:

> Epicurus' criticism of religion is one source, and the most important one, of seventeenth century criticism of religion. Epicurus is conscious of his motive. It is expressly the root first of his criticism of religion and then of his science. Were we not in awe of active and effectual gods, science, according to Epicurus' expressed opinion, would be in essential part superfluous. For Epicurus, the basic aim of knowledge is to achieve a condition of *eudaimonia*, by means of reasoning. This *eudaimonia* does not consist in the scientific investigation itself; science is no more than the indispensable means of attaining the condition. (CR 38)

[47] I will not repeat here the account of the tradition that reads epicureanism as naturalism, given that I have already done so in section 1 of the Introduction.

This original 'moral' motive is peace of mind or tranquillity, what Strauss designates as *eudaimonia*, although the most common word in describing it is *ataraxia*, as I explain in Chapter 1. That's the end of the epicurean moral attitude. Scientific knowledge is only the means toward that end. Atheism precedes theoretical knowledge – which is a mark of epicureanism, according to Strauss. Despite the different terminology, Strauss's point agrees with my reading of epicureanism as taking practical knowledge to be primary.[48]

The next move in Strauss's argument is where our positions about epicureanism visibly diverge. Strauss's move consists in a frontal assault on this moral attitude of monism. Strauss does so through the qualitative distinction between two senses of morality, the monist/epicurean one and the religious/Jewish one. He asserts a 'moral antagonism' due to 'the Jewish designation of the unbeliever as Epicurean' because 'from every point of view Epicureanism may be said to be the classic form of the critique of religion and the basic stratum of the tradition of the critique of religion' (CR 29). The morality that is opposed to a metaphysics of revelation is simultaneously heretical and epicurean.[49] Strauss wastes no time in castigating the epicurean morality: 'Epicureanism can lead only to a *mercenary morality* whereas traditional Jewish morality is not mercenary. . . . Epicureanism is so radically mercenary that it conceives of its theoretical doctrines as the means for liberating the mind from the terrors of religious fear, of the fear of death, and of natural necessity' (CR 29, emphasis added). Epicurean morality is 'mercenary' in the sense that it does not rely on principles but on the calculation of utility. This calculation is described as the overcoming of fear. It is mercenary because it consists in the instrumental pursuit of happiness.[50]

Strauss repeatedly returns to the question of miracles because Spinoza's refutation of miracles is the key to the choice between faith and the 'mercenary morality' of epicurean monism that rejects creation *ex nihilo*. Strauss thus stages the 'moral antagonism' between epicureanism and religion in terms of miracles: 'With the doctrine of the eternity of the world the denial of miracles is given, with the doctrine of the creation of the world the possibility of miracles is admitted' (CR 151). There is either the rejection of creation *ex nihilo*, or creation and, if the latter, then there are miracles, because 'creation of the world is the pre-condition of miracles' (CR 186). Where Strauss himself stands at this binary is clear as he repeats three times

---

[48] See section 2 of the Introduction, as well as section 1 of Chapter 1.
[49] See Montag, 'Lucretius Hebraizant'.
[50] The accusation that epicurean morality is mercenary becomes prevalent following Cicero's attack in *De Finibus*, 2.50.

that the epicurean rejection of miracles is an attitude that consists in merely laughing them off (*CR* 29, 144 and 146).

Let me summarize Strauss's critique thus far. First (this is the insight from Jacobi), Strauss holds that Spinoza cannot assert monism as the fact that there is nothing outside our rational capacity to know, unless a belief heterogeneous to reason is presupposed. Second, Strauss discerns a moral attitude as being more primary than any theoretical contemplation in Spinoza's monism. And, third, Strauss designates this monism as epicurean and disparages its 'mercenary morality'. The antagonism against the mercenary epicurean morality is insufficient unless Strauss denies it any effectivity whatsoever.

Strauss makes this fourth move by forcefully rejecting any *political motives* to monism. Spinoza's monism is, to use Strauss's words, 'not at all political' (*CR* 227). Strauss justifies this position by indicating that the political motives associated with the tradition of the critique of religion are averroist and machiavellian, which are 'traditions of very different origin' than epicureanism (*CR* 48–9). This seems like a weak argument given Strauss grants that 'after the rediscovery of Epicurean philosophy by the humanists' these traditions merged (*CR* 48).[51] Nonetheless, according to Strauss, it is only epicureanism that is monist. Hence, the strong point here is to deny monism any political import.[52]

So, where can the political impulse of the *Theological Political Treatise* be located if not in Spinoza's epicureanism? The only possibility of a Spinozan politics in *Spinoza's Critique of Religion* arises in chapter 9, where Strauss argues for the importance of the statesman as the wise man separated from the multitude (*CR* 229).[53] This is the opposite of the essentially anti-authoritarian impulse in epicureanism. Strauss can arrive at this position by separating monism from the other two themes of Spinoza's epicureanism.

---

[51] I have already dealt with Machiavelli's influence on the *Theological Political Treatise* (see Chapter 2). I discuss how the *Treatise* deals with averroism in the first section of the next chapter.

[52] The rejection of the political import of epicureanism on the grounds that tranquillity of the mind is not political is a constant theme that runs throughout Strauss's works. For instance, see his *Natural Right and History*, 109–13; *Hobbes Critique of Religion and Related Writings*, 67–9; as well as his essay 'Notes on Lucretius', in *Liberalism Ancient and Modern*, 76–139.

[53] This idea from the 1930 book is further developed a couple of decades later in Strauss's influential chapter 'How to Study Spinoza's *Theologico-Political Treatise*' from *Persecution and the Art of Writing*. This is the essay in which Strauss develops his thesis about an esoteric and an exoteric reading of the *Theological Political Treatise*. Of the many critiques of Strauss's reading, the most detailed one is perhaps Nancy Levene's 'Ethics and Interpretation, or How to Study Spinoza's *Tractatus Theologico-Politicus* without Strauss'.

The result of this separation in Strauss's interpretation is that authority well and truly predominates over utility in Spinoza. It is as if the authority of the statesman disavows the epicurean 'mercenary morality' of Spinoza's monism and atheism. It is as if – to put it differently – Spinoza saves himself from epicureanism by developing a politics that is thoroughly incompatible with his monist metaphysics and the 'mercenary morality' they entail. Spinoza saves himself from his own epicureanism.

There is something highly paradoxical – I almost said unbelievable – in this move whereby Spinoza recuperates himself through a spectacular self-amputation. It is surely one thing to say that a philosopher cannot be entirely consistent over a whole oeuvre, and another to impute such a schizophrenic split between Spinoza's ethics – his 'mercenary morality' – and politics. It is doubtful that Strauss would have been able to make such a radical claim had he not been following in the footsteps of two and a half centuries of reception of Spinoza's monism as apolitical. Following the line of interpretation popularized by Bayle, Strauss simply has to append a politics that is distinct from Spinoza's metaphysics, a gesture that complements the earlier reception history that could not account for Spinoza's obvious interest in politics in the two treatises.

One of the most radical shifts in the reception of Spinoza since 1968 is arguably the insight that his metaphysics and his politics are inseparable. After the work of Gilles Deleuze, we know that Spinoza is critical of the metaphysical hierarchies characterizing Platonism and the political hierarchies modelled on them.[54] Perhaps even more significant is the work of Antonio Negri, who has systematically argued that a metaphysics of necessity implies a politics and that it is a political decision to remain oblivious to this fact.[55] Balibar also starts from the premise that Spinoza's politics and metaphysics are inextricable, even though his reading is different from Negri's.[56] Finally, perhaps the most thorough examination of the way in which naturalism is political is Hasana Sharp's *Spinoza and the Politics of Renaturalization*. Sharp argues that the concept of nature is not divorced from history and politics because 'being natural [in Spinoza] means being situated within a particular time, place, and causal nexus'.[57]

---

[54] Deleuze, *Expressionism in Philosophy: Spinoza*; see also his 'Lucretius and the Simulacrum', published as an appendix to *The Logic of Sense*.

[55] See, for instance, Negri, *The Political Descartes*, and, specifically for Spinoza, *The Savage Anomaly*.

[56] Balibar, *Spinoza and Politics*.

[57] Sharp, *Spinoza and the Politics of Renaturalization*, 8.

The ascription of a political agenda to monism still does not explain the epicurean nature of his politics. This pertains, I contend, in the priority of utility over authority. We can only see this if we discern the co-implication of the three epicurean themes.

Spinoza paves the way for the co-implication of the epicurean themes in chapter 5, when he turns to the question of the kind of narrative Scripture is. He argues there – just as he argues about ceremonies and miracles – that there are essentially two ways of knowing, one that is practical and relies on Scripture and the other that is through reason. The former 'relies on experience', the latter on a 'process of deduction solely from intellectual axioms'. Given that Scripture is concerned to teach as many people as possible, and given that the correct use of reason is 'rarely to be found among men', Scripture reverts to teaching with appeal to experience (66). Scripture is an historical narrative because it appeals to practical knowledge or knowledge from experience. Such an historical narrative has one drawback, namely, that 'experience can give no clear knowledge of these matters [i.e. that philosophical content of Scripture that leads to monism], and cannot teach what God is and in what way he sustains and directs all things and cares for humans'. But this does not stop it from being useful, since 'it can still teach and enlighten men as far as suffices to impress on their minds obedience and devotion' (67). In terms of how we act, Scripture is sufficient as it leads to obedience, that is, to authority. This is not merely an ethical outcome of the historical narrative of Scripture, it is also political as Scripture was first given to a specific people contributing to the establishment of their state, the Hebrew state.

We see here, then, all three epicurean themes: an account of the establishment of authority that is related to monism and to the practical knowledge of the people who receive Scripture. We also encounter again the two ways of acting in the world, either by following reason or by obeying the dictates of historical narratives. We can express the same point in the political vocabulary used only a couple of pages earlier in chapter 5, according to which an instituted community either relies on obeying sovereignty or on the correct operation of instrumental rationality – that is, a community either adheres to authority or to the model of natural democracy. The two different kinds of knowledge of how to be in the world arising from the co-presence of the three epicurean themes correspond to the two possible regimes of power that Spinoza posits earlier.

Significantly, Spinoza wants to argue that there are *only* two conceivable ways of being with others. Soon after having established the co-presence and parallel operation of the three epicurean themes, Spinoza adds the following remark: 'he who is neither acquainted with these biblical narratives nor has any knowledge from the natural light, if he be not impious or obstinate [*non impium, sive contumacem*], is almost inhuman [*inhumanum tamen*] and close to being a beast [*paene brutum*]' (67/78). This is not a simple humanist assertion that the human is characterized by the use of rationality. Rather, Spinoza asserts here that there are two ways of acting. One is through the kind of obedience that historical narratives instil, and the other is through the operation of reason. To be obstinate is to reject for self-serving reasons both of these ways – an idea that Spinoza will develop further in the second part of the *Theological Political Treatise*, and to which I will return in the next couple of chapters. So Spinoza is saying that someone is almost inhuman and a beast when they act by neither obeying nor using their reason. Differently put, someone is inhuman or a beast if their behaviour cannot be accommodated in the tripartite thematic unity that constitutes epicureanism for Spinoza. There is no way of acting that Spinoza can admit which is 'human' that does not conform to the co-presence and parallel operation of the three epicurean themes.

When we turn to chapter 6, we learn not only that the exercise of reason that affords us a conception of God as one and of his natural laws as immutable is a rare capacity for humans, but also that even if one has such a capacity, still natural or divine laws 'are not all known to us [*omnes nobis notae non sint*]' (73/83). Not only are they not known – more precisely, they are no knowable. We see here the move that I described in the Introduction and in Chapter 1 as facilitating the transition from the second to the third epicurean theme. I described this with reference to Epicurus's idea of the totality (*to pan*) as it is related to phronesis.[58] From monism we posit that knowledge is impossible unless we presuppose a totality. This is the epicurean principle of the immutability of natural laws that was so crucial for empiricism and the rise of scientific inquiry in modernity.[59] It is essentially the argument against miracles: if we do not take the laws of nature as perfect but as mutable or as subject to the whims of meddling gods, then no knowledge can be derived as anything we know can change all of a sudden and without warning through miracles. From monism we also need to infer that not everything is knowable. We cannot know everything that happens, nor all the laws of nature – as this would lift our knowledge on a par to the knowledge of God, which is impossible. This is why for Epicurus the

---

[58] Diogenes Laertius, 'Epicurus', X.39.
[59] See Lange, *Geschichte des Materialismus und Kritik seiner Bedeutung in der Gegenwart*; and Wilson, *Epicureanism at the Origins of Modernity*.

primary form of knowledge is phronesis, which is the source of all virtue.[60] This is why, in other words, monism requires the primacy of practical knowledge or the calculation of utility.

It is instructive to notice how the entire chapter 6 is framed. The multitude (*vulgus*) understands an occurrence to be a miracle when its causes are unknown. Significantly, Spinoza does not stop here, since ultimately no one has the capacity to know all causes that operate within the totality – as we saw above. Thus, Spinoza adds: 'particularly if such an event is to their profit or advantage [*lucrum aut commodum*]' (71/81). The human inability to know all causes necessitates a comportment to the world that consists in starting with the calculation of utility. From this practical perspective, miracles are useful in helping the multitude form practical judgements.

The same point is raised at the end of the chapter. I quote the entire passage that summarizes the discussion about monism and the rejection of miracles:

> Consequently [*quare*], on these matters [i.e., on miracles] everyone is entitled to hold whatever view he feels will better bring him with sincere heart to the worship of God and to religion. This was also the opinion of Josephus, for towards the end of Book 2 of his *Antiquities*, he writes as follows: 'Let no one baulk at the word miracle, if men of ancient times, unsophisticated as they were, see the road to safety open up through the sea, whether revealed by God's will or of its own accord. Those men, too, who accompanied Alexander, king of Macedon, men of much more recent times, found the Pamphylian sea divide for them, offering a passage when there was no other way, it being God's will to destroy the Persian empire through him. This is admitted to be true by all who have written of Alexander's deeds. Therefore on these matters let everyone think as he will.' Such are the words of Josephus, showing his attitude to belief in miracles. (85/96)

Spinoza quotes Josephus here as agreeing with him in the sense that it does not matter whether miracles really occur or not, so long as they are believed to occur in such a way as to motivate the right kind of action.[61]

---

[60] Diogenes Laertius, 'Epicurus', X.132.
[61] The reference to Josephus is significant. We will see in Chapter 8 the importance of Josephus – whose books Spinoza owned – for the discussion of the construction of the Hebrew state. Josephus is a major source for Spinoza's account of the social and political formation the Hebrew state.

It little matters if the waters parted through divine intervention to let the Jews or the Macedonians through – what matters is that the Jews and the Macedonians believed that there was a divine intervention, which motivated them to achieve their respective ends. Thus, miracles are not concerned with theoretical knowledge about God and the immutable natural laws. Rather, miracles are means that partake in the operation of the instrumental reasoning of those who perceive them as miracles.

If monism is positioned within its epicurean framework, not only does it *not* eradicate particularity and history, as the reception of Spinoza following Bayle holds. Rather, monism entails that knowledge does not reside in the subject's mind as it perceives external objects but rather in the effects that this knowledge produces, which makes monism political through and through. Thus, to refer to one of Bayle's examples I cited above, epicurean monism is not concerned with the chemical constitution of the body burned at the stake, but rather with the motivations of those who thought it prudent that such an auto-da-fé would be beneficial to the society. In other words, the question for Spinoza is not how the alive and the burnt body both refer to a common substance, but rather how the impossibility of knowing that common substance can lead to chains of reasoning that justify the exercise of capital punishment.

Further, epicurean monism is not a 'mercenary morality' that rejects all political motives in the service of personal self-interest, as Strauss contends. To the contrary, epicurean monism shows that any attempt to side-line utility leads to the political affirmation of an authority that 'knows better than us' and whom we therefore have to obey – which is precisely what Strauss proposes. Differently put, epicurean monism shows that authority cannot be separated from utility and, moreover, that utility precedes authority as the human response to the totality that can never be fully known. It is this priority of utility that prevents authority from ever becoming absolute. In Spinoza, there is no metaphysical monism, there is only *political* monism.

* * *

According to Foucault, power requires resistance. This leads to a materialist account of power, but it also creates two problems: counter-resistance and the ruse of sovereignty; resistance can be duped into doing the bidding of power and resistance needs to presuppose power in order to have something to resist. In terms of the epicurean dialectic we have been examining in this book, Foucault's conception posits the priority of authority over utility.

By reversing that priority, whereby utility takes precedence over authority, Spinoza can describe the ineliminable conflict between two forms of power regimes, namely, natural democracy and a state of authority. This way, Spinoza does not merely describe or critique existing power formations, but rather recognizes that such formations are malleable and in a state of continuous flux. Their agonistic relation is the articulation of historical vicissitude. Thus, Spinoza's framework sidesteps both counter-resistance and the ruse of sovereignty because his epicurean dialectic does not depart from pre-existing conditions responding to them, but rather examines the possibilities for advancing utility in the future by the way that past power relations articulate in the present. The priority of utility over authority indicates that there is no pure monism. Rather, monism is for Spinoza always accompanied by the effects of the calculations of utility in specific circumstances, and as such monism is always political.

5

Love your Friend as Yourself: The Neighbour and the Politics of Biblical Hermeneutics (chapters 7 to 13)

The first part of the *Theological Political Treatise* is concerned with the genesis of personal authority exemplified by the prophets, who are defined in terms of the communication they effect. Theirs is a one-way communication through revelation: they interpret God's message for the people. But their authority is premised on a series of errors that also permeate the conceptions of identity of the people and the source of legality. Spinoza structures the second part of the *Treatise* by explaining how the errors that underlie the personal authority of the prophets are overcome.

This does not mean that Spinoza rejects authority as such. Rather, he develops a new notion of authority. This new notion of authority is informed by changes brought forward by the Reformation when authority's relation to communication shifts from the person – such as the absolute authority of the Pope to interpret Scripture – to the authority of Scripture itself, or *sola Scriptura*. The changed conditions about interpretation in the aftermath of the Reformation influence the notion of authority. I call this authority that is created in conjunction with hermeneutics *Reformed authority*.

It would be deficient, however, to resolve the intricacy of Spinoza's argument with reference solely to the historical context. Reformed authority is situated within the argumentative structure of the *Theological Political Treatise*. The notion of neighbourly love is pivotal in the *Treatise*'s presentation of authority. In chapters 7 to 13, Spinoza returns three times to neighbourly love, mobilizing it in such a way as to function as the cypher of his conception of Reformed authority. The key to this conception, as it is exemplified by the first use, is that Reformed authority overcomes the distinctive error of the prophets in the course of establishing their own authority – namely, the error of imagining God as a ruler and lawgiver or ascribing *potestas* to the divine. Reformed authority no longer relies on a transcendent source to prop itself up. Rather, it relies on reason and as such it is an authority whose function is to teach; it is a *didactic authority*, as Spinoza calls it.

The political element remains strong in this notion of Reformed authority. As we saw in the last chapter, Spinoza argues in chapter 5 of the *Theological Political Treatise* that there are two viable arrangements for the polity, natural democracy in which people render obedience to themselves and decide as if by one mind, and a state of authority that relies on obedience as it is regulated by the sovereign but with the utility of the people in mind. The question that inevitably arises at this point is about the nature of the obedience that the new, Reformed authority requires. After the wane of personal authority, who is obeyed? And how does interpretation, and specifically biblical hermeneutics, inform this new kind of obedience?

We will see that to answer these questions neighbourly love is polemically mobilized against a series of positions so as to conceive of an authority no longer in conflict with the utility of the community. Or, to put this point in positive terms, neighbourly love is the concept that demonstrates the reciprocity of utility. No calculation of utility, no exercise of phronesis, can ever be correct, without taking the other into account.

This conjunction of neighbourly love and reciprocal utility may appear entirely anomalous in the tradition. Neighbourly love is usually understood as referring to an other that is distinct from any calculative process. This creates a sharp contrast between Spinoza's position on neighbourly love and other conceptions of alterity, such as that of Emmanuel Levinas, one of the major critics of Spinoza's ethical theory in post-war European philosophy. To explain where Spinoza derives his conception of the reciprocal utility of neighbourly love from in such a way as to contradict the position that philosophers such as Levinas defend, I will turn to the epicurean conception of friendship. The epicurean injunction to 'love your friend as yourself' may appear to mirror the biblical injunction but, as I will argue, radically departs from it.

1. Monism and Interpretation: No Meaning Outside the Text

Chapter 7 contains Spinoza's hermeneutical theory, presented as a theory of meaning. How does this theory of meaning lead to Reformed authority? We need to start from the double distinction that organizes Spinoza's theory of meaning. There is a distinction between true and false meaning, and between 'true meaning and the truth of things [*verum sensum cum rerum veritate*]' (89/100). I will start with the latter distinction.

Scripture is concerned with true meaning whereas philosophy is concerned with the truth of things. This distinction is repeated throughout the chapter and it refers to the distinction between practical reason connected to meaning and reason as it arrives at adequate ideas. Let me present the most telling ways in which Spinoza formulates this distinction. The first significant use says: 'For human nature is so constituted that what one conceives by pure intellect [*puro intellectu*], one defends only by intellect and reason [*intellectu et ratione*], whereas what originates from the affects of the heart [*ex animi affectibus*] are affectively defended' (87/98). Reason is distinguished here from the affects. The effects of each are different. Given that Scripture is communicating with the people who may not be schooled in reasoning, it 'treats of matters that cannot be deduced from principles known by the natural light' (87). In other words, it relies on affects to communicate its message, whereby it is an historical narrative – as Spinoza argues in chapter 5 and as he repeats several times in chapter 7.

If we recall chapter 5, the fact that Scripture is an historical narrative does not mean that it is separated from reason altogether. Rather, instead of dealing with adequate ideas, it deals with the practical kind of instrumental reason that concerns itself with moral decisions – what I have been calling the calculation of utility or phronesis. Spinoza stages this contrast in the course of discussing several difficulties arising from the fact that Scripture is an historical narrative. Specifically, as an historical narrative it relies on understanding the language of the text and the intentions of the historical actors. Spinoza is not envisaging a complete reconstruction of what historical figures thought but rather that words and actions of the past are amenable to 'clear intellectual conception [*clarum possumus facile formare conceptum*]' (98/111). We need to be able to read and understand the means and ends relations that historical narratives express to arrive at their meaning.[1] By contrast, when it comes to a theorem in Euclid, we need neither 'a thorough knowledge of the language' nor a comprehension of the conditions in which Euclid wrote the book so as to understand the instrumentality involved, since instrumental reasoning is of no consequence to the adequate ideas expressed in geometry (98).

The distinction between true meaning and the truth of things needs to be understood in the context of the discussion of historical narratives and miracles in the two previous chapters of the *Theological Political Treatise*. If the truth of things refers to the use of reason so as to arrive at the idea of monism, whereby nothing can be added to nature and its law, then it presupposes the move we have seen, whereby monism requires the operation

---

[1] This is akin to Georg Gadamer's observation in *Truth and Method* about the presupposition of a completeness of meaning for any hermeneutical situation to arise.

of instrumental rationality. This is the move between the second and third themes of Spinoza's epicureanism: the totality of nature is the precondition of knowledge, but as we can never completely know that totality, we have to approach it with a practical comportment. This is the anthropological principle that requires the primacy of phronesis. Chapter 7 adds that phronesis can generate true meaning.

From this vantage point, the much debated methodology of Spinoza's biblical hermeneutics appears straightforward: 'the method of interpreting Scripture is no different [*haud differre*] from the method of interpreting nature, and is in fact in complete accord with it [*cum ea prorsus convenire*]' (87/98). Ignoring the distinction between true meaning and the truth of things leads easily to misunderstandings of Spinoza's hermeneutics. For instance, Emmanuel Levinas holds that Spinoza is ignorant of the Talmudic tradition that requires the reader to actively participate 'in the production of meaning . . . of the text' – which is, in Levinas's reading, precisely what Spinoza's method precludes.[2]

Such confusions are avoided as soon as the methodology for Spinoza's biblical hermeneutics is placed in the context of his epicureanism. According to the second principle of Spinoza's epicureanism, any kind of knowledge needs to presuppose monism. Thus, the phronesis that underlies true meaning as it is found in Scripture needs to be in accord or converge with the monist understanding of nature. The key epistemological insight of monism is that nothing can be added to nature. This is mirrored in the method of interpreting Scripture: 'knowledge of . . . all the contents of Scripture must be sought from Scripture alone, just as knowledge of Nature must be sought from Nature itself' (87). Any knowledge of Scripture has to avoid contradicting monism. Differently put, the true meaning of Scripture relies on phronesis, but for phronesis, as understood by epicureanism, to be possible, monism needs to be presupposed. Both knowledge of nature and knowledge of Scripture – different though they might be, since one strives for the truth of things and the other for the truth of meaning – presuppose a totality outside of which nothing exists.

Ignoring the epicurean background can only lead to a cascade of misunderstandings. For instance, Spinoza insists that to read the Bible as an historical narrative requires that we identify the intentions of its characters. This does not mean, as Levinas and others have supposed, a subjectivism that requires a complete reconstruction of the agents' intentions.[3] Rather,

---

[2] See Levinas, 'Spinoza's Background', in *Beyond the Verse*, 168 and 173.
[3] Cf. Levinas, 'Spinoza's Background', 172.

it points to the Lucretian argument in Book 5 of On the Nature of Things according to which it is part of human nature to act by calculating utility and consequently it is possible to approach historical events by reconstructing this instrumentality.[4] There is no suggestion here that a complete reconstruction of the agents' intentions is either possible or desirable. There is, rather, an insistence on the operative presence of phronesis in history. Far from a subjectivist view, this entails that the historical actors are responsive to their environment and that their judgements are determined by their material circumstances. So long as the interpreter has an understanding of these circumstances, an understanding of the instrumental rationality employed by the historical actors is possible – thereby generating historical meaning. Meaning is produced through phronesis.[5]

The epicurean background of the distinction between true meaning and the truth of things also mobilizes the epicurean theory of language as reliant on use. The link between utility and language as it affects biblical hermeneutics is encapsulated in Spinoza's observation that 'it could never have been to anyone's utility [ex usu] to change the meaning of a word' (93/105). Linguistic usage develops alongside the communal determination of utility. It does not rely on a personal authority who confers a mysterious, deep meaning to selected words. The best epicurean account of language relying on use occurs in Lucretius's On the Nature of Things, which Warren Montag explicitly links to Spinoza's own theory of language.[6] Use here does not mean only linguistic convention. Rather, the epicurean theory of language foregrounds the effects of linguistic usage – effects that are social, political, legal, religious, philosophical no less than hermeneutical.[7]

Louis Althusser is attuned to the fact that Spinoza's hermeneutics places the onus on the reader to use language, which is to say, to produce a meaning whose *effects* are historical: 'The first man ever to have posed the problem of *reading*, and in consequence, of *writing*, was Spinoza, and he was also the first man in the world to have proposed both a theory of history and a philosophy of the opacity of the immediate. With him, for the first time ever, a man linked together in this way the essence of reading and the essence of

---

[4] See section 2 of Chapter 1. We can find a similar argument in Collingwood, *The Idea of History*.
[5] I explain in section 2 of Chapter 2 how this argument is derived from Book 5 of Lucretius's *On the Nature of Things*.
[6] Montag, *Bodies, Masses, Power*, 9.
[7] The other famous argument about language as use is developed by the late Wittgenstein in the *Philosophical Investigations* – although Wittgenstein seems to be unaware that the epicureans had developed a similar approach.

history in a theory of the difference between the imaginary and the true.'[8] The most sustained analysis of the materialism of Spinoza's hermeneutic method – that Althusser himself never developed – is provided by Warren Montag, who points out that 'Spinoza rejects the notion of a method prior and therefore external to the process or activity of knowledge itself', and consequently, instead of speaking of the meaning of Scripture, 'we ought to be speaking of the effects it produces as a body among other bodies'.[9] In other words, reading impacts the understanding of the reader's present predicament. Or, differently put, the message of Scripture is moral, as Spinoza says, as it produces practical effects.

This practical knowledge that arises from the examination of the true meaning of Scripture contains an 'indubitable [*certo*] doctrine' (90/102), whose utility Spinoza underscores: it is a 'doctrine eternal and most useful for all mortals [*omnibus mortalibus utilissima doctrina*]' (91/102). This doctrine is: 'that God exists, one alone and omnipotent [*unicus et omnipotens*] . . . who loves above all others those who worship him and love their neighbours as themselves [*proximum tanquam semet ipsos amant*]' (91/102). The useful message of Scripture, then, is the combination of monism and neighbourly love.

Spinoza also immediately adds that 'Scripture does not teach formally' questions such as 'what God is' (91), that is, Scripture does not teach monism – it is up to philosophy and true reasoning to arrive at a definition of God within the purview of monism. Scripture is historical and is concerned solely with the moral precept of charity (*caritas*) or neighbourly love. Nonetheless, the strong point made here about neighbourly love is that it cannot be disentangled from the conception of God as 'one alone and omnipotent'. Neighbourly love – with all its ethical and political implications – is only possible if monism is maintained, regardless of whether monism is properly argued for philosophically.

If we take the idea of neighbourly love as denoting that we are who we are by virtue of our relations with others, then we have encountered this idea before. For instance, practical judgement as phronesis requires this intersubjective relationality that leads to a differential identity of the self. The human is naturally predisposed to calculate its utility in relation to others. We encounter this idea in chapter 5 of the *Theological Political Treatise*, expressed in different terminology, in the argument I reconstructed

---

[8] Althusser and Balibar, *Reading Capital*, 16–17. Following on this suggestion, Pierre Macherey paid particular attention to the materialism of his method in comparing Hegel and Spinoza. See Macherey, *Hegel or Spinoza*, chapter 2.

[9] Montag, *Bodies, Masses, Power*, 2 and 5.

in Chapter 4 about the origin of community in the reciprocal calculation of utility even in the absence of a formalized legal system (63). This idea is also prominent in the *Ethics*. Thus, according to Proposition 37 of Part IV: 'The good which everyone who seeks virtue wants for himself, he also desires for other men; and this desire is greater as his knowledge of God is greater.' Given that the good for Spinoza is that which is useful (*E* IV, D1), we see again here expressed the idea of a mutual aid as determinative of human interaction. This is an important insight for Spinoza as demonstrated by his assertion in Scholium 1 of the same Proposition, where he points out that he has 'shown what the foundations of the state are'.[10] And as Proposition 37 again stresses, in conformity with chapter 7 of the *Treatise*, this neighbourly love is inextricable from God understood in monist terms.

Neighbourly love, then, touches upon many different topics of Spinoza's thought in such a way as to make them resonate with each other. This convergence is due to the way in which neighbourly love, as the outcome of the true meaning of Scripture, is indispensable in defining Reformed authority. It does so by combining phronesis, sociality and the political. It is this convergence that Spinoza signifies as the moral teaching of Scripture. The authority that this convergence denotes is no longer personal, as the utility is something shared with others. Usefulness is something enjoyed with my neighbour as the precondition of society and of a state that relies on obedience to achieve the good for its citizens. In other words, neighbourly love is the social and political face of phronesis as it is presented in Scripture.

There is, however, a problem. Scripture may teach an indubitable doctrine that is easy to comprehend and hence shows everyone 'the path to salvation [*salutis viam*]', and yet still 'people [*vulgus*] make no attempt whatsoever to live according to the Bible's teachings' (86/97). This observation introduces a further distinction within Reformed authority. Reformed authority can lead to truth – either of its meaning (which is the province of Scripture) or the 'truth of things' (which is the province of philosophy) – but it can also lead to falsity.

Significantly, Spinoza does not castigate the 'fickle multitude' as responsible for this false meaning – as is the usual move in the philosophical tradition at least since Plato.[11] Instead, he immediately points the finger to the theologians for deviating from the fundamental teaching of Scripture. His argument proceeds in two stages, both of which refer to authority. First, the theologians employ 'their own arbitrarily invented ideas [to interpret

---

[10] I look at Proposition 37 in detail in the next chapter.
[11] See the discussion of stasis in section 3 of Chapter 1.

Scripture], for which they claim divine authority [*divina authoritate*]' (86/97). They invent ideas that are unrelated both to neighbourly love and to what is useful and, consequently, are in contradiction to historical reality as well as the divine law – even though *qua* theologians they claim divine authority for their fanciful interpretations. Second, the reason they do this is, in a nutshell, to further their 'own personal authority [*eorum . . . authoritas*]' (86/97). They want to make the people their voluntary slaves. In other words, the supposition of a divine authority is in fact the basis of the personal authority of those who instigate the false interpretations of Scripture such as to exploit the fears of the people and to imbue them with superstition.

We already know the source of this argument: it is the discussion of *religio* in Lucretius's *On the Nature of Things*. Personal authority is constructed by the theologians.[12] Spinoza applies this general framework to his biblical hermeneutics. The argument is straightforward: those who construct a false meaning in order to further their own personal authority flaunt Spinoza's own method, according to which nothing should be added to Scripture. There is an unmistakable polemical intent here – one that pivots around the determination of the good and virtue, which are, according to the *Ethics* (E IV, D1), determined by utility. It is not that the false meaning of Scripture forgets utility; rather, utility is personalized, thereby obscuring the fact that it is for the entire community. Differently put, the personal advantage that the false interpretations of Scripture derive is incompatible with neighbourly love.

Initially, Spinoza singles out the 'Pharisees' – Spinoza's term for the Talmudic tradition – and the Pope as purveyors of the false meanings of Scripture. Their method of interpreting Scripture relies respectively on a tradition that claims to go back to the prophets and on papal infallibility, that is, on different articulations of personal authority. 'However, as we cannot be sure', underscores Spinoza, not without a modicum of irony, 'either of the tradition in question [*hac traditione*] or of the authority of the Pontiff [*Pontificis authoritate*], we cannot base any certain conclusion on them' (93/105). Both institutionalized forms of religion effectively seek authority and personal power for their representatives by denying that interpretation relies on its effects and hence constructing God as creator or denying monism, which in turn requires that their interpretations demand obedience in the guise of the people suspending their phronesis. In other words, the Judeo-Christian tradition is built on the mistake about personal authority generated and propagated by the prophets.

---

[12] See the discussion in section 2 of Chapter 1.

Spinoza analyses two particular techniques generating the false meaning of Scripture in the Judeo-Christian tradition, both of which deny monism. In chapter 15, Spinoza calls these two techniques the sceptical and the dogmatic. They represent the two positions in the medieval debate about the relation between theology and philosophy. The sceptic affirms the priority of theology, the dogmatist the priority of philosophy, but they both do so by introducing unwarranted additions to Scripture.

The sceptic introduces a 'supernatural light' as necessary to arrive at Scriptural meaning (99). The supernatural is that which exceeds nature and hence denies that there is a totality outside of which nothing exists. Spinoza identifies Jehuda Alpakhar as a representative of this position, since he holds that reason should conform to Scripture (165). If biblical interpretation relies on its effects, then what is the effect of the sceptical position? Spinoza puts it succinctly in chapter 15: 'whatever Scripture teaches as a doctrine and quite expressly affirms must be accepted as absolutely true simply on its own authority [*ex sola ejus authoritate*]' (166/181). In other words, the effect of asserting a supernatural meaning in Scripture is the production of personal authority. I note the irony here of ascribing the Reformation principle of Scriptural authority – or, *sola Scriptura* – to the sceptical position. As both Samuel Preus and Susan James note, Spinoza has contemporary Calvinists in mind.[13]

Carlos Fraenkel convincingly shows that Spinoza's conception of dogmatism is in conversation with averroism.[14] Averroes's key move consists in the distinction between the pedagogical import of Scripture and its philosophical content. Both for Averroes and for Maimonides, who is working in the averroist tradition, this entails the primacy of the philosophical interpretation over the pedagogical one that is directed to the masses. The key methodological principle is that everything that is not clear in Scripture can be interpreted allegorically to conform to rationality. Consequently, the averroist tradition posits theology as the handmaiden of philosophy (*ancilla philosophiae*).[15] Fraenkel notes a divergence between Averroes and

---

[13] For the details, see Preus, *Spinoza and the Irrelevance of Biblical Authority*, chapter 5; Preus, 'A Hidden Opponent in Spinoza's *Tractatus*'; and James, *Spinoza on Philosophy, Religion, and Politics*, chapter 7.

[14] Carlos Fraenkel argues that Spinoza received averroism primarily from Elijah Delmedigo, whose book, *Examination of Religion*, was in Spinoza's library. See Fraenkel, 'Reconsidering the Case of Elijah Delmedigo's Averroism and Its Impact on Spinoza', in Akasoy and Giglioni (eds), *Renaissance Averroism and Its Aftermath*, 213–36.

[15] See Fraenkel, *Philosophical Religions from Plato to Spinoza*; and, Fraenkel, 'Spinoza on Philosophy and Religion', in Fraenkel, Perinetti and Smith (eds), *The Rationalists: Between Tradition and Innovation*, 27–44.

Maimonides. Averroes restricts the use of scriptural allegory to the philosophers, whereas Maimonides insists that allegories must become accessible to the masses through legislation.[16] What both Averroes and Maimonides recommend is the establishment of an inviolable authority – either the philosopher or the legislator – through the introduction of allegory in biblical hermeneutics.

It is instructive to examine here Spinoza's engagement with Maimonides in chapter 7. It shows how Spinoza strictly adheres to his hermeneutical methodology and how he dismisses the dogmatist position because of the kind of authority that it implies – an authority premised on the rejection of monism.

The extract from Maimonides's *Guide of the Perplexed* quoted in chapter 7 is the largest continuous-text citation in the *Theological Political Treatise*.[17] In the cited passage, Maimonides explains why he rejects the view that the world is eternal – that is, that there is nothing outside nature or monism. It is clear from the context that Maimonides is considering the description of monism in Ecclesiastes that Spinoza invokes in support of monism in his discussion on miracles (84). Maimonides provides two reasons for the rejection of monism. First, 'the eternity of the world has not been proved; so it is not necessary to do violence to the Scriptural texts and explain them away merely because of a plausible opinion, when we might incline to a contrary opinion with some degree of reason' (100). Whereas other obscure passages of Scripture need to be interpreted allegorically, Maimonides exempts the idea of the eternity of the world, since the contrary position can be reasonably maintained. Second, 'the belief that God is incorporeal is not contrary to the basic tenets of the Law, whereas the belief that the world is eternal ... destroys the very foundations of the Law' (100). The entire structure of obedience and command that sustains Jewish law hinges on accepting God as a creator who acts like a lawgiver. Without that, Maimonides argues – that is, if we lapse into monism – the conception of divine law as ordained by God is impossible.

We see how this is an excellent illustration of the kind of hermeneutics Spinoza rejects through his methodology. The general framework is the following: the interpretation of Scripture is the same as the interpretation of nature in the sense that true meaning has to accord with the monism that is never proved in the Bible. If the dogmatist adds something to biblical

---

[16] Fraenkel, 'Spinoza on Philosophy and Religion', 33.
[17] In fact, I cannot think of a longer continuous citation anywhere else in Spinoza's works.

meaning – that is, allegory – he can also refuse to add allegory, especially at the crucial point of the assertion of monism in Ecclesiastes. But this means that any additions or omissions are purely arbitrary. Let us now follow closely Spinoza's riposte.

He first draws attention to the arbitrary choice by Maimonides *not* to interpret as allegorical the passages from Ecclesiastes that support the view that the world is eternal. If Maimonides cannot disprove the rejection of creation *ex nihilo*, then 'he cannot be sure of the meaning of Scripture' (101). Why? 'For as long as we are not convinced of the truth of a statement, we cannot know whether it is in conformity with reason or contrary to it, and consequently neither can we know whether the literal meaning is true or false' (101). In the absence of a refutation, the rejection of an idea as untrue is merely capricious – and, we may add, it is merely a way for Maimonides to effect the legitimation of his preferred law. The effect is that the one who institutes the hermeneutic exception – or, 'decides on the exception', as Carl Schmitt puts it – derives personal authority from it.[18] The exception relies on personal proclivities that strengthen one's power.

Spinoza's argument amounts to saying that Maimonides implicitly understands reason here as instrumental rationality. Maimonides *in practice*, through his decision to treat the eternity of the world as an exception to the rule of allegorical interpretation so as to practically support the 'foundation of the law', adopts Spinoza's position about the priority of phronesis. But this epicurean position that Maimonides's argument entails presupposes monism – which is precisely what Maimonides's allegorical interpretation of the Scripture to establish the authority of the law cannot tolerate.

Spinoza further accentuates the tension within Maimonides's position by showing next that the dogmatist position in fact reverts to scepticism, since, 'if this view were correct, I would unreservedly concede that we need a light other than the natural light [*alio praeter lumen naturale*] to interpret Scripture' (101/114). What is this 'other light' other than the technique of appealing – arbitrarily, exceptionally – to the supernatural as a way of shoring up one's authority? The exception is equivalent to miracle, as Carl Schmitt observes.[19] Even though the sceptic and the dogmatist appear to be diametrically opposed, in fact their procedures are the obverse sides of the same coin, namely, the institution of personal authority through interpretation.

Spinoza's critique culminates in an attack on the kind of personal authority entailed in the rejection of monism. If 'nearly all the contents of Scripture

---

[18] Schmitt, *Political Theology*, 5.
[19] Schmitt, *Political Theology*, 36.

are such as cannot be deduced from principles known by the natural light' (101) but require additions by the philosopher or the legislator, then the 'common people [*vulgus*]', who are unschooled in logic and reasoning, 'have to rely solely on the authority and testimony of philosophers [*ex sola authoritate et testimoniis philosophantum*] for their understanding of Scripture' (101/114). In other words, the authority of *sola Scriptura* now masquerades as the authority of *sola Philosophia*. The dogmatist posits the 'philosopher' as a new pontiff whose interpretations are infallible and beyond contestation. Spinoza stops employing arguments at this point and just observes what the effects of such an hermeneutics ought to be: 'This would indeed be a novel form of ecclesiastical authority [*Ecclesiae authoritas*], with very strange priests or pontiffs, more likely to excite common people's [*vulgus*] ridicule than veneration' (101/114). Laughter – the surest way to undermine authority, as Arendt puts it – will be the revenge of the *vulgus* on the philosopher-theologian who wants to submit the people to his own interpretative authority, introducing arbitrary additions that pass for infallible doctrines.[20] The oft-maligned *vulgus* can have the last laugh, according to Spinoza.

We see then that the distinction between the true meaning of Scripture and the pursuit of philosophical truth leads to a hermeneutics that is practical or moral and that is expressed through its effects, namely, neighbourly love. Even though the calculation of utility as reciprocal is distinguished from the rationality required to prove monism, still monism is presupposed for understanding virtue in terms of utility. We see, further, that the pursuit of a false meaning of Scripture is nothing but an attempt to change the meaning and use of neighbourly love so as to consolidate personal authority. Both techniques Spinoza discusses seek personal authority through the rejection of monism.

The two distinctions that organize the entire discourse of chapter 7 can be understood as describing relations between the three epicurean themes. The distinction between the truth of meaning and truth of things traces the relation between monism and utility, that is, between the second and the third epicurean themes. And the distinction between the truth and falsity of meaning addresses the relation between authority and utility, the dialectic formed through the interaction of the first and second themes. Thus, this first use of neighbourly love becomes the pivot of the initial distinctions within Reformed authority that Spinoza draws in chapter 7 to outline the convergence of authority and communication, which Spinoza achieves by determining all the significant concepts within his epicurean framework.

[20] Arendt, *On Violence*, 45.

2. Didactic Authority: The Universal as Communication

Spinoza's concern with authority remains the focus for the next three chapters dealing with the *authorship* of the Pentateuch, a point which is clear as soon as we recall that *authoritas* means both authorship and authority. A new important distinction within the true meaning of Scripture is not introduced until chapter 11 – and it is a distinction that also has significant repercussion for the delineation of Reformed authority in relation to utility. Let me provide some context.

In chapters 11 and 12 Spinoza argues that Scripture contains a universal message that is moral. The universalism of Scripture is a practical one. Given the distinction we have already seen between the true meaning of Scripture and the truth of things that philosophy is concerned with, one may be tempted to argue that Spinoza stages here the distinction between the different universalities of faith and reason. The clash of faith and reason is a critical site of conflict that arises in modernity and is determinative of the understanding of authority in the aftermath of the Reformation, as Herbert Marcuse convincingly shows in *A Study on Authority*. Significantly, Marcuse demonstrates, this conflict between faith and reason is not simply the other side of the 'secular' conflict between Church and state. The antagonism between faith and reason, writes Marcuse, appears 'in the most varied forms in the ambivalence of bourgeois relationships of authority: they are rational, yet fortuitous, objective, yet anarchic, necessary, yet bad'.[21] Given this, the crisis in the relation between faith and reason becomes the site of intense speculation, from Kant to Hegel, from Weber to Benjamin, and more recently from Negri to Derrida.[22] One could argue, then, that Spinoza is staging here the familiar conflict between faith and reason.

This impression will be dispelled as soon as we realize that Spinoza does

---

[21] Marcuse, *A Study on Authority*, in *Studies in Critical Philosophy*, 55.

[22] The literature on this topic is enormous, so I provide here only some key pointers. Regarding Kant, see essays such as 'The Conflict of the Faculties' and 'Religion within the Bounds of Reason' collected in *Religion and Rational Theology*. For Hegel, see *Faith and Knowledge*. For Max Weber, see *The Protestant Ethic and the Spirit of Capitalism*. For Walter Benjamin, 'Capitalism as Religion', in *Selected Writings*, vol. 1, 288–9. The concept of the crisis of modernity is central to Negri's project, e.g. in his book with Michael Hardt, *Empire*. Derrida provides his own interpretation of this topic in the influential 'Faith and Knowledge: The Two Sources of "Religion" at the Limits of Reason Alone', in Anidjar (ed.), *Acts of Religion*, 42–101. Michael Naas's *Miracle and Machine: Jacques Derrida and the Two Sources of Religion, Science, and the Media* is not only a detailed reading of Derrida's essay, but also an insightful and original approach to this thorny topic.

not ascribe universality either to faith or to reason but to communication.[23] What is universal arises neither from revelation nor from reason, but from what can be communicated to everyone. This universally communicable message turns out to be neighbourly love. Let us see how Spinoza constructs this argument.

The argument about universal communication proceeds through a distinction within the true meaning of Scripture. This is the distinction between 'prophesizing or teaching' (138), or between the prophets and the apostles. Spinoza writes that the apostles are 'far removed from the authoritativeness of prophecy [*ab auctoritate prophetica*]' (138/151). The reason is that whereas 'the apostles everywhere employ argument ... the authority of a prophet does not permit of rational argumentation [*prophetae auctoritas ratiocinari non patitur*]' (139/152). The same contrast is drawn a bit later between Moses and Paul. The former, 'the greatest of the prophets', was 'never engaged in logical argument, whereas the norm in Paul is lengthy chains of logical argumentation such as we find in the Epistle to the Romans' (140). The reason for this difference pertains to the utility of the message. Unlike the prophets, whose calling was to reach a specific people and hence to provide utility to a limited community, 'the Apostles were called to preach absolutely to everyone [*omnibus absolute*]' (141/154). This is possible because their teaching was not based on 'the attestation of signs' that are restricted to the specific circumstances of the recipients of the message but on 'natural knowledge' that is common to all (141).

This difference of communication entails a shift in the nature of authority between apostles and prophets. As Spinoza explains in the opening of chapter 1 of the *Theological Political Treatise*, prophecy is a one-directional communication from God to the people via the interpretation offered by the prophets. This imbues the prophets with personal authority, as it is only they who can interpret and communicate that particular divine message. This personal aspect is absent in the teaching conducted by the apostles. Their 'calling' to reach all humankind provides the apostles with 'an authority to teach [*auctoritas ad docendum*]' (141/155). This didactic authority enables them to communicate their message to absolutely everybody.

Spinoza further emphasizes the universality of communication through didactic authority by arguing that the apostles 'were teaching true religion [*veram docere religionem*]' (141/155). The emphasis here is not on the

---

[23] This argument is indebted to Étienne Balibar, even though we do not look at the same texts, and our conclusions are not identical. See especially the last chapter of *Spinoza and Politics*.

verum but on the *docere*, inserted between the adjective and the noun. The religious teaching is true, or is a truly religious teaching, because it is transmitted or communicated to everyone, irrespective of their particular circumstances. There is no true religion as such if religion is understood as a doctrine or static system of beliefs. There is a teaching that communicates religion to the entirety of humankind, it reaches potentially everyone, and it is this possibility of a universalized communication that makes both the teaching and the religion taught true. The term 'true religion' in the *Theological Political Treatise* signifies the conditions of the possibility of a universal communication.

This universal communicability is possible because the true meaning of Scripture 'can be readily grasped by everyone by the natural light of reason [*unusquisque lumine naturali*]' (142/156). Spinoza adds a note at this point stressing that the entire philosophical message of Scripture can be reduced to Christ's Sermon on the Mount contained in Matthew (237, note 27). This clarifies what Spinoza means by 'the natural light of reason'. The Sermon on the Mount was crucial for modern epicureanism because Christ's 'golden rule' contained in it was interpreted as equivalent to the calculation of utility.[24] In the middle of the nineteenth century, John Stuart Mill is still making the same point: 'In the golden rule of Jesus of Nazareth, we read the complete spirit of the ethics of utility. To do as one would be done by, and to love one's neighbour as oneself, constitute the ideal perfection of utilitarian morality.'[25] The 'natural light of reason' that Spinoza has in mind here, then, is not reason insofar as it leads to adequate ideas, but practical reason as *prudentia* or *phronesis*, which is moreover linked to neighbourly love.[26] The universality of the apostolic communication assumes the calculation of utility as a capacity held by all humans, making it the basis of ethics.

This possibility of a didactic authority capable of communicating a moral message that everyone can potentially understand requires a further move in Spinoza's hermeneutics. This is not surprising because, as I said at the beginning of the chapter, Reformed authority is inextricable from the process of communication and interpretation – it is inextricable from hermeneutics. Spinoza introduces this new move in his hermeneutics in chapter 12 by

---

[24] See Brown, *The Return of Lucretius to Renaissance Florence*, 128; and Brown, 'Lucretian Naturalism and the Evolution of Machiavelli's Ethics', in del Lucchese, Frosini and Morfino (eds), *The Radical Machiavelli*, 112.

[25] Mill, 'Utilitarianism', in *The Collected Works of John Stuart Mill*, vol. 10, 218.

[26] This is an important point as it suggests that the calculation of utility cannot be the same as the second kind of knowledge that requires adequate ideas to arrive at truth. I take up this issue in the following chapter.

accentuating the contrast between the text as such and its use. He argues that the 'true handwriting of God [*verum . . . Dei syngraphum*]' (145/158) is the human mind. Conversely, those who venerate the Bible 'worship likenesses and images [*simulacra et imagines*], that is, paper and ink [*chartam et atramentum*]' (146/156). And, 'Scripture . . . is sacred, and its words divine, only as long as it moves men to devotion towards God; but if it is utterly disregarded by them . . . it is nothing more than paper and ink [*chartam et atramentum*], and their neglect renders it completely profane [*absolute profanatur*]' (147/161). 'Paper and ink' are merely particular articulations of Scripture and they do not coincide with its message – they merely express it in a contingent way. The argument that Spinoza puts forward here follows from his move to understand the universal in terms of the possibility of communication. But still, it is not clear exactly where he is heading with this argument. What is the purpose of rejecting any interpretation that relies on 'paper and ink'?

The reason becomes clear as we read on in chapter 12. It is to further nuance the effectivity of the true meaning of Scripture or, to remain closer to Spinoza's own vocabulary, the way that the message of Scripture is realized through its use: 'A thing is called sacred and divine when it is destined [*destinatum*] to foster piety and religion, and it is sacred only for as long as men use it [*utuntur*] in a religious way' (146/160). The inference is that 'nothing is sacred or profane or impure in an absolute sense apart from the mind [*nihil extra mentem absolute*]' (147/160). Or, to put it the other way round, something is sacred when the mind can calculate that it is useful. Just as linguistic expression is contingent because its utility depends on historical circumstances, as Spinoza argues in chapter 7, similarly he argues here that a text is sacred depending on its use. The specific example Spinoza provides to support his point pertains to the Tablets of the Law. The Tablets Moses carried when he descended from Mount Sinai the first time were sacred only to the extent that 'on them was inscribed the Covenant under which the Jews had bound themselves to obey God' (147).[27] But as soon as they started venerating the Golden Calf, they chose not to use the 'covenant [*pactum*]', whereby the tablets became useless and thus 'merely stones' (147/161). This emphasis on use makes Reformed authority and the calculation of utility

---

[27] As I note in section 3 of Chapter 2, Spinoza never explicitly mentions the capital punishment for those venerating the Golden Calf that Moses orders when he descends from Mount Sinai the first time. This moment, however, is of critical import to Spinoza's argument, as we see here too, and as will become even clearer in Chapter 8, where I examine the reasons Spinoza offers for the destruction of the Hebrew state.

work together – but now their dialectic no longer traces a trajectory that is detrimental to the polity; instead, in the context of the universality of communication the kind of authority Spinoza describes and utility work co-operatively in tandem.[28]

This argument about universality as residing in the usefulness of communication is important for the second time that Spinoza employs neighbourly love in the second part of the *Theological Political Treatise*. 'From Scripture itself we learn, without difficulty or ambiguity, that its message is in essence this, to love God above all, and one's neighbour as oneself [*Deum supra omnia amare, et proximum tanquam se ipsum*]. ... This is the basis of the whole structure of religion [*totius religionis fundamentum*]' (151/165). Hence 'no hasty or errant pen' (151) can distort this message since it is a 'fundamental principle [*fundamentum statuendum*] [that] is uncorrupted' (151/165). Neighbourly love expresses the meaning of Scripture as it persists independently of its contingent, linguistic expression – that is, independently of any interiority that is accessible only to a particular individual. Neighbourly love expresses a message that is universal because it is useful regardless of contingent circumstances.

Neighbourly love, as the fundamental principle of Scripture, is not a matter of faith nor a matter of reason, if faith and reason are understood as aspiring for opposing senses of universality. Rather, the fact that piety resides in its use entails that universality is ascribed in its communicability and that it requires the calculation of utility; it requires the operation of phronesis, but in such as a way as to acknowledge that utility is reciprocal. Thus, in this second distinction regarding Reformed authority – between prophesying and teaching, or between the particularity of personal authority and the universality of didactic authority – we see again that neighbourly love is the crucial term. It is again the pivot that regulates the distinction, since without it the universal message of Scripture would lose its utility and hence its moral import. We see at this point that Reformed authority and the calculation of utility converge, creating a dialectic, which makes possible the state of authority reliant on phronesis that Spinoza envisages in chapter 5.

3. Universality without Transcendence: Levinas contra 'Spinozism'

Understanding universality in terms of communication is a move that leaves several questions unanswered, none more pressing than the relation between

---

[28] We will see in Chapter 7 the importance of use for the social contract or *pactum*.

universality and transcendence. This is a particularly pressing question in the context of the employment of the notion of the neighbour as the universal meaning of Scripture, since in the Jewish tradition, where it originates from, the neighbour is customarily understood as transcendent. How can this square with Spinoza's materialism? And how does it inform his conception of Reformed authority? Spinoza does not explicitly raise this problematic, but he gives us enough clues nonetheless to reconstruct his position. Emmanuel Levinas is pivotal here since his own philosophically brilliant appropriation of the Jewish notion of the neighbour as transcendent and its transformation into the figure of the Other is coupled with a stinging animosity toward Spinoza and a vehement denunciation of what he calls 'Spinozism'.

Let us approach this problematic about the relation between universality and transcendence with reference to the use of neighbourly love in chapter 13. There, Spinoza supports his position that the universal message of Scripture consists in neighbourly love with reference to Paul's Epistle to the Romans:

> Scripture demands nothing from men but obedience, and condemns not ignorance, but only obstinacy [*contumaciam*]. Furthermore, since obedience to God consists solely in loving one's neighbor [*solo amore proximi*] (for he who loves his neighbor in obedience to God's command has fulfilled the Law [*Legem implevit*], as Paul says in Romans chapter 13 v. 8), it follows that Scripture commands no other kind of knowledge [*nullam aliam scientiam commendari*] than that which is necessary for all men before they can obey God according to this commandment, and without which men are bound to be obstinate [*contumaces*], or at least unschooled to obedience. (154/168)

We see here the clear articulation of Spinoza's conception of Reformed authority insofar as it is related to the Bible and to biblical hermeneutics. The sole purpose of the Bible is to instil obedience, that is, to establish a sense of authority. This is no obedience to a person or to a political entity. Rather, it is obedience to a single, specific law, namely, to love one's neighbour. Anything else is contumacy, says Spinoza, a word that he consistently uses to designate the pursuit of false meaning in Scripture.

So, in the first step of his determination of Reformed authority, Spinoza associates it with the true meaning of Scripture as distinguished from false meanings and from philosophical pursuits; in the second, he specifies it as the didactic kind of authority that can communicate the universal message of neighbourly love, unlike the particularized communications of the prophets; and here, in the third step, he adds that this universal message is to be understood in terms of law.

In this context, Spinoza's appeal to Paul's Romans for support of this position may appear tenuous. According to Romans, to love one's neighbour is the fulfilment of the law, or, in Greek πλήρωμα νόμου. In other words, Paul, following a Jewish tradition – for, as Spinoza insists, the New Testament may have survived in Greek but its 'idiom is Hebraic' (88) – does *not* designate neighbourly love as a law. A law proscribes something *specific* that can be obeyed or disobeyed, whereas Paul is referring to something universal.[29] The *fulfilment* of the law is the sense of justice that supports the law but is not identical with it. For instance, a law may be unjust, whereby it demands obedience, but a sense of justice may also call for its overturning. Or, differently put, whereas a law is something that is particular in the sense of informing the decisions we make about obeying and disobeying, justice is something that is both universal and transcendent, something that is always present and yet irreducible to a specific command.

The Jewish idea of neighbourly love as the fulfilment of the law has often been misrepresented. Thus, Freud, for instance, questions in *Civilization and its Discontents* why it is that one should love one's neighbour. One has to earn love. Otherwise, it may lead to self-contradictory situations. Freud puts it as a counterfactual: 'If it will do [my neighbour] any good he has no hesitation in injuring me.'[30] The neighbour may be good, but also may be destructive, says Freud, summarizing his point with the invocation of Hobbes's judgement on human nature: *homo homini lupusi* (man to man is an arrant wolfe).[31] Thus, according to Freud, the law to love one's neighbour cannot possibility attain to universality. Slavoj Žižek not only accepts Freud's verdict but amplifies it by arguing that the forgetting of the potential for violence in relation to the neighbour is symptomatic of high capitalism's compulsion toward tolerance.[32]

A closer look at Paul's text, however, makes it clear that the key to neighbourly love is not the exclusion of violence but rather how it precedes the law. Freud starts from the law, noting that it can never be divorced from particularity so as to attain universality. Paul would have gladly granted

---

[29] See Badiou, *Saint Paul: The Foundation of Universalism*.
[30] Freud, *Civilization and its Discontents*, 300.
[31] Freud, *Civilization and its Discontents*, 302.
[32] See his contribution in Žižek, Santer and Reinhard, *The Neighbor: Three Inquiries in Political Theology*.

Freud this point, since for him neighbourly love as the fulfilment of the law is a universal that precedes and informs any particular proscription. The command and obedience model that characterizes the law presupposes faith: 'a man is justified by faith without the deeds of the law' (Romans 3:28). This move allows Paul to both advocate for neighbourly love *and* for justified violence: 'the carnal mind [is] enmity against God: for it is not subject to the law of God [τῷ γάρ νόμῳ τοῦ Θεοῦ οὐχ ὑποτάσσεται]' (Romans 8:7). The 'children of the flesh' are not under God's law. This is what justifies the violence exercised by those who are His children and who can be our neighbours. The protection of our neighbours – as the 'fulfilment' of the law – justifies violence against those who do not adhere to the just principle of neighbourly love.[33] We can analyse the entire history of violence in the Judeo-Christian tradition by tracing the varied determinations of the 'children of the flesh' who cannot be 'our neighbours'.

If we understand neighbourly love strictly as a law, then the neighbour does indeed participate in the parallel founding and transgression of the law and hence both needs to exclude violence and yet cannot.[34] But the notion of 'fulfilment' or πλήρωμα of the law is not merely a founding. Rather, it signifies something that is heterogeneous – *qualitatively* – from the law itself. It is the transcendence of the law, or what Levinas calls the Jewish notion of justice. Neighbourly love is not a law that can proscribe for or against violence. Rather, neighbourly love signifies the transcendent space that precedes and justifies any such proscription. Neighbourly love, thus, is irreducible to specific laws that are developed and practised in specific historical circumstances. From this perspective, neighbourly love in the Jewish tradition has a certain affinity with Kant's categorical imperative that is also transcendent, heterogeneous to natural causality and yet, because of that, determining of action. As Levinas puts it, 'to adhere to an ethics without worrying about its doctrinal presuppositions, to set one's metaphysics according to categorical imperatives – is surely to proceed in the way most in keeping with the Biblical spirit'.[35] In this tradition, then,

---

[33] See Derrida's comments on the theological provenance of protection in 'Faith and Knowledge'.

[34] Žižek et al., *The Neighbor*.

[35] Levinas, *Alterity and Transcendence*, 80. Levinas often links the responsibility to the Other to Kant's categorical imperative. Just to give one more example: 'as a relationship out of which responsibility arises, exercised in initiatives, and eventually in thematizations, cognitions and actions, the relationship with the other is an a priori fact preceding the a priori forms or conditions for the possibility of experience. Somewhat as in Kant, where the subjection to law – the fact of the categorical imperative

the transcendence of alterity – of the other or the neighbour – is that which enables universality.

I quote Levinas to suggest that he is following a certain Jewish tradition in understanding the neighbour as the Other, that is, as something transcendent that is irreducible to a physical presence, and the love toward the neighbour as the expression of a universal justice.[36] Levinas summarizes this point in his essay 'A Religion for Adults': 'The Justice rendered to the Other, my neighbour, gives me an unsurpassable proximity to God. . . . Justice is the term Judaism prefers to terms more evocative of sentiment. For love itself demands justice, and my relation with my neighbour cannot remain outside the lines which this neighbour maintains with various third parties. The third party is also my neighbour.'[37] The Jewish concept of the neighbour is used here as a synonym of Levinas's notion of the Other as an entity that is separated from the I because of its transcendence, which is signified by its proximity to God. At the same time, this is only possible because the neighbour/Other are constitutive of the universality of justice – of the fulfilment of the law and not of law as such.

The contrast with Spinoza here is sharp. Not only have we learned earlier, in the discussion of the divine law (or justice), that it is conceivable in terms of utility, and as such it cannot be transcendent; it is a 'logic of living', that is, it affects our being in the world. More importantly, we learn in the passage quoted at the beginning of the present section that neighbourly love is inextricable from obedience, that is, from the law. Thus, the fulfilment of the law as interpreted by Spinoza is not transcendent and is irreconcilable with the Jewish idea of justice Levinas draws on. Little wonder, then, that Levinas in 'The Spinoza Case' accuses Spinoza of being 'anti-Jewish' as well as of a 'betrayal' of Judaism.[38] This contrast also makes sense of the seemingly more ambiguous position in 'Have you Reread Spinoza?' that admits redeeming features to 'Spinozism', namely, that in it 'absolute thought also tried to be an absolute religion'.[39] This assertion appears in a section of the essay

---

– precedes and makes possible the legislative activity of autonomous subjectivity, precedes even its intrinsic forms.' Levinas, *Otherwise than Being or Beyond Essence*, 4.

[36] Cf. Bernasconi, 'Who is my Neighbor? Who is the Other? Questioning "the Generosity of Western Thought"', in Katz and Trout, *Emmanuel Levinas: Critical Assessments of Leading Philosophers*, Vol. IV, 5–30.

[37] Levinas, *Difficult Freedom*, 18.

[38] Levinas, *Difficult Freedom*, 107, 108.

[39] Levinas, *Difficult Freedom*, 117. On this point, see de Vries, 'Levinas, Spinoza, and the Theological-Political Meaning of Scripture', in de Vries and Sullivan (eds), *Political Theologies*, 232–48.

devoted to obedience. Here, obedience to the 'Word of God', as Levinas puts it, is an ethical imperative that again comes from a transcendent source. 'Spinozism' – Levinas is loath to write 'Spinoza' – may have redeeming features, but still completely misses transcendence and hence universality because of the insistence on seeing Scripture as a human creation.[40]

Levinas's critique of Spinozism crystallizes in two positions that amount to an insistence on the universality of the transcendence of the Other. First, Spinozism leads to a crude conception of immanence: 'Spinoza is the first messenger of the death of a God. . . . The divinity of being or nature consists in the pure positivity of *esse* . . . for there is nothing beyond that positivity and that *conatus*, no value in the sense of a surpassing of being by the good; it is a totality without *beyond*.'[41] Here, Levinas's understanding of Spinoza is remarkably close to Deleuze's, whose *Expressionism in Philosophy* makes the most forceful case yet that Spinoza is a philosopher of immanence – irrespective of the fact that this is something negative for Levinas whereas it is highly laudable for Deleuze.[42]

The most common way in which Levinas expresses this reduction to immanence is by referring to the conatus, or the 'conatus essendi', as he prefers to phrase it, and which he understands as the idea of *self*-preservation before any concern for others, that is, the I's concern for its own survival before any consideration of its neighbour. The problem with the conatus, as he puts it in *Otherwise than Being*, is that it entails 'superindividuation', which consists in a lack of 'sharing' the concern for preservation with others.[43] The ultimate result is nothing less than the preponderance of war.[44] According to Levinas, founding ethics on finitude as opposed to transcendence leads to death and destruction.[45] No wonder, then, that Levinas compulsively alludes to Spinoza in order to designate one of the greatest adversaries of his ethical position on the grounds that the 'conatus essendi' reduces ethical relations to finitude.[46]

---

[40] Levinas, *Difficult Freedom*, 116.
[41] Levinas, *Proper Names*, 84.
[42] Deleuze, *Expressionism in Philosophy: Spinoza*.
[43] Levinas, *Otherwise than Being*, 118.
[44] Levinas, *Otherwise than Being*, 4.
[45] Cf. Derrida, 'Violence and Metaphysics', in *Writing and Difference*, 97–192.
[46] In his lectures immediately after the publication of *Otherwise than Being*, Levinas ascribes this Spinozist point about the deficiencies of the 'conatus essendi' explicitly to other key philosophical figures, such as Heidegger and Descartes, as if Spinoza, or Spinozism, is the greatest enemy in – or rather, *throughout* – the history of philosophy, the cipher of the history of philosophy that a conception of ethics as responsibility to

Second, the transcendence of the Other means that there is, according to Levinas, an asymmetrical relation to the neighbour. *Totality and Infinity* expresses this point by talking about the 'Other as my Master'. The universality of the neighbour consists in this asymmetrical relation. Because of Spinoza's insistence on immanence, this mastery of the other is lacking in 'Spinozism', which is why, for instance, Levinas describes the conatus essendi as an 'inversion'.[47] By making the Other transcendent, Levinas wants to avoid at all costs giving any sense of ethical propriety or justice to a sense of mastery that is malleable or ambiguous. The relationship to the other as the neighbour in the Jewish tradition that Levinas develops in his philosophy has to be asymmetrical and one-directional.

Ethics is only possible as the transcendence of the Other, according to Levinas's philosophical formulation of the Jewish tradition of the neighbour. Spinozism is described in *Totality and Infinity* as the opposite of this position: 'Thought and freedom come to us from separation and from the consideration of the Other – this thesis is at the antipodes of Spinozism.'[48] In the interview 'The Proximity of the Other', Levinas summarizes his position in *Totality and Infinity* about the one-directionality of the relation of mastery that the Other requires as an overcoming of Spinozism: 'To address someone expresses the ethical disturbance produced in me, in the tranquility of the perseverance of my being, in my egotism as a necessary state, by the interruption of the "conatus essendi."'[49] And, in the late essay 'Philosophy and Transcendence' from 1989, Levinas is still using Spinozism as the counter-point of his ethics, in this instance of his conception of responsibility: 'The responsibility for the other is not reducible to a thought going back to an idea given in the past to the "I think" and rediscovered by it. The natural *conatus essendi* of a sovereign *I* is put in question before the face of the other.'[50] The 'Spinozism' Levinas constructs consists in the rejection of the neighbour as the transcendent other that forms the universal basis of ethics.

These two positions that delineate the ethical transcendence of universality amount to Levinas's religious faith – as opposed to Spinoza's 'betrayal' of Judaism. This is presented succinctly in an essay fittingly titled 'On Jewish Philosophy':

> the other ought to conquer. See Levinas, *God, Death, and Time*: for Heidegger, see 22 and 25, and for Descartes 188. These courses were delivered in 1975 and 1976, whereas *Otherwise than Being* was published in 1974.

[47] Levinas, *Otherwise than Being*, 70 and 75.
[48] Levinas, *Totality and Infinity*, 105.
[49] Levinas, *Alterity and Transcendence*, 97.
[50] Levinas, *Alterity and Transcendence*, 32.

My entire effort consists in separating myself, so to speak, from ontology, in which the meaning of the intelligible is attached to the event of being, because it would be *in itself* like *presence*, culminating in its repose and perseverance in itself, self-sufficient – a perfection that, in Spinoza's view, is its divinity. It is the human self, master and possessor of the world, all powerful in strength and knowledge, who would thus be divinized. To understand the for-the-other in a radical and original way as first philosophy – this involves asking oneself whether the intelligibility of the intelligible is not *prior* to the possession of the self by itself, prior to the 'hateful self', and (without having previously evaluated what one is and has, before having made the assessment of oneself) caring for the other, whose being and death are more important than my own.[51]

We can summarize Levinas's critique of Spinoza in terms of a failure to secure universality. The universal disappears in pure immanence, which renounces faith in justice because it substitutes the transcendent other or neighbour for an obsessive concern with the self. As such, the conception of the neighbour as master of the self disappears, and with it any pretence to a universal message of Scripture is nothing but a spectacular failure in the service of an instrumental reason that leads to violence. Understanding neighbourly love as a law – instead of as an expression of justice – condemns Spinoza to an ontology of mastery that is not worthy of ethics.

If we consider neighbourly love as I have reconstructed it in Spinoza's argument thus far, Levinas's critique may appear tenuous. Spinoza's conception of neighbourly is universal because it communicates a certain usefulness that is reciprocal, that is, never personal or selfish. In other words, there is neither universal communication nor utility if they are centred around the self, which contradicts what Levinas says when he reconstructs Spinoza's argument. Thus Spinoza and Levinas would agree that the relation to the neighbour is not selfish. Their disagreement resides in the fact that Levinas constructs a transcendent universal as the basis of ethics that is incompatible with Spinoza's dialectic of authority and utility. The reason is twofold. First, Spinoza's didactic authority cannot accommodate the one-directional notion of mastery that Levinas's Other requires to secure its transcendence; and, second, the two-directional notion of authority that Spinoza develops requires that neighbourly love is understood as a law – not as justice, as is the case in the Jewish tradition.

Let me start with the divergence around the notion of mastery or authority.

---

[51] Levinas, *In the Time of the Nations*, 178.

If Spinoza were to respond to Levinas, he would object to constructing an ethics on the principle that the 'Other is my master'. Spinoza describes such a one-directional power relation as the personal authority exemplified by the prophets. I will not repeat the argument here that I presented in Chapter 2 as to how Spinoza rejects any sense of transcendence in this one-directional relation. The reason is that this relation is premised on a communication with God that is interpreted by the prophets. Thus, the relations signified by authority unfold because of an activity – the prophets' interpretation – that is mediated and constructed. Instead, Spinoza explains the one-directional authority in terms of error: first on the part of the people who misunderstand the cognitive capacity of the prophets as some kind of potentia superior to the natural knowledge that is common to all; and further by the prophets themselves who mistake God's power for potestas, thereby imagining him as a lawgiver who transfers his authority to them. Both of these errors require that communication is particularized. In other words, the transcendence of the Other is constructed by denying the possibility of communication as universal.

The only prophet who does not rely on a mediated interpretation according to Spinoza is Christ: 'God revealed himself to Christ . . . without mediation [*immediate revelaverit*] . . . as in the case of the prophets' (54/64). This allows Spinoza to introduce the universality of communication, which he elaborates in chapters 11 and 12, as we saw in the previous section. Specifically, Spinoza writes that 'Christ was sent to teach [*docendum*] not only the Jews but the entire human race [*totum humanum genus*]. Thus it was not enough for him to have a mind adapted to the beliefs of the Jews alone; his mind had to be adapted to the opinions and doctrines universally held by all humans [*opinionibus et documentis humano generi universalibus*], that is, to those notions that are common to all and true [*notionibus communibus, et veris*]' (54/64). Spinoza does not take this to mean that Christ's revelation as such is universal. When Christ is faced with people who are ignorant and obstinate, he is compelled to communicate the revelation, just like Moses, in the form of laws (54). That is, Christ may avoid the error of the previous prophets, but circumstances also force him from time to time to communicate in the manner that the prophets of old did.[52] Consequently, the universality of the revelation does not consist in its content; rather, it consists in its communication. Christ becomes a *teacher* to communicate Scripture's true message to all the humans. This ability to

---

[52] That's why his teaching is particular and universal at the same time (91–2). See Balibar's insightful analysis of this point in *Spinoza and Politics*, 40.

teach distinguishes the *effects* of Christ's communication with the people in comparison to all other prophets. That's the notion of didactic authority that I described earlier.

We discern here the clear divergence between Levinas and Spinoza. For Levinas, universality is preserved in a one-directional relation of mastery: the Other is my master. For Spinoza, universality as communication requires a two-way mastery: the one who has didactic authority is my master. The advantage of Levinas's position is that it places a significant ethical responsibility on the self to respect the other. The shortcoming is that it appears of limited political value as political power relations are rarely one-directional.[53] It is this shortcoming that Freud and Žižek exploit in their critiques of the Jewish conception of neighbourly love, as I mentioned earlier. Conversely, the weakness of Spinoza's position is that there is no universal ethical imperative as such. The advantage is the recognition that the ethical and the political can never be thoroughly separated, which means that *pace* Levinas there is no autonomy of the ethical. The cross-pollination of the ethical and the political is presented through the multidirectional sense of mastery implied in the usefulness of didactic authority. Thus, when the master teaches the pupil, a didactic authority is established. Since the teaching is communicable and can be fully appropriated by the pupil, who may even surpass his master, there is the possibility that mastery will be reversed. Levinas's position cannot tolerate this 'inversion', as he calls it, but for Spinoza it is indispensable so that the ethical would not be cut adrift from the political.

This leads to the second issue, namely, the question about how such an ethico-political relation can be maintained through the reciprocity of utility – that is, when neighbourly love is understood not as justice, but as a law that demands obedience. It is in the purview of this problem that Spinoza relies on the intellectual background of his conception of the neighbour – a background that is epicurean. No wonder then that Levinas accuses Spinoza of a betrayal of Judaism and of heresy, as we saw earlier, given that the words heretic and epicurean are the same in Hebrew.[54]

Spinoza describes the operation of the reciprocal calculation of utility that characterizes neighbourly love in terms of the imitation of affects. We can find this theory presented in Part III of the *Ethics*. For instance, according to Proposition 27, 'if we imagine a thing like us, toward which we have

---

[53] Despite his efforts to present a Levinasian politics, Howard Caygill does not address this point in *Levinas and the Political*.
[54] See Montag, 'Lucretius Hebraizant: Spinoza's Reading of Ecclesiastes'.

had no affect, to be affected with some affect, we are thereby affected with a like affect'. This theory of the imitation of the affects is crucial for Spinoza because of the initial distinction that he draws in the context of Reformed authority, namely, between true meaning and the truth of things. As we saw, Spinoza's distinction relies on a separation between pure rationality and the affects. I quote again a passage that I cited earlier: 'For human nature is so constituted that what one conceives by pure intellect, one defends only by intellect and reason, whereas what originates from the affects of the heart are affectively defended' (87). Pure intellect – such as employed by philosophers – can only cause effects when it engages with pure intellect, and the phronesis that characterizes the affects only when it engages other affects. This is a consequence of Spinoza's so-called parallelism (E II, P7).

The same point is repeated in chapter 13 by saying that God does not expect humans to know 'his nature as it is really in itself' because this is 'a nature which a certain human logic of living cannot imitate [*quam naturam homines certa vivendi ratione imitari non possunt*]' (156/171). This means that 'the intellectual knowledge of God . . . has no bearing on the practice of a true way of living [*ad veram vivendi*]' (156–7/171). The theory of the imitation of the affects describes the mechanism whereby interaction is possible at the affective level – that is, at the level of the true meaning of Scripture that shows us the 'true way of living'. Thus, this theory from *Ethics* is supplemented with a significant discussion at the end of chapter 13 of the *Theological Political Treatise*. Unlike in the *Ethics*, Spinoza is not concerned here to show how imitation works but concentrates instead on how 'charity [is] the only means of making God manifest' (156), that is, how *caritas* or neighbourly love encapsulates the true dispensation of imitation – imitation describes how the reciprocity of utility or neighbourly love can come into effect. In fact, the last quoted passage is Spinoza's paraphrase of the passage from John's First Epistle that functions as the epigram to the *Treatise*.[55] This indicates how crucial for the entire argument of the *Treatise* this discussion of imitation in terms of charity or neighbourly love is.

When the imitation of the affects leads to a true way of living, then it is God's 'charity' that 'humans can imitate through a certain logic of living [*certa vivendi ratione imitari possunt*]' (156/170). We see here – as well as in the quotation from the same page cited in the previous paragraph – Spinoza using the expression 'ratio vivendi' that is the predicate of his definition of

---

[55] I have already shown in section 2 of the Introduction that Spinoza uses this passage from John's First Epistle to refer to the co-operation of the three epicurean themes. I will return to the quotation used in the epigram again in the following chapter.

the law in chapter 4 of the *Theological Political Treatise*. This 'logic of living' is – as I explained in section 1 of Chapter 3 – synonymous with phronesis or the calculation of utility. So neighbourly love or charity does indeed instil obedience to the law but without recourse to anything transcendent. The 'logic of living' or *ratio vivendi*, as we saw in Chapter 3, describes the correlation of law and phronesis that is the rational activity unfolding in specific historical circumstances and as a response to them.

We are now in a position to generalize Spinoza's point about the imitation of the affects. The true message of Scripture, its universal message irrespective of circumstances, is that circumstance is determinative. Neighbourly love is a law in the sense that it has to be actualized in human action. This is not a message amenable to Judaism – or, at least, in Levinas's conception of it – but the reason is not because it promotes an ethics of violence. Rather, the reason is that if the true message of Scripture concerns the universality of the given circumstances, then this message is a call to act by being cognizant of the reciprocity of utility. It does not require abstract thought, it rather requires being able to recognize the other's affects. The imitation of the affects is the form that communication can take when it is reliant on the reciprocity of instrumental reasoning. To put it differently, Spinoza's conception of universality does not require the separation of transcendence and immanence.[56] Instead, universality resides in material relations of communication – the material is the universal.

Spinoza derives this opposition to the Jewish tradition of the neighbour from epicureanism. To see this, we need to turn to the most extensive epicurean discussion on friendship contained in Cicero's *On Ends*.[57] From all the derivative sources of epicureanism, Cicero's *On the Nature of Gods* and *On Ends* are the most important, the former for the epicurean theory of nature and the latter for its ethical theory.[58] *On Ends* is an ethical treatise in the form of three dialogues. Cicero presents in each dialogue the position of one of the dominant schools of philosophy and then puts it under scrutiny. The epicurean position is represented by Lucius Torquatus in the first dialogue, and it contains the most detailed epicurean account of friendship that has survived from antiquity. Lucius Torquatus defends the position that

---

[56] Catherine Malabou argues this too – albeit via a different route – in 'Before and Above: Spinoza and Symbolic Necessity'.

[57] For the context, see Mitsis, 'Cicero on Epicurean Friendship'.

[58] Cicero's books are, as I explain in the Introduction, primary sources of the two premodern interpretations of epicureanism, the physicalism of its physics and the sensualism of its ethics.

all virtues are means to the end of attaining happiness. This instrumental conception of virtue relies on the metaphysical principle that there is nothing outside being.[59] People act by calculating their utility or their advantage.[60] Such calculation is necessary for virtue to function as a means. This whole discourse concludes with a discussion of friendship, describing it as the greatest of all the means to happiness.[61]

The reason friendship is the culmination of the epicurean sense of virtue is that it extends the logic of the calculation of utility to include the other: 'friendship is the most trustworthy preserver and also creator of pleasure alike for our friends and for ourselves'.[62] Friendship in the epicurean sense shows that phronesis is shareable – and this sharing is not a contingent characteristic but a predicate of phronesis. It shows that utility is not personal but rather reciprocal. Lucius Torquatus continues, noting the social import of friendship: 'it is not possible to secure uninterrupted gratification in life without friendship, nor yet to preserve friendship itself unless we love our friends as much as ourselves [*nisi aeque amicos et nosmet ipsos diligamus*]'.[63] The exigency to 'love your friend as yourself' is not a law independent of the given circumstances; rather, it is the indispensable precondition of maximizing our utility in the given circumstances by recognizing that utility is never personal but only ever reciprocal. The fulfilment of utility is in friendship.

Lucius Torquatus sketches a theory of the imitation of the affects as the mechanism of the articulation of the love of one's friend as oneself:

> For we rejoice in our friends' joy as much as in our own, and are equally pained by their sorrows. Therefore the wise will feel exactly the same towards their friend as they do towards themselves, and will exert themselves as much for their friend's pleasure as they would for their own.[64]

Friendship is the condition of sharing affects. Compare here Proposition 31 of Part III of the *Ethics* that summarizes the theory of the imitation of affects: 'If we imagine that someone loves, desires, or hates something we ourselves love, desire, or hate, we shall thereby love, desire, or hate it with greater

---

[59] This point is repeated throughout Lucius Torquatus's discourse. See, for instance, Cicero, *De Finibus*, 1.33, about how it applies to the wise person, or the summary of the argument in 1.54.
[60] Cicero, *De Finibus*, 1.34.
[61] Cicero, *De Finibus*, 1.65.
[62] Cicero, *De Finibus*, 1.67.
[63] Cicero, *De Finibus*, 1.67.
[64] Cicero, *De Finibus*, 1.67–8.

constancy.' The imitation of the affects describes the condition of epicurean friendship. It signifies that the reciprocity of utility is accompanied by the reciprocity of affect. No epicurean theory of virtue could do without this step, given that – as I have repeated several times already – phronesis or the calculation of utility is presupposed by the epicurean construction of virtue. But phronesis is rationality and emotion working in tandem. The 'law' to 'love your friend as yourself' discloses the mechanism to articulate this epicurean conception of virtue.

This is not confined to the ethical realm: 'wise people have made a sort of compact [*foedus*] to love their friends no less than themselves'.[65] If there is a notion of social contract in epicureanism, such a contract explicitly rejects the necessity for a political authority – the sovereign – who calculates social utility on behalf of the citizens. To the contrary, it is the co-calculation of utility that binds friends together.[66] Thus, Reformed authority, as it is constructed in Spinoza's *Theological Political Treatise*, shows a convergence of the ethical and the political that is mediated by the calculation of utility and the imitation of the affects. To love one's neighbour as oneself then means constructing a community on the basis of mutual need and aid. What is to be obeyed is the logic of living that governs such a reciprocity. No external personal authority can make an absolute claim to obedience, nor can authority be purely external or transcendent.

Spinoza will further elaborate this Reformed authority in the rest of the *Treatise*, as we will see in subsequent chapters. This elaboration requires that we are aware of the three steps in which he constructs neighbourly love as the universal message of Scripture: first, as a moral or practical message distinct from both false interpretations that aim to adumbrate personal authority and from philosophical concerns directed toward adequate ideas or the second kind of knowledge; second as a universal message because it can be communicated; and, third, as reliant of the reciprocation of utility or imitation of affects entailed in phronesis. All three steps rely on neighbourly love as the useful message of Scripture, whereby the Reformed authority described here and utility are shown to be able to work together.

Spinoza can take the third step because of his reliance on the epicurean discourse on friendship. He translates epicurean friendship into the biblical discourse of neighbourly love. This allows him to make a political point that adheres to his epicureanism while expressing it in a language derived from

---

[65] Cicero, *De Finibus*, 1.70.
[66] I discuss much further the Spinozan (and epicurean) connection between the social contract or *pactum* and utility in section 2 of Chapter 7.

the Bible. We can thus read his biblical hermeneutics as a prompt for the reader to perform a translation in the reverse direction, namely, the translation of biblical terms such as 'God', 'neighbour' and 'charity' back into the language of epicurean politics. This reverse translation is required if we are to follow his own hermeneutical method of adding nothing to the text of the *Theological Political Treatise*, that is, of presenting neighbourly love in such a way as to accord with monism – the monism of the second theme of his epicureanism.

6
The Freedom to Philosophize: The Two Paths to Virtue (chapters 14 and 15)

It would be convenient to regard chapters 14 and 15 of the *Theological Political Treatise* as merely transitional chapters that summarize and at most refine the arguments of the previous thirteen chapters. There is a modicum of truth in this. For instance, the figure of the sceptic drawn in chapter 7 is here developed in detail. But the important interpretative and discursive reason for viewing these chapters as transitional would be to explain the persistence of one of the major exegetical disagreements about the *Treatise*, namely, the question whether Spinoza believes that the state ought to be based on piety and obedience, or whether alternatively it should be grounded on the exercise of reason. It is in these two chapters that Spinoza directly confronts the question of the relation of faith as based on the imagination and the emotions, and reason as based on the pursuit of truth. If these are transitional chapters, then it would be understandable that they do not settle the relation of faith and reason, which in turn justifies the persistence of this disagreement in the reception of the *Treatise*.

As opposed to that view, I hold onto the centrality of these chapters for Spinoza's political enterprise. I will show that, even though Spinoza announces the clear separation of faith and reason in the title of chapter 14, still the fact that their relation remains complicated is critical for his conception of neighbourly love and for how the 'freedom to philosophize' is to be understood. The intricate relation between faith and reason as presented here also paves the way for the most critical move we will discover in the last two chapters of the *Treatise* that articulates Spinoza's conception of democracy, as I will explain. Finally, the way Spinoza presents the relation of faith and reason can be understood – or, more emphatically, is only understandable – within the framework of his epicureanism.

1. 'Finally'? The Politics of the Distinction between Faith and Reason

The title of chapter 14 could not appear clearer on the question of the relation between faith and reason. It states that 'faith is finally separated [*tandem separatur*] from philosophy'. This seems to announce the definitive and irrevocable separation of faith and reason. And yet, the finality suggested by the title seems to be refuted by the text itself. Spinoza argues that they are separated because they have different aims. The aim of Scripture is obedience whereas the aim of philosophy is the attainment of truth. Or, in the words of the text itself, the 'aim [*intentum*] of Scripture is only [*tantum*] to teach [*docere*] obedience' and 'not to impart knowledge' (159/174).[1] This distinction is undermined if we consider the trajectory of the argument thus far. There are three significant reasons:

First, this separation has been announced several times previously. For instance, we saw in chapter 7 the distinction between the true meaning of Scripture and the pursuit of the truth of things characterizing philosophy. In general, it has been a leitmotif of the argument thus far that religion and faith are not concerned with philosophical – what Spinoza also calls 'mathematical' – proofs. But in the course of suggesting this separation previously, Spinoza persistently employs arguments both from faith and reason to argue for the same position. For instance, we saw that in chapter 5 of the *Theological Political Treatise* Spinoza argues that the origin of ceremonies is not the divine law. He does so initially through biblical references and then 'through a universal basis [*ex universalibus fundamentis ostendam*]' (62/73). Or, in chapter 6, he argues against miracles first through the way that reason requires monism or the idea that there is nothing outside God, and then with reference to Ecclesiastes. Thus, the already proclaimed separation of faith and reason is accompanied by Spinoza's repeated employment of two distinct argumentative strategies, one from faith and obedience and the other from reason, both of which reach the same conclusion. As a result, one is led to doubt whether a 'final' separation of faith and reason can actually be achieved if their respective argumentative strategies converge.

Second, the separation becomes even more problematic as soon as we consider the nature of the obedience that characterizes faith. Spinoza does not equivocate on this point: 'the entire law consists in this alone [*totam*

---

[1] The same distinction through their respective aims is repeated throughout chapter 14. For instance, just to give one more example: 'The aim of philosophy is, quite simply, truth, while the aim of faith . . . is nothing other than obedience and piety' (164).

legem in hoc solo consistere], to love one's neighbor' (159/174). This is the fundamental commandment of Scripture. The reason is that 'Scripture was written and disseminated not just for the expert [*non solis peritis*] but for all humans [*omnibus*] of every time and race' (159/174). This means that even though not every one may have the capacity to reason from axioms and first principles so as to arrive at knowledge through adequate ideas, still everyone has the capacity to exercise charity (*caritas*) or neighbourly love. The inference that Spinoza draws from this is again unequivocal: 'Thus [*quare*] this commandment is the one and only guiding principle for the entire universal faith [*hoc ipsum mandatum unica est totius fidei catholicae norma*], and through this commandment alone should be determined all the tenets of faith [*solum omnia fidei dogmata*] that everyone is bound to accept' (159/174–5). We can summarize this chain of thought by saying that the aim of faith is to instil obedience to neighbourly love as the indispensable commandment of Scripture.

An effect of this narrow determination of the obedience of faith and piety as obedience to the fundamental principle of neighbourly love, however, undermines the distinction between faith and reason. As we saw in the previous chapter, in the course of distinguishing between prophesying and the teaching that characterizes the apostles, Spinoza defines didactic authority in chapter 11 in terms of the use of 'chains of logical argumentation' (140). This didactic authority is universal in the sense that it teaches a universally communicable message, namely, neighbourly love. The message about neighbourly love is universally communicable precisely because it is based on reason and hence transcends the peculiarities of place, time, idiom, personality, customs and so on. So either neighbourly love is universally communicable and therefore its aim has recourse to reason, or neighbourly love is separated 'finally' – that is, with finality, completely – from reason and hence it is not universally communicable.

We can express the same *ad absurdum* with recourse to Spinoza's epicureanism. Neighbourly love – as we saw in the previous chapter – adds something significant to the third epicurean theme, namely, practical judgement or the calculation of utility. Neighbourly love teaches us that utility is never personal but rather is always interpersonal. One calculates one's utility on condition that one recognizes that one's utility is connected to the utility of others. Or, succinctly, utility is reciprocal. If that is indeed the case, then the calculation that includes the other cannot be a matter of sheer obedience. For the calculation to take account of the other's utility, one must exercise some level of reasonableness. Thus, neighbourly love as a *calculation* and as a *judgement* cannot be separated from reason. This is why the epicurean dialectic Spinoza constructs is between authority that demands obedience and utility that questions that obedience and problematizes it in various ways, some of which we have explored in the previous chapters.

Third, Spinoza himself does not seem entirely convinced of the 'finality' of the separation of faith and reason in chapter 14, or he would not have returned to the topic in chapter 15 – if the separation is characterized by finality then the final word on it would have been said and no more discussion would have been required. Of particular importance in chapter 15 is the question whether the fundamental commandment of Scripture, that is, neighbourly love, can be proved. To sustain the separation of faith and reason, Spinoza would have to argue that it is indeed impossible to prove it rationally. Instead of relying on argumentation from axioms, Spinoza insists on empirical grounds that we can be sure of the fundamental importance of neighbourly love: it leads to our salvation (169) and provides moral certainty (170); it would be folly to refuse it (171) and it is a commandment that benefits everyone (171). From this, Spinoza concludes that 'although this fundamental principle [*fundamentum*, i.e. neighbourly love] underlying all theology and Scripture cannot be demonstrated with mathematical exactitude, we may yet accept it with sound judgment' (171/187).

Not only do these inductive arguments not prove the validity of neighbourly love, furthermore, as Spinoza explains, the separation of faith and reason depends on the impossibility of proving neighbourly love: 'If we accept this fundamental principle [*fundamentum*, i.e. neighbourly love] without reason, blindly, then we too are acting foolishly without judgment; if on the other hand we assert that this fundamental principle can be proved by reason, then theology becomes a part of philosophy, and inseparable from it' (169/185). Spinoza is implying that if we say that neighbourly love, as the foundation of faith, is unrelated to reason, then we will lapse into the sceptical position that seeks recourse to something supernatural to ground faith. If, on the other hand, we try to prove it through reason, then we will lapse into the dogmatist position that subordinates faith to philosophy. The difficulties that arise for the sceptic and the dogmatist, as I presented them in the previous chapter, are not adequately tackled through the empirical approach advocated in chapter 15, since, as Spinoza himself argued against Maimonides's rejection of the completeness of the world in chapter 7, if we cannot prove truth or falsity, then we cannot know whether a position is in conformity with reason and whether it would be sound judgement to follow it (101).[2]

---

[2] I discuss Spinoza's distinction between the sceptic and the dogmatist as well as his engagement with Maimonides in detail in section 1 of Chapter 5.

The same argument can be applied, *mutatis mutandi*, to Spinoza's admission that the fundamental principle of religion and faith cannot be proved.

Immediately after arguing that neighbourly love cannot be proved without lapsing to either scepticism or dogmatism, Spinoza summarizes his position: 'I maintain absolutely [*absolute*] that this fundamental dogma of theology cannot be investigated by the natural light of reason, or at least [*saltem*] that nobody has been successful in proving it' (169/185). There is a dizzying movement from the 'finally' of the title of chapter 14, to the 'absolutely' that affirms and strengthens that 'finally' in this sentence in chapter 15, to the 'at least' in the very next sentence that casts doubt on it. Spinoza starts this argument by saying that he *finally* shows the separation of faith and reason. Then he reinforces this separation on the grounds that neighbourly love as the fundamental principle of faith *absolutely* cannot be proved by philosophy. And he concludes that such a proof has *at least* not been offered as yet. The reader could legitimately wonder at this point: Does this actually mean that if there is a proof of this fundamental dogma of religion that consists in the reciprocity of utility, then faith and reason can *never* be finally separated?

As if this dizzying movement is not enough to unsettle the reader and to cast aspersions upon the entire trajectory introduced by the 'finally' in the title of chapter 14, the reader would be decidedly surprised then when they turn to the *Ethics* to find not one but two demonstrations of this fundamental principle of religion! I am thinking here of Proposition 37 of Part IV of the *Ethics*, whose importance Spinoza underscores in the first Scholium where he claims that this Proposition shows 'what the foundations [*fundamenta*] of the state [*civitatis*] are'. Proposition 37 reads: 'The good [*bonum*] which everyone who seeks virtue wants for oneself, one also desires for others; and one's desire is greater as one's knowledge of God is greater.' The idea of the reciprocal good as virtue may not be explicitly called here charity or neighbourly love. But if we recall that the good is defined as that which is useful or has utility in definition 8 of Part IV of the *Ethics*, then this reciprocity of utility is precisely how neighbourly love is defined in the *Theological Political Treatise*, which is also the reason why it is the fundamental principle of faith. In an unusual move, Spinoza provides two separate proofs for Proposition 37.

The second Demonstration proves the reciprocity of the pursuit of the good in terms of the affects: 'The good which one wants for oneself and loves, one will love more constantly if one sees that others love it (by IIIP31). So (by IIIP31C), one will strive to have the others love the same thing. And because this good *is* common to all (by P36), and all can enjoy it, one will therefore (by the same reason) strive that all may enjoy it. And this striving will be the greater, the more one enjoys this good (by IIIP37), q.e.d.' It is significant that the argument here relies on Proposition 31 from Part III of the *Ethics*, that is, the proposition that concludes the discussion of the imitation of the affects. It is precisely the imitation of the affects that Spinoza appeals to at the end of chapter 13 to describe neighbourly love as a logic of living, and it is the same imitation of the affects that justifies the epicurean idea of loving one's friend as oneself in Cicero's *De Finibus*, as we saw in the previous chapter.[3] Here the same mechanism of the imitation of the affects is mobilized to prove the reciprocity of good as the sign of virtuous conduct.

The first Demonstration proceeds not from the affects but rather from reason. I quote here only the beginning of the first Demonstration as I will return to it in more detail in the following section: 'Insofar as men live according to the guidance of reason, they are most useful to man.' So what we have here is not only a proof of that which the *Theological Political Treatise* claims absolutely cannot be proved. Moreover, we have two proofs, one from the framework of faith – the imitation of the affects that underlies the obedience made possible by neighbourly love – and one from reason itself. Further, not only does this not settle 'finally' the question of the relation between faith and reason, it also displaces the entire problematic to politics since it is presented as addressing the foundations of the state (*E* IV, P37S1).

It is Étienne Balibar's singular achievement to have noted the importance of this double proof of Proposition 37 of the *Ethics* and its far-reaching political implications. I will concentrate here on three of Balibar's works to outline his extrapolation of the double proof of neighbourly love, because Spinoza is addressed explicitly in these three works, but the idea plays a significant role in a number of other writings by Balibar.[4] These three works span a period of over three decades, starting with *Spinoza and Politics* (first published in 1985, hereafter abbreviated as *SP*); followed by his lecture at the Spinoza Society, *From Individuality to Transindividuality* (originally delivered in 1993 and then published in 1997, hereafter abbreviated as *IT*); and, finally, a long essay 'Philosophies of the Transindividual' that deals with Spinoza alongside Marx and Freud (from 2018, abbreviated as *PT*).[5]

Balibar frames the double proof of neighbourly love in Proposition 37 in terms of the question of the source of sociality and of the political. In the tradi-

---

[3] See section 3 of Chapter 5.
[4] I should note that Balibar himself does not explicitly note the link between neighbourly love and Proposition 37, although he frequently uses the language of the neighbour and the friend when discussing these passages.
[5] A translation of all of Balibar's essays on transindividuality is currently in preparation for Edinburgh University Press, *Spinoza, the Transindividual*.

tion of political philosophy, there are two divergent answers as to the origins of the political. One sees the origins in the natural proclivities of the individual to be social – for instance Aristotle, Bossuet and Marx all pursue different versions of this argument (SP 77). The other sees sociality as something entirely artificial, as something instituted to curb the naturally anti-social proclivities of the individual. Good examples here are Hobbes and Kant (SP 77). Balibar wants to argue that Spinoza evades these two traditional responses: for Spinoza 'the alternative between "nature" and "institution" is no longer binding' (SP 78). In *From Individuality to Transindividuality* Balibar refers to this overcoming as 'transindividuality', while acknowledging 'the intrinsic difficulty which readers had (and still have) in understanding a doctrine which virtually escapes (or dismisses) the basic antinomies of metaphysics and ethics which arise from ontological dualism: individualism vs holism (or organicism), but also the opposite ways of understanding the human "community" itself, in which either "intersubjectivity" or "civil society", "interiority" or "exteriority", is given primacy' (IT 6–7).

Within this framework, it is hard to underestimate the importance of the double proof of Proposition 37. Instead of two competing origins of society, one in 'natural man' and the other in 'rational institution', the double proof of Proposition 37 suggests that the two origins, if appropriately reconfigured, can in fact work together to explain sociality. As Balibar puts it, the sociality that 'human nature' strives for is, according to Proposition 37, 'defined both by reason and by ignorance' (SP 83). This insight is critical in the development of the concept of transindividuality – not only in Balibar but in other theorists too. For instance, in his significant work on transindividuality, Jason Read acknowledges Spinoza's important contribution: 'Spinoza's critical transindividual perspective begins by demonstrating that the idea of an autonomous individual is itself the product of an originary ignorance.'[6] The importance of this idea has generated valuable research in recent years.[7] Essentially, then, the two proofs of Proposition 37 point to a 'double genesis' – Balibar's term – for sociality, thereby avoiding a series of dualisms that mark the metaphysical tradition and the conception of the political in the Occident.

Let me provide a long quotation from his more recent 'Philosophies of the Transindividual' that summarizes Balibar's position on the 'double genesis' of the social:

---

[6] Read, *The Politics of Transindividuality*, 37.
[7] See, for instance, the articles on transindividuality collected in the *Australasian Philosophical Review* 2:1 (2018), ed. Mark Kelly and Dimitris Vardoulakis; and Morfino, *Plural Temporality*.

if man's essence always pertains to his individual singularity, this, in reality, cannot be isolated from a network of relations with other individuals that *determines* it, and in which this essence is always simultaneously active and passive. But this reciprocity is itself legible according to two modalities, to which Spinoza analytically correlates the two competing 'demonstrations' he proposes for Proposition 37: the modality of passionate exchanges for which the motor is the ambivalent desire of each person to identify himself to others and that of others to identify themselves to them (*ambitio*), and the modality of rational calculation that leads each person to understand that their own utility resides in the existence of a society where the forces of all make up a superior power to act (and to conserve everyone). Taken together, these two components of Spinoza's reasoning combine to show that 'social human nature' is a compound, in variable proportions, of dispositions and actions that 'obey reason' and others that 'proceed from passion'. The upshot of this is that the affective composition of singular individuality and the conjunction, in the institution of the city, of rational 'forces' and passionate forces are simply the front and reverse sides of the same question, because individual dispositions themselves have a *relational* essence, whether this follows the modality of imitation or that of utility. They are at one and the same time causes and effects of the 'social' relation in which each individual finds themselves always already with all the others, and therefore these effects *express* this relation. (*PT* 13)

Not only does this summary of the 'double genesis' of sociality point to Balibar's more general project of a philosophical anthropology, thereby taking Spinoza's insight as the foundation of a long and detailed philosophical project – as Balibar adds to the above-quoted passage, this 'reversibility is the very object of philosophical *anthropology*, to which the reversibility confers from the outset a political character' (*PT* 14).[8] In addition, and more significantly for our purposes, this reciprocity between humans coupled with the reversibility between reason and affect – or, in short, transindividuality – pertains to the centrality of communication in Spinoza. The reader can recall at this point that I have laid great stress on the importance of communication in Spinoza, both in how prophets and power are determined in the opening three chapters of the *Theological Political Treatise* (see Chapter 2)

---

[8] On Balibar's political anthropology, the most significant works, amongst many, are perhaps *Citizen Subject: Foundation for Philosophical Anthropology*, and *Equaliberty: Political Essays*.

and in how Spinoza conceives of the universality of neighbourly love on the grounds that it is universally communicable (see Chapter 5). I acknowledged earlier Balibar's influence on my thought on this point, and I note here the textual sources of that influence.[9]

Let me provide a significant clarification: the idea that the subject is differentially determined in Spinoza has often been noted in the most insightful readings of Spinoza. For instance, Alexandre Matheron's monumental *Individu et Communauté chez Spinoza* starts from this point to develop a Marxist reading of Spinoza. Or, Antonio Negri in *The Savage Anomaly* emphasizes the creative process of production in Spinoza. This process is shared in such a way as to establish the political community, or, in other words, it is an intersubjective creativity. Balibar's insight is that this differential identity provides society with a double origin that confounds the two paradigmatic accounts in the history of thought of how the social and the political are formed (see *SP* 85 and 87; and, *IT* 27–8).[10]

My own further point is that this double origin as it is articulated in Proposition 37 points to the notion of neighbourly love from the *Theological Political Treatise*. As such, it is pivotal in understanding the relation between faith and reason that is meant to be settled 'finally' in chapter 14, and which according to chapter 15 is meant to be 'absolutely' impossible to prove. My suggestion is that Spinoza is partly correct: maybe – *concesso non dato* – from a narrow cognitive perspective there is either obedience or reason – there is, in the terminology that I have been using, either authority or utility. But in fact, as Proposition 37 makes abundantly clear and as Spinoza's own uncomfortable hesitations in the *Treatise* betray, as soon as obedience and reason are overlaid on the political – and when is it that obedience and reason are non-political? – they are no longer separated nor separable, but only distinct in such a way that shows the intertwining of authority and utility. The fact that I call this relation a dialectic is also indebted to Balibar (see *IT* 10), with the caveat of course – as I have noted from the beginning – that this is a non-teleological dialectic.

---

[9] I should clarify: Balibar tends to talk about the importance of communication in the *Ethics*. The points about communication as defining of prophecy and personal authority as well as of the universality of neighbourly love are my own readings of the *Theological Political Treatise* – readings that bear the mark of Balibar's thought.

[10] I ought to add here a lesser known but for my purposes more pertinent analysis of transindividuality, one that can be found in Hill and Montag, *The Other Adam Smith*, chapter 2. The difference of this analysis of transindividuality in Smith and Spinoza is that it focuses on interest – or, that 'one's own interest includes . . . the interest of others' (109). This approximates the idea of reciprocal utility I have been developing here.

To put this somewhat differently, the distinction but non-separation of faith and reason indicates that society can be conceived – to put it in the terminology from Chapter 4 of the present book – both as a natural democracy and as a state of authority. These are two ways in which a social formation unfolds that do not exclude each other. They are two *paths* that express, in Balibar's words, 'the unity of contraries' (*SP* 88) because they are '*distinct* from one another and yet express the *same* necessity' (*SP* 81). This common necessity is the reciprocity of human relations, or neighbourly love. If this does not give a final answer to the question of the separation of faith and reason, that's because there is no finality in how this common necessity is articulated or in what its effects are. The two paths to sociality 'finally' show the lack of finality – that is, the lack of a telos bestowed from some mysterious 'above' as to how we should supposedly relate to each other.[11]

2. The Necessary Rebel: The Transversal of Faith and Reason

As soon as we accept that there are indeed here two paths to sociality and to virtue – faith as neighbourly love and reason – then the problem of the relation between them only intensifies. What is the nature of this relation? How does this ante-secular connection work?[12] To tackle this topic that implicitly contradicts the 'finally' of the title of chapter 14, Spinoza uses an unexpected figure, the 'necessary rebel'.

Immediately after the definition of faith in terms of its aim – that is, faith as the obedience to the commandment to love one's neighbour as oneself – Spinoza draws various consequences. All of them revolve around the idea that faith is articulated in works. This is not a new idea. For instance, Spinoza articulates it at the end of chapter 5: 'We cannot know anyone except by his works [*nisi ex operibus*]. He who abounds in . . . charity . . . whether he be taught by reason alone or by Scripture alone [*sive ex sola ratione, sive ex sola Scriptura*], is in truth taught by God, and is altogether blessed [*omnino beatus*]' (70/80). Both faith and reason, on their own, can lead to blessedness or virtue and the good. This is possible because of the effects of one's actions. Or, to put the same point in the epicurean terminology used in the previous chapter, use and its effects determine piety – regardless if this use is produced by obedience to neighbourly love (or faith), or by the exercise of reason (or philosophy).

---

[11] That's why I have talked sometimes of Spinoza's politics as a promise. A promise remains a promise so long as there is an attempt to realize it but it is not actually attained. See section 3 of the Introduction and section 2 of Chapter 7.

[12] For ante-secularism, see the discussion in section 2 of Chapter 1.

This same idea is repeated in chapter 14 of the *Theological Political Treatise* in all the consequences of the determination of faith as obedience. Thus, according to the first consequence, 'faith on its own without works is dead [*fidem per se absque operibus mortuam esse*]' (160/175). This is the epicurean point that we have seen before, namely, that something exists by virtue of its use. A similar point is made later: 'only by works can we judge anyone to be faithful or unfaithful [*neminem judicare posse fidelem, aut infidelem esse, nisi ex operibus*]' (160/175). This emphasis on work indicates that for Spinoza the two paths concern not solely the sources of sociality or its 'double genesis', as Balibar puts it. In addition, and more significantly, Spinoza's *two paths describe two ways in which people can attain the good or virtue through works.* Differently put, if there is a sense of origin in Spinoza, then that origin does not precede action, but rather articulates itself through the effects of how we act. It is not an origin that can never be cashed in – rather, it is an origin that always needs to be recreated through our actions. It is a performative origin or an origin as performative. This is very much in keeping with the idea of the origin of the social in terms of use and utility, as we find it in chapter 5 of the *Treatise*.[13]

The various consequences that Spinoza draws from this origin that is inscribed in our actions culminate in the insight that faith 'does not expressly demand true [*vera*] dogmas [*dogmata*], but only such as are necessary for obedience [*ad obedientiam necessaria sunt*]', that is, those that strengthen the will to love one's neighbour. Such dogmas may lack even 'a shadow of truth [*nec umbram veritatis*]', adds Spinoza, almost provocatively, suggesting that knowledge is only one path to good and virtue and that obedience is a different and equally legitimate path (161/176). Nothing new thus far – we have already seen that there are two distinct paths, one through the affects that requires obedience and the other through reason.

At this precise point, Spinoza introduces a qualification that presents a thought that is prefigured in the idea of agonistic democracy in chapter 5 and which will be of critical import in the political part of the *Theological Political Treatise*, especially in chapters 19 and 20 that develop it in detail. Obedience, says Spinoza, is unconcerned as to the truth of beliefs, 'provided [*dummodo*] that he who adheres to them is ignorant of the fact that they are false [*falsa esse ignoret*]; otherwise [*alias*], he would necessarily be a rebel [*rebellis necessario esset*]' (161/176). What matters are the effects of actions. This does not require knowledge of the chain of causality, only a calculation of the resultant effects. But it does not also suggest that ignorance is to

---

[13] See section 1 of Chapter 4.

be celebrated – it is not a calculation of the 'blessed are the poor in spirit' kind that we find the Bible (e.g. Matthew 5:3 or Luke 6:20). Knowledge cannot be eliminated as a determinative factor in how the good is achieved. Chapter 15 puts this as a rhetorical question: 'who can give mental acceptance to something against which his reason protests [*reclamante ratione*]?' (167/182). We see an implication of the strict adherence to the epicurean insistence on the inseparability of mind and body. The affects may be able to control us but they will never be able to eliminate the possibility that 'reason protests' thereby rising into a 'rebellion'.

This signifies not merely that the two paths are distinct yet inseparable, but also that under certain conditions there is a *transversal* between the two paths. When rationality transgresses into faith – for whatever reason, we are not concerned with this question yet, Spinoza will return to it in chapters 19 and 20 – then the two paths of faith and philosophy cross, and reason is inscribed in the operation of the affects. It is this transversal that Spinoza understands as rebellion or protest, as it is the act that registers *dis*obedience. Significantly, it is a disobedience not to the commandment to love one's neighbour, but to the various 'dogmas' – we can also say, 'laws' – that are 'false' in the sense that they contravene the fundamental principle of faith. In this instance, it is not the affects themselves that effect this transversal but the inscription of reason into the operation of the affects, that is, the inscription of philosophy into the path of faith and obedience – not in order to contradict that path but in order to safeguard the reciprocity of utility that virtue requires.

Given the critical importance of this transversal of the two paths, I need to pause to clarify it further, both in terms of what we have already seen and in terms of how it works. The six clarifications that I present here are not meant to cover the entire gamut of implications of this transversal but rather to pave the way for the more detailed discussion later.

First, let me endeavour a summary of the transversal of the two paths from the perspective of the account of the origin of society that we saw in chapter 5 of the *Theological Political Treatise* – as I explicate it in Chapter 4. We discovered there that Spinoza admits two possible socio-political formations, natural democracy and the state of authority. Further, we saw that the two are both inseparable and related agonistically. Here, the question arises: How are these two regimes of power related to the two distinct paths that lead to the good and to virtue we have discovered in chapters 14 and 15 and in Proposition 37 of Part IV of the *Ethics*? As soon as we view the distinction between the two regimes of power and the complex relation of faith and reason together, the answer to the above question appears straightforward:

natural democracy corresponds to the path of reason, and the state of authority to the path of faith. The transversal of the two paths corresponds to the agonistic relation between natural democracy and the state of authority we saw in chapter 5. Thus, what we discover in chapter 5 of the *Treatise* accords with our reading of chapters 14 and 15. In fact what remained still abstract in chapter 5, because there Spinoza argued from 'universal principles' (62), is now given thickness as he details in the second part both the practice of communication and the historical development of how people interpret the fundamental commandment of faith.

Second, this agonistic relation between faith/the state of authority and reason/natural democracy leads to necessary rebellion. There is no suggestion in Spinoza's text that he is thinking here of a grand Revolution. There is also no grand narrative of the 'event' that ruptures reality. Besides Spinoza's customary caution that prevents such grandiose gestures, he is also strictly adhering to the epicurean point about body and mind working together. This leads to the position that the two paths are never 'pure'. The path of faith may rely on the imitation of the affects and the path of reason on striving for the truth, but the two contaminate each other as they transverse. Thus, to conceptualize political change, Spinoza promotes an image of impurity as opposed to a fundamental, violent rupture. In other words, the necessary rebellion that Spinoza talks about can unfold at any time because it is an effect of the errors – analysed in detail in the first six chapters of the *Treatise*, as I explained earlier – that arise from the fallibility of practical judgement and that are constitutive of political activity. If I hesitate to call this Spinozan position a 'permanent revolution', that's because the process is strictly non-teleological and there is even no guarantee that it leads to the good. It can be both progressive and regressive.

Third, the political relation between natural democracy and the state of authority is grounded on a relational ontology where the process of change is understood as the interminable and non-teleological process of creation and destruction. Balibar describes with remarkable clarity this non-teleological process that the interaction of the affects and reason instigates. He begins his description by insisting that transindividuality is not a state of being but a 'process' (*IT* 16) that leads to a 'relationship of forces . . . between destructive and constructive effects' (*IT* 18). This process means that the individual in relation to the other – that is, as the condition of neighbourly love – is always in 'virtual decomposition' of itself (*IT* 19). Or, more starkly, 'the complete concept of an individual is that of . . . a *metastable* equilibrium which must be destroyed if it is not continuously recreated' (*IT* 22). Jason Read presents this point clearly: 'Individuation, of both the collective and the individual, is nothing other than the constitution, and destruction, of this particular relation of ideas, affects, and desires.'[14]

Antonio Negri notes this point approvingly but also points to its limitations. He argues that transindividuality 'offers an excessively monistic perspective, constituting the strongest image of the immanent refusal of any socio-political contract and thereby preventing any possible transfer of power toward political domination'.[15] Transindividuality offers an account of the individual and the collective whose process of constitution and deconstitution resist absolute authority. But Negri also insists that the power that the transindividual expresses 'is proportional to the extension of the union' with others, that is, it cannot be resolved in relation to constituted power.[16] In other words, Negri suggests that there is not enough scope for political change here. I regard this criticism as missing the critical point, namely, that Balibar is not attempting an account of political change *per se* but rather a description of relations of being or of 'communication', as he calls it, that are a process without a telos. Or, differently put, it is not a normative argument but an ontological argument that informs our conception of history.

I will only add here that we have already seen this idea in Lucretius. His ontology is also relational, relying on a process of mutual composition and decomposition: 'the whole consists of a body subject to birth and death [*totum nativo ac mortali corpore constat*]', writes Lucretius in an extended discussion of the incessant and non-teleological process of creation and destruction.[17] This insight in Book 5 of *On the Nature of Things* is critical for Lucretius's conception of history as a movement of simultaneous progression and retrogression.[18] In other words, there is a process that requires a continuous struggle or conflict as primary over any grand ruptures or any supposedly final aims. Importantly, then, this relational ontology is critical to the ontological outlook of the epicureans.

Fourth, the first presentation of the transversal of the two paths leading to the good and to virtue is framed by two references to the epigram of the *Theological Political Treatise*. The epigram links neighbourly love to the relation between the second and the third themes of Spinoza's epicureanism.

---

[14] Read, *The Politics of Transindividuality*, 34.
[15] Negri, 'Spinoza: A Different Power to Act', in Kordela and Vardoulakis (eds), *Spinoza's Authority*, Volume 1, 136.
[16] Negri, 'A Different Power to Act', 137.
[17] Lucretius, *On the Nature of Things*, 5: 321.
[18] The discussion of the process of creation and destruction occupies a large portion of Book 5 and it is presented as an inference from atomism (see 5: 181ff.). I discuss the importance of this point for epicureanism in section 2 of Chapter 1.

Monism is inscribed within the process of the transversal indicated as the activity of the necessary rebel.

The epigram is from John's First Epistle, chapter 4. In chapter 13 of the *Treatise*, Spinoza alludes to the epigram – without specifying the reference, simply calling attention to 'that passage in John' and prefiguring that he will return to it later. Spinoza uses the epigram to point out that God manifests in the world through *caritas* or neighbourly love. The passage in the King James translation is as follows: 'No man hath seen God at any time. If we love one another, God dwelleth in us, and his love is perfected in us. Hereby know we that we dwell in him, and he in us, because he hath given us of his Spirit' (1 John 4:12–13). Spinoza immediately clarifies that 'spirit' in this context means love, a point that is confirmed if we turn to the Greek text: 'ὁ Θεὸς ἐν ἡμῖν μένει καὶ ἡ ἀγάπη αὐτοῦ τετελειωμένη ἐστὶν ἐν ἡμῖν', or, in my translation, 'God is in us and his love is completed in us.'[19] After this clarification, Spinoza extrapolates the epigram as follows: 'since nobody has seen God he [i.e. John] concludes therefrom that it is only through love of one's neighbor that one can perceive or be conscious of God' (160). Knowledge of God is displaced to the idea that faith consists in a practical comportment that is related to neighbourly love.[20] Since it is impossible to know that which has no outside or the totality of being – what Spinoza calls God or Nature – then we can proceed by practical knowledge. And the kind of practical knowledge that accords with God is not only the calculation of utility, but the recognition that utility does not belong to one individually but only exists reciprocally. In other words, the calculation of utility requires neighbourly love.

I have already described several times this relation between the supposition of totality as the precondition of knowledge (monism as the second theme of Spinoza's epicureanism) and the admission that practical knowledge or phronesis is required due to the impossibility of a complete knowledge of the totality (the anthropological principle as the third theme of Spinoza's epicureanism). This relation is derived from Epicurus, according to whom the totality or *to pan* cannot be known or perceived. Just like God in the quotation from John's First Epistle, the only way to know the totality is through

---

[19] I do not want to go here over the issue of Spinoza's sources of the New Testament. As is well known, Spinoza did not read Greek and his main source for the New Testament was Immanuel Tremellius's translation from Aramaic. See Edwin Curley's 'Editorial Preface' in *The Collected Works of Spinoza*, vol. 2, 64.

[20] Spinoza makes the same argumentative move in 1675, when he uses the same passage from John in his letter to Alfred Burgh (*Ep.* 76).

its effects, that is, through the practical kind of knowledge that Epicurus calls phronesis – as I explained both in the Introduction and in Chapter 1. Spinoza adopts this idea and further develops it, in particular, by socializing the function of phronesis through neighbourly love, as we saw in the previous chapter. Here we see the same move in terms of faith: one is faithful when one's works contribute to neighbourly love. Such a love is the kind of praxis that compensates for the fact that we cannot know God as such.

These works that fulfil faith include the possibility of the necessary rebel, that is, the transversal between the two paths to virtue. After discussing that under certain conditions one must 'necessarily be a rebel' (161), Spinoza returns again to the figure of neighbourly love, 'this love, as John says [i.e., in the epigram], that every man is in God, and God in every man' (161). Framed by the only detailed extrapolation of the *Treatise*'s epigram and its repetition, the figure of the 'necessary rebel' then is placed in a unique position in Spinoza's narrative. This repetition of the epigram functions like a spotlight from either side that places necessary rebellion, or the transversal of the two paths, at centre stage of the argument.

Significantly, the epigram is placed on either side of a position – the necessary rebel – that is incommensurable with the a 'final' separation between faith and reason. At the very least, the necessary rebel shows that the separation is unstable and fragile and that it can be bridged through specific works. At its most emphatic, the necessary rebel shows that in actuality there is no such separation of faith and reason at all and to talk about such a separation is merely a convenient tactic – one that brings into play the other epicurean theme, authority, as we will see in the next section.

The fifth clarification has broader implications for Spinoza's epistemology and its connection to action – and hence ethics and politics. If we accept the position that faith and reason can never be completely separated – either because the separation can be bridged or because in actuality there is no such separation – then it becomes impossible to account for the relation between the two paths to virtue based on the typology of the three kinds of knowledge contained in Part II of the *Ethics* – specifically, based on the relation between the first kind of knowledge, or the imagination that employs the emotions and that is required by faith, and reason that is employed by philosophy and that seeks the truth through adequate ideas. This is the one, but significant, drawback of the otherwise brilliant interpretation by Balibar. Instead, the epicurean conception of the relation between monism and phronesis is indispensable, as shown by the fourth point above.

Let me start with a description of Balibar's position. In all three works by Balibar that I have been referring to here, there is an assumption that the 'double genesis' of sociality corresponds to the first and second kinds of knowledge, namely, the imagination and reason. Even though this is stated on occasion – for instance, Balibar writes that sociality is 'founded on an astonishing "parallelism" of the first two "kinds of knowledge"' (*PT* 13) – still it is never argued for. Thus, Balibar states that 'one cannot be rational without being reasonable' (*IT* 28), but this merely assumes that what I call phronesis is part of the second kind of knowledge, which is far from obvious.

Let me pause for a moment to provide a quick sketch of the distinction between the first two kinds of knowledge, the imagination and reason. The distinction is drawn largely in terms of imagination consisting in inadequate ideas whereby its images are neither true nor false (see, e.g., *E* II, P17S), whereas reason has adequate ideas whereby it can lead to truth or falsity (see, e.g., *E* II, P34). Thus, to use Balibar's terms, one can certainly be 'reasonable' without having adequate ideas. Consequently, the distinction between the two origins as that between 'the logic of imitation [of the affects] and the logic of utility' (*PT* 16) cannot parallel the distinction between the first and the second kinds of knowledge. The reason is that the calculation of utility or phronesis cannot be, strictly speaking, a form of the second kind of knowledge as it is not concerned with adequate ideas.

A whole host of questions, both exegetical and of philosophical substance, arise at this point, which can be summarized in the following one: Is the distinction between the three kinds of knowledge overcome in the discussion of utility in Part IV of the *Ethics*? To answer this question requires a detailed reading of the *Ethics* – which I cannot do here.[21] I simply note that it seems to me that Spinoza is aware of the issue, even if he does not address it explicitly. We can see this by turning to the first Demonstration of Proposition 37 – that is, the Demonstration from the perspective of reason.

---

[21] An analysis of intuition or the third kind of knowledge, as it is presented in Part V of the *Ethics*, will be critical in any such discussion. It is noteworthy that the relation between emotion and reason is presented in the opening of Part V (Propositions 1 to 20) as the relation of the first and second kinds of knowledge, which is possible because the entire argument is framed in terms of causality. Any discussion of instrumentality or utility – which is the central concern of Part IV – is bracketed out here. This is possible because Spinoza notes early on (e.g. *E* I P33 and its scholia) that it is possible to view things both in terms of their necessity, that is, through the chain of causality, and in terms of their contingency, that is, from the way in which humans act by calculating means and ends. Thus, if the relation between imagination and adequate ideas is delineated only in terms of causality, where does that leave instrumentality? The whole issue then becomes what role the intuition plays in Part V in answering this question, that is, in escaping the narrow frame of causality employed in the first 20 propositions of Part V. This is a complex topic for another occasion.

I am citing the first Demonstration in its entirety:

> Insofar as people live according to the guidance of reason, they are most useful [*utilissimi*] to each other (by P35C1); hence (by P19), according to the guidance of reason, we necessarily strive to bring it about that humans live according to the guidance of reason. Now, the good which everyone who lives according to the dictate of reason (i.e., by P24, who seeks virtue) wants for himself is to be intelligent [*intelligere*] (by P26). Therefore, the good which everyone who seeks virtue wants for oneself, one also desires for others.
>
> Next [*deinde*], desire [*cupiditas*], insofar as it is related to the mind, is the very essence of the mind (by Def. Aff. I). Now the essence of the mind consists in knowledge [*in cognitione*] (by IIP11), which involves knowledge of God (by IIP47). Without this [knowledge the mind] can neither be nor be conceived (by IP15). Hence, as the mind's essence involves a greater knowledge of God [*majorem Dei cognitionem*], so will the desire also be greater by which one who seeks virtue desires for another the good one wants for oneself, q.e.d.

The Demonstration is divided into two parts. The first examines the maximization of utility when it is reciprocal. This is described in terms of *intelligentia* and is supported with reference to propositions from Part IV that are concerned to demonstrate the reciprocity of utility. The second part of the Demonstration – indicated by the *deinde* – is concerned with knowledge or *cognitio* of God. The second part is supported by references to Part II of the *Ethics*, for instance to Proposition 47 that argues that the human mind can have an adequate knowledge or *cognitio* of God (*mens humana adaequatam habet cognitionem aeternae et infinitae essentiae Dei*). This division in itself suggests two distinct yet related functions of rationality – one social that strives toward the reciprocity of utility, one cognitive that strives toward a knowledge of God. This is the distinction between instrumentality and causality I have been insisting upon all along.[22]

It is noteworthy at the same time that Spinoza introduces the transition to the second part of the Demonstration with reference to Proposition 11 of Part II of the *Ethics*. The reader may recall that I use this Proposition in the Introduction to show the relation between the second and the third themes of Spinoza's epicureanism. The Proposition reads: 'The first thing which constitutes the actual being of a human mind is nothing but the idea

---

[22] See in particular sections 1 and 2 of Chapter 1 and section 3 of Chapter 2.

of a singular thing which actually exists [*rei alicujus singularis actu existentis*].'
Mental activity requires a reference to being. Further, this still requires, as
the Corollary makes clear, that 'the human mind is a part of the infinite
intellect of God', even though this thinking that is tied to singular things or
to the contingent objects of our existence 'perceives the thing only partially,
or inadequately'. As I argued earlier, this is the point where the transition
from monism to phronesis takes place: God – understood in monist terms
as the totality or substance outside of which nothing exists – is required for
knowledge to be possible, but practical knowledge, as a response to one's
particular circumstances, is primary. The first Demonstration of Proposition
37 hinges on this relation between monism and practical judgement that
requires – and presupposes – the distinction between instrumentality and
causality.

Balibar faces two significant difficulties as a result of failing to draw the
distinction between practical knowledge, understood as the calculation of
utility, and the second kind of knowledge. First, he reaches the conclusion
that 'the *preference* in favour of reason is striking' (*PT* 16). If the relation
between the paths of obedience and reason is seen as privileging the latter,
the difficulty is that Spinoza insists throughout that the majority of the people
or the multitude are not able – for whatever reason – to think according to
adequate ideas. At the same time, Spinoza never presents any argument that
claims that the multitude need to train themselves for participation in the
polity. As we have seen, his conception of democracy is not perfectionist.[23]
Asserting the primacy of reason in the absence of a perfectionist argument,
and given that 'in every age virtue has been exceedingly rare' (146), could
only lead to pessimism. And – I do not believe that Spinoza is a pessimist
political philosopher (and neither does Balibar, I think).

Second, in order to avoid giving the impression that the preference for
reason leads to a dialectical teleology, Balibar adduces that 'imagination and
reason form, in the political field . . . a *chiasm*' (*PT* 16). I completely agree
with Balibar when he describes this chiasm as follows: 'The idea of a city
entirely constituted by logics of passionate *imitation* is absurd: a rational utility

---

[23] Let me cite one passage from chapter 16 that is incompatible with a perfectionist understanding of democracy: 'just as the wise man has the supreme right to do all that reason dictates [*sapiens jus summum habet ad omnia, quae ratio dictat*], i.e. to live according to the laws of reason [*ex legibus rationis*], so, too, a man who is ignorant and weak-willed has the highest right to do all that is urged on him by appetite [*ignarus, et animi impotens summum jus habet ad omnia, quae appetitus suadet*], i.e. to live according to the laws of appetite [*ex legibus appetitus*]' (174/190). Both the laws of reason and the laws of appetite are legitimate, whereby hierarchies depending on personal enlightenment are erased.

must not only be "immanent" but *recognized* by the citizens, which is the function of *institutions*. But the idea of a *rational city*, without an affective and imaginary "base", is just as devoid of signification' (*PT* 16). I fully concur. In fact, I myself will use the language of the chiasm in Chapter 9 to describe the relations between the state of authority and natural democracy. But there is also a crucial difference. Basing the chiasm on the separation between imagination and the second kind of knowledge does not give Balibar the means to describe how the transition between two takes place.[24] What is it that motivates the operation of the chiasm? It is one thing to say that each path on its own is nonsensical (with which I agree), and it is another to describe how the two paths contaminate each other in the process of transversal. This latter explanation is lacking in Balibar.[25] Maybe this has to do with his preference for turning to the *Ethics* to discover this chiasm that characterizes the 'constitutive instability' of the polity (*PT* 17), whereas in fact Spinoza describes the mechanism of their relation as a form of agonism in the third part of the *Theological Political Treatise*, especially in the concluding two chapters – as we will see in Chapter 9. Ultimately, the issue of reciprocal utility – or neighbourly love, or transindividuality – will remain trapped in the relation between the first and second kind knowledge, unless we recognize the importance of the distinction between instrumentality and causality and hence the importance of practical judgement or the calculation of utility for Spinoza.[26]

So, to summarize the fifth point, the concept of utility that Spinoza employs in the *Theological Political Treatise* and develops further in Part IV of the *Ethics* cannot be accommodated within the distinction between the first and second kinds of knowledge as described in Part II of the *Ethics*. Rather, the calculation of utility is a practical kind of intelligence (*intelligere*) that is neither pure imagination nor purely adequate knowledge (*cognitio*). This neither/nor effects the link between monism and practical judgement, that

---

[24] This is *mutatis mutandi* the same problem facing Pierre Clastres about the relation between a society without a state and the state, as I outline the problematic in section 2 of Chapter 4.

[25] Another way of putting this point is by saying that Balibar's account of political change is inadequate. See Vardoulakis, 'Conflict as the Quasi-Transcendental'.

[26] I should note in passing the impact that Deleuze's interpretation of Spinoza has had in covering over the importance of the distinction between instrumentality and causality. Deleuze attempts to derive the entirety of Spinoza's politics through the relation of the first and second kind of knowledge. Responding to a paper I presented, an exasperated Deleuzian told me once that the entire philosophy of Spinoza is contained in Parts I and II of the *Ethics*, with a bit of assistance from the beginning of Part III. I think this summarizes my dissatisfaction with the Deleuzian line of interpretation pretty accurately.

is, between the second and third themes of Spinoza's epicureanism. The productive effect of this link is that instrumentality is inserted in the relation between imagination and adequate knowledge.

As I have stated from the very beginning, I prefer the language of the dialectic of authority and utility – instead of an opposition between the imagination and the second kind of knowledge – so as to avoid the above problems. Phronesis, as we have seen, is inscribed in both. We have seen, for instance, that the prophets communicate so as to lead the people to certain actions in response to given circumstances. Their authority is concerned with the utility of the polity. Also, the utility of the polity both requires the operation of practical judgement by its members and also recognizes that it may be in the utility of the people to defer judgement to someone else on certain issues. Utility does not preclude authority, which is to say that neither can be preferred over the other.

This latter observation leads to my sixth and final clarification. If there is no intrinsic preference between authority and utility or their corresponding political regimes, namely, the state of authority and natural democracy, then how are we to understand the transversal or chiasmus that characterizes their agonistic relation? I contend that their relation is that of a cross-pollination – nay, better, a process of *mutual contamination*. If theirs is a dialectical relation, it is a dialectic of the *pharmakon*, that is, both remedy and poison.[27] The figure of neighbourly love, or of reciprocal utility, is fundamental in understanding this poisonous and yet therapeutic relation. At the same time, given that this dialectic requires phronesis to be inscribed in the agonistic relation since it is operative both in the state of authority and in natural democracy, and given that the freedom to judge is characteristic of democracy, this dialectic indicates the primacy of democracy over all other constitutional forms – democracy, that most aporetic, that most poisonous yet therapeutic form of instituting reciprocal utility. This is the inevitable political inference from his epicureanism that Spinoza – as we will see – draws on in the final part of the *Theological Political Treatise*, and which he further develops in the *Political Treatise*.

3. The Freedom to Philosophize: Freedom from Personal Authority and the Freedom to Transverse

We find at the end of chapter 14 the first reference to the freedom to philosophize since the title page of the *Theological Political Treatise*. We saw in

---

[27] See Derrida, 'Plato's Pharmacy', in *Dissemination*, 61–171.

Chapter 1 of the present book that Spinoza employs 'the freedom to philosophize' in an unexpected way in the subtitle. The first part of the subtitle seems to affirm the commonly held view in secular modernity that the freedom to philosophize – just like faith – is a personal matter, something that is conducted introspectively, and separated from the reason of the public sphere. The second part of the subtitle, however, suggests that no polity can be successful unless the freedom to philosophize is adhered to, thereby making philosophizing more than an introspective exercise. I explained in Chapter 1 that Spinoza substitutes the freedom to philosophize with the freedom of judgement in the Preface to the *Treatise*, thereby mobilizing the epicurean tradition that understands freedom in terms of the exercise of phronesis. I will bring these insights together while further elaborating on the notion of freedom in Spinoza. This will pave the way to the final part of the *Treatise*.

The single use of the expression 'the freedom to philosophize' in chapter 14 is the first time that the expression from the subtitle is used in the body of the text: 'faith allows to everyone the utmost freedom to philosophize [*fides igitur summam unicuique libertatem ad philosophandum concedit*]' (164/179). This is situated in a summary of the ostensible point of the chapter, namely, that Spinoza has 'finally' separated philosophy from faith due to their divergent aims, the pursuit of truth for the former and the attainment of obedience and piety for the latter. Shortly after, as a concluding remark, Spinoza observes that 'what I have here demonstrated forms the most important part of the subject of this treatise [*quae hic ostendimus, praecipua sunt, quae in hoc tractatu intendo*]' (164/180). So, it is clear that the position Spinoza wants to present himself as holding is that the freedom to philosophize is due to the separation between philosophy and faith, whereby one does not infringe upon the other. This secular separation between reason and faith is both presupposed and reinforced by the freedom to philosophize.

The problem is, however, that, as we saw in the first section of the present chapter, the 'finally' only dissimulates finality. In actuality, Spinoza's position is thoroughly incompatible with such a separation. There may be a distinction between faith and reason, but no separation. Further, we saw in the second section that there is a clear and necessary possibility of communication between faith and reason. One is able to act basing one's judgements and actions on either, and if one bases them on faith but recognizes that the truth belies one's faith, one is compelled to become a 'necessary rebel' who uses reason to determine how to act. From this it follows that the 'final' separation of faith and reason is neither a sufficient means nor a good end to establish the freedom to philosophize.

I will argue that the freedom to philosophize is incompatible with the conception of freedom that arises in secularism and which consists in a split between the inner self and its external actions. This shows that the real motivation for Spinoza is to mobilize the first theme of epicureanism in the context of the discussion of the freedom to philosophize. We have seen thus far in this chapter how the relation between faith and reason can be traced onto the third theme – the calculation of utility – and the second theme – monism. The freedom to philosophize introduces into the discussion the critique of authority, thereby introducing into the relation of faith and reason the dialectic of authority and utility.

The short answer to the question 'what constitutes the freedom to philosophize?' is a double sense of agonism that leads back to authority. Let us explore both of these senses.

The first agonism is related to Spinoza's rejection of the free will. The chapter opens by asserting that 'for a true comprehension of faith, it is essential to understand that Scripture is adapted [*accommodata*] to the intellectual level not only of the prophets but of the unstable and fickle Jewish masses [*varii et inconstantis . . . vulgi*]' (158/173). The important word here is the verb *accommodare* – a verb that recurs throughout the chapter. Faith is not defined in terms of a set of revealed beliefs but by how it accommodates the 'fickle masses'. Faith is important for those who do not have the mental capacity to reach the good through the operation of rationality and instead require the historical narratives of Scripture. Thus, whereas reason effects a universal communication – as we saw in the previous chapter – faith is inextricable from utility and the operation of phronesis – that is, from the process that accommodates rationality to one's material reality.

Spinoza then immediately draws a distinction: 'One who indiscriminately [*promiscue*] accepts everything in Scripture as being the universal and absolute teaching about God, and does not distinguish precisely what is adapted to the understanding of the masses [*vulgi accommodatum sit*], is bound to confuse the beliefs of the masses with divine doctrine, to proclaim as God's teaching the figments and arbitrary opinions of men, and to abuse Scriptural authority [*Scripturae . . . auctoritate . . . abuti*]' (158/173). The adverb *promiscue* registers the operation of the free will. Some think that they have the right or the freedom to make any choices they like about the interpretation of Scripture. The individual assumes a free will to determine the meaning of Scripture. The effect of this operation of the free will is that faith will not be accommodated to the people, thereby subverting the aim of Scripture.

Spinoza persists in describing the effects of such an exercise of the free will. He calls *sectarios* those who indiscriminately (*promiscue*) adapt Scripture to their interpretations without regard for the masses (158/173). The substantive *sectarius* comes from the verb *seco* meaning to cut. The *sectarios* are the factionaries, those who act as the internal enemies that ravage the city by dividing it or cutting it into opposing fighting factions. Spinoza clarifies further: the *sectarios* are not impious when they accommodate Scripture 'to their own beliefs if they feel that this will enable them to obey God'. Rather, they are impious because they refuse 'to grant this same freedom to others [*eandem libertatem reliquis nolunt concedere*]' (158/173). The effect of this refusal to grant the same freedom means that the free will of the factionaries castigates as enemies of God (*Dei hostes*) all those with dissenting opinions. This is not a theological matter but a political one, as 'nothing ... more fraught with danger to the state [*reipublicae magis perniciosum*] can be devised' (158/173).

I need to remind the reader of a number of arguments that we have seen already and which are condensed in this discussion that links the freedom of the will with internal discord at the opening of chapter 14.

First, the profound subversion of the entire tradition of the enemy internal to the state – that I noted in section 3 of Chapter 1 when discussing the notion of voluntary servitude from the Preface – is fully realized here. The internal enemies are traditionally those who oppose the state because they are positioned outside the structure of power (*potestas*) and political authority. By contrast, Spinoza indicates as internal enemies those who have theological and hence political authority, and who also strive to strengthen their grip on authority through the exercise of the free will. Since the Preface, Spinoza has been consistently associating sedition with the propagation of personal authority leading to authoritarianism.[28]

Second, Spinoza explains who fits the description of the factionary. It is those who create disputes in the Church, as he 'recounted at the beginning of chapter 7' (159). As we saw there, it is the theologians that indiscriminately adapt Scripture to further their claims to authority, thereby leading to interstitial conflict (86). Now, chapter 7 distinguished the pursuit of truth – either through Scripture that strives for true meaning, or of philosophy that strives for the truth of things – from the falsity that characterizes the interpretations of Scripture that lead only to personal authority. The additional

---

[28] Machiavelli, who expresses a similar idea in chapter 29 of Part III of the *Discourses*, may be the source of this argument. 'By no means should princes complain about any sin committed by the people they have in charge, because such sins of necessity come either from a prince's negligence or from his being spotted with like faults.' Machiavelli, *Discourses on the First Decade of Titus Livius*, 493.

point Spinoza makes here is to link the discourses of personal authority and freedom. Those who pursue personal authority presuppose a freedom of the will all the while refusing to grant (*concedere*) that same freedom to others. By contrast, faith, in Spinoza's sense, grants (*concedere*) the freedom to philosophize, as he insists at the end of the same chapter.

Third, I have already discussed in Chapter 1 the idea from Moira Gatens and Genevieve Lloyd according to which 'freedom fundamentally is [for Spinoza] the emergence from the illusion of freedom – that is from the illusion of free will'.[29] Free will signifies two things at once. There is a separation between mind and body, and the mind is in control of the body. The paradigmatic story of the creation of the free will is the Fall, as we further saw in Chapter 3. God endows Adam and Eve with the capacity to choose between good and evil.

There is a notable tension between Spinoza's animosity toward the free will and the secular concept of freedom developing with the Reformation. As Herbert Marcuse puts it, the notion of authority developing in the aftermath of the Reformation 'leads back to the concept of freedom', as the Reformation is concerned with 'the practical freedom of the individual, his social freedom and its absence'. This conception of freedom relies on the 'union of internal autonomy and external heteronomy'.[30] This freedom is inextricable from the division of the subject into an interiority and an exteriority.[31]

The well-known argument about the production of freedom through this division of the subject that is essentially the production of the free will parallels the separation of faith and reason: the subject is endowed with an internal spirituality separated from external realities. Spiritual freedom is only possible in this interior realm. At this point, autonomy, freedom and individuality become largely overlapping concepts. The individual is autonomous so long as it enjoys a personal freedom guaranteed by its internal spirit. Opposed to this interiority of autonomy and freedom is the exteriority of heteronomy and unfreedom. The world is not spiritual, it is material, and that is what is responsible for the enslavement of the subject. Material objects as well as material relations, all the way from the family to the state,

---

[29] Gatens and Lloyd, *Collective Imaginings*, 51.
[30] Marcuse, A Study on Authority, in *Studies in Critical Philosophy*, 51.
[31] According to Michel Foucault, this 'empirico-transcendental doublet' is a constitutive feature of modernity's conception of the human. See the chapter 'Man and his Doubles' in *The Order of Things*. For a discussion, see Vardoulakis, *The Doppelgänger*, 70–2.

are confined to the exterior and hence can only ever approximate the real freedom that is enclosed inside the individual.[32]

This articulation of the secular separation of faith and reason into the concept of the free will has political repercussions. The division between the interiority and the exteriority of the subject is reproduced in the 'secular' division between the moral realm where the subject is free to exercise its beliefs, and the political realm where the subject has to submit to the law and authority of the state – that is, it is reproduced in the separation of Church and state. Or, to put it differently, political freedom, or civil liberty, or positive freedom – without wanting to conflate the different meanings of these terms in their specific contexts – all rely on the division between the inside and the outside of the subject so that they can signify the political sphere, that is, the sphere of external relations. Conversely, the inner spiritual or moral realm is separated from these external relations. The attempt is always to find a bridge between the inside and the outside. Thus, Kant goes to great lengths to describe the connection between the moral realm from the *Critique of Practical Reason* and its political articulation in the 'Doctrine of Right', an effort that is also discernible in a series of other writings such as the essay on 'Perpetual Peace'. What remains invariable is the initial separation – in Kant's terminology, the incompatibility between the moral law that is inside us and the natural causality outside, or, as he puts it in the Conclusion to the *Critique of Practical Reason*, 'the starry sky above me and the moral law within me'.[33]

Marcuse's verdict on the construction of freedom upon the distinction between the inside and the outside is stark: 'Freedom . . . is the condition of unfreedom.'[34] The purest example of this move can perhaps be found Kant. In Marcuse's words, 'the transcendental freedom of man, the unconditional autonomy of the rational person, remains the highest principle in all dimensions of Kant's philosophy'.[35] But, the fact that this autonomy ultimately seeks to justify the state means 'that coercion was made the basis of freedom, and freedom the basis of coercion'.[36] As Kant puts it, the gallows is a handy – external – reminder of the necessity to comply with the moral – i.e., inner

---

[32] This is the notion of freedom that the first part of the subtitle of the *Theological Political Treatise* seems to suggest and which the second part confounds, as I explain both at the opening of the present chapter and in Chapter 1.
[33] Kant, *Critique of Practical Reason*, in *Practical Philosophy*, 269.
[34] Marcuse, *Authority*, 52.
[35] Marcuse, *Authority*, 90.
[36] Marcuse, *Authority*, 91.

– freedom made possible by the categorical imperative.[37] This is the authoritarian underbelly of the notion of freedom as the free will produced by the separation of the inside and the outside of the subject within the context of secularism.

As I argued in Chapter 1, Spinoza is unequivocally opposed to freedom understood as the free will. For instance, we read in the Scholium to Proposition 2 of Part II of the *Ethics*: 'when people say that this or that action of the body arises from the mind, which has dominion over the body, they do not know what they are saying, and they do nothing but confess, in fine-sounding words, that they are ignorant of the true cause of that action, and that they do not wonder at it'. Spinoza rejects both premises of the free will, namely, the separation of mind and body and the control of the body by the mind. Thus, as I suggested in Chapter 1, Spinoza develops a notion of freedom as freedom from the free will.

What we learn here in addition is that Spinoza positions the freedom to philosophize in such a way that it is incompatible with the two dominant senses of freedom as free will that emerge in the aftermath of the Reformation, namely, the liberal and the republican. This is a huge topic and there is an enormous variety in both of these conceptions of freedom, to which I cannot possibly refer in any detail here. The basic positions are nonetheless clear. The liberal conception of freedom requires the freedom of the individual as the bearer of rights and as the figure in whose image humanity is conceived. No such conception of the individual is possible in Spinoza, since an individual is defined in relation to the other, that is, in terms of neighbourly love. The republican conception of freedom starts from the idea of freedom from domination, which may at first glance appear as akin to Spinoza's. But there is a crucial difference here too, in the sense that the republican idea derives freedom from the legitimacy of the state, whereas for Spinoza freedom arises from phronesis, which precedes any form of established authority, as I argued in Chapter 3. Ultimately, both the liberal and the republican conceptions of freedom require a notion of the free will to play a positive role in the definition of liberty, whereas for Spinoza the free will is the negative against which any conception of liberty measures itself.

Instead of a liberal or a republican conception of freedom, Spinoza's conception should be understood in agonistic terms, specifically as opposed to any notion of freedom of the free will that leads to forms of personal authority. In short, for Spinoza, freedom is *freedom from the free will*. The free will and personal authority are intertwined, and the epicurean conception

---

[37] Kant, *Practical Philosophy*, 163. Cf. Adorno, *Negative Dialectics*, 224.

of practical judgement or the calculation of utility is opposed to both insofar as they promote the interests of 'theologians' or anyone who 'promiscuously' choses passages from the Bible to promote their power. This is to say that the notion of freedom Spinoza develops is positioned in such a way as to oppose personal authority.[38] Freedom from the free will contributes to an understanding of our being with others that is agonistically comported against personal authority. Or, differently put, freedom from the free will is an *effect* of the operation of the dialectic of authority and utility.

The second characteristic of freedom that is implied in the freedom to philosophize pertains to the relation between philosophy and faith. Let me quote again the sentence that contains the expression 'freedom to philosophize': 'faith allows to everyone the utmost freedom to philosophize' (164). The intertwinement of faith and philosophy – the fact that they can never 'finally' be separated – is indispensable for this freedom to philosophize. This means that a host of other positions about freedom are rejected here. For instance, Spinoza rejects the Stoic position according to which 'philosophy encompasses the aim of politics'.[39]

So, why is it that faith grants the freedom to philosophize, according to Spinoza, and not the other way round? The answer to this question requires that we start from Spinoza's own pragmatic starting point, namely, that 'virtue is exceedingly rare', whereby the regimes of power customarily rely on authority. If this authority does not seek to further its personal utility but approximates, rather, what I have been calling 'a state of authority', then the fact that faith grants authority means that the freedom to philosophize needs to be granted in the kind of regimes of power that predominate. Even if the multitude is 'fickle', still such a freedom needs to be granted.

Such a freedom needs to be granted, especially, as a right to disobey, or as the necessity of rebellion – to use the language from chapter 14. Differently put, granting the freedom to philosophize is nothing but the recognition on the part of authority that the two paths to the good or virtue transverse each other. The freedom to philosophize, then, indicates the mobilization of the chiasmus between the two paths. If the former sense of the freedom to philosophize – freedom as opposition to personal authority – is dealt with in detail in the first two parts of the *Theological Political Treatise*, the freedom that arises from the chiasmus of the two paths still needs to be tackled in any detail. This will be the main aim of the third part of the *Treatise*, comprising chapters 16 to 20.

---

[38] Cf. del Lucchese, *Conflict, Power, and Multitude in Machiavelli and Spinoza*.
[39] DeBrabander, *Spinoza and the Stoics*, 129.

Thus, in defining faith as neighbourly love or reciprocal utility in chapters 14 and 15, Spinoza can bring together a number of discursive threads that have run through the *Treatise* thus far. These amount to the idea of freedom from the free will, which implies an agonistic comportment against personal authority. At the same time, in the course of determining the freedom to philosophize in terms of the relation between faith and reason, Spinoza points to the idea that is critical for the rest of the *Treatise*, namely, the chiasmus between the two paths that lead to virtue. This implies a different kind of agonism, one that prevents the dialectic of authority and utility from settling in a final telos and which suggests the interminable parallel and ambiguous operation of the state of authority and of natural democracy. It is in the interstices between the agonism against personal authority and the agonism as the articulation of the transversal of the two paths that Spinoza will develop his conception of agonistic democracy.

7

Fear and Power: Natural Right and Authorization in Spinoza and Hobbes (chapter 16)

There is a distinctive change of tone in chapter 16 – the first chapter of the third part of the *Theological Political Treatise*. It is as if Spinoza suddenly becomes more direct, freer and bolder. He notes that 'up to this point our object has been to separate philosophy from theology and to show that the latter allows freedom to philosophise for every individual'. This is the task that is announced as 'finalized' in chapter 14, and yet, as we saw, it is not finalized in the sense that faith and reason are separated; rather they are distinguished yet interminably entangled. This is the conclusion of a trajectory that includes the critique of personal authority in the first part of the *Treatise*, as well as the development in the second part of Reformed authority that is no longer opposed to the calculation of utility. Then, Spinoza explains what he intends to do in this third part: 'It is therefore time to enquire what are the limits of this freedom of thought, and of saying what one thinks, in a well-conducted state.' This part, then, will present the double sense of agonism that pertains to the freedom to philosophize, as we saw in the previous chapter, that is, the agonism against any false sense of meaning that promotes personal authority, and the transversal or chiasmus between the two paths that lead to the good and virtue. The latter, in particular, will be the focus of the third part. Spinoza further indicates how he will accomplish this task: 'To approach this question in an orderly way, we must discuss the basis of the state, and prior to that . . . we must discuss the natural right of the individual' (172). The first concern, then, is natural right.

Spinoza immediately proceeds to define right in terms of power. First, this definition is articulated in terms of nature: 'Nature's right is co-extensive with its power [*jus naturae eo usque se extendere, quo usque ejus potentia se extendit*]' (173/189). And then in terms of individuals: 'the right of the individual is co-extensive with its determinate power [*determinata potentia*]' (173/189). It is passages such as these that give a sense of boldness to chapter

16. For the coextensivity of right and power may give the impression that it is repeating Thrasymachus's argument from the *Republic*, according to which justice consists in the right of the strongest – a position almost unanimously rejected in the philosophical and theological tradition.¹ As Socrates shows, as soon as 'might is right', there is no longer any foundation of just action other than force, which is nothing other than the justification of violence and the pursuit of immorality. Following the standard liberal readings of Spinoza's notion of right as repeating Thrasymachus's position, Steven Smith draws the inevitable conclusion that Spinoza's coextensivity of right and power is 'amoral'.² Differently put, the coextensivity of right and power suggests, according to the liberal interpretation, first, a distinction between natural power or potentia and instituted power or potestas; and, second, the transfer of all right to potestas, which is amoral as it gives absolute licence to potestas to act as it wills.

There is, at the same time, a diametrically different approach to the notion of right in Spinoza, a radical democratic one, according to which the coextensivity of right and power shows the prevailing of potentia over potestas.³ The most original and distinctive exponent of this line of interpretation is Antonio Negri, whose reading of the coextensivity of right and power is carried out in chapter 5 of *The Savage Anomaly*. Departing from the distinction between potentia and potestas, Negri argues that Spinoza's conception of natural right is distinct from the entire political philosophical tradition that includes Hobbes, Rousseau, Kant and Hegel.⁴ The crucial point of differentiation is that Spinoza never reconciles right with the function of the state. Differently put, right is confined exclusively to the function of potentia.

In the liberal reading of Spinoza's right, potentia disappears and the entire political field is abandoned to potestas. In the radical democratic reading, potentia rises over potestas and determines the constitution of the political. It is startling that in fact the liberal and the radical democratic interpretations agree on one critical point, namely, they reject the possibility that there is a persistent relation between potentia and potestas in Spinoza. They are committed instead to separating them by privileging either one or the

---

¹ Plato, *Republic*, 338c.
² Smith, *Spinoza, Literalism, and the Question of Jewish Identity*, 124.
³ For the most perspicacious presentation of the radical democratic reading of Spinoza that is also critical of some of its positions, see Martin Saar's *Die Immanenz der Macht: Politische Theorie nach Spinoza*.
⁴ Negri, *The Savage Anomaly*, 114.

other. And yet, the intertwinement of potentia and potestas is a distinctive feature of the social contract tradition, according to which the people transfer their right to sovereignty thereby *authorizing* it to exercise executive power and to legislate.

There is some justification for the liberal and for the radical democratic readings. The distinctively early modern conception of authorization, so crucial for the conception of representative democracy, is constantly under threat from being understood as promoting 'might is right'. Isn't the authorization of the sovereign ultimately a sanction to act 'above the law' and to use force – in the guise of established institutions, such as the army – to enforce decisions? This threat to the social contract tradition is foremost in the minds of the political philosophers of the seventeenth century, including the most influential of them all, Thomas Hobbes. This explains why for Hobbes potentia and potestas are never completely separated, for if that were the case, the two possible outcomes would have been unpalatable: either potestas prevails in which case 'might is right' triumphs, or potentia predominates whereby 'might is right' disappears as if in a magician's trick.

To explore the conjunction of potentia and potestas in Spinoza's conception of right, I will argue that chapter 16 of the *Treatise* was written with *De Cive* on Spinoza's desk so as refute Hobbes's nodal points of the entanglement of potentia and potestas. Let me be clear: I am not making a biographical or philological point. It does not concern me whether Spinoza actually had *De Cive* on the desk while writing chapter 16 – although we certainly know that he held it in his library. Rather, I am concerned to explore their radically different co-articulations of potentia and potestas by exploring the antitheses of *De Cive* and the *Theological Political Treatise*. This is important philosophically – which is what concerns me – for the transformation of the notion of authority in the contract theory tradition, which understands the sovereign in terms of *authorization*. As Alexandre Matheron demonstrates, what is at stake in Hobbes's and Spinoza's divergent accounts of right is nothing less than the conceptualization of authorization.[5]

Three questions are important for discerning the conjunctions and disjunctions between right and authorization in Spinoza. First, how does the intertwinement of potentia and potestas inform human sociality? Second, how does it contribute to the establishment of the social contract? And, lastly, how does right carve out a space that is incommensurable with sover-

---

[5] Matheron, 'The Theoretical Function of Democracy in Spinoza and Hobbes', in Montag and Stolze (eds), *The New Spinoza*, 206–17.

eignty, thereby avoiding the old problem of power from the *Republic*? I will take these questions in turn.⁶

1. Epicurean Communities: Fear and Utility

There is little doubt that Spinoza was aware of Hobbes's work. Abraham van Berkel, who was a Collegiant friend, published a Dutch translation of the *Leviathan*.⁷ But the influence of *De Cive* on the *Theological Political Treatise* ought to have been more significant because of the publication history.⁸ We know that Spinoza held in his library a copy of *De Cive* that appeared first in Latin, and its second edition was actually published in Amsterdam in 1647. The *Leviathan* was published in English in 1651 but Spinoza did not read English. The Dutch translation of the *Leviathan* was published in 1667 and the Latin edition a year later. But by that time most of the *Theological Political Treatise* would have been written, or at least its argument would have been worked out. There is also textual evidence – in particular the example of the highway robber that I will discuss in the following section – that points to a dialogue between *De Cive* and the *Treatise*.

Hobbes is not mentioned by name in the *Theological Political Treatise*, except in note 33, added after the publication of the book. The most significant reference to Hobbes is Letter 50 to Jelles, dated 2 June 1674, that is, well after the publication of the *Treatise*. In that letter, Spinoza writes that 'the difference between Hobbes and myself ... consists in this, that I always preserve the natural right in its entirety, and I hold that the sovereign power in a State has right over a subject only in proportion to the excess of its power over that of a subject'. That may be true – although I will return to this statement later to show that Spinoza exaggerates the difference – but the letter remains silent on what they might share in common.

In particular, Spinoza remains silent about their common commitment to materialism, or, more accurately, to epicureanism. Hobbes's epicurean kind

---

⁶ This is to situate authorization within the discourse of authority developed by epicureanism, as elaborated throughout the present book. There is a different, narrower use of authorization in discussions of Hobbes. Thus, Zarka argues that authorization is lacking in *De Cive* as the sovereign is pre-existing, while in *Leviathan* the sovereign is authorized, which is to say created, by the people's renunciation of right. See Zarka, *Hobbes and Modern Political Thought*, 45–6. I do not use authorization here in this technical sense.

⁷ See van Bunge, *From Stevin to Spinoza*, chapter 4.

⁸ Hobbes, *On the Citizen*, hereafter abbreviated as C and cited by chapter followed by paragraph number.

of materialism is well documented.⁹ There are biographical details that support this view, such as his association with Gassendi and other materialists at the Cavendish salon in Paris.¹⁰ But neither the physicalist interpretation of epicureanism – its corpuscularianism – nor its sensualism – the hedonistic interpretation of epicureanism – are the most important common ground for Spinoza's and Hobbes's epicureanism. Rather, the critical similarity is that they both place practical judgement understood as the calculation of utility at the centre of their conception of human nature. This propensity of the individual to calculate the 'greater good or the lesser evil' (C 5.1) among its options for action is definitive of human nature, according to Hobbes. That's why there are remarkable similarities to Epicurus's doctrines about justice and the law.

An indication of Hobbes's epicureanism in terms of phronesis is his use of the 'golden rule' from the Sermon on the Mount (Matthew 7:12) to express the idea of utility. 'Do not do to another what you could not have done to you' (C 4.26). I indicate – in the Introduction and elsewhere – the importance of the 'golden rule' for modern epicureanism as it was believed to affirm the epicurean principle about the centrality of utility for understanding human nature. Such use of the 'golden rule' is still made in the mid-nineteenth century by utilitarians, and by Spinoza himself in chapter 16 of the *Theological Political Treatise*, according to which one ought 'to do to no one what they would not want done to themselves, and to defend another's right [*jusque . . . alterius . . . defendere*] as they would their own' (175/192). It is noteworthy that Spinoza articulates the 'golden rule' here in terms of natural right. I will return to this point later.

The distinctive feature of Hobbes's epicurean use of phronesis is that it is explicitly linked to the drive for self-preservation or the conatus. It is this conjunction that is definitive of human nature, according to Hobbes, and which grounds natural right. Thus, we read that 'each man is drawn to desire that which is Good for him and to Avoid what is bad for him, and most of all the greatest of natural evils, which is death; this happens by a real necessity of nature as powerful as that by which a stone falls downward' (C 1.7). There is, on the one hand, the calculation that seeks to maximize the good and to minimize the bad, which is typical of how phronesis is formulated in the seventeenth century; and there is, on the other hand, the conjunction of this formulation with the conatus. Hobbes calls this conjunction of phronesis and the conatus 'the first foundation of natural right' (C 1.7). Natural

---

⁹ Lange, *Geschichte des Materialismus und Kritik seiner Bedeutung in der Gegenwart*.
¹⁰ Wilson, *Epicureanism at the Origins of Modernity*.

law is also defined within the same framework: it is the 'right reasoning' that 'may conduce to his advantage or to other men's loss' and which is concerned with 'the longest possible preservation of life and limb' (C 2.1). This conjunction of phronesis and the conatus makes perfect sense within an epicurean framework. If 'death is nothing to us', as Epicurus and Lucretius put it, that's because there is no afterlife for the spirit, so that when we are dead there is nothing any longer that we can be concerned about. The other side of this principle is that our utility is better served by remaining alive. Bluntly put, there is no utility for us if we die. Nothing much new here, thus far.

Hobbes's distinctive innovation arising from the conjunction of the calculation of utility and the conatus consists in privileging one emotion, fear, in the determination of phronesis. Two notes are important here. First, from antiquity, practical judgement understood as phronesis indicates a combination of emotion and rationality. For instance, this is one of the key points in the discussion about the truth of phronesis as it is presented in Book VI of Aristotle's *Nicomachean Ethics*, and the same holds for Epicurus, as we saw in the Introduction and in Chapter 1. No particular emotion is privileged in this tradition. Privileging fear is Hobbes's innovation. Second, fear is not understood simply as a feeling that arises from an immediate stimulus. Fear is also future directed, which explains why it is linked to rationality. An impressionable image of the use of fear offered at the very beginning of *De Cive* is about fear at night: 'on going to bed, men lock their doors' because they calculate that someone may enter their home threatening their life (C 1.2). Fear includes anticipation because of the operation of phronesis.[11] And the ultimate fear is the fear for one's life – the fear that arises from the operation of the conatus.

We can readily discern the challenge Hobbes poses to Spinoza at this precise point. Not only is fear associated in the epicurean tradition, at least since Lucretius, with the establishment of 'religio' and personal authority – an insight fully shared by Spinoza and developed primarily in the first part of the *Theological Political Treatise*. Moreover, phronesis as the foundation of virtue in the epicurean tradition indicates the co-presence of rationality and emotion without privileging any kind of emotion – as I mention above. This insight is fundamental, for instance, in Spinoza's argument for the two paths to the good or virtue, the path of the emotions that relies on obedience and the path of reason where everyone can render obedience to themselves.

---

[11] Fear is the fear of the worse, as Jacques Derrida – here closely following Hobbes – puts it. Derrida and Borradori, 'Autoimmunity: Real and Symbolic Suicides', in Borradori, *Philosophy in a Time of Terror*, 96–7.

This distinction means that Spinoza cannot privilege any one emotion – the kind of emotions at play are dependent on the specific circumstances that make obedience possible. Thus, Hobbes poses a double challenge: both to the way the epicurean tradition uses fear as a negative emotion leading to superstition and personal authority, and to the construction of instrumental rationality in Spinoza specifically. Hobbes departs from the epicurean definition of human nature in terms of phronesis by introducing a deviation – the privileging of fear – that threatens the epicurean conception of the political, at least in how it is conceived by Spinoza. It is around this challenge that I locate the dialogue between Hobbes's *De Cive* and chapter 16 of the *Theological Political Treatise*.

The deviation introduced by fear results in a profoundly different articulation of sociality in Hobbes and Spinoza. Whereas for Spinoza, as we have seen, our relations to others are determined by the principle 'love your neighbour as yourself', in Hobbes this principle is rendered meaningless if not dangerous. A Hobbesian re-articulation of charity might be: 'if you love yourself and your life – which you should, as this is constitutive of your human nature – then fear your neighbour'.[12] The reason is that in the state of nature – that is, the state wherein the human can express its nature without restrictions – 'man to man is an arrant wolfe'.[13] There is no reciprocity in the calculation of utility, there is only ever personal self-interest. This leads to a war of all against all whose effect is fear for one's life. This existential threat forms the foundation of Hobbes's entire political project.

We can express this difference in terms of right and power. Right (the freedom to act afforded by the absence of law in the state of nature) is coupled with power (the actions one performs depending on one's desires and calculations). By linking right to power, Hobbes leads a materialist charge against the Platonic sources of the understanding of right as indicating a value independent of experience – and in this Spinoza is in

---

[12] Cf. Vardoulakis, *Sovereignty and its Other*, 84–93.

[13] The complete quotation from the famous dedication of *De Cive* is as follows: 'There are two maxims which are surely both true: Man is a God to man, *and* Man is a wolf to Man. The former is true of the relations of citizens with each other, the latter of relations between commonwealths' (C 3–4). Of course, this means that man can be 'god' to man according to Hobbes only under the compulsion of the state. By contrast, the relations between different states, which mirror the state of nature, is the condition of universalized enmity. Without being able to go into an analysis of *Ethics* Part IV here, the point that I am making and which is also clear from chapter 16 is that Spinoza does not accept the distinction that Hobbes draws in the dedication of *De Cive*.

agreement. Their disagreement pertains to the inferences Hobbes draws about human nature and phronesis from the linking of right and power. Whereas Spinoza accepts this link to argue that the other is part of the calculation that one forms, so that – to use the words of the *Ethics* – 'man is a god to man' (*E* IV, P35S), the instrumental rationality that characterizes individuals according to Hobbes is destructive. Thus, whereas for Spinoza the calculation of utility yields a constructive articulation of sociality, the articulation is destructive for Hobbes. In his narrative of the state of nature, Hobbes is adamant that the instrumental rationality characterizing the human leads to a violence that dissolves the social bonds in a war of all against all.

As the distinctive emotion of instrumental rationality, fear plays a positive role in Hobbes's account of the origins of social interaction. This is the first point that Hobbes makes in the opening of chapter 1 of *De Cive*. He articulates this positive function of fear as the absurdity of the principle of neighbourly love: 'if man naturally loved his fellow man, loved him, I mean, as his fellow man, there is no reason why everyone would not love everyone equally'. But this is not the case because in one's relations with others 'everyone is looking for profit not for friendship'. And given that these 'public affairs' rely on pervasive egotism or the pursuit of self-interest, 'a kind of political relationship develops, which holds more mutual fear than love' (C 1.2). There is no community based on love. The idea of a benevolent neighbour is a delusional fiction because the calculation of the individual's personal interest is conducted at the expense of others. Calculations of utility derive from the base instincts of the human that, when left unchecked in the state of nature, lead to pure violence (C 1.11). Therefore, it is not love but 'mutual fear' that characterizes the relation between humans due to how phronesis operates.

The fear generated by everyone's inherent egotism is indispensable not only for Hobbes's anthropology – developed most remarkably in the opening chapters of the *Leviathan* – but also for the foundation of society: 'no one should doubt that, in the absence of fear, men would be more avidly attracted to domination than to society. One must therefore lay it down that the origin of large and lasting societies lay not in mutual human benevolence but in men's mutual fear' (C 1.2). Love as a social virtue and love of neighbour as the basis of law and of command are – 'no one should doubt' – a recipe for conflict between humans. Conversely, it is only fear of the neighbour, or 'mutual fear', that can lead to the preservation of society. Fear marks the origin of society, according to Hobbes. In other words, it is fear that drives humans to the realization that exercising natural right is detrimental to social interaction. If the calculation of utility is prone to violence, it is its primacy emotion, fear, that seeks to rectify this inimical impulse.[14]

The moment fear becomes central, authority is required to manage and regulate that fear in the service of achieving order, peace and stability. This is what instigates the process of authorization, whereby people transfer their right to a sovereign who can transform the fear of the other into the fear of punishment to ensure laws will be followed and people will avoid harming each other. To put this in terms of power, according to Hobbes, potentia without potestas entails pure, unadulterated violence. Because of its inherent violence and the fear that this violence engenders, human capacity or potentia is inextricable from sovereignty or *summa potestas*. Leo Strauss clearly recognizes this point when he writes that 'only *if potentia* and *potestas* essentially belong together, can there be a guaranty of the actualization of the right social order' for Hobbes.[15] 'Mutual fear', or the fear of the neighbour, brings together potentia and potestas so as to lead to the authorization that establishes the political order.

To recapitulate Hobbes's argument, the process of arriving at the commonwealth has three stages, all determined by fear due to the conjunction of phronesis and the conatus. In the state of nature, humans fear for their lives from others; in the social stage they realize that mutual fear can lead to productive interpersonal relations because it curtails the existential threat to one's life; in the political realm, the sovereign is authorized to transfigure the existential fear of death and mutual fear into the fear of punishment as a way of securing the law and the lives of subjects.

We have already seen the emphasis Spinoza puts on neighbourly love. It is not only the fundamental principle of religion, as we learn in the second part of the *Treatise*.[16] In addition, the reciprocity of utility is the origin of sociality, according to the argument in chapter 5 that we examined earlier.[17] I will not repeat all that here. Instead, let us see how Spinoza develops his argument through his exposition of right.

Spinoza differentiates his exposition of right from Hobbes's from the beginning. Hobbes begins *De Cive* with reference to the idea from Aristotle's

---

[14] The centrality of fear in Hobbes's account is well known. For instance, Carl Schmitt and Leo Strauss agree on the importance of fear in Hobbes's philosophy, despite the implicit polemic conducted through their respective books. See Schmitt, *The Leviathan in the State Theory of Thomas Hobbes*; and Strauss, *The Political Philosophy of Hobbes*.

[15] Strauss, *Natural Right and History*, 194.

[16] See, for instance, section 1 of Chapter 5 or section 1 of Chapter 6.

[17] See sections 1 and 2 of Chapter 4.

politics that the human is a political animal. Whereas Aristotle holds that sociality is something natural to the human, Hobbes wants to prove that society is an artificial construct. Nonetheless, starting with Aristotle means that Hobbes's entire account of right is anthropocentric. Fear is human fear. Potentia is human power. Conversely, Spinoza's starting point is antihumanist in the sense that potentia is linked to nature. 'Nature's right is co-extensive with her power. For Nature's power is the very power of God [*Naturae enim potentia est ipsa Dei potentia*], who has the highest right over all things [*summum jus ad omnia*]' (173/189). Individuation or singularity are premised on this antihumanism: 'By the right and established order of Nature [*Per jus et institutum naturae*] I mean simply the rules governing the nature [*regulas naturae*] of every individual thing, according to which we conceive it as naturally determined [*naturaliter determinatum*] to exist and to act in a definite way [*ad certo modo existendum et operandum*]' (173/189).

This antihumanist account is thoroughly materialist and it can lead to violence. According to the first example Spinoza uses to illustrate the coextensivity of right and power, 'fish are determined by nature to swim, and the big ones to eat the smaller ones. Thus it is by the supreme natural right [*summo naturali jure*] that fish inhabit water, and the big ones eat the smaller ones' (173/189). Just as in Hobbes, right is what one can do given the specific circumstances in which one finds oneself in. One's capacity is determined by one's nature – both one's personal nature and in relation to others. And this contains within itself the possibility of violence.

The introduction of the human entails that desire and knowledge intervene in the coextensivity of right and power. 'The natural right of every human is determined not by sound reasoning [*non sana ratione*], but by its desire and its power [*sed cupiditate et potentia*]' (174/190). It is useful to recall here the definition of desire in the *Ethics*. *Cupiditas* is the essence of the human and it consists in the coupling of an appetite with the consciousness of that appetite. In other words, desire as that which delimits the potentia of the human is an emotion or passion – something that the human undergoes, or something that determines the human – accompanied by the rational calculation as to how that determination affects the human. It is not 'sound reason' that operates here, in the sense that it is not reason concerned with adequate ideas. It is rather the practical kind of reason that is concerned with means and ends. This is the notion of phronesis that since Aristotle and Epicurus couples emotions to the calculation of utility – in other words, it is the anthropological principle of Spinoza's third epicurean theme.

Importantly, *cupiditas* or desire does not have a privileged emotion according to Spinoza. The combination of emotion and rationality in the exercise of phronesis can take many forms that are all valid from the perspective of natural right. From that perspective, all emotions are on an equal footing, according to Spinoza. This means that phronesis as the *potentia* of the human's natural right is as such – that is, irrespective of a specific emotional comportment – the necessary and sufficient condition for the formation of society. Human natural right is coextensive with commonality. This is a profoundly empowering gesture. It may not free the human from the violence that is inherent in nature – whence its materialism that avoids all idealization of morality – but it offers the possibility of a reciprocal conception of utility. Let us see how Spinoza describes this sociality.

It may be the case that 'reason can claim no more right than hatred and anger', but still from the perspective of phronesis 'there cannot be any doubt as to how much more it is to the human's utility [*utilius*] to live in accordance with the laws and sure dictates of our reason, which, as we have said, aim only at the true utility of the human [*verum hominum utile*]' (175/191). The reason concerned with utility aims at the human's self-preservation – it is linked to the conatus. This means that phronesis is not a function of each individual on its own. Rather, it is that which brings individuals together: 'in order to achieve a secure and good life, humans had necessarily to unite in one body [*in unum conspirare*]'. (175/191). Unlike Hobbes, for whom the conjunction of phronesis and the conatus leads to fear for one's life, here the conjunction leads to the reciprocity of utility.[18] Spinoza continues: 'They therefore arranged that the unrestricted right naturally possessed by each individual should be held collectively [*collective haberent*], and that this right should no longer be determined by the strength and appetite of the individual, but by the power and will of all together [*ex omnium simul potentia, et voluntate*]' (175/191). The sociality made possible by the reciprocity of utility is the basis of the political – which is the argument that we saw also in the analysis of Proposition 37 from Part IV of the *Ethics* in section 1 of the previous chapter.

The coextensivity of right and power culminates in the imperative that one ought 'to do to no one what they would not want done to themselves, and to defend another's right [*jusque . . . alterius . . . defendere*] as they would their own' (175/192). The first clause articulates the fundamental

---

[18] On the conjunction of power and the conatus, see Cesare Casarino's compelling 'Grammars of Conatus', in Kordela and Vardoulakis (eds), *Spinoza's Authority, Volume 1*, 57–85. I would like to acknowledge the discussions with Joshua Visnjic that have helped me crystallize my thinking on the relation of phronesis and the conatus in Spinoza.

principle of religion or neighbourly love, expressed as the 'golden rule' from the Sermon on the Mount. This familiar epicurean move that highlights the importance of the calculation of utility – a use that Hobbes himself makes, as we saw above – is articulated in the second clause in terms of right. Reciprocal utility extends to the exercise of right. The imperative of natural right, according to Spinoza, is to defend the rights of the other. For Spinoza, unlike Hobbes, we can have common desires that are constructive. These enable the sharing of one's right with others and lead to the imperative to defend the other's right. This sharing – which is strictly impossible in Hobbes because of his privileging of fear – is enough for Spinoza to link natural right to the formation of society.

2. The Robber in the Night: On the Promise

Hobbes's conception of the social contract requires the combination of fear and the promise. Fear needs to combine with promise for the formulation of the social contract. Fear is, according to Hobbes, responsible not only for the relations that we form with others but also for how these relations are instituted in legal and governmental institutions. The material cause that forges the transition from the state of nature through the social bond to the civil state is fear.[19] The Hobbesian account goes as follows: because human nature makes people fear for their lives and because they realize that their utility is served by authorizing a power to guarantee their self-preservation, people transfer their rights to a sovereignty that overseas adherence to the law through the threat of punishment. Thus the social contract transforms the fear for one's life due to the unfettered violence of the neighbour into the fear of punishment from the sovereign. The political sphere is formed through this transformation of fear.

The concept of the promise is critical in this account. In chapter 2 of *De Cive* Hobbes defines the concept of the contract as the act that establishes the political sphere. A contract occurs when 'the trusted party promises to make performance later; and a promise of this kind is called an AGREEMENT [*pactum*]' (C 2.9). The promise is required for the *pactum* – which can signify both agreement in general and the social contract more narrowly. Such a promise can only take place for the agreement to be valid if reasoning about

---

[19] For a fascinating discussion of Hobbes's materialism according to which the contemplation of causality is inadequate for materialism and what is also needed is the thought that arises from known effects – or what I have called earlier the distinction between causality and instrumentality – see Lee, *The Thought of Matter*, chapter 4.

one's advantage or disadvantage is operative: '*Promises* therefore which are made in return for *good* received (such promises too are *agreements*) are signs of will, that is . . . signs of the last act of deliberation by which the liberty not to perform is lost; consequently they are obligatory' (C 2.9). He recapitulates this train of thought as follows: 'Agreements are made only about actions which are susceptible of deliberation; for an agreement requires the will of its maker, and will is the final act of deliberation. *Agreements are therefore only about possible, future things*' (C 2.14). This reference to the future is what makes them a promise. A *pactum* is a specific kind of promise that involves the 'will', that is, the calculation of one's utility. But this is 'the last deliberation' in the sense that in making a *pactum* one promises to *cease* calculating one's utility about the matter agreed upon. To put it in terms of the dialectic that concerns us in the book: a *pactum* according to Hobbes is the calculation of utility to transfer authority or to *authorize* someone else to deliberate on our behalf and the *promise* to obey the person endowed with that authority. The key element is that the promise is realized: 'deliberation' is suspended and obedience occurs. This kind of agreement that realizes the promise is what Hobbes understands as the social contract.

The combination of fear and the promise raises a difficulty that bothers Hobbes. He acknowledges it as an imaginary objection immediately after concluding his description of the agreement or *pactum*: 'The question is often asked whether *agreements* extorted by fear are obligatory or not.' To demonstrate the necessity of the combination of fear and the promise for contractual arrangements, Hobbes uses an extraordinary example. He considers a highway robbery: 'For example, am I obligated if, to save my life, I make an *agreement* with a highway robber to pay him a thousand gold pieces tomorrow, and to do nothing that might result in his arrest and arraignment?' Hobbes's answer is unequivocal: an agreement or *pactum* 'will not be invalid simply because it was motivated by fear' (C 2.16). The conjunction of fear and the promise does not invalidate the agreement. As the example of the robber shows, the calculation to promise money in exchange for one's life relies on the principle of self-preservation. A promise given in fear of one's life is certainly obligatory, according to Hobbes.

Hobbes continues by drawing an analogy between the agreement with the highway robber that combines fear with the promise and the social contract:

> [If agreements through fear were invalid,] this would imply that the *agreements* by which men unite in civil life and make laws are invalid (for one's submission to government by another person is motivated by fear of mutual slaughter); and that one is not acting rationally in putting one's

trust in an agreement with a captive on the price of his ransom. The truth is that agreements are universally valid once the benefit has been accepted, and if the act and the content of the promise are licit. And it is licit to make a promise to ransom my life and to give anything I like of my own to anyone, even to a robber. Thus we are obligated by agreements motivated by fear, unless a civil law forbids it by making what is promised illicit. (C 2.16)

There are two conditions that validate an agreement or *pactum*. First, an agreement is valid if its 'benefit has been accepted'. This is the epicurean idea that an agreement relies on its utility. It also has to be 'licit', meaning that it conforms to the law. Hobbes's frankness is disarming. Given his premises, Hobbes's inference is valid – 'we are obligated by agreements motivated by fear'. But the example itself is unsettling, even horrifying, to law-abiding citizens, since the example presents the sovereign as analogous to a highway robber. The presence of fear essentially indicates that the promise needs to be cashed in. The nature of the authorized party – the robber or the sovereign – is entirely irrelevant to the promise, that is, to the agreement to suspend judgement for certain future actions in exchange for a certain benefit, namely, self-preservation.

In *De Cive*, fear transforms right into a promise effecting the transition to the political. This is only further intensified in the *Leviathan*, where the metonymic personification of the authorized party is no longer the highway robber but rather the mythical monster, the leviathan.[20] The reason that Hobbes employs this mythical monster is, as he explains, its description in the Bible as the 'king of the Proud', that is, as the one who can stand above all others who are only concerned for themselves – and this standing above others is due to its not being subject to fear.[21] Fear defines the position both of the citizen and the sovereign – the former being subject to fear of the law, and the latter being fearless.[22]

We see the figure of 'might is right' rearing it head at this point. Does not this account of the promise suggest the absorption of morality into the political sphere? This same example of the threatening outlaw from *De Cive* has been used to argue not only for the inseparability of morality

---

[20] I should note that the example of the highway robber is repeated in the *Leviathan* but in a much less stark manner. It no longer plays the crucial role it had in *De Cive*. See Hobbes, *Leviathan*, 98.
[21] Hobbes, *Leviathan*, 221.
[22] I deal with this point in detail in my *Sovereignty and its Other*, chapter 3.

from politics but, more emphatically, for the priority of the moral over the political. Benjamin Constant confronts Immanuel Kant with the objection that it is impossible to adhere to the moral duty of his theory, according to which one ought always to be truthful. Constant's example is of an armed outlaw who is knocking on one's door looking for a friend that the outlaw wants to kill. Constant asks Kant whether one still ought to be truthful to such an assassin. Kant responds that one still needs to be truthful, even if the friend is hiding inside, because 'truthfulness is a duty that must be regarded as the basis of all duties to be grounded on contract, the law of which is made uncertain and useless if even the least exception to it is admitted'.[23] Unless a moral imperative precedes and grounds the political, the basis of the political community – the social contract – is undercut. And if being truthful means betraying a friend to an armed outlaw, still that would be the right political action because it adheres to the moral precept of truthfulness and morality precedes and grounds politics.[24] According to this approach, the right of the strongest articulates itself as the authorization to exercise force or violence by disregarding the priority of morality.[25]

Hobbes's epicureanism leads to a different extrapolation of the highway robber. The emphasis in Hobbes is on the *use* of the agreement. There is nothing about 'duty' in the way Hobbes presents the example of the robber. The basis of the agreement is totally different. The utility of the contract – that is, the authorization involved in the promise to preserve one's life – appropriates any sense of morality, whereby, so long as the sovereign – or the robber – respect the agreement to preserve one's life, they remain authorized to legitimately act on its conditions. Moral duty disappears, ceding its place to legal injunction. And yet, there is also a startling similarity between Hobbes and Kant. Despite their divergent accounts of the conditions of an agreement, they still agree that the promise needs to be kept. Whether that's because it enables the use of the contract, or in order to adhere to a moral duty, the connection between the agreement and the promise remains inviolable.

[23] Kant, 'On a Supposed Right to Lie from Philanthropy', in *Practical Philosophy*, 613.
[24] Robert Paul Wolff makes a similar point about the separation of morality and politics, using the example of 'a thief who is holding me at gunpoint'. According to Wolff, the moral imperative is to exercise one's autonomy. Political legitimacy is guaranteed only when authority guarantees the autonomy of the individual. Wolff uses the example of the highway robber to forge the distinction between the moral and political. See Wolff, *In Defence of Anarchism*, 4.
[25] For a more detailed analysis, see Vardoulakis, 'The Freedom to Lie'.

Spinoza challenges this inviolability through his recounting of the example of the highway robber as an analogy for the one who is authorized through the social contract.[26] The difficulty of Spinoza's argument and the reason that it has been so misunderstood is its bare simplicity. Spinoza has no recourse to duty, like Kant, to explain the nature of agreement. Like Hobbes, he follows the epicurean position that emphasizes use. Unlike Hobbes, he has no use of fear as the primary emotion of phronesis leading to the binding nature of the contract. Instead, for Spinoza all that matters is utility. In this, he closely follows Epicurus, who argues that the laws are binding only so long as they are useful.[27] How does that impact on his conception of the promise? *What is Spinoza's promise?* Let us read closely his recounting of the confrontation with the robber.

Spinoza, like Hobbes, starts the discussion of the social contract by pointing to the human's inherent drive to calculate its utility, but he thereby arrives at a different sense of the promise. Spinoza asks what ensures the 'stability and validity' of the 'social contract [*pactum*]' (175/191). He immediately turns to a discussion of the calculation of utility: 'it is a universal law of human nature that nobody rejects what he judges to be good except through hope of a greater good or fear of greater loss, and that no one endures any evil except to avoid a greater evil or to gain a greater good' (175).[28] The ground of the political is the anthropological principle or the third theme of Spinoza's epicureanism. After this, Spinoza introduces the figure of the promise: 'Now from this law [i.e., that the human calculates its utility] it necessarily follows that nobody is going to promise to give up one's unrestricted right unless through deception [*absque dolo*], and in general nobody is going to keep any promises whatsoever, except through fear of a greater evil or hope of a greater good' (176/192).[29] This may appear to be close to Hobbes's idea that the agreement relies on the benefits it confers. But what about the idea of the promise? Does the promise make the agreement or *pactum* obligatory, as is the case in Hobbes?

At this precise point, Spinoza repeats Hobbes's example of the highway robbery in order to address the issue of the promise:

---

[26] Vittorio Morfino correctly argues that Machiavelli is an inspiration for Spinoza's argument. See his *The Spinoza-Machiavelli Encounter*.

[27] See Diogenes Laertius, 'Epicurus', *Lives of Eminent Philosophers*, X.152–3. I discuss this passage in section 1 of the Introduction.

[28] Recall here Hobbes's similar formulation that I quoted earlier. It is common in the seventeenth century to formulate phronesis as the calculation of the better of two good alternatives or the least of two evils. See also *E* IV, P65 and P66.

[29] I examine the notion of 'dolo' in this passage in Vardoulakis, 'The Freedom to Lie'.

> To make the point more clearly understood, suppose that a robber [*latronem*] forces me to promise [*promittam*] to give him my goods at his pleasure. Now, since, as I have already shown, my natural right is determined by power alone, it is quite clear that if it is within my power [*si possum*] to free myself from this robber by deceit [*dolo*], promising him whatever he wants [*quicquid velit, promittendo*], I am permitted [*licere*] by natural right to do so, that is, to pretend to agree to whatever he wants [*dolo scilicet, quicquid velit, pacisci*]. (176/192)

It is not the obligation to keep one's promise that validates the agreement but rather the possibility that the promise will be broken as soon as it is no longer useful. There is no other basis for the social contract other than its utility:

> the validity of an agreement relies on the calculation of its utility [*ratione utilitatis*], without which the agreement has no force [*pactum nullam vim habere*]. (176/192)

And also:

> nobody makes a contract [*contrahit*] or is bound to abide by an agreement [*pactis*], except through hope of some good or apprehension of some evil. If the basis is removed, the agreement annuls itself [*pactum ex sese tollitur*]. (180/196)

Phronesis on its own is the necessary and sufficient condition for the agreement. No special affective condition is required, such as fear, nor the cashing out of the promise in an inviolable obligation to obey.

Not only does this not forget the connection between phronesis and the conatus, it in fact reinforces it and moreover in a way that is critical of Hobbes's necessary connection between fear and the promise. Immediately after the example of the highway robber, Spinoza gives another example:

> Or suppose that in all good faith I have promised somebody [*absque fraude alicui promisisse*] that I will not taste food or any other nourishment for twenty days, and that I later realised that I had made a foolish promise [*stulte promisisse*] which could be kept only with considerable hurt to myself [*nec sine damno maximo promisso stare posse*]. Since by natural right [*ex jure naturali*] I am bound to choose the lesser of two evils, I have the

sovereign right to break faith with the agreement [*possum ergo summo jure fidem talis pacti rumpere*]. (176/192)

According to Hobbes, the agreement or *pactum* requires the combination of fear and the promise to guarantee self-preservation. According to Spinoza, on the contrary, it is because of the concern with self-preservation that the promise can never be secured. If the conditions change, or if we realize that we have made the wrong calculation, the agreement's utility evaporates and we have every right to break our promise so as to preserve our life. It is because of the conatus that 'everyone has the natural right to act deceitfully and is not bound to keep his agreements [*dolo agere potest, nec pactis stare tenetur*] except through hope of greater good or fear of greater evil' (176–7/193).

Just as in the case of the robber in Hobbes's example, Spinoza's own examples are 'particularly relevant in the institution of a state [*in Republica instituenda*]' (176/192). Spinoza's concept of the social contract, then, rests on a minimal condition, namely, the utility of the agreement. And this means that the moment there is no utility, the agreement is no longer useful and we can forego our promise. Spinoza agrees on the indispensability of the promise for the social contract, but the promise is understood here as something that can never be realized. Or – which amounts to the same thing – the condition of the possibility of the promise is that it can be broken. The promise of the social contract consists in its violability.

This is the same argument about utility that we saw Spinoza using in the distinction between the true meaning of Scripture and its actual words (its 'ink and paper'). As we saw when discussing chapter 11, Spinoza argues that when Moses descends from Sinai with the Tablets of the Law and sees the Jewish people venerating the Golden Calf, he smashes the Tablets because they are no longer sacred but 'merely stones', since the actions of the Jews effectively annulled the 'covenant [*pactum*]' (147/161). No fear, no obligation, no duty – and we may add other conditions, for instance, no sanctity, no blood-ties, no holy alliances and so on – is the basis of the *pactum*. The social contract rests *only* on its utility. The simplicity of this thought, the purity of the social and political function of utility, which is derived from Epicurus, makes it hard to discern, perhaps because the entire social contract tradition does not exhibit the same boldness as Spinoza in stripping the *pactum* of any additional conditions other than use.

Thus, I disagree with Antonio Negri, who finds in these references to the social contract in chapter 16 the inherent limitation of the *Theological Political Treatise*, supposedly overcome only in the *Political Treatise* where the social contract is never mentioned.[30] If my interpretation above is correct, a more plausible reason for the disappearance of the social contract from the *Political Treatise* is prudence. After the publication of the *Theological Political Treatise* and the hostile reception it received, Spinoza could have realized that it was too provocative to assume with Hobbes the analogy between the outlaw and the sovereign, and to further add that, by retaining a right to judge, by basing the social contract entirely on the calculation of utility, we are authorized to break our promise. This boldness in Spinoza may explain the apocryphal anecdote about Hobbes's opinion on Spinoza: 'When Spinoza's *Tractatus Theologico-Politicus* first came out, Mr. Edmund Waller sent it to my lord of Devonshire and desired him to send him word what Mr. Hobbes said of it. Mr. H. told his lordship: *Ne judicate ne judicemini* [do not judge so that you are not judged yourself]. He told me he had outthrown him a bar's length, for he durst not write so boldly.'[31]

The boldness of Spinoza's argument consists in the realization that a promise is a promise only if it cannot be absolutely adhered to. Hobbes is correct that an agreement is a promise, which means that it relies on how it determines the will in the future. But he draws the wrong inference from this, namely, that this makes the promise obligatory. Much more pragmatic, Spinoza points out that we cannot know the future. No matter how much we may try, no matter how hard we may calculate, we may later realize that our instrumental rationality erred and that what we promised was wrong. Grounding the *pactum* on phronesis that is a fallible kind of judgement entails that the authorization produced by the agreement is founded on the possibility of *de-authorization*.[32]

The impossibility of realizing one's promise robs – and I am using this verb intentionally – sovereignty of a secure basis. If Hobbes's sovereign is a robber because he robs the citizens of their right or *potentia* to break faith and renege on their promise, Spinoza's promise, by contrast, robs the sovereign of any security, robs potestas of any absoluteness, because it insists that the calculation of utility authorizes the people to break their promise. This promise

---

[30] For instance, Negri insists on the 'disappearance in the [*Political Treatise*] of any reference to the contractarian horizon' as a significant advancement over the *Theological Political Treatise*. Negri, '*Reliqua desiderantur*: A Conjecture for a Definition of the Concept of Democracy in the Final Spinoza', in *Subversive Spinoza*, 30.

[31] Clark (ed.), *Brief Lives, Chiefly of Contemporaries, set down by John Aubrey*, vol. 1, 357. For a detailed examination of Aubrey's statement, see Curley, '"I Durst Not Write So Boldly"', in Bostrenghi (ed.), *Hobbes e Spinoza, Scienza e Politica*, 497–593.

[32] This argument mirrors the argument about the foundation of the law in disobedience, as we saw in section 3 of Chapter 3.

in Spinoza makes the future fragile and unstable – but also it opens up hope and possibility because it refuses to reconcile potentia and potestas. Thus, it may be by natural right that the big fish eats the small fish – as we saw Spinoza reminding us of the violence that is inherent in the natural right. But the irreconcilability of potentia and potestas entailed by the possibility of breaking one's promise also means that it is by natural right that the small fish can judge that, if it is in their utility and within their power to form an alliance to resist the big fish, then they retain the right to do so. Many small fish may eat a big one. Do I need to say any more about the radical potential of Spinoza's conception of the social contract?

Just as Spinoza uses the name 'God' so as to subvert the use of the same name by religion, similarly he uses the name 'pactum' to subvert the idea of the promise that underlies the notion of the social contract.[33] His most subversive political insight is that the promise is violable. Authorization is sanctioned by the possibility of its de-authorization.

3. The Right to Resist or the Fallibility of Judgement? On the Limits of Authorization

To persuasively dispel the suspicion that Hobbes and Spinoza follow the principle that 'might is right', we need to show what limits they set to the power of the sovereign. Let us start with Hobbes. The operation of fear leads to the promise that is part of the agreement authorizing the sovereign to decide on behalf of the people on certain matters. But if there are no limits to the power of the sovereign, then indeed the authorization is nothing other than the assertion of might is right.

Hobbes makes an ingenious move to guard against this possibility. Just as the transformation of fear – from the existential fear for one's life to the fear of punishment when the law is broken – institutes the political sphere, it is also fear that delimits sovereignty. The fear of one's life remains a possibility in an organized political community and grants the subject the right to resist any action of the sovereign that poses an existential threat to it. Differently put, the transformed fear in the commonwealth cannot completely eliminate

---

[33] It is worth recalling here how Althusser describes Spinoza's strategy about the use of the name God: 'he began by taking over the chief stronghold of his adversary, or rather he established himself there as if he were his own adversary, therefore not suspected of being the sworn adversary, and redisposed the theoretical fortress in such a way as to turn it completely around, as one turns around cannons against the fortress's own occupant'. Althusser, 'The Only Materialist Tradition, Part 1: Spinoza', in Montag and Stolze (eds), *The New Spinoza*, 10–11.

the fear in relation to self-preservation that characterizes nature. Conatus remains operative even when the sovereign offers protection. Consequently, if the sovereign does not account for one's self-preservation, then the subject has the right to resist.

Hobbes introduces the right to resist immediately after the example of the highway robber: 'No one is obligated by any *agreement* he may have made not to resist someone who is threatening him with death.' After arguing that agreements based on fear are valid, he turns to the right to resist that delimits the power of sovereignty. What the social contract cannot eliminate is the fear for one's life. This is why 'in the civil state, where the right of life and death and of all corporal punishment are the responsibility of the commonwealth, this very right of killing cannot be allowed to a private person'. Only the sovereign has the prerogative of life and death – or the 'right of killing'. Hobbes continues by underscoring how this right does not invalidate the individual's right to self-preservation: 'Nor need the commonwealth itself require of anyone, as a condition of punishment, an agreement not to resist, but only that no one protect others' (C 2.18). The right of resistance posits a limit to sovereign power. Significantly, this limit passes through the individual, not through others. The individual can protect itself but no one has the right to 'protect others'. Thus, the right to resist is not a political but a personal right, one that does not pertain to the protection of the polity but to the preservation of the individual itself.

The existential fear arising from the threat to the *individual*'s self-preservation entails both the social contract and the right to resist. The sovereign is authorized to protect the community while the individual retains the right to resist. The conjunction of phronesis and the conatus through fear entails that if the contract asks one to agree not to resist, then the contract will take away the basis upon which the contract itself is founded, namely, the calculation of utility: 'an obligation not to resist is an obligation to choose what will seem the greater of two present evils. For certain death is a greater evil than fighting. But it is impossible not to choose the lesser of two evils. Hence by such an agreement we would be obligated to the impossible, and that is contrary to the nature of agreements' (C 2.18). The same point is repeated in the *Leviathan* at the key moment when Hobbes introduces the social contract with the qualification that an agreement is invalid if it threatens one's self-preservation.[34] The confluence of the calculation of utility and the conatus is retained in the political sphere but it is strictly confined to the individual.

---

[34] Hobbes, *Leviathan*, 98.

The self-preservation of the individual introduces the only exception to the authorization of sovereignty. Thus the right to resist is responsible for the concept of the individual in Hobbes. Without that right, there is no notion of self-preservation, and consequently no fear that prompts the establishment of both the social and the political spheres. Even though the right to resist has received a lot of attention in the secondary literature on Hobbes, its importance as I sketch it here rarely comes to the fore.[35] The reason may be the profound influence of the interpretation of Hobbes as a 'possessive individualist', that is, the interpretation that the individual in Hobbes is defined through its calculations to achieve its personal utility.[36] This line of interpretation acknowledges Hobbes's materialism that relies on a conception of the instrumental rationality of the individual, but it is one-sided because it does not acknowledge the intersubjective element.[37] Phronesis in Hobbes is inextricable from natural fear and hence from the right to resist when one's self-preservation is at stake. Thus phronesis can lead to contradictory outcomes: the calculation of utility can create both egotism requiring the strong rule of the sovereign *and* it can also undermine the rule of the sovereign and even invalidate – and that is Hobbes's word – the social contract. The exceptionality of the sovereign – the fact that the sovereign stands above the law – relies on the exceptionality of the individual – on the conatus articulated as the individual's right to resist. The two exceptionalities are part of Hobbes's articulation of a dialectic of authorization and utility that creates sovereignty and individuality as part of the same process. The mutual limitation of the potentia of the individual and the potestas of the sovereign – this synchronized and unified action – structures Hobbes's entire political philosophy. The right to resist essentially means that right is not completely transferred to the sovereign – which is why Hobbes rejects 'might is right'.

Thus Spinoza is actually wrong to ascribe to him in Letter 50 the position

---

[35] For the most thorough account of the right to resist in Hobbes, see Suzanne Sreedhar's *Hobbes on Resistance*.

[36] The classic study here is C. B. MacPherson's *The Political Theory of Possessive Individualism*. I should also note the influence of this interpretation of Hobbes in studies on the relation between Hobbes and Spinoza. For instance, the only limitation of the otherwise excellent study by Aurelia Armstrong is the presupposition of the interpretation about Hobbes's possessive individualism. See Armstrong, 'Natural and Unnatural Communities: Spinoza Beyond Hobbes'.

[37] For a different interpretation of Hobbes's materialism that is acutely aware of the limitation of the interpretation of Hobbes as an individualist, see Frost, *Lessons from a Materialist Thinker*.

that there is a complete transfer of right for the formation of the commonwealth. The individual's right to resist posits the limit to sovereign power. And if we dig a little deeper, we will uncover further similarities. According to their common epicureanism, right is inextricable from the calculation of utility. In *De Cive* Hobbes explains the transference of right in terms of the coordination of the utility of the individual and the people: 'I transfer my right to the people, for your benefit, on condition that you transfer your right to the people for my benefit' (C 7.7). This entails the primacy of democracy in Hobbes, as Alexandre Matheron argues.[38] Precisely this mutual utility allows Spinoza to say that democracy is 'the most natural form [*maxime naturale*] of state [*imperii democratici*]' (179/195). Further, it is on the basis that right belongs to the people in their totality that the other constitutions are defined. Thus, Hobbes defines aristocracy as the election of a body of representatives based on 'the total right of the whole *people*' (C 7.8). This is the move that Spinoza makes in the *Political Treatise* where he defines democracy as the absolute regime of power because the utility of the people is determinative of every regime of power.[39]

The prevarication of Letter 50 is symptomatic not of the erasure of the difference between Spinoza and Hobbes – far from it. Rather, it is symptomatic of a difficulty Spinoza is facing when he defines utility as reciprocal – that is, by deriving obedience from the principle of neighbourly love. The right of resistance is easy for Hobbes to articulate as every *individual* seeking to preserve itself. With Spinoza's move to *transindividuality* – to use the term from the previous chapter – the preservation of one individual as opposed to another can create conflict and the determination of utility as a whole is much harder. To compound this, Spinoza holds, as we have seen, that there are two paths to the attainment of good and virtue. Is self-preservation to be determined according to the imitation of affects characterizing the path of obedience, or according to the rationality of the path of reason? Differently put, because the emphasis in Spinoza shifts away from the individual, he does not have recourse to the right of resistance. This makes it harder for Spinoza than for Hobbes to show the limits of sovereign power. It is symptomatic of this difficulty that Spinoza ascribes a wrong position to Hobbes in Letter 50.

---

[38] Matheron, 'The Theoretical Function of Democracy in Spinoza and Hobbes'.

[39] Thus James Martel is correct to point out a democratic core in Hobbes's thinking that is comparable to Spinoza's. See his *Subverting the Leviathan: Reading Thomas Hobbes as a Radical Democrat*; and 'Hobbes and Spinoza on Scriptural Interpretation, the Hebrew Republic and the Deconstruction of Sovereignty', in Kordela and Vardoulakis (eds), *Spinoza's Authority*, Volume II, 67–100.

Still, the problem remains for Spinoza. How can he – without recourse to the right to resist – delimit the power of potestas so as avoid lapsing into the position that 'might is right'? He needs to find a different way to delimit the authorized sovereign's power. This consists, I hold, in showing how the fallibility of phronesis helps delimit both the people and the sovereign. In other words, Spinoza persists with his minimalist approach of determining the political by defining every significant concept with recourse to phronesis. Let us see how he manages to show the limits of sovereignty using this strategy.

Immediately after introducing the robber example to show the necessity of the violability of the promise in the conjunction of phronesis and the conatus, and inferring from this that 'the validity of an agreement rests on its utility', Spinoza adds that these considerations are 'particularly relevant in considering the constitution of a state [*in Republica instituenda*]' (176/192). Essentially, what is relevant is the use of practical judgement in the polity. How the state is instituted depends on the use of phronesis. The first possibility Spinoza entertains is that 'all humans could be readily induced to be guided by reason alone [*solo ductu rationis*]' (176/192). As he quickly notes, however, 'that is by no means the case' (176). Judgement fails. There may be many reasons for this failure – for instance, when emotional surges cloud the judgement of the people. These are instances where the utility of the people is better served by authorizing someone to judge for them. That's where the figure of the sovereign is important in Spinoza's argument. People can 'transfer some of their individual power [*quantum unusquisque potentiae*]' to the person who holds 'supreme power [*qui summam habet potestatem*] whereby he can compel all by force and coerce them by threat of the supreme penalty, universally feared by all' (177/193). The authorized sovereign has the prerogative of life and death to threaten with punishment those who break the law. The authorized potestas functions as a check on the failed judgements of potentia. *Potestas delimits potentia*.

But the delimitation is mutual: when the sovereign's judgement fails to cater for the utility of the people, they have the right to de-authorize. Spinoza adds immediately after the quotation above: 'This right sovereignty will retain only as long as [*quamdiu*] it has this power of carrying into execution whatever it wills; otherwise its rule will be precarious, and nobody who is stronger will need to obey it unless they so wish' (177/193). Notice the conditional. Spinoza repeats this idea twice more in the next few pages: 'sovereign powers [*summis potestatibus*] possess the right of commanding whatever they will only for as long as [*quamdiu*] they do in fact hold supreme power [*summam habent potestatem*]' (177/194). And: 'This contract will remain in force for as long as [*quamdiu*] its basis – namely, the consideration of danger or utility – persists' (180/196). This repeated qualification – so long as, *quamdiu* – underscores the continuing operation of right in the fact that the people can still calculate their utility even after they promise to transfer their right thereby entering into the social contract. Whereas utility is confined to the fear of the life of the individual in Hobbes, here Spinoza makes it a communal right that checks and delimits the power of the sovereign. The right to resist is thus exponentially expanded. It is now not only the expression of self-preservation as a result of the fear of physical annihilation, but in addition the expression of the ineluctable capacity to calculate utility reciprocally that creates the potential of de-authorization. *Potentia also delimits potestas.*

One may press Spinoza at this point, and insist that he has still not answered the crucial question, namely, what ought to happen when the sovereign acts against the utility of the people. And how is the reciprocity of utility to be calculated? Isn't that Spinoza's problem all along? He concedes that this is a valid question, but it is instructive to note how he frames it:

> We may now be asked, 'What if the sovereign's command contravenes religion and the obedience we have promised to God by express covenant [*Deo expresso pacto promisimus*]? Should we obey the divine or human command [*imperio*]?' As I shall later be dealing with this question in more detail, I shall here make only this brief reply: we must obey God before all things when we have a sure and indubitable [*certam, et indubitatam*] revelation. But in matters of religion humans are especially prone to go astray [*maxime errare solent homines*]. (182/199)

The question about the adherence to the social contract is framed in terms of the incommensurability of the two paths, that of reason and that of obedience. Shall we obey the divine command, that is, our human nature that consists in the exercise of practical reason? Or shall we obey the one authorized to command? This is not a clear choice when the sovereign's command contravenes the fundamental principle of religion, namely, the reciprocity of utility. Unlike in Hobbes, the question is never only about the individual's utility, it is primarily about the reciprocity of utility. But this is framed as the choice between the two paths. Further, this contrast between the two paths is determined by the fallibility of judgement – we are 'prone to go astray'. Spinoza, then, essentially indicates that the framework for answering the question in full is the way in which the two paths transverse each other, but he defers a complete answer, announcing that he will deal with it in the rest of the book. We will see indeed how crucial the figure of the chiasmus of the two paths is for the rest of the *Theological Political Treatise* in the last chapter, and how it addresses specifically Spinoza's reformulation of the right to resist into the authority to abrogate.

It is instructive to return here briefly to Negri's treatment of potentia. In *The Savage Anomaly* Negri rejects the Hobbesian solution of merging potentia within potestas. Instead, the relation between potentia and potestas is presented as an antithesis that has an ontological basis. Spinoza, says Negri, 'poses potentia against potestas'.[40] Notably, this is initially presented as an ontology whose main feature is antagonism. The clearest description of this occurs in chapter 5 of *The Savage Anomaly*, that is, the chapter devoted to the discussion of natural right and power in Spinoza. The phrase Negri uses to describe this antagonistic ontology is 'the horizon of war', which he explains as follows: 'the antagonism among individuals ... maintains its nature at the level of developed sociality ... Natural antagonism constructs the concrete historicity of society.'[41] The more the agonistic element recedes in Negri's writings, correspondingly the relation between potentia and potestas fractures into a mutual exclusion. Thus, in *Insurgencies*, constituent power, as the new name used for potentia, is described in opposition to legalist conceptions of power, in such a way that the 'constitutive strength [of constituent power] never ends up as [constituted] power'.[42] By the time that Negri co-authors *Multitude* with Michael Hardt, not only has potentia or constituent power found a new name – the multitude – but also, and more importantly, antagonism is confined to the social realm, while in the political realm there is the stark separation between the constructive multitude that is against war and capitalism, and potestas that favours war. There is no possibility of a relation between these two powers specifying two political alternatives.[43] This accords with Negri's theory of the two modernities: Machiavelli, Spinoza and Marx stand for potentia, the multitude and hence for democracy, while Hobbes, Rousseau, Kant and Hegel stand for the tradition of potestas or sovereignty.[44] These two political alternatives never meet. They are antithetical to each other, and they are, insists Negri, profoundly incompatible.

---

[40] Negri, *The Savage Anomaly*, 140.
[41] Negri, *The Savage Anomaly*, 112.
[42] Negri, *Insurgencies*, 14.
[43] Hardt and Negri, *Multitude*.
[44] The theory of the two modernities is central in Negri's philosophy. See, for instance, Murphy, *Antonio Negri: Modernity and the Multitude*, 8–18.

Negri remains blind to the positive possibilities contained in obedience because he is blind to the constructive possibilities entailed by the fallibility of judgement. It is this fallibility that both protects Spinoza from the abuse of power contained in 'might is right', and propels the antagonism between the two regimes of power – natural democracy and the state of authority – that can never be completely separated. It is this fallibility that propels the dialectic of authority and utility. Conversely, despite the tremendous insights contained in Negri's engagement with Spinoza, he has a tin ear for any mention of the calculation of utility and the necessity of practical judgement in Spinoza's epicurean materialism.[45]

Let us return to the fallibility of the calculation of utility as the means Spinoza uses to mutually delimit potentia and potestas. This mutual delimitation resulting from the fallibility of judgement registers the operative presence of the dialectic of authority and utility, which is the distinctive feature of Spinoza's epicureanism, as I have argued from the beginning of the book. This is the dialectic that shows how authority and utility both cannot tolerate each other and cannot do without each other. The new element added in chapter 16 is that this dialectic allows for the foregrounding of phronesis as a way of determining democracy – which is named here for the first time. Spinoza is consistent throughout chapter 16 about the centrality of phronesis. His understanding of democracy as the possibility of judgement is a move that makes democracy coterminous with the political field. Thus, Spinoza writes that 'a community's right [*societatis jus*] is called a democracy, which can therefore be defined as a united body of humans [*coetus universus hominum*] that collectively [*collegialiter*] possesses sovereign right over everything within its power [*summum jus ad omnia, quae potest, habet*]' (177/193). This right that is possessed by everyone is designated with the expression *summum jus ad omnia* that recalls the discussion of the right of nature at the beginning of the chapter. This democracy is coterminous with the capacity to judge that characterizes human nature.

This power of democracy holds sovereignty accountable to the extent that, even if the regime is not designated as democratic as such – for instance, it may be a monarchy – still the power to check potestas drives it to the right decisions. This is the reason why, says Spinoza, 'it is exceedingly rare for governments to issue quite unreasonable commands; in their own interest and to retain their rule, it especially behoves them to look to the public good and to conduct all affairs under the guidance of reason' (177–8). In other

---

[45] This is the same deficiency characterizing all the naturalist interpretations of epicureanism, as I explain in section 1 of Chapter 1.

words, it is in the utility of the government in any specific constitutional form – a monarchy, an aristocracy, or a democracy – to act for the utility of the people, because the calculation of that utility gives the people the right to de-authorize those who hold the reins of government. The calculation of phronesis, as that which is common to all, delimits any particular government. But it is the capacity to judge that defines human nature and politically democracy as 'the most natural constitution' (179). Thus, every government has its basis on democracy. Spinoza develops this idea further in the *Political Treatise*, culminating in the designation of democracy as 'absolute' (11.1). Thus, instead of a right to resist, Spinoza keeps on emphasizing the fallibility of practical judgement to discuss democracy in terms of the dialectic of authority and utility.

Spinoza does not stop here. He further complicates the fallibility of judgement. The text presents two different forms of failed judgements, namely, the wrong judgements of the multitude that lead to sovereignty as a positive articulation of potestas, and the various wrong judgements of those who hold potestas that lead to their de-authorization. These are productive failures in the sense that they delimit the power of both the people and the sovereign, and give rise to the democratic. This mutual delimitation is characteristic of the dialectic of authority and utility, and it is not confined to Spinoza's use of this epicurean dialectic. Machiavelli, for instance, claims in an important passage in chapter 2 of the *Discourses* that the perfection of the Roman republic is caused by 'the discord between the people and the Senate'.[46] The famous definition of authority in Cicero's *De Legibus*, which I cited in the Introduction, says that the people have power and the Senate has authority.[47] Within this framework, Machiavelli is referring to the discord between utility and authority as the source of the greatness of the Roman republic. Thus, the epicurean dialectic of authority and utility leads to a conflictual or agonistic politics that Spinoza explicitly associates with democracy – and even though Machiavelli does not explicitly use that word, others have shown how the conflict at the heart of his thought leads to the democratic.[48] Chapter 16 of the *Theological Political Treatise* offers the additional insight that the conflict or agonism is premised on a fallibility of judgement as the motor of the dialectic of authority and utility.[49] And this

---

[46] Machiavelli, *Discourses on the First Decade of Titus Livius*, 200–1.
[47] Cicero, *De Legibus*, 492.
[48] See del Lucchese, *Conflict, Power, and Multitude in Machiavelli and Spinoza*.
[49] I have examined the productive function of fallibility many times – see, for instance, the discussion about the production of authority in Chapter 2.

dialectic is responsible for the chiasmus between the two paths to political virtue – the paths of the emotion and of reason – whereby democracy is also presented as an effect of this fallibility.

Such a fallibility offers no normative criteria for a correct practical judgement. Not only is Spinoza unconcerned with searching for any normative criteria to secure judgement; to the contrary, he reintroduces the figure of the slave that amplifies the fallibility of judgement. Spinoza defines the slave as one who acts without consideration for personal utility. The slave is one who fails to exercise phronesis. In Spinoza's words, a slave is understood in terms of 'the reasons for one's actions [*actionis ratio*]': specifically, 'if the purpose of the action is not to the utility [*utilitas*] of the doer but of him who commands, then the doer is a slave [*servus*], and is unconcerned with his or her utility [*sibi inutilis*]' (178/194). This inability to calculate one's utility, this self-renunciation of the ability to judge, is the apex of the fallibility of judgement, signifying one who is acting for their servitude as if they are acting for their salvation – to recall the formulation of voluntary servitude from the Preface. Here, Spinoza not only does not seek to resolve the issue of how to recognize a correct judgement. To the contrary, he raises the stakes by moving from a potentially failed judgement to the failure to judge altogether. Why does Spinoza need to make this move?

He does not give us an answer but we can reconstruct one. Spinoza rejects the free will in his definition of freedom – as we saw in Chapter 1 and again in Chapter 6. This presents him with the problem of how to motivate action. In the absence of the free will to ground action, and given that personal authority relies on depriving people of their ability to judge, how can an individual be motivated to act in the political realm? More pressingly, what can motivate a community of slaves to rise from their slumber and start calculating their utility?

My contention is that the precariousness of judgement, and in particular its intensification in the image of the voluntary slave, provides one with the existential impulse to act. When one has no security that one's judgements will be correct, one continuously faces an imperative to calculate before one acts. And when one knows that one cannot determine absolutely whether one's ratiocinations are correct, one can only intensify one's efforts. The threat of the slave is the motivating factor for action. The threat of the slave is the material articulation of Spinoza's minimal condition for the political, that is, the operation of phronesis.[50]

---

[50] I should note here that I have only touched on the complexity of the figure of the slave in Spinoza. As Michael Polios has shown me, there is a profound paradox in the figure

Let me summarize Spinoza's response to how the power of sovereignty is delimited by returning to the figure of the promise that is so crucial in his conception of the social contract. The promise to adhere to an agreement can never be fully realized because of the fallibility of judgement. The inability of the people to properly calculate their utility means that it can be useful to authorize someone competent to make decisions on their behalf. Simultaneously, sovereignty's failure to cater for the utility of the community can lead to its de-authorization. We see, then, that the two paths to the good – the path of obedience and the path of reason – responding to the two regimes of power – the state of authority and natural democracy – are co-implicated in this mutual delimitation that prevents Spinoza's argument from lapsing into the position that 'might is right'.

At the same time, the threat that the slave poses is the danger that the polity will be overwhelmed by a personal authority concerned for its own utility. Authority transforms into authoritarianism or despotism. This is a threat to the possibility of judgement and as such to the existence of a political sphere. This threat functions as the motivating factor for action. One exercises one's freedom by seeking to account for this threat.

In these two moves we meet again the two senses of agonism that are imbued in Spinoza's dialectic of authority and utility. They are, first, the tension between the two regimes of power; and, second, the struggle against authoritarianism. What we learn in addition in chapter 16 is that this agonism is constitutive of Spinoza's conception of the social contract. There is no instituted community without this double sense of conflict. Étienne Balibar perfectly captures the centrality of conflict in Spinoza's agonistic politics: 'no body politic can exist without being subject to the latent threat of civil war ("sedition").... This is the cause of causes, which ultimately determines the efficacy of every other cause [in the political].'[51] Thus, the promise of Spinoza – that is, the fact that there is no obligation to adhere to the agreement of the social contract unless it promotes our utility and no promise can be realized because of the fallibility of judgement – is the observe side of Spinoza's agonistic politics.

We see a clear fork in the road at this point. It is the choice between

---

of the slave in the sense that strictly speaking no one in Spinoza's anthropology should be totally unable to form judgements about their utility. See Polios, 'Natural Right and the Failure to Calculate'. I am noting this to indicate that I am not exhausting the import of the figure of the slave in Spinoza's thought. Rather, I am only pointing out its structural position vis-à-vis Spinoza's account of democracy in the *Theological Political Treatise*.

[51] Balibar, *Spinoza and Politics*, 68.

Hobbes and Spinoza. I am using the figure of the fork in the road because while we have seen other positions that differ from Spinoza's — such as those espoused by Arendt, Strauss or Levinas — all start out from different presuppositions. In Hobbes, Spinoza encounters a fellow epicurean in the sense that they both describe the anthropological principle in terms of instrumental rationality. But the calculation of utility spawns a radically different political epicureanism in the two thinkers. For Hobbes, phronesis is motivated by fear, ending up in the authorization of potestas that is only checked by the right of the individual to resist. In Spinoza, the entire political field is determined by the operation of phronesis. The ontological principle that right is co-extensive with power can be translated into the political by saying that right is co-extensive with the operation of phronesis or the calculation of utility. The key here is to discern the importance of the fallibility of phronesis. This prevents the realization of the promise to adhere to the agreement of the social contract and instigates Spinoza's agonistic politics. Thus, even though Spinoza starts from a minimal description of the political as the exercise of phronesis, the agonistic politics that arises is much more complex than the opposition between authorization and the right to resist.

Anyone who seeks to espouse an epicurean position needs to contend with these two alternatives: the conception of the political arising from fear; and the conception of the political as a result of the inherent inability to make the correct judgement. Do our interpersonal relations inscribe a mutual fear? Or are our personal limitations responsible for all sorts of mistakes that our best intentions cannot avoid? One concerned primarily with one's individual utility might be inclined to fear. One attuned to the existential comedy that is life might concentrate on the errors that govern our being.[52] The advantage of the former is that it introduces a 'mass psychology' into the political. The advantage of the latter is that it is more pragmatic as it is based on the inevitability of error in practical judgement, while not precluding the possibility of a psychology built upon this basis. It is its joyfulness and pragmatism that make Spinoza's materialism more appealing.

---

[52] Cf. section 3 of Chapter 3.

8

Theocracy:
On the State of Authority (chapters 17 and 18)

To understand what Spinoza is aiming at as he returns to a discussion of the Hebrew state in chapters 17 and 18, we need to consider the structure of the third part of the *Theological Political Treatise*.

In chapter 16, Spinoza focuses on what I have called (since section 2 of Chapter 4) natural democracy. Immediately after defining democracy as 'the most natural form of state', Spinoza adds: 'For in a democratic state nobody transfers one's natural right to another so completely that thereafter one is not to be consulted; one transfers it to the majority of the entire society [*in majorem totius Societatis*] of which one is part. In this way everyone remains equal, as they were before in a state of nature' (179/195). The democratic state is characterized by the exercise of right in an organized political community. We could express this by saying that in such a society natural right is determinative of civil law. There is an equality of people in such a community. This is identical with the description of what I called natural democracy in Chapter 4. Spinoza then adds the following methodological remark: 'And there is this further reason why I have chosen to discuss at some length only this form of state [*solo imperio*]: thereby my main purpose is best served, which is to discuss the utility of freedom in a commonwealth [*de utilitate libertatis in Republica agere constitueram*]' (179/195). This is the *only* form of state that Spinoza discusses in chapter 16. The examination of natural right or how useful phronesis is to society *only* allows for an examination of democracy.

This methodological observation needs to be situated in terms of the distinction between the two regimes of power that Spinoza identifies in chapter 5 of the *Theological Political Treatise*, namely, natural democracy as the regime that relies on equality, and the state of authority as the regime that relies on obedience. As I explained in Chapter 4, both of these regimes of power require that the people calculate their utility.[1] Further, as we saw Balibar arguing earlier, the good or political virtue can be attained by following either of two distinct paths: the path of reason or the path of the emotions.[2] Differently put, the political community is based either on the fact that everyone participates in the calculation of utility, or on the imitation of the affects that becomes the vehicle for a cohesive community through obedience. Now, if the discussion of natural right as calculation of utility corresponds to the regime of natural democracy and the path of reason, then the Hebrew state is used in chapters 17 and 18 to address the other path and the state of authority. (We will see in the next chapter that the concluding two chapters of the *Treatise* primarily address what I called in Chapter 4 'agonistic democracy', namely, the conflictual relation of natural democracy and the state of authority as a way of articulating the dialectic of authority and utility.)

Thus, the question that Spinoza raises in chapters 17 and 18 is the following: How is it possible to conceive of a well-functioning political community that relies on obedience? Or, differently put, what does a successful state of authority look like? In yet another formulation: How does a society that relies on authority also cater for the utility of the people?

1. Josephus: The Anti-authoritarianism of Theocracy

Spinoza describes the Hebrew state as one in which 'civil law and religion ... were one and the same thing' since the tenets of religion were 'laws and commands' (189). He repeats this point a few lines later – 'there was considered to be no difference whatsoever between civil law and religion' – to indicate that this form of government is called a 'theocracy [*theocratia*]' (189/206). The point seems to be clear: whereas democracy is the approximation of natural right and civil law, the theocracy of the Hebrew state is the coincidence of civil and religious law.

But this distinction is not entirely informative since it does not explain what a theocracy is nor why it is important that Spinoza uses this term to describe the Hebrew state. Let me provide some historical and conceptual background: What is a theocracy? Its compounds are *theos* (God) and *kratos* (power), signifying the rule or sovereignty of God. The word 'kratos' does not signify a transcendent kind of sovereignty, such as the rule of God in 'heaven'. Rather, *kratos* signifies an immanent rule, such as the rule of a sovereign on earth. And what is the purchase of theocracy in the political

---

[1] See sections 1 and 2 of Chapter 4.
[2] See Chapter 6.

debates of early modernity? To answer this question, we need to delve a little deeper.

The word 'theocracy' was coined by Josephus, a first century A.D. Jew who defected to Rome, and who under the protection of the emperor Flavius composed a number of works on Jewish history and culture. The most important are *The Jewish War*, which provides an account of the Jewish revolt against the Romans in 66 to 70 A.D., an event that Josephus witnessed; *Jewish Antiquities*, which expounds on Jewish history and customs all the way from creation to the time of the book's composition; and, *Against Apion*, which adumbrates a defence of Judaism. These works were written in Greek and the first time the originals were made available widely was in 1544, edited by the Dutch humanist Arnoldus Arlenius. Spinoza held copies of Latin translations of Josephus's books in his library. Even though Josephus is named only once in chapters 17 and 18, he is one of the authors most often mentioned in other chapters of the *Treatise*, and Spinoza's account of the Jewish state is heavily influenced by him.[3]

The impact of Josephus and the rise of so-called 'Josephism' in the sixteenth and seventeenth centuries has a number of parameters.[4] These provide a background to chapters 17 and 18, even the basis upon which their argument is constructed. I offer here a schematic typology of the issues that arise through the coining of the neologism 'theocracy' in Josephus insofar as they relate to the description of the Hebrew state as paradigmatic of a state that operates by relying on obedience.

First, Josephus's impact can be discerned in the context of the rise of biblical hermeneutics in the aftermath of the Reformation. To support the principle of *sola Scriptura*, or the authority of the text of the Bible itself as opposed to the personal authority of the Pontiff to interpret the Bible, Protestant theologians start to develop interpretative methodologies. The historical positioning of the biblical text is an important part of this effort. In this context, the discovery of Josephus's texts is hugely important. These books are the only detailed source of the culture, history and customs of

---

[3] Omero Proietti has done a remarkable job in creating a matrix of classical references in Spinoza's work in '"Adulescens luxu perditus": Classici latini nell'opera di Spinoza'. It is a pity that Josephus is not included in this list because he does not strictly qualify as a 'classical' author. It seems to me that the influence of Josephus is just as, if not more, important than the classical authors in the *Theological Political Treatise*. It would be a worthwhile exercise, for instance, to trace the influences of *Jewish Antiquities* on Spinoza's account of the Hebrew state.

[4] On Josephism and Spinoza, see Abolafia, 'Spinoza, Josephism and the Critique of the Hebrew Republic'.

the Jews written by a Jewish eye-witness from the time in which Christ lived and the New Testament was composed, and thus they became in the sixteenth and seventeenth centuries the most important sources for the study of the cultural milieu of the Bible.[5] Anyone interested in interpreting the Bible without deferring to an external ecclesiastic authority had recourse to Josephus's books, which rapidly became indispensable for any revisionist reading of the Bible – which explains Spinoza's possession of these works.

Second, Josephus's writings also had a profound influence on political philosophy from the sixteenth century onward. This is due to the fact that they overturn a dominant orthodoxy in political philosophy since at least the time of Plato and Aristotle. I am referring to the ingrained position that there are three constitutional forms: monarchy, aristocracy and democracy. The distinction between them is quantitative. In monarchy there is one ruler, in aristocracy a few, and in democracy many – a distinction that the Greek names of these constitutional forms clearly describe.[6] A large body of literature develops all through antiquity and the Middle Ages departing from this distinction between three pure constitutional forms, even though it is generally acknowledged that in actuality states have mixed forms of constitution. Nonetheless the distinction between the three pure forms remains the basis of any philosophical or political discussion of constitutional forms.[7] Spinoza's own *Political Treatise* is structured according to this typology, devoting separate sections to monarchy, aristocracy and democracy.

This orthodoxy is further adumbrated in early modernity. The rediscovery of Polybius's *Histories* and their publication in Florence at the end of the fifteenth century has a profound impact on political thought – if proof is needed, one can simply trace the influence of Polybius in the opening chapters of Machiavelli's *Discourses*.[8] According to Book 6 of Polybius's *Histories*, the three constitutions – monarchy, aristocracy and democracy – conform to a natural cycle of mutation. None of them is absolute, but all are liable to decay, ceding their place to one of the others. Polybius expresses this under the concept of *anakyklosis*, the revolution or rotation of constitutions.[9] This provides a dynamic account of the movement between constitutions that also gives political philosophy concerned with constitu-

---

[5] For instance, Josephus refers to Christ as a historical figure of the time.
[6] See for instance Aristotle's *Politics*.
[7] See von Fritz, *The Theory of the Mixed Constitution in Antiquity*.
[8] Cf. del Lucchese, *Conflict, Power, and Multitude in Machiavelli and Spinoza*, 67–8.
[9] Polybius, *The Histories*.

tional forms the opportunity to develop a historical account explaining the transmutation of political regimes.[10]

Josephus acknowledges this tradition when he writes that 'some peoples have entrusted the supreme political power to monarchies, others to oligarchies, yet others to the masses'. But he immediately adds: 'Our lawgiver, however, was attracted by none of these forms of polity, but gave to his constitution the form of what – if a forced expression be permitted – may be termed a "theocracy," placing all sovereignty and authority in the hands of God.'[11] It is this sentence that for the first time introduces the word theocracy. Josephus constructs his neologism by echoing other similar compounds like democracy and aristocracy. But there is a significant difference from the other constitutions identified by classical Greek political thought, namely, that in the Hebrew state God himself is the sovereignty. This idea breaks the shackles of the orthodoxy about the three pure constitutional forms and has a liberating effect on political philosophy.

Third, Josephus's designation of theocracy makes the Hebrew republic into a special case of a political regime that was unique and unrepeatable, thereby elevating it to a significant example in political philosophy. During the sixteenth and seventeenth centuries, philosophers consistently refer to the Hebrew state as a way of displacing politically sensitive discussions to a relatively neutral territory – to an example situated in a remote past and beyond reproach as it is a polity of divine rule. This is the case, for instance, with the use of the Hebrew state in Grotius's *De republica emendanda*, where it is compared it to the Dutch republic. In general, the Hebrew republic becomes a consistent point of reference or an important example for all significant political philosophers of the seventeenth century, including Hobbes and Locke. The key in this tradition is that political points can be made about the theocracy of the Hebrew state that have a direct relevance to contemporary politics, but which cannot be raised explicitly without fear of offending the theological or political authorities. The Hebrew state offers protection precisely because it is a theocracy – a state whose sovereign is God.

The *Theological Political Treatise* participates in this tradition of using the Hebrew state as an example. The Hebrew state is – in the schema I outlined above – Spinoza's paradigmatic state that relies on obedience and the path

---

[10] It is interesting to consider here the similarities between the biological metaphors of *anakyklosis* in Polybius and auto-immunity in Derrida. See Vardoulakis, 'Autoimmunities: Derrida, Democracy and Political Theology'.

[11] Josephus, *Against Apion*, II.164–5.

of the emotions leading to virtue. At the same time, it is noteworthy that the last thing Spinoza mentions before he concludes his discussion of the Hebrew state at the end of chapter 18 is a comparison with the Dutch republic. This is an important reference for an additional aspect of the use of Josephus and the revival of interest in the Hebrew state. Spinoza writes:

> As for the Estates of Holland, as far as we know they never had kings, but counts, to whom the right of sovereignty was never transferred. . . . They have always reserved to themselves the authority to remind the said counts of their duty, and have retained the power to uphold this authority of theirs and the freedom of the citizens, to assert their rights against the counts if the latter proved tyrannical, and to keep them on such a tight rein that they could do nothing without the permission and approval of the Estates. From this it follows that sovereign right was always vested in the Estates, and it was this sovereignty that the last count [i.e. the King of Spain] attempted to usurp. Therefore it is by no means true that the Estates revolted against him, when in fact they recovered their original sovereignty which had almost been lost. (210–11)

The Hebrew state is compared here with the founding story of the Dutch republic. The estates of Holland, just like the Hebrew theocracy, never had mortal kings, which provided a legitimation for their opposition to Spanish rule. There is an anti-monarchical and anti-authoritarian thrust here.

Fourth, this anti-authoritarian use of the Hebrew state develops in the sixteenth and seventeenth centuries. As Eric Nelson has recently shown, republican authors who were concerned to argue for freedom from coercion, and hence were anti-monarchists, used the idea of theocracy to argue against monarchy.[12] Of particular importance to their argument was the interpretation of 1 Samuel 8 in Josephus as well as in biblical commentaries in Hebrew, according to which God was the sovereign of the Hebrew republic until the people asked Samuel for a mortal sovereign, just as any other nation (1 Sam. 8.5). In other words, they did not wish to have God as their sovereign any longer. Samuel, as the high priest, consults with God, who responds by enumerating the evils that a mortal king will bring upon the Hebrews: a king will exploit their sons and daughters (1 Samuel 8.11–13), and he will take ownership of the land, the slaves and stock (1 Samuel 8.14–17). The inference drawn by the republicans was that this response positions monarchy as equivalent to the sin of idolatry – since ultimately

---

[12] Nelson, *The Hebrew Republic*, chapter 1.

God will abandon the state with a mortal sovereign (1 Samuel 8.18). We will see how the entire discussion of the Hebrew state is premised on the distinction between a state of authority that caters for the utility of the people, and tyranny as a form of authoritarianism that is only ever detrimental. This strong anti-authoritarian thrust derived from the tradition is critical to Spinoza's determination of theocracy and the Hebrew state as paradigmatic of how the path of the emotions can achieve the good and virtue.

Five, there is an additional element that plays a critical role in Spinoza's argument. When Josephus's idea of theocracy as the state whose sovereign is God is combined with the anti-monarchical interpretation of 1 Samuel 8, we arrive at the idea that there is a primary constitutional form – or a form of the constitution – that is characterized by the freedom of the individual citizens. Nelson refers to this idea as 'republican exclusivism', which for him ultimately testifies to the rise of the idea of liberal democracy as the most perfect constitution. Nelson argues that 'exclusivism' became an 'alternative' to the idea that there are only three pure constitutional forms – monarchy, aristocracy and democracy – and it 'became a powerful force by the end of the seventeenth century and ultimately emerged victorious in the West after the great eighteenth-century revolutions'.[13] I do not want to comment here on the historical dimension of this argument that side-lines historical complexities – for instance, how do the revolutionary movements of the nineteenth century or the anticolonial struggles fit in this picture? And it will certainly be difficult to make Spinoza's account fit this overarching historical narrative.[14] In any case, the idea of a form of the constitution in Spinoza is incommensurable with Nelson's description of exclusivism.

Spinoza determines the form of the constitution within his epicurean framework. The idea of a connection between the Hebrew state, theocracy and a primary constitution that provides the form of different constitutions without being reducible to any one of them proves pivotal in Spinoza's argument. Immediately after introducing the term 'theocracy' (189/206), Spinoza comments that 'the Hebrews retained their sovereign right completely.... Since the Hebrews did not transfer their right to any other man, but, as in a democracy [*ut in democratia*], they all surrendered their right on equal terms ... this covenant [i.e. the theocracy] left everyone completely equal

---

[13] Nelson, *The Hebrew Republic*, 53.
[14] Nelson does refer to Spinoza in his book, but in another chapter, in relation to the question of toleration, and then only briefly and – one senses – that he is uncomfortable in his use of Spinoza, which does not fit neatly into his narrative. But Nelson does not mention Spinoza at all in connection to what he calls 'republican exclusivism'.

[*hoc pacto aequales prorsus mansisse*]' (190/206). The basis of both natural democracy and of the state of authority is the same, namely, an equality that is premised not on legal norms, but on the retention on one's natural right – that is, the retention of one's power and the ability to calculate one's utility. Differently put, the substratum that underlies any constitutional arrangement is the operation of the dialectic of authority and utility. I will return to this idea later, as it plays a critical role in the last two chapters of the *Theological Political Treatise*.

To recapitulate, we can discern five distinct uses of theocracy as it enters the vocabulary of thought in the sixteenth century and further develops in the following century. First, the discovery of Josephus's works contributes to the development of biblical hermeneutics by becoming the source of the cultural context of the New Testament as well as the historical narrative of the Hebrew state. Second, the Hebrew state becomes a favoured example in political philosophy to challenge and complicate the doctrine of the three constitutions. Third, as a consequence of the previous point, political philosophers can use the Hebrew state as a foil to talk about their present political predicament. Fourth, the growing anti-monarchical movement utilizes the Hebrew republic and specifically the references to the disastrous decision by the Jews to ask for a mortal king in 1 Samuel 8. And, fifth, there is a form of the constitution that underlies both natural democracy and the state of authority – that is, both the path of reason and the path of the emotions leading to the good and virtue – that consists in the operation of the dialectic of authority and utility. These five points provide the context of theocracy within which we can read Spinoza's description of the Hebrew state as a state of authority that relies on obedience.

2. Between Tyranny and Revolution: The Limits of the State of Authority

To indicate the transition to a different but related topic – that is, from the analysis of natural democracy in terms of natural right to the examination of the state of authority as it relies on obedience – Spinoza introduces his theme in chapter 17 by using language echoing that of chapter 16. Earlier natural right is determined by how far it extends in relation to power. Here, as Spinoza puts it, he is concerned with 'a proper understanding of how far extends the state's right and power [*imperii jus et potestas se extendat*]' (185/201). Thus, the conversation shifts from the limits of right to the limits of the state or *imperium*.

As I noted earlier, the state of authority is characterized by the exercise of obedience. What is absent in chapters 17 and 18, however, is the determination of obedience in terms of its genetic relation to authority. As I explained in Chapter 2, Spinoza is concerned at the beginning of the *Theological Political Treatise* to ask whether it is authority that leads to obedience – which is the theological conception of the genesis of authority – or whether it is instead obedience that causes authority – which is the political conception of authority. As I explain there, Moses is the paradigmatic figure of authority because he combines both the theological and the political. His authority is theological because he receives the Tablets of the Law through revelation, and it is also political as he is the founder of the Hebrew state. This concern from the first part of the *Treatise* – namely, whether authority causes obedience or vice versa – is absent in the third part, when Spinoza returns to the historical presentation of the Hebrew state as a way of describing its political constitution. The reason is that the coincidence of religious and civil law – the definitive feature of the Hebrew state as I noted in the previous section – provides a framework that escapes the genetic question. For the Hebrew theocracy, just as for the figure of Moses, the theological and the political are intertwined, which means that neither is privileged over the other, and as soon as civil and religious law are the same it does not even make sense to raise the question as to whether authority or obedience comes first.

So if the question of obedience is no longer framed in the way it was in the earlier part of the *Treatise*, then how are we to approach the presentation of the state of authority? How is the function of obedience framed within the Hebrew state as paradigmatic of the path of the emotions that lead to virtue and of the state of authority? To grasp the way Spinoza proceeds we need to take literally the way he frames the question at the beginning of chapter 17. The question is, as I say above, about the limits of the state; it is about how far the power of the state extends.

Spinoza returns to the same question to refine it further at a critical point of his argumentation. Having argued that the Hebrew state is a theocracy in the sense that it combines civil and religious law (189), he returns to its theocratic nature when he considers whether it remains a theocracy after the death of Moses (194–5). Spinoza insists that it does remain a theocracy but with a difference. Whereas Moses encompasses both theological and political authority, his succession planning consists in fracturing the theological and the political. Theological authority resides only with the priests taken from a single tribe, the Levites – a crucial point that I will return to in the next section – whereas political authority is divided between the captains of each tribe that is allocated a specific land.

Within the context of the discussion of these arrangements about the distribution of authority after Moses's death, Spinoza determines the limits of the Hebrew state according to 'how far a constitution framed on these lines [i.e. the theocracy of the Hebrew state after Moses's death] was able to exercise control over the minds of subjects and *to so restrain both rulers and ruled* that neither would the latter rebel nor the former become tyrants' (195, emphasis added). This provides the new frame for the question of obedience. It consists in the mutual delimitation of rulers and ruled. The delimitation of the power of the state in terms of the mutual limitation between rulers and ruled suggests that, when the state instils obedience by exercising control over the subjects' minds, then it is possible to avoid two perils: the danger that the people will revolt if they come to the conclusion that their interests are no longer served by the sovereign; and the danger that if the state gathers too much authority in its hands it will turn authoritarian and establish a tyranny. The limits of the state are established to avoid these two perils – both ingrained in the possibility of a state based on obedience.

This idea of a mutual delimitation between rulers and rules is not unique to Spinoza. As Stathis Gourgouris argues, the mutual delimitation of ruler and ruled, or *archon* and *archomenos*, is critical for Aristotle and is clearly stated in his *Politics*.[15] But from this we do not need to conclude, following Gourgouris, that such a mutual delimitation leads to an anarchic politics. To the contrary, as I have explained above, the thrust of the complex relation between rulers and ruled presented by Spinoza is to frame the question of obedience in such a way that its origins are untethered from personal authority. This does not obviate the need for obedience, and it does not lead to an anarchic position. Rather, it establishes a framework within which it becomes possible to subject authority to the scrutiny of practical judgement – which is to say, it becomes possible to be critical of authority. This is the reason why Spinoza suggests, as I will explain, a distinction between the state of authority and what I will call authoritarianism.

We have encountered this idea already. For instance, as I have noted several times since Chapter 4 when introducing the idea of the state of authority, a state based on obedience does not exclude the possibility of the calculation of utility. To the contrary, the calculation of utility is foundational for such a state based on obedience – a point that Spinoza makes very clearly in chapter 17 too, as we will see later. If we combine this insight with Spinoza's persistent position that utility is reciprocal, this leads to an idea

---

[15] Gourgouris, 'Arche', in Bernstein, Ophir and Stoler (eds), *Political Concepts: A Critical Lexicon*, 5–24.

that should be familiar by now: that the sovereign has no absolute power but is rather subject to the judgements of the people. The sovereign needs to include in its considerations, at the very minimum, how its decisions will be received by the people. Thus, the delimitation of the state in terms of the mutual delimitation of rulers and ruled is premised on the operative presence of phronesis or instrumental rationality.

The mutual delimitation of rulers and ruled within the Hebrew state as the exemplary state of authority that relies on obedience articulates into a series of complex and interconnected concerns in chapter 17. These are often particularly resonant with concerns in contemporary political philosophy. I identify here four such concerns:

First, Spinoza's epicurean dialectic of authority and utility can only operate if – as we saw in the previous chapter – the calculation of utility forms the basis of the social contract. Thus, Spinoza insists that the pivotal characteristic of the Hebrew state that mediated the relation between rulers and ruled is that the state catered for the utility of the people:

> there was another feature of this state, peculiar to it and of indisputable weight [*solidissimum*], which must have been most effective in deterring citizens from contemplating defection and from ever wanting to desert their country, to wit, the calculation of utility [*ratio utilitatis*], the strength and life of all human action [*quae omnium humanarum actionum robur et vita est*]. This, I say, was a feature peculiar to this state [*in hoc imperio singularis*]. Nowhere else did citizens have a stronger right to their possessions than did the subjects of this state, who had an equal share with the captain in lands and fields, and were each the owners of their share in perpetuity. For if any man was compelled by poverty to sell his farm or field, it had to be restored to him when the jubilee came round, and there were other similar enactments to prevent the alienation of real estate. Then again, nowhere could poverty have been lighter to endure than there, where charity to one's neighbor [*charitas erga proximum*], that is, to one's fellow citizen, was a duty to be practiced with the utmost piety so as to gain the favour of God, their king [*Deum suum Regem*]. (198–9/215–16)

Of utmost significance (*solidissimum*) for the Hebrew state, according to Spinoza, is the cultivation of the calculation of the utility (*ratio utilitatis*) for the people. The most obvious point here is that the path of authority is not separated from phronesis. This is a point I drew attention to in Chapter 4, when discussing the distinction between natural democracy and the state of authority in chapter 5 of the *Theological Political Treatise* (63–4). Thus, there is no authority on its own. Authority and utility are intertwined and inseparable. They are in a dialectical relation.

The utility of the state for the Hebrews takes two specific forms, according to Spinoza. The first is an instituted equality of land ownership. The Hebrew state did not suffer a complicated land redistribution, like Athens in the time of Solon, or the pain of trying to implement agrarian laws, like the Roman republic. Rather, the equality of land was instituted from the moment of the state's foundation. This entailed that all the citizens saw value in the state. In addition, the religious command to love one's neighbour as oneself was inscribed in the theocratic state's laws. As such, the utility enacted within the Hebrew state was not self-centred interest but rather reciprocal utility, whereby the citizens recognized the value of their fellow citizens for their own personal utility. These two facets of utility make the Hebrew state unique (*imperio singularis*), according to Spinoza.

Second, the state of obedience presents an inchoate materialist theory of ideology as the primary means of the exercise of its power. Chapter 17 opens with the assertion that no individual can completely give up their right because a sovereign cannot 'command [*imperaret*]' a subject to act contrary to its emotions – one cannot be commanded to love something they hate or to hate something they love (185/201). In other words, the path of the emotions does not imply unconditional obedience. Authority is not absolute. Spinoza articulates this idea through a qualitative distinction. He writes that the power of the state is 'not strictly confined to its power of coercion by fear, but rests on all the possible means by which it can induce men to obey its commands. It is not the rationale for obeying, but obedience that makes the subject [*non enim ratio obtemperandi, sed obtemperantia subditum facit*]' (185/201–2). Obedience is not concerned with why people obey – which includes the question of whether they obey through fear, which is Hobbes's argument, as we saw in the previous chapter. They in fact may have totally wrong motives or reasons for obeying. The key to a well-functioning authority is to avoid demanding obedience through threats that instil fear. In a passage that recalls Machiavelli, Spinoza further specifies that the reasons for obedience are secondary if not irrelevant – they can be, says Spinoza almost flippantly, 'fear of punishment, hope of reward, love of country or any other emotion [*affectu*]' (186/202). All that matters are the effects that follow from the obedience.

It is not hard to discern here a theory of ideology *in nuce*: 'From the fact, then, that a man acts from his own decision, we should not forthwith conclude that his action proceeds from his own right, and not from the right of the government [*ex suo, et non imperii jure*].' The reason is that 'obedience is not so much a matter of outward action as of the internal acts of the mind [*obedientia non tam externam, quam animi internam actionem*]'. And this means that 'whoever reigns over the subjects' minds holds the most powerful dominion [*maximum tenere imperium*]' (186/202). We see here the appeal that Spinoza exercised on theorists of ideology in the twentieth century, starting with Althusser and many thinkers subsequently.[16] Ideology is the reproduction of the existing network of power without the need for physical coercion, simply through the control of the minds of the subject.

We see at this point the radical materialism that characterizes Spinoza's philosophy. The subject cannot rise above the given circumstances to assert a 'free will' that liberates it from materiality. Nor can the rulers assert their power arbitrarily, through their own sovereign decisions. Both ruled and rulers are dependent on the fact of obedience. Differently put, what matters is not the intentions of the political actors but the effects of their actions. These effects enable the maximum obedience when people are not coerced through violent means but when their minds are controlled, which is to say, when they believe that they are exercising their free will whereas in fact their actions conform to what those in authority want them to do. That's why, Foucault insists, the free will is a key pillar of neoliberalism.[17] There is no more effective tool for the implementation of obedience than the illusion of the free will.[18]

This suggests that for identifying the limits of the political – the imperative to avoid both rebellion and tyranny – it is crucial to avoid a voluntaristic account of action. Let me underscore this point, as it suggests also a difference from theories of ideology such as Althusser's or theories of power such as Foucault's. Spinoza's dialectic of authority and utility does not reject authority as such. Rather, it draws a distinction between authority and authoritarianism. If authority can instil obedience that can contribute to the well-being of the subjects, authoritarianism seeks to use the subjects' free will to turn them into voluntary slaves so as to 'pursue their servitude as if they are striving for their salvation'. The contrast between these two possibilities for authority becomes a motivating factor for action, as I explain at the end of the previous chapter. At the same time, it is precisely this distinction between authority and authoritarianism that is missing in Althusser and Foucault. Concepts such as the 'system' supported by ideology

---

[16] See Estop, 'Beyond Legitimacy: The State as an Imaginary Entity in Spinoza's Political Ontology', in Kordela and Vardoulakis (eds), *Spinoza's Authority*, Volume 1, 87–111.

[17] See Foucault, *The Birth of Biopolitics*.

[18] For an analysis of Spinoza's critique of the free will, see Chapters 1 and 6.

or power incorporate both senses of authority. The effect of this is that neither Althusser nor Foucault have recourse to the dialectic of authority and utility. And without a concept of practical judgement and instrumentality they find it difficult to conceptualize a democratic politics.

This materialist presentation of ideology does not lapse into a functionalism according to which we are simply trapped within the apparatuses of power. Spinoza does not consider such an idea in chapter 17. Instead the framework is still provided by the relation of rulers and ruled, which leads to the following problematic: it is unclear what the means for effecting obedience are if 'both rulers and ruled, are but human, and as such certainly prone to forsake labor for pleasure [*omnes namque tam qui regunt, quam qui reguntur, homines sunt ex labore scilicet proclives ad libidinem*]' (187/203). It is important that the question of obedience is not confined to the people but extends to the rulers too. Humans – both rulers and ruled – fall victim to bad judgements because they are swayed by their emotions. Thus, the 'fact of obedience' is always a negotiation between rulers and ruled, to the point that the control of the people's minds is only possible if the desires of the people also dictate the desires and decisions of the rulers. Obedience indicates a reciprocal influence between authority and its subjects.

At the same time, the significance – even necessity – for the path of the emotions and the state of authority is indicated by the fact that the 'fickle disposition of the multitude [*tantum varium multitudinis ingenium*]' drives those who consider politics to 'despair' (187/203). The people are swayed by this or that emotion and they forget to calmly calculate their utility. It is this fact that makes the state of authority necessary. But recognizing the problem is not the same as fixing it. A solution to the conundrum of how to make the fickle multitude obey – 'this is the task, this the toil [*hoc opus, hic labor*]' (187/203), says Spinoza.[19]

It is noteworthy what Spinoza suggests has been taken as the solution to this problem historically: 'kings who in ancient times seized power, tried to persuade men that they were descended from the immortal Gods [*se genus suum a Diis immortalibus*], thinking that if only their subjects and all men should regard them not as their equals but should believe them to be Gods, they would willingly suffer their rule and would readily obey' (188/204). Political authority is insufficient on its own. Authority also requires the support of the theological – be that through ancestry or through revelation. This was the ploy, for instance, that Alexander the Great employed, claiming that he was the son of Jupiter. Considering an episode from Curtius, Spinoza

---

[19] This expression is a quotation from Virgil's *Aeneid* (6:129).

notes Alexander's response when his blood ties to Jupiter were challenged by Hermolaus. Alexander responded that 'public opinion [*fama*] is an important factor, and a false belief has often done duty for truth [*quod falso creditum est, veri vicem obtinuit*]' (188/204). Alexander is aware here that it is not the motives of obedience that matter but rather the fact of obedience itself. Further, he is aware that for obedience to be effective, authority requires both a political and a theological origin. In other words, authority and the obedience it generates can contribute to the utility of the community, and to effect this it is perfectly legitimate to use any means at one's disposal to strengthen authority, which means to construct it as theologico-political.

It should come as no surprise that Spinoza insists on the theologico-political support for a figure of authority. I have drawn attention to this point already in the Introduction, and I have also shown its importance for the adumbration of prophecy as well as the figure of Moses in Chapter 2, where I indicated that Moses was the paradigmatic figure of the theologico-political authority in the sixteenth and seventeenth centuries, as he received the law – the Decalogue – through revelation while he was also the Hebrew state's founder. I also explained how the production of theologico-political authority in the first few chapters of the *Theological Political Treatise* is determined through error – for instance, by the people's mistaken belief that the prophets are somehow superior because the people mistake prophecy as a superior form of knowledge because it is rare, whereas in fact it is a species of natural knowledge which is common to everyone. These errors, however, can be perfectly useful, such as when they contribute to the establishment of the Hebrew state. Thus, as I noted in the Introduction, one of the ways in which the dialectic of authority and utility articulates is through the recognition that on certain occasions it is to the utility of the community to suspend the calculation of utility and to submit to authority.

Such a positive unfolding of the dialectic of authority and utility is familiar, but what surprises is the rhetoric at this point. The chapter concerns the Hebrew state and its founder, Moses, the exemplar of theologico-political authority throughout the *Treatise*. But Spinoza does not turn to Moses to determine the theologico-political origin of authority. Rather he turns to Alexander, which allows him to show the importance of the effects of obedience *irrespective* of the veracity of the belief in the theological origin of authority. Thus, Spinoza may be suggesting here that, just like Alexander, it little matters whether Moses did actually receive his theological authority through revelation. From the perspective of authority and the obedience it inculcates, all that matters is the public perception (*fama*) of its theological provenance. To put it in the vocabulary from Machiavelli, what matters for authority is not its veracity but its effective truth. Authority's utility is registered in its effects.

Third, clearly, this ideological dimension is insufficient to guarantee that there is no rebellion of the ruled. What is needed in addition is an account of how such a theocracy achieves social and political cohesion. This steers Spinoza's argument about the theocratic coincidence of religious and civil law in a direction that resonates with contemporary accounts of biopolitics.

After insisting that the Hebrew state served the utility of the people, Spinoza offers the following remark: 'Thus the Hebrew citizens could enjoy a good life [*bene esse poterat*] only in their own country; abroad they could expect only hurt and humiliation' (199/216). There are various elements to this attachment to the Hebrew state enjoyed by its citizens, but they all point to its usefulness 'in avoiding civil war' (199). The most significant reason for this is that in such a theocracy civil and religious laws overlap. As such, the law spreads into every aspect of living. The positive side is that people feel that their utility is fulfilled by the state. The other side is that they can only achieve this utility within the Hebrew state and by adherence to the state religion. Thus 'one who forsook his religion ceased to be a citizen [*civis*] and by that alone became an enemy [*hostis*]' (189/206). This attachment to a land and a religious way of life identical with civil life was the reason why the Hebrews enjoyed 'an ardent patriotism' that was 'fostered by their daily rituals' determined by law (197). The well-being they enjoyed as a result of following all these laws meant that 'their life was one long habituation in obedience [*vita continuus obedientiae cultus*]', but because of the benefits they derived, 'obedience must have appeared no longer as bondage, but freedom [*non amplius servitus, sed libertas*]' (199/216). Thus, in the Hebrew state, theocracy creates the conditions of a happy life by an expanded system of laws and regulations that dictate every aspect of living. In this path of the emotions, rebellion is prevented by regulating emotion to such an extent that the people's desire is free only to the extent that it coincides with obedience – that is, their desire is sublimated in the theologico-political law of the state.

The effects of this coincidence of desire with the law that is both religious and civil are multifarious. For instance, it determines citizenship of the Hebrew state, both in terms of the movements of the citizens themselves, but also in relation to what is not acceptable as a legitimate punishment for those who disobey the law. The coincidence of civil and religious law to which every citizen ought to adhere prevents movement outside the state: 'it was regarded as utterly disgraceful [*flagitio*] even to live outside the state [*extra patriam tantum habitatum*], for the religious rites which it was their constant duty to practice could be performed only on their native soil [*non nisi in patrio solo exerceri*]' (197/214). Simultaneously this imposes a limit to the punishment that the state can deliver: 'no citizen was condemned to exile [*nullus civis . . . exilii damnabatur*]; for the wrongdoer does indeed deserve to be punished, but not to be disgraced [*flagitio*]' (197/215). Leaving the state, either voluntarily or as a form of punishment, is disgraceful and an outrage because it forces those migrating or being exiled to break the link between civil law and religion that defines them as Hebrews. We see how citizenship is determined in a theocracy through the limitations that are placed reciprocally upon rulers and ruled – neither travel outside the state nor exile are an acceptable form of punishment.

We can discern the importance of this conception of citizenship for a state relying on authority and obedience if we recall the importance of exile for the democratic constitution of ancient Athens. Exile is an Athenian institution that promotes agonism. This is done through two famous laws. First, there is Solon's law of stasis, according to which those who do not participate in the conflicts of the polity lose their citizenship and are expelled from the city.[20] Second, there is the law of ostracism, whereby someone who accumulates too much power and influence is expelled, so as to preserve, as Nietzsche explains this law, the agonistic spirit of the Greek polis – since there is no agonism when someone has amassed too much authority.[21] Both of these forms of political exile require a sense of citizenship that is determined through the operation of practical reason, through the search for what is right and wrong, and hence the possibility of rising up and resisting when one is called to obey something that is against one's utility. The incompatibility of the Hebrew state with this logic of exile is symptomatic of a sense of citizenship relying on obedience. It suggests that in the Hebrew state the path of reason in which right approximates law is cast adrift from the path of the emotions relying on obedience and authority. The emotional identification of desire and law has the effect of repressing any agonistic impulse – which may protect the state from rebellion, but also stifles the flourishing of democratic possibilities.

Such a stifling is not surprising if we recognize the similarities of the Hebrew theocracy with what has come to be called in the twentieth century 'biopolitical power'. In the famous lecture in which Foucault introduces

---

[20] Aristotle, *Athenian Constitution*, 8.5. I discuss this law in 'Stasis: Notes Toward Agonist Democracy'.
[21] See Vardoulakis, *Stasis Before the State*; and, Nietzsche, 'Homer's Contest', in *On the Genealogy of Morality and Other Writings*, 174–81.

the term biopolitics, he contrasts it with classical sovereign power. Whereas sovereignty is characterized by the prerogative of life and death, that is, by the exercise of power so as to punish anyone who opposes constituted power, biopolitics is characterized by the control and normalization of life. The effect of this move is that power is now distributed across the entire population, and it appears as if it has no outside since it regulates every facet of life.[22] Foucault could have used Spinoza's account of the coincidence of civil and religious law to illustrate his point, namely, that the Hebrew religion regulated actions such as when the Hebrews could plough or sow the land, or which days they could rest (199). The effect of this in both Foucault's and Spinoza's analyses is that the state encroaches upon every facet of life, whereby nothing outside the state is conceivable – which is another way of saying that the possibility of rebellion is eradicated.[23]

This confluence of what Spinoza calls theocracy and what Foucault calls biopolitics is significant on many levels. From an historical perspective, it suggests that biopolitics is not simply the latest expression of power, but rather a form – for Spinoza, the exemplary form – of power relying on obedience that can be contemporaneous and exist in parallel with, even supporting in certain circumstances, other forms of power.[24] From the perspective of the discourse on political theology that has flourished in the past few decades, this suggests that there is no contradiction or incompatibility between the decisionism characteristic of the sovereign in those political theologies that depart from Carl Schmitt, and the biopolitical theories following in Foucault's footsteps. Rather, Spinoza's analysis of obedience entails that what underlies them both is the operative presence of authority, albeit articulated in different ways. The personal authority of the sovereign requires a genetic account – that is, of how the decisions of the sovereign lead to obedience – whereas the biopolitical account relies on the confluence of theological and political norms so as to expand the field of regulation to the entire field of living. The insight of the seventeenth-century political philosophers that theocracy can be just as relevant to their day holds equally true for us today. I return to this idea at the end of the chapter.

The coincidence of desire and the law characteristic of the Hebrew theocracy has an additional effect, namely, it promotes one particular affect over every other. That affect is hatred – in fact, a double hatred. The Hebrews

---

[22] See the last lecture of Michel Foucault's *Society Must be Defended*.
[23] For the issue of how to conceive something outside the state, see Vardoulakis, *Stasis Before the State*.
[24] I discuss this point at length in chapter 5 of *Sovereignty and its Other*.

come to hate others because 'their daily worship was not merely quite different, making them altogether unique and completely different from other peoples [*diversus omnino erat*], but also absolutely opposed [*absolute contrarius*] to others. Hence this daily invective, as it were, was bound to engender a lasting hatred [*continuum odium*]' (197–8/215). But the insularity of the Hebrews also provoked the hatred of others toward the Hebrews: 'this [i.e. the hatred] was reinforced by the universal cause of the continuous growth of hatred, to wit, the reciprocation [*reciprocatio*] of hatred; for the other nations inevitably held them in bitter hatred in return [*contra odio infensissimo*]' (198/215). Their self-perception of their uniqueness made them hate others and others hate them back. Thus, while the coincidence of religious and civil law may allow desire to be sublimated in the law and thereby avoid the prospect of rebellion, the price the Hebrews pay for their entirely singular society is insularity and the rise of the affect peculiar to it, namely, hatred. The harnessing of hatred in the obedience of the theologico-political law finds an outlet in a single emotion, hatred, that functions as a *pharmakon*, both protecting the state and infecting it from the inside, threatening its very existence.

The coincidence of religious and civil law – the chief characteristic of theocracy – protects the Hebrew state from its own people rebelling against it. This protection from rebellion arises from the unique institution of the Hebrew state – or, at least, unique insofar as one accepts that God was its sovereign, since it is not as unique if the expansion of the law is viewed in biopolitical terms. It provides a cohesive body of citizens who are patriotic and supportive of the state.

Fourth, the protection from tyranny – that is, the limit on the rulers – is determined by one main characteristic that the Hebrew state shares with other states, namely, the fact that the most powerful entity in a polity is the people. Spinoza repeats this point four times in chapter 17, the first three as a general point not specific to any state, and the last one being explicitly associated with the limitations on the political leaders of the Hebrew state.

The first time the point is raised is at the beginning of the chapter: 'This is shown, I think, quite clearly by actual experience [*ipsam etiam experientiam*]; for men have never transferred their right and surrendered their power to another so completely that they were not feared by those very persons who received their right and power, and that the government has not been in greater danger from its citizens [*propter cives*], though deprived of their right, than from its external enemies [*propter hostes*]' (185/201). The fact that the most political power rests with the people who are the most fearful entity for the rulers not only contradicts Hobbes's description of the sovereign as the one who is to be feared the most, but also asserts the impossibility of establishing a secure tyranny. This is a point of view that we can find in Machiavelli's *The Prince* too, where the sovereign is given licence to do anything to perpetuate power except provoke the hatred and resentment of the people. I am suggesting that it is not enough to associate this comment with Spinoza's famous castigation of Hobbes in Letter 50, addressed to Jarig Jelles: 'With regard to political theory, the difference between Hobbes and myself . . . consists in this, that I always preserve the natural right in its entirety.' To stay at the level of the different conception of natural right does not tell us yet about the limits of the state, which is the important question in chapter 17.

In the next few pages, Spinoza compulsively returns to the idea that the people are the entity with the most power in a polity. It is used here to assert the limits of the power of the rulers, to show that their power can never be absolute: 'there can never be any state so mighty that those in command would have unlimited power to do anything they wish [*potentiam absolute ad omnia, quae velint, habeant*]' (186/203). The reason is that 'if the strongest dominion [*maximum tenerent imperium*] were held by those who are most feared [*maxime timentur*], then it would assuredly be held by tyrants' subjects [*tyrannorum subditi*], for they are most feared by their tyrants' (186/202). Thus, it is the threat of rebellion when the rulers do not satisfy the utility of the ruled that prevents tyranny: 'the position has never been attained where the state [*imperium*] was not in greater danger from its citizens [*propter cives*] than from the external enemy [*hostes*], and where its rulers were not in greater fear of the citizens than the enemies' (187/204–5). The same point is raised in the course of the discussion of what the limits to the power of the captains of the Hebrew state were. Spinoza highlights the importance of an independent citizen soldiery – as opposed to mercenaries – since the citizen-soldiers do not obey arbitrary commands by their leaders (196). Essentially, this solution to the limits of the state's and the sovereign's power due to its delimitation by the superior power of the people is the articulation of the final point about Josephism that I raised at the end of the previous section, namely, that there is a form of constitutional forms. The power of the people or the multitude is critical for Spinoza's articulation of this idea.

It is noteworthy that this idea is not confined to the *Theological Political Treatise*; rather, it is stated as a principle in the *Political Treatise* (e.g. 6.6) and it becomes the motor of the argument there. For instance, drawing on the same argument when he talks about monarchy in the *Political Treatise*, Spinoza infers that 'the king's sword or right [*regis gladius, sive jus*] is in reality the will of the multitude itself or of its stronger part [*ipsius multitudinis*, *sive validioris ejus partis voluntas*]' (7.25). I noted in Chapter 1 how we first encountered this idea in the Preface to the *Theological Political Treatise* immediately after Spinoza asserted the threat of voluntary servitude. The idea is further developed in terms of the limits on the power of the rulers in a state of authority in chapter 7, and it then becomes the organizing concept of the discussion of monarchy, aristocracy and democracy in the *Political Treatise*.

The link to the *Political Treatise* is significant because it clearly demonstrates a point that is present in the *Theological Political Treatise* but it is couched there in much more cautious terms and hence is easy to miss. The point is about the 'absoluteness of democracy', to use the vocabulary from the last chapters of the *Political Treatise*. It is the point that natural democracy as it is linked to the foundational impulse of the political – namely, the operative presence of the calculation of utility – appears in one clear, powerful and universal effect: the power of the people. This power is not enough, as Spinoza well recognizes. What is needed in addition is an account of the relation of democracy to forms of authority – or what I called in Chapter 4, agonistic democracy. Spinoza will develop this point in the last two chapters of the *Theological Political Treatise*.

To recapitulate, the Hebrew state shows how it is necessary to have a reciprocal sense of obedience that delimits the power of both the rulers and the ruled. First, the state of authority remains grounded on the calculation of utility. No community or polity can operate, according to Spinoza, without some practical judgement exercised by the people and without the rulers taking that into account. Second, this is possible on condition that obedience is not coercive but rather is exercised over the minds of the people, which is best effected by the combination of the theological and the political sides of authority. Third, the coincidence of religious and civil law protects the community from internal rebellion. In a description that recalls the biopolitical normalization of the population, Spinoza explains how this creates a cohesive citizenry. And, fourth, the community is protected from the spectre of tyranny due to the fact that the most powerful element in any polity is the people. This is the framework that both sustains the state based on obedience and retains natural democracy as the primary constitution underlying the operation of a state of authority.

3. The Fragmentation of Authority: On the Reasons for the Destruction of the Hebrew State

If what makes the Hebrew state a model polity relying on obedience is the authority derived from the law, why then – ponders Spinoza – do the

Hebrews so often forsake the law (200)? With this question, Spinoza introduces the reasons for the dissolution of the Hebrew state. That dissolution ultimately has one main cause that produces a multiplicity of detrimental effects: the cause is the deficient articulation of authority. There are three steps that establish the authority that characterizes the Hebrew theocracy. The third one is by far the most important insofar as the causes of the destruction of the Hebrew state are concerned, and it will occupy the bulk of the discussion in the present section.

The first step concerns the form of constitution that we saw from two different perspectives at the end of the first and at the end of the second section of the present chapter. Specifically, the initial social contract or *pactum* that established the theocratic state was in fact not all that different from democracy: 'as in a democracy [*ut in democratia*] . . . this covenant [with God] left them all completely equal [*hoc pacto aequales prorsus mansisse*], and they all had an equal right to consult God, to receive and interpret his laws; in short, they all shared equally in the government of the state [*absolute omnem imperii administrationem omnes aeque tenuisse*]' (190/206). It appears as if the only difference from a democracy as the 'most natural state' is that, in addition to the equality between the citizens due to the equal distribution of natural right, the Hebrews had a covenant with God, which really does not amount to much if God – from the monist perspective – is the same as nature and if the power of nature is articulated through each individual's singular natural right. In fact, there is not even an authority over the Hebrews in this theocracy, since God – as we saw in chapters 2 and 3 of the *Treatise* – does not have, strictly speaking, any constituted power or any *auctoritas*: God can neither be obeyed nor disobeyed.[25]

The second step immediately changes all that. When the first chance comes for the Hebrews to consult with God, they are terrified by his voice and 'they thought that their last hour had come' (190). In this state of being 'overwhelmed with fear' (190) – and, as I explain in Chapter 1, fear is the cause of authority in the epicurean tradition – they turn to Moses asking him to represent them to God. This significant move that creates Moses's theologico-political authority is not paraphrased in the text. Instead, Spinoza cites the passage from Exodus that describes the Jews' request to Moses. Fear, then – the cause of the production of authority – is coupled with error – the fact that the Jews mistake their benevolent God for something threatening. This combination of fear and error creates Moses's authority, in an account that resonates with the errors that produce authority as I described

---

[25] See, e.g., the discussion in Chapter 2.

them in Chapter 2. With the second step, theocracy becomes dissimilar to democracy.

The third step – which will concern us for the rest of the section – is the crucial one for the reasons leading to the destruction of the Hebrew state. It consists in an evolution of the articulation of authority in the Hebrew state that Spinoza singles out as the ultimate cause of its destruction: 'In order that we may rightly understand ... the cause of the destruction of the [Hebrew] state [*causa vastationis imperii*], we should observe that it had first been intended to entrust the entire ministry of religion to the firstborn, not to the Levites (Num. ch. 8 v. 17); but when all except the Levites had worshipped the calf, the firstborn were rejected and defiled [*repudiati et impurati*], and the Levites were chosen in their place [*Levitae eorum loco electi*] (Deut. ch. 10 v. 8)' (200/218). To understand why Spinoza places so much emphasis on the fact that the Levites were the only Israelite tribe that did not venerate the Golden Calf, we need to have in mind the way he describes the preservation of authority after the death of Moses. Only then will it be possible to return to the biblical passages that Spinoza is thinking about here to make sense of his assertion.

After the establishment of the state, Moses recognizes that if someone is to replace him through whatever means – for instance, if the leadership of the Jews were to be inherited – then 'the state would have become simply a monarchy' (191). According to Spinoza, Moses is well aware of this and he tries to maintain the theocratic nature of the state by fragmenting authority between its theological and its political components. The Levites are chosen as the priests. They are entrusted with the administration of the temple and charged to communicate with God, but they are deprived of any land ownership (191). The land is divided between the other twelve tribes, establishing a confederation – Spinoza adds that it is similar to the confederation of the Estates of the Netherlands – while each tribe retains relative autonomy and has a captain to lead it politically (192–4). The tribes and their captains live autonomously, and do not interfere with each other's affairs, with only one exception: 'If he [i.e. the captain of a tribe] rebelled against God, it was the duty of the other tribes to attack him as an enemy who had violated the terms of his agreement, not to pass judgment on him as a subject' (194). Renouncing God and the religious basis of the state would place a captain and his tribe outside the covenant and hence make them *external* enemies to the Hebrew confederation. This fragmentation of authority is successful to the extent that when Moses died the Hebrew state – emphasizes Spinoza – 'was left neither a monarchy nor an aristocracy nor a democracy, but ... a theocracy' (194–5).

We should pay attention to one crucial detail of this split authority instituted by Moses that makes it incommensurable with the idea of a secular separation between ecclesiastical and temporal powers. The Levites – that is, the priests – are made solely responsible for the interpretation of the law (195). The Hebrew theocracy places the law in the hands of the priests. This may be an expediency on the part of Moses, who wants to limit the political power of the captains. Spinoza emphasizes how constraining (*continere*) on both rulers and ruled is the fact that the priests are in charge of the law – another factor that limits the power of the state and prevents both rebellion and tyranny. Besides its expediency, this is also a measure consistent with the nature of theocracy, namely, the fact that religious and civil law coincide. It is because of this coincidence and because of the position it accords to the priests as guardians of the law that 'no one can imitate now [*nemo jam imitari potest*]' the Hebrew state, as Spinoza says at the opening of chapter 18 (205/221). The fragmented authority that places the law in the hands of the priests is the critical historical feature that makes the Hebrew state both unique and inimitable.

Keeping in mind the critical role of the splitting of authority into its theological and political constituents, let us return to Spinoza's biblical sources. After the Hebrews ask Moses to be their representative to God because of their fear, Moses climbs Mount Sinai to receive the law. While wandering for forty days, the Hebrews despair at his absence and turn to the veneration of an idol, the Golden Calf. Upon his return, Moses is outraged at the sight of this idolatry. Here is how Moses's reaction to the veneration of the Golden Calf is described in the King James translation: 'Then Moses stood in the gate of the camp, and said, Who is on the Lord's side? [let him come] unto me. And all the sons of Levi gathered themselves together unto him. And he said unto them, Thus saith the Lord God of Israel, Put every man his sword by his side, and go in and out from gate to gate throughout the camp, and slay every man his brother, and every man his companion, and every man his neighbour. And the children of Levi did according to the word of Moses: and there fell of the people that day about three thousand men' (Exodus 32:26–8). We see here the reason why the Levites are chosen as priests – they are the only ones who are not defiled by venerating false idols.

This passage from Exodus describes the massacre following Moses's first descent from Mount Sinai. As I explain in Chapter 2, it is a passage famous with political philosophers in early modernity, but Spinoza himself never explicitly mentions this violence.[26] The closest he comes is in his reference

---

[26] The massacre described in Exodus 32 also has an important function in recent discussions of the figure of Moses. The most influential of these discussions is Jan Assmann's

to the Levites becoming the priests of the Hebrew state, which can only be understood if the reader knows the biblical passage from the Exodus I cite above. Even though Spinoza never cites or paraphrases this passage, we see here how pivotal to his argument it is. It explains why authority is fragmented between the Levites and the rest of the tribes – the key point about authority in the Hebrew theocracy after Moses. What Spinoza never explicitly cites but to which he heavily alludes is the fact that the Levites achieve their theological authority – their religious purity by refusing to venerate the calf – through the same sequence that puts the sword in their hands to execute the sovereign prerogative of life and death, that is, the punishment of those who have defiled God. The first assertion of their authority is a political one – it is the violence of execution that is foundational for the Hebrew state. Thus, their theological (and legal) authority after the death of Moses is tainted with the political from the very beginning, even before the Hebrew state is founded, through this act of violence that they justifiably execute as representatives of political authority. To put it in the visual metaphorics of the frontispiece from the *Leviathan*: they can hold the crosier because they initially held the sword. Their *theological* authority is steeped in blood because initially they were instruments of Moses's *political* authority. The Levites become representatives of theological authority only as a result of first being representatives of political authority by carrying out Moses's order for the massacre. Thus, the fragmentation of authority pursued by Moses to secure the Hebrew state as a theocracy after his death is doomed to failure because – suggests Spinoza – there is no such thing as an unalloyed theological or a purely political authority.

All the various secondary causes for the destruction of the Hebrew state that Spinoza identifies refer back to this impurity of the constituent components of the fragmented authority that characterized the Hebrew state since Moses's death. The most significant one is that the citizens of the state viewed the priestly tribe as 'a constant reminder of their [i.e., the other tribes'] defilement and rejection [*continuo suae impuritatis, et repudiationis arguebant*]' (201/218). The Levites are a constant reminder of the defilement and rejection that the rest of the tribes suffer for having venerated the Golden Calf – as well as of the *political* fate of those who were executed by the Levites as a result. This is compounded by other factors, such as the

The Price of Monotheism. Exodus 32 is one of Assmann's key examples for what he calls 'the Mosaic distinction', namely, the key characteristic of monotheism to be inimical both toward any deviation from 'true' religion within itself as well as toward any other 'false' religion.

resentment arising from having to provide for the priests, or from the fact that the priests did not hesitate in rebuking the other tribes when they thought that their actions did not conform with the law as they interpreted it.

This is further compounded by the animosity between the captains and the priests. The animosity between the political and the theological authorities of the Hebrew state was due to the fact that the political authorities, notes Spinoza, felt that it was intolerable for the Levites to be the interpreters of the law, as this created a 'state within a state' (202, 203). All these factors gradually erode the notion of authority underlying the Hebrew state from the inside. And with the diminished belief in the value of the separation between the theological authority of the Levites and the political authority of the captains comes the questioning of the value of the theocratic constitution that is based on this fragmentation.

The result is the request of the Jewish people to have a mortal king. This is described in 1 Samuel 8, where the Jews ask the high priest to request that they obtain a mortal king, as opposed to having God as their sovereign. As I mention in the first section of the present chapter, this is a prominent reference used to support anti-authoritarian sentiments. Spinoza never explicitly cites this request, made in 1 Samuel 8:4–5, but he mentions it repeatedly, once in chapter 17 (202) and four more times in chapter 18 (on 207 twice, 208 and 209). Neither does Spinoza explicitly cite God's response enumerating the evils that follow from monarchy, which was, as I mentioned, so important for the anti-monarchical movements of the sixteenth and seventeenth centuries that referred to the Hebrew state as a way of talking about their contemporary political situation. But Spinoza's brief references to the transition from theocracy to monarchy – such as the incredible bloodshed and internecine war that it precipitated (207) – leave the reader in no doubt of the catastrophic consequences that followed. Spinoza describes the re-founded Hebrew state as a mere shadow of its former self and refrains from describing in detail its structure. This is consistent with his sharp distinction between authority and authoritarianism. It is clear that Spinoza participates in the anti-monarchical tradition that characterizes the use of Josephus.

It is instructive to note the way in which the Hebrew state, as the paradigmatic state of authority, gradually dissolves because of the mutation of authority. Originally, authority is deferred to God and everyone is equal – which means that theocracy is similar to democracy and which is arguably the reason why the Hebrew state is the paradigmatic form of a state of authority. Soon, however, authority is transferred to Moses, who subsequently splits authority into a theological component enjoyed by the Levites and a political component attributed to the captains. This fragmentation is meant to safeguard theocracy from monarchy, but it is impure from the beginning – it is contaminated by the exercise of political authority by the Levites in the process of carrying out Moses's order for the punishment of those who venerated the Golden Calf. That which is meant to protect the theocracy – the fragmentation of power – contaminates the Hebrew state from within, like an autoimmune disease, leading to the eventual dissolution of theocracy into a monarchy.

As if this is not bad enough, Spinoza notes a final and most pernicious turn in this unfortunate sequence that has led from authority to authoritarianism. This consists in the eventual usurpation of *political* power by the priests. This re-constitution of the theological and the political components of authority does nothing to rescue a notion of productive authority that caters for the utility of the people, leading instead to tyranny: 'after they had acquired the power to transact government affairs and had added to the priesthood the right of secular rule, they each began to seek self-glorification both in religious and secular matters [*unusquisque tam in religione, quam in reliquis sui nominis gloriam incepit quaerere*]. They extended pontifical authority [*pontificali authoritate*] to all areas [*omnia*], and in the field of religious rites, dogma and all else they continually issued new decrees for which they claimed neither less sanctity nor less authority [*non minus sacra, nec minoris authoritatis*] than for the laws of Moses' (206/222). In language steeped in contempt, Spinoza describes the 'pontifical' authority that the priests sought to obtain as well as their hubris in pretending to emulate the theologico-political authority of Moses. Spinoza's verdict on this state of affairs is damning: 'As a result [*ex quo factum*], religion degenerated into destructive superstition [*in exitiabilem superstitionem*], and the true meaning and interpretation of the laws was corrupted' (206/222).

This is the constitution of authority not on the basis of the utility of the people but on the basis of the self-glorification and arbitrary rule of those in authority, who thereby turn into tyrants. In discussing the evils of tyranny, Spinoza underscores how it undercuts the central principle of religion, namely neighbourly love. This has pernicious effects throughout the polity, all of which amount to undercutting the utility of the people. For instance, it means that authority infringes on the freedom of the people to exercise their judgement (208–9). The rise of authoritarianism threatens to derail the dialectic of authority and utility that determines the political field, according to Spinoza's epicureanism.

This corruption of the political field is best encapsulated in what I call elsewhere the 'ruse of sovereignty'.[27] This is the idea that there is nothing outside such an authoritarian rule, whereby the only possibility of political change consists in the substitution of one authoritarian rule with another. Spinoza repeats this point three times, once in chapter 17 and twice in chapter 18. Thus, he describes how the change of those in control of political authority does not change the nature of their authoritarianism: 'for even though they removed a tyrant, the causes of tyranny remained. Thus they merely succeeded in installing a new tyrant at the cost of much citizen blood' (203). The second reference draws attention to the state of a people accustomed to obey too much: 'there is also no less danger involved in removing a monarch, even if his tyranny is apparent to all. The people, accustomed to royal rule and constrained by that alone, will despise and mock a lesser authority; and therefore, on removing one king, will find it necessary to appoint another in his place' (209). And the third instance describes the logic of the substitution of one monarch with another: if the causes of tyranny are not addressed, warns Spinoza, 'a people has often succeeded in changing tyrants, but never in abolishing tyranny or substituting another form of government for monarchy' (210). The great political problem is how to evade tyranny after it has been established. This is a far cry from the authority originally established in the Hebrew theocracy – an authority that resembled natural democracy.

Thus, the Hebrew state, far from being the ideal state for the path of obedience, proves at the end to be a ruse for the perpetuation of tyranny. The morphing of authority into authoritarianism turns obedience into a self-destructive activity. The state of authority relying on obedience and the path that leads to virtue through the emotions seem here hopelessly mired in a futile trajectory of self-destruction. But Spinoza is not one content with identifying a problem and then lamenting it. We will see in the following chapter how he offers a solution – one that is so paradoxical that it has not been noted in the secondary literature. This consists in the way that the two paths – the path of reason and the path of the emotions – and the two corresponding regimes of power – natural democracy and the state of authority – cross each other. We have seen this idea earlier, for instance as the freedom to transverse discussed in Chapter 6. The political import of this idea finds its fulfilment in the final two chapters of the *Theological Political Treatise*.

* * *

If we take theocracy in the strict sense defined in the *Theological Political*

---

[27] Vardoulakis, *Stasis Before the State*.

Treatise, namely, as the identity of religious and civil law, then, as I suggested, this can lead to some reflections on our contemporary political predicament. I will attempt to do so here in a sketchy – suggestive rather than systematic – way, given that I am running out of space. I will organize my thoughts in the guise of five 'theses' on *theocratic biopolitics*.

Thesis 1: Authority cannot be completely eliminated.
Even though theocratic biopolitics starts with the death of the figure of authority still it does not eliminate authority completely. The king's head has still not rolled, as Foucault put it. The priests in the Hebrew state seek authority for themselves through the interpretation of the law and through their meddling in politics, as we have seen Spinoza argue. This suggests that biopolitics is not a form of power separated from other forms of power, such as sovereignty, in such a way that we have either biopolitics or sovereignty.

Example: Foucault in certain passages talks about biopolitics as a completely new formation of power that supersedes older ones, but in others he equivocates or even suggests explicitly that is not the case. In the famous last lecture of *Society Must be Defended*, in which he coins the term biopolitics, Foucault writes: 'one of the greatest transformations political right underwent in the nineteenth century was precisely that, I wouldn't say exactly that sovereignty's old right – to take life or let live – was replaced, but it came to be *complemented* by a new right which does not erase the old right but which does *penetrate* it, *permeate* it. This is the right, or rather precisely the opposite right. It is the power to "make" life and "let" die.'[28] I develop and defend this insight in *Sovereignty and its Other*, where I argue in detail about the parallel operation of various forms of power that are usually seen as separated.

Thesis 2: Morality has taken the place of religious law in non-confessional theocratic biopolitics.
If we apply Spinoza's definition of theocracy to biopolitics, we get the following result: we have a socio-political arrangement that shows a confluence of religious and civil law, while – and this is the lesson of the Hebrew state – there is a separation of religious and political authority. However, the control of the field of the law remains with religious authority. What happens if we combine this idea with the Kantian insight that we can have a non-confessional faith – a faith that does not rely on the existence of God, since

[28] Foucault, *Society Must be Defended*, 241, emphasis added.

the ontological proof in fact proves nothing, but that relies on humanity as a 'kingdom of ends'? The Kantian insight is that, even though we cannot gain access to the absolute, we can still act as if we did every time we act. Thus, the unwritten – and unwriteable – moral law ought to regulate our actions both at an individual and at a political level. From this perspective, the theocratic feature of modern and postmodern secularism is the putative moral law, whose 'priests' are the real figures of authority behind juridical practice.

Example 1: At the time of writing, one of the major political issues in global geopolitics is the Turkish invasion of the northern Syrian semi-autonomous Kurdish region, enabled by the sudden withdrawal of US troops. The Trump administration's justification for pulling out troops was premised on the principle that the US should not be the 'policeman of the world' and America 'should bring its sons home'. That may be a fine principle in theory, but the question is always how to apply it. Moralizing from general rules is dangerous when it fails to consider the effects of an action – or, more emphatically, when the effects of actions are considered merely as an issue of the application of a principle. The effects matter, such as, in this case, the thousands of Kurds murdered by Turkish paramilitaries. This is the problem with principles: the bloodletting they effect. To take seriously Spinoza's insight that human law is about the self-preservation of the community means that we start by considering the effects of action through instrumental judgements – which is to say, we start by blocking our ears to the Siren call of moralizing.

Example 2: Who are the priests of neoliberalism? Maybe they are those unaccountable figures who control global finance based on the law of the 'invisible hand of the market'. But this principle is not only – as for instance Josef Vogl has shown – steeped in theology.[29] In addition, the free reign of finance is only one side of the supposed 'natural' law of the market that regulates our lives. This 'natural' law also requires the laws and institutions of the state to enable the operation of finance, for instance, by building infrastructure such as travel and communication technologies, or even by keeping the population at bay from rising against the abuses of finance.

Thesis 3: Theocratic biopolitics shows the control, regulation and normalization of both mind and body.
It follows that the definition of biopolitics as the control, regulation and normalization of the *body* is squarely inadequate. Theocratic biopolitics indi-

---

[29] See Vogl, *The Specter of Capital*.

cates also, and simultaneously, the control, regulation and normalization of the mind. It seems to me that the fundamental materialist insight of the inseparability of mind and body is often lost in contemporary discussions of biopolitics. The implication of this is that whatever moral 'laws' or 'principles' are invoked so as to exercise power over the body work by convincing others, irrespective of whether they are completely false – because, to paraphrase Alexander's riposte quoted by Spinoza, 'false belief has often done duty for control, regulation and normalization'.

Example: The newspaper today tells of the story of Katie Hill, a Democrat Congresswoman from California whose estranged husband has leaked nude photographs of her to the right-wing press. These photos accompany a story about Hill's affair with a female staffer before she entered Congress. Despite the fact that Hill has always been open about her sexuality – the articles often refer to her as the first openly bi member of Congress – and regardless of the consensus that 'revenge porn' is an abhorrent way to control and exercise violence against women, the right-wing press has been delighting in the disclosed material. They interview her constituents, for instance, asking them whether Hill is setting a good example for their kids and what kind of role model they want their politicians to be. The control of a woman's sexuality – of her body – is accompanied by the control of the mind of the population she represents. The hypocrisy of the same press supporting Donald Trump, against whom there are several allegations of sexual harassment of an incomparably more serious nature, is part of the control of minds as a way of controlling the female body.[30]

Thesis 4: Theocratic biopolitics exhibits an inverse relation of authority and authoritarianism.
This is the logical extension of thesis 1. The fact that authority cannot be argued with is not entirely arbitrary. It depends on a claim to truth perceived to be made by the figure of authority. The judge delivering a verdict has authority by virtue of the fact that the judge is expected to make truth inferences based on the evidence presented in court. By contrast, when authority wanes in theocratic biopolitics, and as figures such as the priests in the Hebrew state strengthen their power with arbitrary assertions based on an 'interpretation of the law', then authoritarianism increases, as we have seen Spinoza arguing. Mendacity, the friend of authoritarianism,

---

[30] A day after this example was written, Katie Hill was forced to resign her position at Congress.

is the enemy of authority. This is not to say that authority cannot lie – intentionally or unintentionally; rather, it is to say that authority is eroded and undermined when it is perceived as lying, whereas the opposite is the case with authoritarian figures. Thus, the mechanisms that support authority and authoritarianism are different, whereby they exhibit an inverse relation.

Example: I have already mentioned this inverse relation of authority and authoritarianism in the Introduction. There is no clearer example of this than Donald Trump. His authoritarianism is supported by a compulsive mendacity that has completely stripped him of any claim to truth. But because of his constant lying, being perceived as a liar does not undermine him. The example I mentioned in the Introduction was of the world leaders laughing at Trump when he boasted in the UN that he was the greatest president ever. Laughter is a sign that he lacks authority – as Arendt puts it, and as we have seen, laughter is the 'surest way' to undermine authority.[31] But since authority is not something Trump strives for, the laughter did not affect him in the least, and in fact his whole election strategy was based on lacking authority.[32] Mendacity is his game and this means that whenever his lies are exposed, his tried and successful strategy is to keep on lying.

Thesis 5: Democracy can resist theocratic biopolitics.
This is not simply because the people are the most powerful entity in the polity, as Spinoza puts it in chapters 17 and 18 of the *Theological Political Treatise* as well as in the *Political Treatise*. This will never be enough due to the fact that the people can always be ideologically determined. What is also needed is a conception of judgement as agonistically related to the theocratic biopolitics of any regime relying on obedience. In Spinoza's epicureanism, authority and its permutations are in a dialectical relation with the calculation of utility. And natural democracy is the operative presence of practical judgement understood as instrumental rationality.

Example: Steve Bannon, the architect of Trump's victory in 2016 and a leading light of the alt-right, said in an interview that his favourite newspaper is *The Guardian*. He explained to the surprised journalist that he likes 'left' journalism because his own 'economic nationalism' starts from the same premise, namely, a description – often apocalyptic in tone – of the contemporary predicament in the era of neoliberalism. But whereas the 'left', as

[31] Arendt, *On Violence*, 45.
[32] See Vardoulakis, 'Was Donald Trump Elected Because He Is Laughable?'

he sees it, delights in moralizing and sermonizing – the kind of 'political correctness' that so many commentators of the right love to hate – he insists on talking about the interests of the people. Having abandoned the discourse of interest to the right, the left, concludes Bannon, is always bound to lose. Bannon is correct, and we have to ask: what would change if what he calls the 'left' were to re-energize a discourse about interest, that is, a discourse that emphasizes the key characteristic of democracy according to Spinoza, the calculation of utility?

9

The Authority to Abrogate:
The Two Paths to Virtue and the Internal Enemy
(chapters 19 and 20)

Having presented the two regimes of power – natural democracy and the state of authority – following the two paths to the good – the path of rationality and the path of the emotions, respectively – we now find ourselves in a position to inquire about the relation between these two regimes and their co-articulation in two paths. Any answer to the question about the relation between the two paths needs to start from Spinoza's insistence in chapter 17 that neither path is pure. Thus, the opening sentence of the chapter refers back to the previous chapter, saying that the 'picture presented in the last chapter ... though it comes quite close to actual practice and can increasingly be realised in reality, must nevertheless remain in many respects no more than theory [*in multis mere theoretica*]' (185/201). Later, immediately after defining the theocracy of the Hebrew state as the coincidence of civil and religious law, Spinoza observes that nonetheless this is 'a matter of theory rather than fact [*omnia opinione magis, quam re constabant*]' (189–90/206). Thus, both paths to communal virtue made available through the political application of the anthropological principle are, on their own, more theory than praxis. In actuality, neither can be realized in a pure form. Or, differently put, no state can be a pure democracy or a pure authority.

If the two paths are not pure, then they contaminate each other by veering into each other's paths. Each path is not the realization of its end, but a process in which the negotiation with the other path is critical. Thus, the path of reason that is characterized by the operation of right through the calculation of utility is constantly in complex relations with the path of the emotions relying on the imitation of the affects as well as on obedience to authority. We see, then, that the relation between the two paths is Spinoza's way of staging the dialectic of authority and utility at two levels simultaneously – both at the level of political regimes, and at the anthropological level. This suggests that both paths can operate simultaneously in the same actual regime of power, or in the same state. Some people follow the dictates of the sovereign through the exercise of their phronesis, others simply because they obey. It also suggests that the paths can transverse – as I argue in section 3 of Chapter 6 – a point that receives its detailed analysis in chapters 19 and 20.

When I examined for the first time the relation between natural democracy and the state of authority that Spinoza presents in chapter 5 of the *Theological Political Treatise*, I argued that their relation is agonistic.[1] This signifies tensions between the calculation of utility as the basis of natural democracy – as we saw in Chapter 7 – and obedience as the hallmark of the path of the emotions that corresponds to the state of authority. These tensions become particularly acute when the state of authority turns authoritarian, whereby it no longer concerns itself with the utility of the people but rather with the utility of the holders of power. The political conflict within the state is precipitated by authority's articulation of communal utility. This suggests that authority is itself determined by utility, and that agonistic democracy, as the relation between two regimes of power, is the articulation of any actualized political regime. The material manifestation of both natural democracy and the state of authority – which on their own are 'more theory than praxis' – is the relation that I call agonistic democracy.

The conflicts staged by agonistic democracy are what allow for the transversals between the two paths.[2] Three distinct questions arise at this point: What is it that motivates the path of the emotions to cross over to the path of reason? What is it that motivates the path of reason to transverse to the emotions? And finally, what does this agonism that allows for the chiasmus between the two paths tell us about the role of the internal enemy in Spinoza's conception of the political? I will take each of these questions in turn.

1. The Path of the Emotions: Neighbourly Love as a Political Principle

Chapter 19 returns to the discussion of the path to virtue through the emotions. The discussion is about law and about how obedience is possible. This is presented as ostensibly a defence of a well-known erastian principle, namely, that the sovereign should be in charge of the law of the state as well as of religious law. This principle is stated unambiguously at the opening of

---

[1] See section 2 of Chapter 4.
[2] I prefigure this in sections 1 and 3 of Chapter 6.

the chapter, and then repeated throughout: 'Religion acquires the force of law [*vim juris*] only by decree of those who hold the sovereignty [*jus imperandi habent*], and . . . God has no special kingdom over people [*Deum nullum singulare regnum in homines habere*] except through those who hold sovereignty [*imperium tenent*]' (212/228). How is Spinoza's epicurean politics inflected by erastianism? Let us start by contextualizing it.

This erastian principle is well-established in the seventeenth century, especially amongst radical political thinkers. One of its most famous proponents is Thomas Hobbes.[3] The name derives from Thomas Erastus, a sixteenth-century protestant theologian. Even though the erastian principle about sovereignty never becomes an accepted position of the official protestant Churches, its influence is deep in the political philosophy of the seventeenth century.

In the specific context of the Dutch republic, erastianism is introduced by Arminius in the first decade of the seventeenth century, resulting in an anti-Calvinist and anti-monarchical movement usually referred to as the Remonstrants. The major theologico-political conflict in the United Provinces in the seventeenth century is between the Remonstrants and their Calvinist opponents, the Counter-Remonstrants.[4] This takes both an ideological and a political form. The Remonstrant insistence on a sovereign who controls legality and legitimacy does not sit comfortably next to cardinal Calvinist doctrines such as grace and predestination. And whereas the Remonstrants tend to be federalists with republican sympathies, the Calvinists align with the House of Orange and find it expedient politically to support monarchism. All the significant political events in the Dutch republic of the seventeenth century are coloured, in one way or another, by the conflict between these two camps.[5]

One particularly liberal and anti-confessional offshoot of the Remonstrants is the Collegiants. We know that Spinoza is closely affiliated with the Collegiants while he is still in Amsterdam, and his choice of destination after his excommunication is indicative of the close connection: Rijnsburg, a smaller village near Leiden, was a stronghold of Collegiants. The circle of friends, followers and supporters around Spinoza are largely Collegiants or sympathetic to them. For instance, a well-known Collegiant

---

[3] For a discussion of Hobbes's erastianism, see Martinich, 'Interpreting the Religion of Thomas Hobbes'.

[4] For the background and interesting discussions, see James, *Spinoza on Philosophy, Religion, and Politics*; and Nadler, *Spinoza: A Life*.

[5] See Schama, *The Embarrassment of Riches*.

of the time is Meyer, with whom Spinoza exchanges important letters and who writes the preface to Spinoza's *Principles of Cartesian Philosophy*. Thus, when Spinoza argues in chapter 19 that the sovereign should control both civil and religious law, any educated person at the time – that is, anyone who could read the *Treatise* in Latin – immediately recognizes the erastian principle.[6]

Three observations are important in situating the erastianism of chapter 19 within the *Theological Political Treatise*. First, Spinoza's erastianism is situated within the development of his argument. Thus, he insists that because 'justice and charity can acquire the force of law and command only through the right of the state [*justitiam et caritatem vim juris et mandati non posse accipere, nisi ex jure imperii*], I can readily draw the conclusion – since the state's right is vested in the sovereign alone [*jus imperii penes summas potestates tantum est*] – that religion can acquire the force of law only from the decree of those who have the right of sovereignty [*jus imperandi*], and that God has no special kingdom over men [*Deum nullum singulare regnum in homines habere*] save through the medium of those who hold sovereignty [*imperium tenent*]' (213/229). The justice expressed by the law accords – nay, ought to accord – with the fundamental principle of religion, *caritas* or neighbourly love. We have seen already the many uses of neighbourly love in the *Treatise*, and I have already stressed that it has a political import. Here, in chapter 19, neighbourly love assumes its clearest and strongest political articulation. There is a path of the emotions that operates on the model of command and obedience, and it is the responsibility and the duty of the sovereign to preserve that path that is determined by the imitation of the affects characterizing neighbourly love. This politicization of charity will prove crucial – as we will see shortly – for forging a deviation from the path of the emotions.

What I am drawing attention to here is that justice is a property of sovereignty when it is coupled with charity. This entails a conditional. Sovereignty and the law are just if and only if they are linked to neighbourly love. Thus, it would be too precipitous to conclude from Spinoza's erastianism that the political overwhelms or covers over the religious. Rather, there is a reciprocal relation between the two. Neighbourly love, by virtue of being linked to justice, checks and delimits sovereign power, while sovereign power, by virtue of being in control of the law, allows for the actualization

---

[6] For much more detail on this context, see Nadler, *Spinoza: A Life*; Nadler, *A Book Forged in Hell*; James, *Spinoza on Philosophy, Religion, and Politics*; and Preus, *Spinoza and the Irrelevance of Biblical Authority*.

of justice as charity in interpersonal relations. This effects a diminution of or check on the authority of the sovereign. For instance, Spinoza writes: 'since it is established both by reason and experience that the divine law is entirely dependent on the decrees of sovereignty [*jus divinum a solo decreto summarum potestatum pendere*], it follows that sovereignty is also the interpreter of the divine law' (215/232). As we saw in the opening chapters of the *Treatise*, the prophets are the sole interpreters of the communications with God since they have the gift of revelation. The sovereigns lack this gift, thereby lacking the authority that the direct communication with God afforded the prophets. Ultimately, what is obeyed is not the sovereign as such but the principle of neighbourly love that it is the responsibility and duty of the sovereign to sustain through laws. Thus, obedience in the path of virtue passing through the emotions is not absolute but conditional.

I will return in a moment to indicate what this political-theological authority of the sovereign relies on but, second, I want to note something about the nature of sovereignty in chapter 19. Spinoza consistently uses the various terms translated as sovereignty in an impersonal way throughout the chapter. The three terms that he uses to refer to sovereignty here are *imperium*, *respublica* and *summa potestas*. These are not entirely synonymous, as they may highlight different aspects of sovereignty.[7] Importantly, unlike someone like Hobbes, all of these terms point to sovereignty as an impersonal kind of instituted power or *potestas* – there is no sovereign figure who derives his power through the fear that he generates in his subjects. Further, and just as significantly, Spinoza specifies explicitly that sovereignty as he applies the term to the erastian principle can assume any of the three possible constitutional forms: 'In order that the precepts of true reason . . . the very precepts of God, might have the absolute force of law, we saw that every man must surrender his natural right and that they must all transfer that right to the whole community, or to a number of men, or to one man' (213). The obedience to the law can unfold in a democratic, an aristocratic and even in a monarchical constitution. Thus what is at stake in Spinoza's idiosyncratic erastianism is not the particular legal formation or legitimacy of the state. Rather, it is the form in which justification operates to sustain sovereignty's claim to justice and charity.

Third, we have seen this shift from legitimacy to justification in section 3 of Chapter 3 in the course of examining Spinoza's conception of the foundation of the law. We see here further how this shift is linked to the

---

[7] For a more detailed discussion see Vardoulakis and Kordela, 'Introduction', in *Spinoza's Authority*, Volume 2, 1–6.

issue of the conditional nature of sovereign power. The formulation of the erastian principle about the sovereign controlling the entire legal field in the opening of chapter 19 that I cited above continues as follows: 'Furthermore, the practice of religion and the exercises of piety must be accommodated to the peace and utility of the commonwealth [*reipublicae paci et utilitati*]' (212/228–9). Spinoza's erastianism does not determine sovereignty through legitimacy or vis-à-vis a realm of legality. Rather, it determines it through the operation of phronesis. It is how sovereignty accommodates or justifies its actions so as to lead to the utility of the republic that determines sovereignty's conditional power. Sovereignty represents the public face of instrumental rationality.

We know from earlier in the *Treatise* that the exercise of piety relies on a single fundamental principle of religion, namely, neighbourly love. The process of the justification of sovereignty is inextricable from the politicization of neighbourly love. Spinoza returns to this point repeatedly. Thus, for instance, 'the external forms of religion and the entire practice of piety must be accommodated to the peace and preservation of the commonwealth [*reipublicae paci et conservationi debere accommodari*]' (215/232). The neighbourly love that the practice of piety signifies is political to the extent that it accommodates the public articulations of the calculation of utility. Spinoza's erastianism is grounded on his epicureanism.

It is within this context that we should understand Spinoza's pronouncement that 'there can be no doubt that piety [*pietas*] toward one's country [*patriam*] is the highest form of piety that can be shown' (215/232). Here, neighbourly love, as the fundamental principle of religion and the criterion of piety, merges with the utility of the state. This theologico-political perspective is a direct inference from the understanding of the political in epicurean terms as the operative presence of utility. Let me underscore this point: the path of the emotions is *not* separated from rationality. This rationality is not the second kind of knowledge, as I argue in Chapter 6: instrumental rationality stands between adequate knowledge and the imagination but it cannot be reduced to either. It is the operation of phronesis as an awareness of the public good even when the polity is determined by the structure of command and obedience on the path of the emotions. Even if the emotions *predominate*, still instrumental rationality is not completely absent as is evidenced by neighbourly love, that is, by the fact that a community chooses to function communally. I should remind the reader that, even though Étienne Balibar is the thinker who has paid the closest attention to the two paths leading to political virtue, still he is not clear on this point, often suggesting that the path of the emotions is separated from the calculation of utility that, he thinks, is solely operative on the path of reason. My analysis is incompatible with such a position.[8]

Thus, we can summarize Spinoza's epicurean use of erastianism by saying that a) it indicates the politicization of neighbourly love; b) it points to the function of sovereignty as justification; and, c) it inscribes instrumental rationality within the path of the emotions and obedience. This epicurean use of erastianism culminates in drawing its logical inference, namely, the acknowledgement of the impossibility of conceiving the path of the emotions and obedience as pure. It follows from the above that 'there is no act of piety towards one's neighbor that is not impious [*nihil proximo pium praestari posse, quod non impium sit*] if it results in harm to the commonwealth as a whole [*totius reipublicae*]. On the other hand, there is no impious act committed toward the neighbor [*nihil in eundem impium committi*] that must not be accounted as pious [*pietati non tribuatur*] if it is done for the sake of the preservation of the commonwealth' (215/232). This is a remarkable statement. The grammar with the accumulation of negations and double negations creates a sense of vertigo, even nausea, forcing us to slow down and read carefully.

Both sentences concern piety: the acts one performs toward one's neighbour. More broadly, the issue is how the other – as an ethical concern – is also, simultaneously, a political issue concerning the state 'as a whole' and the preservation of the republic. The first sentence can be paraphrased as 'it is pious to be impious if impiety results in the utility of the state as a whole'. What is it that this statement denies? It denies the Jewish sense of the neighbour, according to which – as we saw in section 3 of Chapter 5 – the neighbour is primarily if not exclusively an ethical concern. This politicization of the neighbour that infuriates Levinas – as we saw in the same section – is now pitted explicitly against an exclusively ethical interpretation. The neighbour does not signify a relation between individuals, according to Spinoza, and hence the neighbour cannot indicate the measure of the universalization of the other in one's considerations of how to act. Rather, the neighbour indicates how the calculation of utility is universalizable only in relation to the 'state as a whole'. Or, perhaps it is more accurate to say that the neighbour universalizes the necessity to judge – to exercise phronesis – in the political realm and in considering the utility of the polity. The universal is constructed through the interchange or communication with the other.

The second sentence states that – to paraphrase – 'an impious act is pious if it is conducted with the utility of the community in mind'. Let us ask the

---

[8] For the relevant discussion, see section 2 of Chapter 6.

same question we asked about the first sentence: What is it that this statement denies? It denies a morality that supervenes over the political. It also asserts the importance of instrumental rationality in its political dimension. The fact that certain acts are impious in themselves – which, in Spinoza's vocabulary, means acts against one's neighbour – can be in reality pious given that neighbourly love needs to be determined politically. The act is not measured in relation to an individual – either an actualized other or a transcendent Other such as in Levinas – but rather with reference to all the others that are included in how the judgement about the calculation of utility is formed.

This argument could have come straight out of Machiavelli. For instance, in chapter 9 of book 1 of the *Discourses*, Machiavelli writes about Romulus's killing of Remus: 'It is at any rate fitting that, though the deed accuses him, the result should excuse him; and when it is good, like that of Romulus, it will always excuse him, because he who is violent to destroy, not he who is violent to restore, ought to be censured.' And in the same chapter: 'Romulus deserves excuse and not blame for the death of Remus.'[9] Fratricide is certainly a 'deed that accuses him' or an impious act, and yet the result of the establishment of Rome 'excuses him' since it is pious to achieve the political good. There is a difference from Machiavelli – one that I noted in Chapter 2 – namely, that the Florentine applies this logic to those who hold or seek potestas, whereas Spinoza's example is more generalized and applies to the entire community. Nonetheless, the logic is the same, to wit, the political articulation of the reciprocity of utility determines what is useful in terms of the public good. Or, more emphatically, every act of piety, every ethical act, is pious or ethical by virtue of the fact that it is also, and primarily, political.

Note the effect of this insistent politicization of neighbourly love. We are on the path to virtue through the passions. But neighbourly love can attain its political utility if and only if piety is a matter of calculation that accounts for interpersonal relations and for the utility to the state – *and that is not a sovereign prerogative but the prerogative of everyone exercising their instrumental rationality within the community*. One is pious politically by placing the other within a network of calculations that contribute to the commonwealth's preservation. Remarkably, practical judgement predominates at the moment when piety and impiety become embroiled in this dialectic of the politics of the other. Everyone, not only the sovereign, is *free* to use their instrumental rationality for the advantage of the state. The path of the passions is possible on condition that it is not pure, on condition that it is contaminated by the

---

[9] Machiavelli, *Discourses on the First Decade of Titus Livius*, 1:218 and 220.

other path, the path of reason. It is possible, in other words, on condition that it crosses over to the path of reason.

As soon as he has indicated this transversal, Spinoza uses a remarkable example to highlight its import: 'For example, if someone who is quarrelling with me wants to take my coat, it is an act of piety to give him my cloak as well. But when it is judged [*judicatur*] that this is detrimental to the preservation of the state, it is then a pious act to bring him to justice [*in judicium vocare*], even though he must be condemned to death' (215/232). Here, the personal and the juridical judgement converge toward the utility of the republic. This is not only a rejection of the customary Christian morality of personal suffering. It is also a further radicalization of the politicization of neighbourly love. Surrendering one's coat is a reference to the Sermon on the Mount (Matthew 5:40). Understanding the import of this reference will help us see the force of Spinoza's example.

The Sermon on the Mount is hugely important for the argument of the *Theological Political Treatise*. As I said already in the Introduction, the 'golden rule' in the Sermon – 'all things whatsoever ye would that men should do to you, do ye even so to them' (Matthew 7:12) – is used by modern epicureans to justify the use of phronesis. Further, the Gospel of Matthew has a special position in the *Treatise*. Spinoza argues, as I noted earlier, that the Sermon on the Mount contains the entire philosophical teaching of the Bible.[10] In this context, it is telling that the example of the coat in chapter 19 is the only critical use of the Sermon in the *Treatise* – and Spinoza, who is usually happy to cite Matthew, refrains from doing so here, at the point where he is critical. So why is Spinoza critiquing the Sermon on the Mount at this point and why is he reluctant to do so explicitly?

The reason becomes clear if we recall what comes immediately after the example of the coat: 'Ye have heard that it hath been said, Thou shalt love thy neighbour, and hate thine enemy. But I say unto you, Love your enemies, bless them that curse you, do good to them that hate you, and pray for them which despitefully use you, and persecute you' (Matthew 5:43–4). This advice sits uncomfortably next to Spinoza's position that piety can in fact be impious. The politicization of the neighbour entails that the neighbour can indeed be an enemy. The utility of the state may require that the neighbour is subjected to violence. The imperative according to which 'whosoever shall smite thee on thy right cheek, turn to him the other also' (Matthew 5:39) is indeed ethically significant but it does not account for the political utility of the neighbour that Spinoza's epicurean use of the erastian principle requires.

---

[10] See note 27 of the *Theological Political Treatise* (237).

Spinoza brings all the different threads of this epicurean erastianism together immediately after highlighting that the path of the emotions requires as its condition of possibility that one can cross over to the path of reason:

> This being so, it follows that the welfare of the people [*salutem populi*] is the highest law [*summam esse legem*], to which all other laws, both human and divine, must be accommodated [*accommodari*]. But since it is the duty of the sovereign alone [*sulius summae potestatis officium*] to decide what is necessary for the welfare of the entire people and the security of the state [*saluti totius populi et imperii securitati*], and to command what it judges to be thus necessary, it follows that it is also the duty of the sovereign alone to decide what form piety towards one's neighbor should take [*solius etiam summae potestatis officium esse, determinare, qua ratione unusquisque debet proximum pietate colere*]. (215/232)

This may seem to increase the power of the sovereign – which is, for instance, the use that Hobbes makes of the erastian principle. The law is to be viewed strictly in terms of utility and this applies also to piety since 'no one can exercise piety towards his neighbour in accordance with God's command unless his piety and religion accord with the utility of the public [*publicae utilitati accommodet*]' (216/233). But this means that the calculation of utility can give rise to the internal enemy or stasis if it is deemed that the political aspect of neighbourly love – the utility for the commonwealth and the *salus* of the people – reaches a calculation according to which the sovereign's actions contradict the utility of the community. In other words, by inscribing the erastian principle on the path of the emotions, and making this path cross over or transverse to the path of reason as soon as the politicization of neighbourly love requires rational calculation, Spinoza raises the possibility that the internal enemy must be allowed to resist the sovereign's interpretation of the law when that interpretation contradicts reciprocal utility. Or, to put it in terms of Epicurus's formulation, as soon as the law is no longer contributing to the utility of the city, it loses its legitimacy and becomes defunct.[11]

Far from giving sovereignty an absolute freedom of action, then, the politicization of neighbourly love within the context of erastianism sets strict limits to the power of sovereignty. The material cause of resistance to the decisions of the sovereign is the inclusion of the other in one's rational

---

[11] Diogenes Laertius, 'Epicurus', in *Lives of Eminent Philosophers*, X.153. See the analysis of this in section 1 of Chapter 3 and section 1 of Chapter 4.

calculation. But the efficient cause is the sovereign himself: 'if those who hold the sovereignty [*qui imperium tenent*] choose to go what way they will, then . . . all things, both religious and secular, will go to ruin' (219/234–5). If the cause of internal unrest is the miscalculation of the advantage of the commonwealth, then the responsibility for that rests with the sovereign, precisely because the erastian principle places an enormous amount of responsibility on sovereignty. Spinoza's epicurean erastianism essentially says that it is *impious* to resist the sovereign who has control of the entire legal field, except when the impiety of sovereignty – that is, its failure to actualize the politicization of neighbourly love – precipitates the *pious* act of resisting.

The state of authority can only operate, according to Spinoza, when that authority is embroiled in a dialectical relation with the calculation of utility such that phronesis determines the judgements of those who hold authority. Thus, Spinoza's epicurean erastianism requires a transversal of obedience to the path of reason, which inscribes agonism at the heart of a politics that relies on the emotions.

2. The Path of Reason: The Unendurable in Politics

Whereas chapter 19 explores how the path of the emotions can lead to political virtue, chapter 20 examines the path of reason. Here, it is not law, but rather right that facilitates the ends of the polity. Spinoza summarizes this as follows:

> It follows quite clearly from . . . the basis of the state that its end is not to exercise dominion nor to restrain people by fear and subjecting them to another's right [*alterius juris facere*], but on the contrary to free everyone from fear [*unumquemque metu liberare*] so that all can live in security as far as is possible, that is, so that all can best preserve their own natural right to exist and to act, without harm to themselves and to others. It is not, I repeat, the purpose of the state to transform humans from rational beings into beasts or automata, but rather to enable their minds and bodies to use their reason without restraint and to refrain from the strife and the vicious mutual abuse that are prompted by hatred, anger or deceit. Therefore, the purpose of the state is, in reality, freedom [*Finis ergo Reipublicae revera libertas est*]. (223/240–1)

The path of reason that uses right to arrive at political virtue leads to freedom. This is a familiar conclusion. We saw in Chapter 1 the epicurean emphasis on freedom as the exercise of phronesis that facilitates the liberation from fear. The same idea is repeated here.

There is, nonetheless, an additional element in the citation above. Spinoza also identifies the end of the state where reason and right predominate as freedom. Freedom is the desired end of the operation of reason and right. This would have been recognized in the seventeenth century as a republican position. By the use of the term republican here I do not wish to draw any distinction between classical and modern republicanism.[12] Instead, I am drawing on their common denominator, namely, freedom from domination taken as a foundational political principle that indicates the purpose of the polity. Spinoza is certainly mindful of the particular example of the Dutch republic – the United Provinces gaining independence from Spain in the late sixteenth century on the way to becoming a republic.[13] But Spinoza's concern here has a more universal dimension. He has in mind the freedom he foregrounds in the subtitle to the *Theological Political Treatise* – freedom as co-implicated with the prosperity of the state and with piety, as I show in Chapter 1.

Immediately after arguing that the end of the state is in actual fact freedom, Spinoza proceeds to show that freedom contributes to the protection of the state. The argument has two steps, which echoes the subtitle of the *Treatise*.[14] According to the first step, freedom does not contradict sovereignty. On the contrary, 'everyone surrenders only their right to act as they think fit, and not their right to reason and judge [*ratiocinandi, et judicandi*]. So no one can act against sovereignty's decree without infringing on its right, but everyone can think, judge, and consequently speak out [*sentire, et judicare, et consequenter etiam dicere*] without infringing sovereign right' (224/241). Essentially we see here the operation of the anthropological principle: humans calculate their utility. No law can put an end to this. The second step is to indicate that this is beneficial to the law as well. Spinoza introduces this idea as an example: 'suppose one maintains that a certain law is against sound reason [*sanae rationi*], and therefore advocates its repeal. If one at the same time submits one's opinion to the judgement of the sovereign power (which alone is competent to enact and repeal laws),

---

[12] For classical and modern republicanism, see Guena, 'The Tension between Law and Politics in the Modern Republican Tradition', in Niederberger and Philipp (eds), *Republican Democracy*, 5–40.

[13] For an analysis of Spinoza's thought within this historical context, see Prokhovnik, *Spinoza and Republicanism*.

[14] See Chapter 1 for the problems raised by the subtitle to the *Treatise*.

and meanwhile does nothing contrary to what is commanded by that law [*nihil interim contra illius legis praescriptum agit*], one deserves well of the state, acting as an exemplary citizen [*optimus . . . civis*]' (224/241). This freedom protects the law because it creates exemplary citizens who do not lapse into sedition. Freedom protects the state from internal unrest.

But this creates a problem. We saw in section 2 of Chapter 6 that obedience to the sovereign is possible even when the sovereign acts against the utility of the state, provided that one does not recognize the harmful actions of the sovereign. But when one correctly judges as harmful the acts one is called upon to obey, then one becomes, says Spinoza, a 'necessary rebel' (161). The account of the freedom of thought and judgement thus far in chapter 20 is not problematic simply because of the prima facie contradiction to the idea of the necessary rebel. A graver problem is that the protection from rebellion this conception of freedom affords the sovereign may in fact be counterproductive, since it presents a state that is stuck with whatever decisions, laws and policies the sovereign decrees without recourse to change. Paradoxically, if Spinoza's argument stopped here, the political path to virtue through reason would be inferior to that of the emotions, since the path of reason enables the citizens to judge and articulate their thoughts but not to act, thereby making political change dependent on the will of the sovereign – which in most circumstances would mean that political change is impossible. But Spinoza does not stop here.

He proceeds to interrogate what allows the free thinking, properly judging, exemplary citizen to break through the confines of the right of the sovereign and to take up action: 'Humans in general find that nothing is more unbearable [*nihil magis impatienter*] to them than that the opinions they believe to be true [*opiniones, quas veras esse credunt*] are treated as criminal [*crimine*], and when that which motivates their pious conduct to God and man is accounted as wickedness [*sceleri*]. In consequence, they are emboldened to denounce the laws and go to all lengths to oppose the magistrate [*magistratum*], considering it not a disgrace but most honorable [*honestissimum*] to stir up stasis [*seditiones*] and to resort to any lawless action [*facinus*] to effect this cause' (226/244). Up to this point, there has been no indication that Spinoza is discussing anything other than the path of reason. And yet, the expression '*nihil magis impatienter*' (nothing is more unbearable) deviates the entire experience of freedom to the path of the emotions.

What exactly does 'impatienter' mean here? Shirley translates it as 'resentment'. Curley prefers 'impatience'. While not wrong, neither of these translations really captures the idea that Spinoza is conveying here. 'Impatienter' is an adverbial form related to 'patientia', which in turn is a translation of the Greek term 'pathos'. Patientia and pathos mean suffering in the sense of undergoing certain affections, or of being affected. They denote an experience that one receives from the 'outside', or something that one undergoes. In this sense, an affect or an emotion is the product of patientia or pathos. Impatienter and its cognates, such as the adjective impatiens and the noun impatientia, are constructed by the addition of the privative to patientia. The meaning, then, is literally about the impossibility of suffering or enduring. This may denote a lack of affections in the sense of an extreme impassivity or lack of connectedness to the world, and thus be associated to the Greek term 'apathia'. But such an impassivity is rare and hard to achieve – we are, after all, humans because we have feelings and because we let ourselves be affected; we are humans because our essence, Spinoza says, is desire. Consequently, the primary meaning is about the insufferability of that which must nonetheless be suffered. Thus, Glare's Latin dictionary gives as the only meaning of 'impatienter' the periphrasis 'without being able to endure (the situation)'.[15]

I have used the word 'unbearable' to translate 'impatienter' to denote this double movement: one undergoes an experience that one desires to prevent but cannot do so. Here, it is the experience of having one's true opinions treated as criminal or wicked. The privative 'un-' in this context indicates both the impossibility of not being affected by this experience, and also the impossibility of accommodating the experience within a rational framework that would make the experience something that the agent can handle – that would make it bearable. Differently put, it is a surge of emotion that one cannot square with one's rationality. Or, in a more epicurean formulation, it is the co-articulation of emotions with the rational in the operation of phronesis. This particular configuration of emotion and thought that confronts the human's drive to calculate utility has the capacity, suggests Spinoza, to drive one – an individual but also a body of individuals – into stasis, that is, into conflict with the instituted power that is the cause of the 'impatientia'. And when internal conflict arises in such a way, those who are driven to it are not the disgraceful kind of internal enemy that seeks the devastation of the polity, but 'most honourable' in the sense that the stasis seeks to re-establish the destabilized balance between phronesis and emotion. This adverb, then, 'impatienter', *inscribes emotion into the path of reason and in such a way as to indicate a necessary rebel.* Or, differently put, the cause of necessary rebellion is the emotional surge that overwhelms reason thereby leading to instrumental rationality.

[15] *Oxford Latin Dictionary*, 840. The meaning of 'impatience' in English is a further derivative of the experience that I am describing.

It is worth noting here that Spinoza uses a specific name for this unbearable experience in the *Political Treatise*, the name 'indignation'. This term recurs throughout the *Political Treatise* but the most succinct formulation is in a passage that both affirms the insight of chapter 20 of the *Theological Political Treatise* and also pushes it further:

> matters which arouse great indignation [*plurimi indignantur*] are not likely to fall within the right of the commonwealth [*civitatis jus*]. It is without doubt a natural thing for humans to conspire (i.e., to enact a stasis) as if in one body [*in unum conspirare*] either by reason of a common fear or through desire to avenge a common injury. And since the right of the commonwealth is defined by the common power of the multitude [*jus civitatis communi multitudinis potentia definitur*], undoubtedly the power of the commonwealth and its right [*potentiam civitatis et jus*] is to that extent diminished, as it is itself the cause [*ipsa causas praebet*] for many citizens to join as one in a conspiracy (or, stasis) [*plures in unum conspirent*]. (3.9)[16]

This passage articulates more clearly what the *Theological Political Treatise* also wants to express. The crucial addition here is a clearer description of how the surge of feeling is related to sovereignty. Spinoza describes a double move. On the one hand, the surge of feeling is caused by the actions of the state itself; on the other, the feeling thus aroused does not fall within the right of the state. This double move opens up the space for a further refinement of the position described in the *Theological Political Treatise*. Here it is made explicit that this surge of feeling is not individual. This is implied in the earlier *Treatise* but here it is made explicit that indignation can unite the multitude in opposition to sovereignty – and that united conspiracy or stasis is justified by natural right.

The term indignation is perfectly suited to describe all these moves. It is not by coincidence that the protesters who rushed to the streets in response to the European Union's austerity measures to counter the effects of the financial crisis in the early 2010s were called the 'indignants'. In Greece, for instance, this movement – in Greek, the *aganaktismenoi*, a direct translation of the 'indignants' – was crucial for the collapse of the traditional duopoly of power in Greek politics and the election to government of the grassroots movement of Syriza in the January 2015 election. More generally, the term 'indignation' aptly captures the conjunction of a surge of emotion with the

---

[16] The parenthetical extrapolations are my own.

calculation of utility that Spinoza describes in this crucial passage of chapter 20 of the *Theological Political Treatise*.

We see here, then, a deviation from the path of reason. The deviation does not consist in a heightening of reason itself. On the contrary, it takes place through an upsurge of emotion. We saw a similar deviation from the path of the emotions in the previous section. There, too, the deviation was not caused through the emotions themselves, but through an inscription of heightened rationality within the principle of obedience, namely, neighbourly love. Thus we see that the two paths transverse. Neither is pure, but they rather interact and intersect continuously. This is possible because phronesis or the calculation of utility that is definitive of human nature – as we learned in chapter 16 – is a combination of thought and emotion. Thus, it is through the anthropological principle or the third epicurean theme that Spinoza can give an account of political change as the transversal between the two paths leading to the good and virtue.

This double deviation – from the path of reason to that of the emotions and vice versa – addresses the relation between the two paths to achieve the good. If Spinoza concedes earlier that the purity of the two paths is 'more theory than practice', we see in the last couple of chapters of the *Theological Political Treatise* what real political practice consists in, and in such a way as to account for the possibility of political change. Surprisingly, this reality or actuality of the political consists in the possibility of internal enmity or stasis. The deviation from either path is the possibility of rising up against constituted power. I will return for a last time to this figure of stasis in the final section. I have tried to present schematically all the critical moves of this chiasmus in a diagram that can function as a mnemonic device for Spinoza's idea of an epicurean politics.

3. The Right to Abrogate: The Internal Enemy and Democracy

Given that the chiasmus of the paths of the emotions and reason is precipitated by stasis, we need to return one last time to the figure of the internal enemy. We encountered it for the first time in the Preface to the *Theological Political Treatise* where Spinoza argues that the real internal enemy is whoever abuses the law so as to stifle phronesis, all the while insisting that conflict and contestation are ineliminable from the polity. We have also seen that Spinoza repeatedly insists on the responsibility of sovereignty in the creation of internal enmity. And in chapters 7 and 14, Spinoza defines as internal enmity the use of theology to pursue one's self-interest

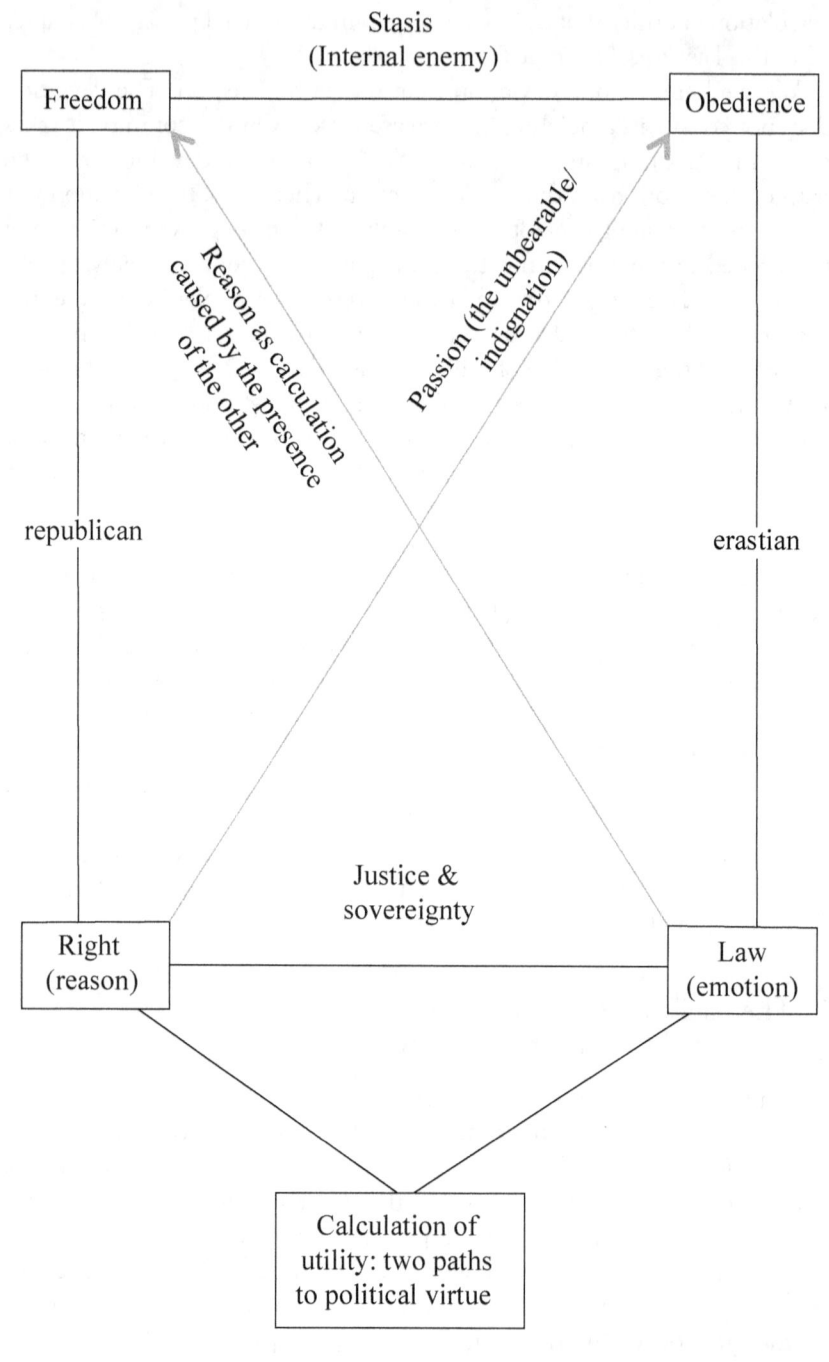

by prosecuting one's opponents.[17] In addition, we see in the present chapter that the internal enemy expresses the conflict between authority and utility – that is, the idea of agonistic democracy. It is at the moments that authority asserts itself by not following what is the true utility of the state and thereby turns authoritarian that indignation arises. And it is the utility accompanying neighbourly love that delimits the authority of political power. Thus, the internal enemy plays a critical role in the way the dialectic of authority and utility is articulated in the chiasmus between the two paths.

It will transpire that internal enmity mirrors the distinction between authority and authoritarianism, which is of such importance to Spinoza. There is an internal enmity – which for brevity I will refer to as stasis – that precipitates the utility of the political community and which propels the transversal from one path to the other. There is also a different notion of internal enmity – which for expedience I will refer to as sedition – that is not only unconcerned with the utility of the community, but also seeks to prevent or pervert the means by which the chiasmus of the two paths takes place. For instance, it may use rational – or seemingly rational – arguments so as to arouse emotions such as fear whose only outcomes are superstition and voluntary submission to those who hold authority. This is the production of voluntary servitude that Spinoza associates with tyranny. Interestingly, Spinoza associates stasis with the people as a whole or with those who are willing to exercise their phronesis but who are not confined to constituted power; while sedition is ascribed to those who strive to strengthen or increase their hold on political power. In other words, the danger of sedition arises within authority.

How does Spinoza manage to draw the distinction between a positive and a negative internal enemy with recourse to the chiasmus between the two paths? We need to follow closely his references to internal enmity in the last two chapters of the *Theological Political Treatise*.

The first point to note is how much of chapters 19 and 20 is concerned with forms of internal enmity that lead to pernicious consequences for the state. In chapter 19, the negative form of internal enmity is understood as the opposition to the erastian principle, that is, 'if private citizens seditiously [*seditiose*] seek to be the champions of religious law' (219/236). The reason that this is seditious is announced from the opening of the chapter: those who 'are making a division of sovereignty are actually paving the way to their own sovereignty [*imo viam ad imperium affectare*]' (212/228). On the path of virtue through the emotions, sedition is the attempt to usurp power

---

[17] See section 1 of Chapter 5 and section 3 of Chapter 6.

by denying that the sovereign has control over both civil and religious law, since that undermines obedience to the law.

This attempt to usurp power, or sedition, utilizes the distinction between justification, legitimacy and judgement. Spinoza uses one of the longest and most important examples in the *Treatise* to illustrate this point. This is his understanding of the political history of Christianity, which is worth examining from the perspective of Spinoza's epicurean erastianism. The starting premise of this history refers back to the principle of didactic authority: 'when we review the origins of the Christian religion, the cause [*causa*] of this phenomenon [i.e. of sedition] is completely revealed. It was not kings who were the first teachers [*non reges primi docuerunt*] of the Christian religion, but men of private station who, despite the will of those who held the sovereignty and were their rulers, were long accustomed to address private religious assemblies, to institute and perform sacred rites, to make all arrangements and decisions on their own responsibility without any regard to the state' (219–20/237). Spinoza adumbrates the notion of didactic authority in chapter 11. It is defined there in contradistinction to personal authority. Whereas personal authority 'does not permit of argumentation' (139), didactic authority relies on the operation of rationality, which makes it universalizable but also subject to contestation. We see at this point the importance of the possibility of contestation for didactic authority. The early Christian fathers used their didactic authority to justify their teaching without recourse to the legitimacy required by sovereign power. From this perspective, the utility of didactic authority – the fact that it teaches the fundamental principle of religion, namely, neighbourly love – enables the clash between authority and utility.

The positive function of didactic authority radically changes, however, when Christianity becomes the official religion in the fourth century, according to Spinoza: 'when their religion began to be introduced to the state [*religio in imperium introduci incepit*], the churchmen were obliged to teach it to the emperors themselves in the form they had given it, from which it was an easy step for them to gain recognition as its teachers and interpreters [*doctores et interpretes*], and furthermore as the pastors of the church and virtually God's representatives' (220/237). The didactic authority of the apostles is now transformed by their successors into a political authority, which essentially consists in controlling the education of the emperors. Or, differently put, moral authority legitimated by dogma supervenes over political authority. Now, instead of seeking to highlight the conflict between authority and utility, didactic authority is used to achieve personal authority and the boundary between the two collapses. Ultimately, this results in the attempt to fracture the authority in control of civil and religious law. The institution of Christianity as the official religion of the state rapidly leads to the violation of the erastian principle – a violation, moreover, that is uncannily similar in structure to the great fault of authority in the Hebrew state, according to the analysis of chapters 17 and 18, namely, that authority is fractured into its theological and political components, while the theological endeavours to dominate the political one.

The mechanism Christian churchmen use to defend the separation of political and religious law consists, according to Spinoza, in the use of rationality in such a way as to confound the pursuit of utility – it is reason without any adherence to the link between phronesis and neighbourly love: 'they multiplied religious dogmas to such an extent [*religionis dogmata ad tam magnum numerum auxerant*] and confused them with so much philosophy [*cum philosophia*] that the supreme interpreter of religion had to be a consummate philosopher and theologian [*summus ejus interpres summus philosophus et theologus*] and to have time for a host of useless speculations [*inutilibus speculationibus*]. This effectively ruled out all but men of private station with abundant leisure' (220/237). In this account of sedition as the separation of ecclesiastical from sovereign power, the speculations of those who have inherited didactic authority are useless (*inutilibus*) because they are not concerned with the utility of the community but rather with their own advantage. It is essentially the tactic of a power grab. From Spinoza's perspective, the theologico-political history of Christianity is nothing but the attempt to inscribe reason in the path to virtue through obedience, not in order to determine one's disposition toward the neighbour, but as a means to furthering the power and interests of one group within the polity, that is, the official Church. Sedition in this context, then, is the self-serving use of reason to circumscribe potestas to a specific group, that is, those who think without concern for utility (*inutilibus speculationibus*).

Sedition in the path of virtue relying on obedience consists in the subversion of reason, that is, of that which allows it to transverse to the other path. Differently put, it consists in the abuse of the means that deviate the path of the emotions to the path of reason. The crossing over to the path of reason that Spinoza advocates consists in an intensification of the operation of rationality in the service of, and as prompted by, a communal sense of utility. There is, then, essentially a *judgement* that the politically expedient action is to disobey. The theologians also intensify the use of reason, but they subvert this use to serve their own advantage by dissociating rationality from the calculation of utility. Reason is now put in the service of a particular group of people – or a faction – who seek to promote their personal authority and to carve out a realm – that of religious law – where they can assert their potestas. The speculative metaphysics of theology denies phronesis only in order to promote the utility of those indulging in speculative metaphysics.[18] It is a deviation that suspends judgement in order to *justify* the power of the Church. This gap between judgement and justification signals the distinction between stasis as the conflict enabling the relation between the two paths, and the reinstatement of personal authority as a form of authoritarianism and tyranny.

The description of sedition in chapter 20 also reinforces the importance of the distinction between judgement and justification for distinguishing between stasis and sedition. And the means are the same as those used on the path of the emotions, namely, the misuse of that element that leads to the crossing or deviation from one path to the other, in such a way as to reinforce personal authority. This intensification of feeling is described here as arousing the emotions of the masses without concern for the utility of the state or for the freedom either of the masses or of those that the aggression of the masses is directed against.

For instance, after arguing that, when the oppression of authority becomes unbearable, the most honourable citizens rise up to resist those executive decisions that are not conducive to the utility of the polity. Spinoza adds: 'if on the contrary the purpose of one's action is to accuse the magistrate of injustice and to stir up popular hatred [*vulgo odiosum reddendum*], or if one seditiously [*seditiose*] seeks to abrogate that law [*legem illam abrogare*] in spite of the magistrate, one is nothing more than an agitator and a rebel [*perturbator est, et rebellis*]' (224/241). The intensification of feeling is registered here in the stirring up of the *vulgus* with the aim being to abrogate the law in order to attack the lawgiver. This demagogical mobilization of feelings makes one an agitator who is not concerned in reality with the utility of the state but rather with their own personal authority that is asserted by making the masses obey them instead of the sovereign.

Spinoza repeats the same argument later to generalize it: 'it is clearer than the sun at noon that the real schismatics [*schismaticos*] are those who condemn the writings of others and seditiously incite the quarrelsome masses against the writers [*vulgum petulantem in scriptores seditiose instigant*] . . . the real agitators [*revera perturbatores*] are those who, in a free commonwealth,

---

[18] In his discussion of phronesis, Heidegger is perfectly correct to point out that the privileging of episteme or universal knowledge is the hallmark of onto-theology. See Heidegger, *Plato's Sophist*. For a further discussion of this point, see Vardoulakis, *The Ruse of Techne* (forthcoming).

vainly seek to abolish freedom of judgment [*libertatem judicii*], which cannot be suppressed' (228–9/246). Here the previous argument about inciting the feelings of the masses to achieve personal authority is not confined to the instances where the sovereign is resisted. In fact, says Spinoza, it applies in all sorts of situations. The real criterion to identify this form of schismatism or sedition is to note that it is an attempt to justify one's power by suppressing the other's right to judge. In other words, sedition is the separation of judgement and justification in such a way as to repress the function and political utility of phronesis.

We see then that sedition always consists, according to the analysis presented in chapters 19 and 20, in the re-inscription of personal authority by subverting the means whereby the two paths to political virtue transverse. This is a significant issue since it raises the problem of how to be sure that any deviation from the path of the emotions or the path of reason is indeed conducted for the utility of the community and for the protection of the freedom to exercise phronesis. Why could one not *pretend* to be acting for the benefit of the polity while furthering one's personal advantage and authority?

Spinoza nowhere gives us the reassurance that it is possible to distinguish self-serving sedition from the stasis that makes democracy possible. Agonism or conflict depend on specific circumstances because phronesis derives its judgements from the contingency of the situation. Thus it is impossible to provide secure normative criteria that will safeguard us from the usurpers of power. The possibility that personal authority will prevail despite the persistence of the calculation of utility, thereby establishing an authoritarian regime, is a real possibility – one that makes the political precarious.

Nonetheless, Spinoza does offer one – and only one – indication of what is the most expedient way in which a democratic polity can safeguard itself from the rise of despotism:

> In a democratic sovereignty [*In imperio enim democratico*] (which comes closest to the natural state [*ad statum naturalem*]) everybody [*omnes*] undertakes to act, but not to reason and to judge, by decisions made in common [*ex communi*]. That is to say, since all humans cannot think alike, they agree [*pacti sunt*] that a proposal supported by a majority of votes shall have the force of a decree, meanwhile retaining the authority to abrogate [*auctoritatem . . . abrogandi*] the same when they see a better alternative. Thus the less freedom of judgment is conceded to men, the further their distance from the most natural state, and consequently the more oppressive the regime. (228/245)

It may be impossible to have normative criteria that help us recognize a justification that leads back to authoritarianism from a judgement that leads to utility. But this does not entail more stringent regulation, according to Spinoza. To the contrary, his advice is for further freedom, advocating an intensification of practical judgement or phronesis. This entails a heightening of the dialectical tension between authority and utility.

It is instructive to note the vocabulary Spinoza uses to put forward this proposition for the intensification of phronesis. He is, first, associating it with democracy. There is sovereignty that is characterized by the creation of a common space for decision making. Second, this is part of a social contract. People agree (*pacti sunt*) to participate in such a process. And, third, the democratic imperative does not eliminate authority – the state of authority characterizing the path of the emotions is a real possibility that can lead to the good. But this is an authority that is distinct from authoritarianism. Such an authority that approximates democracy and is anti-authoritarian, Spinoza designates as the authority to abrogate. The authority to abrogate requires the intensification of judgement – and hence it is an authority that allows for freedom.

Multiple effects follow from this authority to abrogate. Some are spelled out by Spinoza, some remain implicit within his discourse. The most important one is a reaffirmation of the key epicurean insight that 'death is nothing to us': 'Those who are conscious of being honourable [*honestos*] do not fear death as criminals do [*mortem ut scelesti non timent*]. . . . On the contrary, they think it an honor [*honestum*], not a punishment, to die for a good cause [*pro bona causa*], and a glorious thing to die for freedom [*pro libertate gloriosum*]' (227/245). Whoever exercises the authority to abrogate ought to be liberated from fear as the kind of emotion that leads to superstition and servitude.

The fact that, according to the epicureans, 'fear is nothing to us', entails, at the same time, as I argue in Chapter 1, that liberty is understood as the exercise of phronesis unalloyed by the kind of fear that distorts judgement or cripples it altogether. Spinoza is not advocating here some kind of martyrdom. The complete opposite is the case: he is advocating an intensification of judgement that is imbued in living. The free person – according to Proposition 67 of Part IV of the *Ethics* – is concerned with living, not with death. Thus, if those who are free are to die for expressing how unbearable they find unjust laws or for exercising their authority to abrogate, they do so for the sake of living – that is, for the utility of the community – not in the service of some kind of transcendent ideal. They are not martyrs, meaning, literally, 'witnesses' to some otherworldly value or precept. They are active participants in the unfolding of life, and prepared to accept the consequences of their actions. Spinoza's affirmation of liberty as the exercise of phronesis places him firmly within the epicurean tradition of understanding freedom.

At the same time, Spinoza augments that tradition and transforms it in such a way as to draw out the consequences of the anthropological principle of phronesis as it applies to *everyone* – that is, it draws us toward a democratic epicureanism. Spinoza continues from the above citation: 'What sort of lesson [*exempli*], then, is learnt from the death of such people, whose cause is beyond the understanding of those of sluggish and feeble spirit, is hated by those who perpetrate seditions [*seditiosi*], but who the honorable love [*honesti amant*]? The only lesson [*exemplum*] to be drawn from their death is to emulate [*imitandum*] them, or at least to revere them' (227/245). This is a further important insight on the idea of the two paths to virtue. The honourable persons who exercise their judgement without emotional obstacles and with the clear purpose of enhancing the utility of everyone are free because they are operating on the path of reason. But Spinoza readily admits here that these honourable people ought to be imitated. As we saw in Chapter 5, the imitation of the affects is indispensable to neighbourly love and, as we saw further in Chapter 6, Balibar demonstrates that the path of the emotions relies on the imitation of the affects to achieve the good. The inscription of the imitation of the affects in the operation of rationality indicates, therefore, the centrality of the authority to abrogate in the crossing of the two paths.

Indeed, we could say that the point where the two paths transverse is the authority to abrogate. The authority to abrogate indicates, on the one hand, those who revolt from the side of reason: they are the exemplary figures whose indignation leads them to resist those acts that are against the utility of the people. At the same time, these are figures to be emulated. They are exemplars of action. And in that sense they become the models for inciting phronesis within those who are obedient to the sovereign and to the principle of neighbourly love. Thus, the authority to abrogate also affects those who instigate a stasis deviating from the path of the emotions to that of reason. The point of overlap of these two forms of stasis is the authority to abrogate.

Let me also indicate three further effects that are not spelled out by Spinoza. First, the democracy that he has in mind here is not defined primarily with recourse to the people or an established form of potestas. Rather, what is paramount is the freedom of judgement and the establishment of the authority to abrogate – or, the various possibilities of the transversal between the two paths to political virtue. Thus, democracy for Spinoza is not simply a regime of government. Rather, it is the disposition or propensity to realize the anthropological principle, that is, in true epicurean fashion, it is the heightening of the capacity to judge and to exercise phronesis as it unfolds in a dialectical relation to authority.

Second, this means that democracy for Spinoza takes the possibility of conflict as central to the democratic practice. Stasis is paramount for the exercise of phronesis. There is disagreement or dissent and this requires the recognition that disagreement will lead to discord. From this perspective, we can talk about Spinoza's theory of agonistic democracy. But we also need to remember the epicurean provenance of this agonistic democracy because of the emphasis it places on instrumental rationality. Agonistic democracy is here understood as the material actualization of the political in the form of the relation between the two regimes of power – natural democracy and the state of authority – that forms as the paths of reason and the emotions transverse.

Third, we see how the authority to abrogate combines particular concerns with a sense of universality. There is the universal imperative of the political import of neighbourly love. This universal concern entails that phronesis calculates the utility of the community as a whole. However, the community is not an idealized formation or a utopia. And the calculation to be derived has no support from any transcendent criteria. The community is everyone who has agreed to live together and the advantage of this community depends on contingent circumstances that constantly change. Thus, the authority to abrogate establishes a sense of singularity that is both particular and universal. In this, the authority to abrogate is distinct both from the overly particular nature of personal authority and from the overreliance on universality characterizing didactic authority.

So, what is Spinoza's lesson? What does this transversal of the two paths, this authority to abrogate, teach us? Paradoxically, the only 'lesson' we can take away is that there is no final lesson as to how the political is to be instituted. There is no norm or principle that can placate our political anxieties or solve our problems in all given circumstances. Instead, the only constant is the exigency to judge or exercise one's phronesis in such a way as to nurture both rationality and feeling and – significantly – by opposing any misappropriation of either thought or the affects by those who seek to preserve their power by adumbrating their authority. In other words, the only 'lesson' is that our relations to others – both ethical and political relations – are subject to the dialectic of authority and utility.

One way that I put this point earlier was by describing Spinoza's dialectic as a promise. A promise persists so long as it is not realized while its being realized is still held as a possibility. The dialectic of authority and utility is a promise in the sense that it has no final telos. But there is something additional that we find out about the promise in the last part of the *Theological Political Treatise*. If this promise is sustained by the operation of phronesis, and if the calculation of utility is the basis of Spinoza's conception of democracy, then Spinoza's promise is nothing other than the promise of democracy understood as agonistic praxis.

Conclusion:
The Limitation of Spinoza's Epicureanism

Spinoza does a remarkable job in presenting the dialectic of authority and utility in the *Theological Political Treatise*. Not only does this revive an epicurean politics; in addition, it provides a compelling account of a democratic politics that relies on agonism. In this account, the conflict between authority and utility can never be quenched, which makes it the driver of politics. This conflict emerges as more fundamental than any form of government, or than any arrangement of representation, or than any way in which there is a separation of powers within the state.

Through this dialectic of authority and utility, Spinoza participates in the materialist tradition of modernity, not by slavishly following previous ideas but by appropriating and reformulating them. The significant contribution of the *Theological Political Treatise* is that it develops a typology of authority that highlights the importance of democracy for an epicurean politics. The distinction between personal authority, didactic authority and the authority to abrogate provides Spinoza with the basis to both describe and critique constituted power and to delineate a form of agonistic politics characterized by the intensification of the freedom to calculate one's utility.

Further, the reliance of Spinoza's politics on the anthropological principle – or the propensity to calculate one's utility in relation to the utility of the entire community – has a contemporary relevance that is, it seems to me, of urgent significance. There are at least three reasons that this is the case.

First, the anthropological principle, as I describe it, requires that there are two distinct, but not separate, paths to political virtue, the path of the emotions and the path of reason. It seems to me that it is hugely significant to consider a *democratic* politics that does not forget the import of the emotions in the construction of the political. There has been an inordinate emphasis on deliberation and process in the way that the democratic is understood.

The problem with such an overreliance on reason is that it finds it hard to explain so much of the political that is dominated, for the most part, by the emotions.

Spinoza's contribution consists in insisting that even though a political process may be dominated by the emotions, there is always a significant operative presence of reasonableness or phronesis since everyone is so constituted as to calculate their utility. Thus, a politics of the emotions not only does not absolve us from the requirement to provide an explanation, lapsing instead into the crippling left melancholia; to the contrary, from a Spinozan perspective a politics of the emotions is fully realized at the moments it deviates to the path of reason, which require ever more vigilance and the drive to calculate collective utility. It is true that this process can be subverted, but the subversion unfolds by presupposing the connection between emotions and utility.

Let me provide an example of the point I am making: Steven Bannon, the architect of Trump's political victory in 2016, talked about an 'economic patriotism', which essentially asked economically disadvantaged voters to think of their economic predicament and their place in the market in nationalist terms, such as the USA versus China. The triumph of this logic was the conversion of a calculation of an 'economic patriotic' utility into the emotional surge – mostly anger – that propelled Trump to the White House. This process involved a combination of instrumental rationality and the passions, a process Spinoza describes as sedition at various places in the *Theological Political Treatise* – especially the Preface and chapters 7, 14, 19 and 20 – but which is nonetheless more sophisticated and closer to reality than the utopian kind of thinking that presumes the evacuation of the emotions from the political sphere so that rational judgements can be drawn through deliberative processes.

The second reason is that Spinoza's politics is – perhaps eerily – contemporary in that the figure of authority is all the more relevant today. It seems to me that the increasing political success of populist demagogues, of politicians who take advantage of the 'fickle masses', makes Spinoza's insights into authority highly pertinent. This is not to deny that the figure of authority has not been interrogated in the last century. One need only consider thinkers such as Max Weber, Hannah Arendt, Louis Althusser and Michel Foucault. However, what is missing in all the important thinkers of authority and constituted power just listed is the recognition of the importance of the dialectic of authority and utility, which in turn requires the distinction between authority and authoritarianism. Even though they are all materialists in their own ways, none of them is epicurean enough, which is to say, none of them pays particular attention to the importance of phronesis for the political.

The paradox with the above-mentioned thinkers is that even though they have provided unsurpassable analyses of politics and even though they have developed arguably more elaborate – or, at least, more complex – typologies of authoritarianism, the failure to recognize the importance of the calculation of utility in the construction of the political – that is, their deficient epicureanism – made it impossible for them to make a significant contribution in thinking authority and consequently they never arrived at an epicurean conception of democratic agonism. Spinoza's epicureanism may become their ally, helping the epigones of thinkers such as Weber, Arendt, Althusser and Foucault to nuance their insights toward achieving more democratic communities.

Third, we can summarize these two important Spinozan insights by saying that the notion of authority does not simply provide an historical thickness to Spinoza's narrative – that is, the trajectory from revealed religion and the authority of the prophets to universal religion and sovereign authority. This would be a severely limited, even distorted, understanding of Spinoza's position. Rather, Spinoza's point is that earlier forms of authority never completely disappear. Thus, even though there are no longer prophets today, still the structure of personal authority continues to inform our politics. History is not a teleological progress toward some transcendent telos. There are only humanly determined ends dictated by the operation of phronesis.

This insight could be a helpful reminder to those who proclaim deep ruptures and radical new formations of the political, usually under the name of biopolitics or neoliberalism. Significantly, these tend to be proponents – I almost said *prophets* – either of a brave new world or an impending apocalypse. And yet, both options are blind to one simple point, namely, that different forms of authority, either the personal authority relying on particularity or the didactic authority relying on the universality of communication, have haunted politics for a long time and they are responsible for making people obey without even knowing that they are obeying, that is, of turning humans into voluntary slaves. This spectre of the political – the slave – provides us with the impetus and the urgency to calculate our utility in the pursuit of our freedom.

If, then, Spinoza's great contribution is his epicureanism – all the paradoxical conjunctions and disjunctions between authority and utility – I do not mean to thereby suggest that his own thought does not admit of improvement. In fact, it seems to me that there is one significant shortfall in the way he constructs the dialectic of authority and utility in the *Theological Political*

Treatise. Specifically, Spinoza provides a typology of authority, but he does not provide a typology of utility. What are the different ways in which instrumental rationality articulates itself? And how are these informed by different forms of authority?

Perhaps I am being unfair. Maybe we can find a typology of phronesis in the *Theological Political Treatise*. There is, on the one hand, the phronesis that calculates utility from the ethical and democratic side of the neighbour and which aims toward the attainment of the good and virtue. And there is on the other hand the calculation of utility that seeks to justify the power of a person or a group toward establishing their personal authority in such a way that it does not contribute to the utility of the community as a whole. This distinction between two senses of phronesis, one leading to virtue and the other to servitude, is certainly operative in the *Treatise*.

What I am suggesting, then, more accurately, is that Spinoza presents a rather elaborate typology of authority, but nothing like an equally intricate outline of utility. In particular, what is missing in Spinoza is an analysis of the ways in which the justification of power can employ distinct forms of instrumental rationality to achieve either authority or authoritarianism. For instance, if these justifications of power are instrumental, what kind of instrumental relations do they employ? Let me illustrate briefly what I have in mind by turning to a recent example.

We can understand the rise of Trump as the prevailing of distinct forms of instrumental justifications, that is, distinct forms articulating means and ends relations. We can understand the slogan 'make America great again' as positing an end, 'a great America' – whatever that end might mean, and without rejecting the possibility that, just like every transcendent end, it may be totally devoid of meaning, entirely opaque and lacking a signified. This end then functions to justify any belief or action that is mobilized to achieve it. In this form of justification, the end justifies the means. But the relation between means and end is the reverse when it comes to the (in)famous wall that Trump announced throughout his 2016 presidential campaign. Here we have a means – the wall itself – that is mobilized for protection from all those dangers that supposedly threaten the citizens of the United States and the security of the state itself. The means justify the end of the preservation and perpetuation of the state. The instrumental logic in these two examples is different – in the former the end justifies the means, in the latter the means justify the end.

This lacuna in Spinoza's thought is significant for two reasons. First, such a typology of instrumental rationality employed by authority would also enable us to conceive of how judgement or phronesis can be mobilized to critique, deconstruct or – as I prefer to say – dejustify authority's justifications. For instance, it will be one kind of argument that questions whether spurious ends such as the 'greatness of America' actually exist, and it will be another kind of argument employed against the discourse that appeals to the security of the state and the sanctity of its borders. The former kind of dejustification will seek to demystify any ultimate end, while the latter ultimately needs to question whether the Westphalian model of sovereignty is sufficient for understanding political – which is to say, also, interpersonal and ethical – relations.

Second, the lack of a typology of instrumental rationality affects the structure of Spinoza's argument too. The reason is that that both paths to virtue, and their alternative, authoritarianism, rely on the operation of phronesis. This is why, for instance, Spinoza can argue in the *Theological Political Treatise* but also more clearly in the *Political Treatise* that democracy is the basis of every political and constitutional form. But the lack of a detailed typology of the calculation of utility means that Spinoza's conception of democracy is stunted. More needs to be said.

In sum, Spinoza needs to pay much more attention to how instrumental rationality can spawn *both* democratic and despotic forms of being. This calls even more insistently for a typology of instrumental rationality.[1]

It seems to me that Spinoza is aware of the problem of how to account for the causes of different calculations of utility from within the anthropological principle itself, from within phronesis. In fact, we can understand the transition from the *Theological Political Treatise* to the *Political Treatise* as precisely the attempt to address this problem. From this perspective, Spinoza's solution to the problematic is both brilliant and deficient. It is brilliant in that it mobilizes the ancient distinction between the three constitutions – monarchy, aristocracy and democracy – in order to show that there is, in reality, one constitution, democracy, that relies on the judgements afforded by phronesis. In this move, Spinoza reiterates the ancient typology of constitutions only to overcome it by assimilating it in his epicureanism. But this success is also a limitation, as it seems to me that the methodology that relies on the three constitutions is not epicurean enough because it does not draw the distinctions from the dialectic of authority and utility.

Nonetheless the *Political Treatise* is also imbued with a promise. This is the promise of the recognition of the problematic that the calculation of utility bequeaths us. Even if Spinoza himself may have failed to live up to this promise in the *Political Treatise*, the articulation of the dialectic of

---

[1] I attempt to provide such a typology in *Sovereignty and its Other*.

authority and utility in the *Theological Political Treatise* is enough to place the onus on any reader who recognizes the dialectic of authority and utility to aspire toward that promise. Which is to say, to aspire to the promise of epicureanism and its politics of agonistic democracy. Just like any promise, epicureanism is bound to not realize itself in order to remain a promise – it is always to-come. And yet, for this very reason, it becomes the exigency that can direct our thoughts and our actions.

Bibliography

Abolafia, Jacob, 'Spinoza, Josephism and the Critique of the Hebrew Republic', *History of Political Thought* 35.2 (2014), 295–316.

Adorno, Theodor W., Daniel J. Levinson, Else Frenkel-Brunswik and Nevitt Sanford, *The Authoritarian Personality* (New York: Harper & Row, 1950).

Adorno, Theodor, *Negative Dialectics*, trans. E. B. Ashton (London: Routledge, 1990).

Agamben, Giorgio, *Homo Sacer: Sovereign Power and Bare Life*, trans. Daniel Heller-Roazen (Stanford: Stanford University Press, 1998).

Agamben, Giorgio, *Remnants of Auschwitz: The Witness and the Archive*, trans. Daniel Heller-Roazen (New York: Zone, 2002).

Agamben, Giorgio, *The Highest Poverty: Monastic Life and Form-of-Life*, trans. Adam Kotsko (Stanford: Stanford University Press, 2011).

Albiac, Gabriel, 'The Empty Synagogue', in Warren Montag and Ted Stolze (eds), *The New Spinoza* (Minneapolis: University of Minnesota Press, 1997), 108–43.

Althusser, Louis, 'The Only Materialist Tradition, Part 1: Spinoza', in Warren Montag and Ted Stolze (eds), *The New Spinoza* (Minneapolis: University of Minnesota Press, 1997), 3–19.

Althusser, Louis, 'The Underground Current of the Materialism of the Encounter', *Philosophy of the Encounter: Later Writings, 1978–87*, ed. François Matheron and Oliver Corpet, trans. G. M. Goshgarian (London: Verso, 2006), 167–207.

Althusser, Louis, and Étienne Balibar, *Reading Capital*, trans. Ben Brewster (London: NLB, 1970).

Annas, Julia, *The Morality of Happiness* (Oxford: Oxford University Press, 1993).

Arendt, Hannah, *Between Past and Future: Six Exercises in Political Thought* (New York: Viking, 1961).

Arendt, Hannah, *The Origins of Totalitarianism* (Cleveland: Meridian, 1962).
Arendt, Hannah, *On Violence* (New York: Harcourt, 1970).
Arendt, Hannah, *The Human Condition* (Chicago: University of Chicago Press, 1998).
Arendt, Hannah, *On Revolution* (London: Penguin, 2006).
Arendt, Hannah, *The Modern Challenge to Tradition: Fragmente eines Buchs*, ed. Barbara Hahn and James McFarland (Göttingen: Wallstein Verlag, 2018).
Aristotle, *Metaphysics*, trans. Hugh Tredennick (Cambridge, MA: Harvard University Press, 1933).
Aristotle, *The Athenian Constitution; The Eudemian Ethics; On Virtues and Vices*, trans. H. Rackham (Cambridge, MA: Harvard University Press, 1935).
Aristotle, *Politics*, trans. H. Rackham (Cambridge, MA: Harvard University Press, 1998).
Aristotle, *Nicomachean Ethics*, trans. H. Rackham (Cambridge, MA: Harvard University Press, 2003).
Armstrong, Aurelia, 'Natural and Unnatural Communities: Spinoza Beyond Hobbes', *British Journal for the History of Philosophy* 17.2 (2009), 279–305.
Arrow, Kenneth, *Social Choice and Individual Values*, 2nd edn (New York: John Wiley, 1963).
Assmann, Jan, *The Price of Monotheism*, trans. Robert Savage (Stanford: Stanford University Press, 2010).
Augustine, *The City of God Against the Pagans*, ed. and trans. R. W. Dyson (Cambridge: Cambridge University Press, 1998).
Augustine, *On the Free Choice of the Will, on Grace and Free Choice, and Other Writings*, ed. Peter King (Cambridge: Cambridge University Press, 2010).
Badiou, Alain, *Saint Paul: The Foundation of Universalism*, trans. Ray Brassier (Stanford: Stanford University Press, 2003).
Bakker, Frederik A., *Epicurean Meteorology: Sources, Method, Scope and Organization* (Leiden: Brill, 2016).
Bal, Mieke, and Dimitris Vardoulakis, 'An Inter-Action: Rembrandt and Spinoza', in Dimitris Vardoulakis (ed.), *Spinoza Now* (Minneapolis: University of Minnesota Press, 2011), 277–303.
Balibar, Étienne, *Spinoza: From Individuality to Transindividuality* (Delft: Eburon, 1997).
Balibar, Étienne, *Spinoza and Politics*, trans. Peter Snowdon (London: Verso, 1998).
Balibar, Étienne, *Equaliberty: Political Essays*, trans. James Ingram (Durham, NC: Duke University Press, 2014).

Balibar, Étienne, *Citizen Subject: Foundation for Philosophical Anthropology*, trans. Steven Miller (New York: Fordham University Press, 2017).

Balibar, Étienne, 'Philosophies of the Transindividual: Spinoza, Marx, Freud', trans. Mark Kelly, *Australian Philosophy Review* 2.1 (2018), 5–25.

Balibar, Étienne, *Spinoza, the Transindividual*, trans. Mark Kelly (Edinburgh: Edinburgh University Press, 2020).

Barbone, Steven, Lee Rice and Jacob Adler, 'Introduction', in *Spinoza: The Letters*, trans. Samuel Shirley (Indianapolis: Hackett, 1995), 1–58.

Bayle, Pierre, *Historical and Critical Dictionary: Selections*, trans. Richard H. Popkin (Indianapolis: Bobbs-Merrill, 1965).

Beiser, Frederick C., *The Fate of Reason: German Philosophy from Kant to Fichte* (Cambridge, MA: Harvard University Press, 1987).

Benjamin, Walter, 'Capitalism as Religion', *Selected Writings*, vol. 1, ed. Michael W. Jennings et al. (Cambridge, MA: Belknap, 1997), 288–9.

Benjamin, Walter, *The Origin of German Tragic Drama*, trans. John Osborne (London: Verso, 2003).

Benveniste, Émile, *Le Vocabulaire des institutions indo-européennes II: Pouvoir, droit, religion* (Paris: Minuit, 1969).

Berkowitz, Roger, 'Why Arendt Matters: Revisiting *The Origins of Totalitarianism*', *LA Review of Books*, 18 March 2017.

Bernasconi, Robert, 'Who is my Neighbor? Who is the Other? Questioning "the Generosity of Western Thought"', in Claire Katz and Lara Trout (eds), *Emmanuel Levinas: Critical Assessments of Leading Philosophers*, vol. IV, *Beyond Levinas* (London: Routledge, 2005), 5–30.

Bhandar, Brenna, *Colonial Lives of Property: Law, Land, and Racial Regimes of Ownership* (Durham, NC: Duke University Press, 2018).

Bloch, Olivier, *Le Matérialisme* (Paris: Presses Universitaires de France, 1985).

Bottici, Chiara, *A Philosophy of Political Myth* (Cambridge: Cambridge University Press, 2007).

Bottici, Chiara, *Imaginal Politics: Imagines Beyond Imagination and the Imaginary* (New York: Columbia University Press, 2014).

Braidotti, Rosi, *Transpositions: On Nomadic Ethics* (Cambridge: Polity, 2006).

Braidotti, Rosi, 'The Ethics of Becoming Imperceptible', in Constantin Boundas (ed.), *Deleuze and Philosophy* (Edinburgh: Edinburgh University Press, 2006), 133–59.

Braidotti, Rosi, *The Posthuman* (Cambridge: Polity, 2013).

Brown, Alison, *The Return of Lucretius to Renaissance Florence* (Cambridge, MA: Harvard University Press, 2010).

Brown, Alison, 'Lucretian Naturalism and the Evolution of Machiavelli's Ethics', in Filippo Del Lucchese, Fabio Frosini and Vittorio Morfino (eds), *The Radical Machiavelli: Politics, Philosophy and Language* (Leiden: Brill, 2015), 105–27.

Brown, Christopher Leslie et al., *Rembrandt: The Master and His Workshop* (New Haven: Yale University Press, 1991).

Brown, Eric, 'Politics and Society', in James Warren (ed.), *The Cambridge Companion to Epicureanism* (Cambridge: Cambridge University Press, 2009), 179–206.

Brown, Robin Gordon and James Ladyman, *Materialism: A Historical and Philosophical Inquiry* (London: Routledge, 2019).

Brown, Wendy, *Undoing the Demos: Neoliberalism's Stealth Revolution* (New York: Zone Books, 2015).

Brown, Wendy, Peter E. Gordon and Max Pensky, *Authoritarianism: Three Inquiries in Critical Theory* (Chicago: University Chicago Press, 2018).

Calabrese, Omar, *Neo-Baroque: A Sign of the Times*, trans. Charles Lambert (Princeton: Princeton University Press, 1992).

Casarino, Cesare, 'Grammars of Conatus: Or, On the Primacy of Resistance in Spinoza, Foucault, and Deleuze', in Kiarina Kordela and Dimitris Vardoulakis (eds), *Spinoza's Authority, Volume 1: Resistance and Power in the* Ethics (London: Bloomsbury, 2018), 57–85.

Caygill, Howard, *Levinas and the Political* (London: Routledge, 2002).

Caygill, Howard, *On Resistance: A Philosophy of Defiance* (London: Bloomsbury, 2013).

Cicero, *De Legibus*, trans. Clinton W. Keyes (Cambridge, MA: Harvard University Press, 1928).

Cicero, *De Finibus Bonorum et Malorum*, trans. H. Rackham (Cambridge, MA: Harvard University Press, 1931).

Clark, Andrew (ed.), *Brief Lives, Chiefly of Contemporaries, set down by John Aubrey, Between the Years 1669 and 1696* (Oxford: Clarendon Press, 1898).

Clastres, Pierre, *Society Against the State: Essays in Political Anthropology*, trans. Robert Hurley and Abe Stein (New York: Zone Books, 1989).

Clemens, Justin, 'Spinoza's Ass', in Dimitris Vardoulakis (ed.), *Spinoza Now* (Minneapolis: University of Minnesota Press, 2011), 65–95.

Cohen, Herman, *Spinoza on State and Religion, Judaism and Christianity*, trans. Robert Schine (Jerusalem: Shalem, 2014 [1915]).

Coles, Romand, and Lia Haro, 'Understanding Neo-Fascism (Part 1): Trump-shock and Resonant Violence Five Theses for Comprehending

Trumpian Fascism', *Public Seminar*, 17 February 2017, available at <http://www.publicseminar.org/2017/02/understanding-neo-fascism-part-1>

Coles, Romand, and Lia Haro, 'Responding to Neo-Fascism (Part 2): Full-bodied Democratic Power Six Theses for a Robust Resistance to Trumpian Fascism', *Public Seminar*, 21 February 2017, available at <http://www.publicseminar.org/2017/02/responding-to-neo-fascism-part-2>

Collingwood, R. G., *The Idea of History* (Oxford: Clarendon, 1994).

Connolly, William E., *Identity/Difference: Democratic Negotiations of Political Paradox* (Minneapolis: University of Minnesota Press, 2002).

Connolly, William E., *Neuropolitics: Thinking, Culture, Speed* (Minneapolis: University of Minnesota Press, 2002).

Connolly, William E., *A World of Becoming* (Durham, NC: Duke University Press, 2011).

Curley, Edwin '"I Durst Not Write So Boldly", or How to Read Hobbes' Theological-Political Treatise', in Daniela Bostrenghi (ed.), *Hobbes e Spinoza, Scienza e Politica* (Naples: Bibliopolis, 1992), 497–593.

de La Boétie, Étienne, *The Discourse of Voluntary Servitude (Or, Against One)*, trans. James B. Atkinson and David Sices (Indianapolis: Hackett, 2012).

de Vries, Hent, 'Levinas, Spinoza, and the Theological-Political Meaning of Scripture', in Hent de Vries and Lawrence E. Sullivan (eds), *Political Theologies: Public Religions in a Post-Secular World* (New York: Fordham University Press, 2006), 232–48.

DeBrabander, Firmin, *Spinoza and the Stoics: Power, Politics and the Passions* (London: Bloomsbury, 2008).

del Lucchese, Filippo, *Conflict, Power, and Multitude in Machiavelli and Spinoza* (London: Continuum, 2009).

del Lucchese, Filippo, 'Machiavelli and Constituent Power: The Revolutionary Foundation of Modern Political Thought', *European Journal of Political Theory* 16.1 (2017), 3–23.

Deleuze, Gilles, *Spinoza: Practical Philosophy*, trans. Robert Hurley (San Francisco: City Lights, 1988).

Deleuze, Gilles, *The Logic of Sense*, trans. Charles Stivale (New York: Columbia University Press, 1990).

Deleuze, Gilles, *Expressionism in Philosophy: Spinoza*, trans. Martin Joughin (New York: Zone Books, 1992).

Deleuze, Gilles, and Félix Guattari, *Anti-Oedipus: Capitalism & Schizophrenia*, trans. R. Hurley et al. (London: Athlone Press, 2000).

Deleuze, Gilles, and Félix Guattari, *A Thousand Plateaus: Capitalism and Schizophrenia*, trans. Brian Massumi (London: Continuum, 2003).

Della Rocca, Michael, *Spinoza* (New York: Routledge, 2008).

Derrida, Jacques, 'Plato's Pharmacy', in *Dissemination*, trans. Barbara Johnson (London: Athlone, 1981), 61–171.
Derrida, Jacques, 'Violence and Metaphysics: An Essay on the Thought of Emmanuel Levinas', in *Writing and Difference*, trans. Allan Bass (London: Routledge, 2002), 97–192.
Derrida, Jacques, 'Faith and Knowledge: The Two Sources of "Religion" at the Limits of Reason Alone', trans. Samuel Weber, in Gil Anidjar (ed.), *Acts of Religion* (London: Routledge, 2002), 42–101.
Derrida, Jacques, and Giovanna Borradori, 'Autoimmunity: Real and Symbolic Suicides', in Giovanna Borradori, *Philosophy in a Time of Terror: Dialogues with Jürgen Habermas and Jacques Derrida* (Chicago: University of Chicago Press, 2003), 85–136.
Diogenes Laertius, *Lives of Eminent Philosophers*, trans. R. D. Hicks (Cambridge, MA: Harvard University Press, 1931).
Doueihi, Milad, *Augustine and Spinoza*, trans. Jane Marie Todd (Cambridge, MA: Harvard University Press, 2010).
Dumézil, Georges, *Mitra-Varuna: An Essay on Two Indo-European Representations of Sovereignty*, trans. Derek Coltman (New York: Zone Books, 1988).
Edmundson, William A., 'Political Authority, Moral Powers and the Intrinsic Value of Obedience', *Oxford Journal of Legal Studies* 30.1 (2010), 179–91.
Estop, Juan Domingo Sanchez, 'Beyond Legitimacy: The State as an Imaginary Entity in Spinoza's Political Ontology', in Kiarina Kordela and Dimitris Vardoulakis (eds), *Spinoza's Authority, Volume 1: Resistance and Power in the* Ethics (London: Bloomsbury, 2018), 87–111.
Fitzmaurice, Andrew, 'The Genealogy of *Terra Nullius*', *Australian Historical Studies* 129 (2007), 1–15.
Fothergill-Payne, Louise, 'Seneca's Role in Popularizing Epicurus in the Sixteenth Century', in Margaret Olser (ed.), *Atoms, Pneuma, and Tranquillity: Epicurean and Stoic Themes in European Thought* (Cambridge: Cambridge University Press, 1991), 115–33.
Foucault, Michael, 'The Subject and Power', in Hubert L. Dreyfus and Paul Rabinow (eds), *Michel Foucault: Beyond Structuralism and Hermeneutics*, 2nd edn (Chicago: University of Chicago Press, 1983), 208–26.
Foucault, Michael, *The Will to Power*, vol. 1 of *The History of Sexuality*, trans. Robert Hurley (London: Penguin, 1990).
Foucault, Michael, *The Order of Things: An Archaeology of the Human Sciences* (London: Routledge, 2002).

Foucault, Michael, *Society Must be Defended*, trans. David Macey (New York: Picador, 2003).

Foucault, Michael, *The Birth of Biopolitics: Lectures at the Collège de France, 1978–79*, ed. Michel Senellart, trans. Graham Burchell (New York: Palgrave Macmillan, 2008).

Fraenkel, Carlos, 'Spinoza on Philosophy and Religion: The Averroistic Sources', in Carlos Fraenkel, Dario Perinetti and Justin Smith (eds), *The Rationalists: Between Tradition and Innovation* (Dordrecht: Springer, 2010), 27–44.

Fraenkel, Carlos, *Philosophical Religions from Plato to Spinoza: Reason, Religion, and Autonomy* (Cambridge: Cambridge University Press, 2012).

Fraenkel, Carlos, 'Reconsidering the Case of Elijah Delmedigo's Averroism and Its Impact on Spinoza', in A. Akasoy and G. Giglioni (eds), *Renaissance Averroism and Its Aftermath: Arabic Philosophy in Early Modern Europe* (Dordrecht: Springer, 2013), 213–36.

Freud, Sigmund, *Civilization and its Discontents* (Harmondsworth: Penguin, 1991).

Frost, Samantha, *Lessons from a Materialist Thinker: Hobbesian Reflections on Ethics and Politics* (Stanford: Stanford University Press, 2008).

Furley, David, *The Greek Cosmologists: The Formation of Atomic Theory and its Earliest Critics* (Cambridge: Cambridge University Press, 1987).

Gadamer, Georg, *Truth and Method*, rev. trans. Joel Weinsheimer and Donald G. Marshall (New York: Continuum, 1989).

Gatens, Moira, and Genevieve Lloyd, *Collective Imaginings: Spinoza, Past and Present* (London: Routledge, 1999).

Gombrich, E. H., *Art and Illusion: A Study in the Psychology of Pictorial Representation* (London: Phaidon, 1984).

Gourgouris, Stathis, *Lessons in Secular Criticism* (New York: Fordham University Press, 2013).

Gourgouris, Stathis, 'Arche', in J. M. Bernstein, Adi Ophir and Ann Stoler (eds), *Political Concepts: A Critical Lexicon* (New York: Fordham University Press, 2018), 5–24.

Gourgouris, Stathis, *The Perils of the One* (New York: Columbia University Press, 2019).

Greenblatt, Stephen, *The Swerve: How the World Became Modern* (New York: Norton, 2011).

Grotius, Hugo, 'De republica emendanda/On the Emendation of the Dutch Polity', *Grotiana* 5 (1984), 66–121.

Guena, Marco, 'The Tension Between Law and Politics in the Modern Republican Tradition', in Andreas Niederberger and Philipp Schink (eds),

Republican Democracy: Liberty, Law and Politics (Edinburgh: Edinburgh University Press, 2013), 5–40.

Guyau, Jean-Marie, *La Morale d'Épicure et ses rapports avec les doctrines contemporaines* (Paris: Librairie Germer Baillière, 1878).

Guyau, Jean-Marie, *La morale anglaise contemporaine: Morale de l'utilité et de l'évolution* (Paris: Librairie Germer Baillière, 1879).

Guyau, Jean-Marie, 'Spinoza: A Synthesis of Epicureanism and Stoicism', trans. Frederico Testa, *Parrhesia* 32 (2020), 33–44.

Hadot, Pierre, *What is Ancient Philosophy?*, trans. Michael Chase (Cambridge, MA: Harvard University Press, 2004).

Hammill, Graham, *The Mosaic Constitution: Political Theology and Imagination from Machiavelli to Milton* (Chicago: University of Chicago Press, 2012).

Hardt, Michael, and Antonio Negri, *Empire* (Cambridge, MA: Harvard University Press, 2000).

Hardt, Michael, and Antonio Negri, *Multitude: War and Democracy in the Age of Empire* (New York: Penguin, 2004).

Hart, H. L. A., *The Concept of Law* (Oxford: Oxford University Press, 1961).

Hegel, G. W. F., *Lectures on the History of Philosophy*, trans. E. S. Haldane and Frances H. Simson (London: Kegan Paul, 1895).

Hegel, G. W. F., *Faith and Knowledge*, trans. Walter Cerf and H. S. Harris (Albany: SUNY Press, 1977).

Hegel, G. W. F., *Lectures on Logic, Berlin, 1831*, trans. Clark Butler (Bloomington: Indiana University Press, 2008).

Heidegger, Martin, *Plato's Sophist*, trans. Richard Rojcewicz and Andre Schuwer (Bloomington: Indiana University Press, 1997).

Hesiod, *Theogony; Works and Days; Testimonia*, trans. Glenn W. Most (Cambridge, MA: Harvard University Press, 2006).

Hill, Mike, and Warren Montag, *The Other Adam Smith* (Stanford: Stanford University Press, 2015).

Hirschman, Albert O., *The Passions and the Interests: Political Arguments for Capitalism Before its Triumph* (Princeton: Princeton University Press, 1997).

Hobbes, Thomas, *Leviathan*, ed. Richard Tuck (Cambridge: Cambridge University Press, 1999).

Hobbes, Thomas, *On the Citizen*, ed. Richard Tuck and Michael Silverthorne (Cambridge: Cambridge University Press, 2003).

Honig, Bonnie, *Public Things: Democracy in Disrepair* (New York: Fordham University Press, 2017).

Huemer, Michael, *The Problem of Political Authority: An Examination of the Right to Coerce and the Duty to Obey* (New York: Palgrave, 2013).

Israel, Jonathan, *Radical Enlightenment: Philosophy and the Making of Modernity 1650–1750* (Oxford: Oxford University Press, 2001).

Jacobi, Friedrich Heinrich, *The Main Philosophical Writings and the Novel Allwill*, trans. George di Giovanni (Montreal: McGill-Queen's University Press, 1994).

James, Susan, *Spinoza on Philosophy, Religion, and Politics: The Theologico-Political Treatise* (Oxford: Oxford University Press, 2012).

Jones, Howard, *The Epicurean Tradition* (London: Routledge, 1992).

Josephus, Flavius, *Against Apion*, trans. Henry St. John Thackeray (Cambridge, MA: Harvard University Press, 1926).

Kalimtzis, Kostas, *Aristotle on Political Enmity and Disease: An Inquiry into Stasis* (New York: State University of New York Press, 2000).

Kant, Immanuel, *Religion and Rational Theology*, trans. Allen W. Wood and George Di Giovanni (Cambridge: Cambridge University Press, 1996).

Kant, Immanuel, *Practical Philosophy*, ed. and trans. Mary Gregor (Cambridge: Cambridge University Press, 2001).

Klibansky, Raymond, Erwin Panofsky and Fritz Saxl, *Saturn and Melancholy: Studies in the History of Natural Philosophy, Religion and Art* (Nendeln/Liechtenstein: KRAUS Reprint, 1979).

Kojève, Alexandre, *The Notion of Authority (A Brief Presentation)*, ed. François Terré, trans. Hager Weslati (London: Verso, 2014).

Kujula, William, and Burles, Regan, 'The Politics of Ethics: Spinoza and New Materialisms', *Theory & Event* 23.1 (2020), 145–65.

Lambert, Gregg, *On the (New) Baroque* (Aurora, CO: Davies Publishing Group, 2008).

Lambert, Gregg, 'Spinoza and Signs: The Two Covenants and Authority in the *Theological-Political Treatise*', in Kiarina Kordela and Dimitris Vardoulakis (eds), *Spinoza's Authority, Volume 2: Power and Resistance in the Treatises* (London: Bloomsbury, 2018), 153–66.

Lange, Friedrich, *Geschichte des Materialismus und Kritik seiner Bedeutung in der Gegenwart* (Iserlohn: Baedeker [1866], 2nd rev. edn 1887).

Lee, Richard, *The Thought of Matter: Materialism, Conceptuality and the Transcendence of Immanence* (London: Rowan & Littlefield, 2016).

Levene, Nancy, 'Ethics and Interpretation, or How to Study Spinoza's *Tractatus Theologico-Politicus* without Strauss', *Journal of Jewish Thought and Philosophy* 10 (2000), 57–110.

Levene, Nancy, *Spinoza's Revelation: Religion, Democracy and Reason* (Cambridge: Cambridge University Press, 2004).

Levinas, Emmanuel, *Totality and Infinity: An Essay on Exteriority*, trans. Alphonso Lingis (Pittsburgh: Duquesne University Press, 1969).

Levinas, Emmanuel, *Otherwise than Being or Beyond Essence*, trans. Alphonso Lingis (Dordrecht: Kluwer, 1991).
Levinas, Emmanuel, *Beyond the Verse: Talmudic Readings and Lectures*, trans. Gary D. Mole (Bloomington: Indiana University Press, 1994).
Levinas, Emmanuel, *In the Time of the Nations*, trans. Michael B. Smith (Bloomington: Indiana University Press, 1994).
Levinas, Emmanuel, *Proper Names*, trans. Michael B. Smith (Stanford: Stanford University Press, 1996).
Levinas, Emmanuel, *Difficult Freedom: Essays on Judaism*, trans. Seàn Hand (Baltimore: Johns Hopkins University Press, 1997).
Levinas, Emmanuel, *Alterity and Transcendence*, trans. Michael B. Smith (London: Athlone, 1999).
Levinas, Emmanuel, *God, Death, and Time*, trans. Betina Bergo (Stanford: Stanford University Press, 2000).
Lezra, Jacques, and Liza Blake (eds), *Lucretius and Modernity: Epicurean Encounters* (London: Palgrave, 2016).
'*Little Children are Sacred*': *Report of the Northern Territory Board of Inquiry into the Protection of Aboriginal Children from Sexual Abuse*, available at <http://www.inquirysaac.nt.gov.au/pdf/bipacsa_final_report.pdf>
Locke, John, 'An Essay on Toleration', in *Political Essays*, ed. Mark Goldie (Cambridge: Cambridge University Press, 1997), 134–59.
Loraux, Nicole, *The Divided City: On Memory and Forgetting in Ancient Athens*, trans. Corinne Pache and Jeff Fort (New York: Zone, 2006).
Lord, Beth (ed.), *Spinoza's Philosophy of Ratio* (Edinburgh: Edinburgh University Press, 2018).
Lordon, Frédéric, *Willing Slaves of Capital: Spinoza and Marx on Desire*, trans. Gabriel Ash (London: Verso, 2014).
Lucretius, *On the Nature of Things*, trans. W. H. D. Rouse, rev. Martin F. Smith (Cambridge, MA: Harvard University Press, 1924).
Macherey, Pierre, *Hegel or Spinoza*, trans. Susan M. Ruddick (Minneapolis: University of Minnesota Press, 2011).
Machiavelli, Niccolò, *The Prince*, ed. Quentin Skinner and Russell Price (Cambridge: Cambridge University Press, 1988 [1513]).
Machiavelli, Niccolò, *Discourses on the First Decade of Titus Livius*, trans. Allan Gilbert, in *Machiavelli: The Chief Works and Others*, vol. 1 (Durham, NC: Duke University Press, 1989).
Mack, Michael, *Spinoza and the Specters of Modernity: The Hidden Enlightenment of Diversity from Spinoza to Freud* (London: Bloomsbury, 2010).
MacPherson, C. B., *The Political Theory of Possessive Individualism: Hobbes to Locke* (Oxford: Oxford University Press, 1962).

Malabou, Catherine, 'Before and Above: Spinoza and Symbolic Necessity', *Critical Inquiry* 43 (2016), 84–109.

Marcuse, Herbert, *A Study on Authority*, in *Studies in Critical Philosophy*, trans. Joris de Bres (Boston: Beacon Press, 1973).

Martel, James, *Subverting the Leviathan: Reading Thomas Hobbes as a Radical Democrat* (New York: Columbia University Press, 2007).

Martel, James, 'Hobbes and Spinoza on Scriptural Interpretation, the Hebrew Republic and the Deconstruction of Sovereignty', in Kiarina Kordela and Dimitris Vardoulakis (eds), *Spinoza's Authority, Volume 2: Resistance and Power in the Political Treatises* (London: Bloomsbury, 2018), 67–100.

Martinich, A., 'Interpreting the Religion of Thomas Hobbes: An Exchange: Hobbes's Erastianism and Interpretation', *Journal of the History of Ideas* 70.1 (2009), 143–63.

Marx, Karl, *Grundrisse*, trans. Ernst Wangermann, in *Collected Works*, vol. 28 (New York: International Publishers, 1976).

Marx, Karl, *Capital, Volume 1*, in *Collected Works*, vol. 35 (New York: International Publishers, 1976).

Massumi, Brian, *What Animals Teach us about Politics* (Durham, NC: Duke University Press, 2014).

Massumi, Brian, *Politics of Affect* (Cambridge: Polity, 2015).

Matheron, Alexandre, *Individu et Communauté chez Spinoza* (Paris: Minuit, 1969).

Matheron, Alexandre, 'The Theoretical Function of Democracy in Spinoza and Hobbes', in Warren Montag and Ted Stolze (eds), *The New Spinoza* (Minneapolis: University of Minnesota Press, 1997), 206–17.

Melamed, Yitzhak, 'Acosmism or Weak Individuals? Hegel, Spinoza, and the Reality of the Finite', *Journal of the History of Philosophy* 48.1 (2010), 77–92.

Melamed, Yitzhak, 'Why Spinoza is Not an Eleatic Monist (Or Why Diversity Exists)', in Philip Goff (ed.), *Spinoza on Monism* (London: Palgrave, 2011), 206–22.

Mill, John Stuart, 'Utilitarianism', in *The Collected Works of John Stuart Mill*, ed. John M. Robson (Toronto: University of Toronto Press, 1982), vol. 10.

Milner, Jean-Claude, *Le sage trompeur: Libres raisonnements sur Spinoza et les Juifs. Court traité de lecture 1* (Paris: Verdier, 2013).

Mitsis, Phillip, 'Cicero on Epicurean Friendship: A Reappraisal', *Politeia* 1.2 (2019), 109–23.

Moder, Gregor, *Hegel and Spinoza: Substance and Negativity* (Evanston: Northwestern University Press, 2017).

Montag, Warren, *Bodies, Masses, Power: Spinoza and his Contemporaries* (London: Verso, 1999).
Montag, Warren, 'Who's Afraid of the Multitude? Between the Individual and the State', *South Atlantic Quarterly* 104.4 (2005), 655–73.
Montag, Warren, 'Lucretius Hebraizant: Spinoza's Reading of Ecclesiastes', *European Journal of Philosophy* 20.1 (2012), 109–29.
Montag, Warren, *Althusser and his Contemporaries: Philosophy's Perpetual War* (Durham, NC: Duke University Press, 2013).
Montag, Warren, 'From Clinamen to Conatus: Deleuze, Lucretius, Spinoza', in Jacques Lezra and Liza Blake (eds), *Lucretius and Modernity: Epicurean Encounters* (London: Palgrave, 2016), 163–72.
Moreau, Pierre-François, *Spinoza et le Spinozisme* (Paris: PUF, 2014).
Morfino, Vittorio, 'Tra Lucrezio e Spinoza: La "filosofia" di Machiavelli', in Stefano Visentin et al. (eds), *Machiavelli: immaginazione e contingenza* (Pisa: ETS, 2006).
Morfino, Vittorio, *Plural Temporality: Transindividuality and the Aleatory Between Spinoza and Althusser* (Leiden: Brill, 2014).
Morfino, Vittorio, 'The Five Theses of Machiavelli's "Philosophy"', in Filippo Del Lucchese, Fabio Frosini and Vittorio Morfino (eds), *The Radical Machiavelli: Politics, Philosophy and Language* (Leiden: Brill, 2015), 145–73.
Morfino, Vittorio, 'Memory, Chance and Conflict: Machiavelli in the *Theologico-Political Treatise*', in Kiarina Kordela and Dimitris Vardoulakis (eds), *Spinoza's Authority, Volume 2: Resistance and Power in the Political Treatises* (London: Bloomsbury, 2018), 7–26.
Morfino, Vittorio, *The Spinoza-Machiavelli Encounter: Time and Occasion*, trans. Dave Mesing (Edinburgh: Edinburgh University Press, 2019).
Murphy, Timothy S., *Antonio Negri: Modernity and the Multitude* (Cambridge: Polity, 2012).
Naas, Michael, *Miracle and Machine: Jacques Derrida and the Two Sources of Religion, Science, and the Media* (New York: Fordham University Press, 2012).
Nadler, Steven, *Spinoza: A Life* (Cambridge: Cambridge University Press, 1999).
Nadler, Steven, *A Book Forged in Hell: Spinoza's Scandalous Treatise and the Birth of the Secular Age* (Princeton: Princeton University Press, 2011).
Nail, Thomas, *Lucretius I: An Ontology of Motion* (Edinburgh: Edinburgh University Press, 2018).
Negri, Antonio, *The Savage Anomaly: The Power of Spinoza's Metaphysics and Politics*, trans. Michael Hardt (Minneapolis: University of Minnesota Press, 1991).

Negri, Antonio, *Insurgencies: Constituent Power and the Modern State*, trans. Maurizia Boscagli (Minneapolis: University of Minnesota Press, 1999).

Negri, Antonio, *Subversive Spinoza: (Un)contemporary Variations*, trans. Timothy S. Murphy et al. (Manchester: Manchester University Press, 2004).

Negri, Antonio, *The Political Descartes: Reason, Ideology, and the Bourgeois Project*, trans. Matteo Mandarini and Alberto Toscano (London: Verso, 2006).

Negri, Antonio, 'Spinoza: A Different Power to Act', trans. Giuseppina Mecchia, in Kiarina Kordela and Dimitris Vardoulakis (eds), *Spinoza's Authority, Volume 1: Resistance and Power in the* Ethics (London: Bloomsbury, 2018), 135–45.

Nelson, Eric, *The Hebrew Republic: Jewish Sources and the Transformation of European Political Thought* (Cambridge, MA: Harvard University Press, 2010).

Nietzsche, Friedrich, *On the Genealogy of Morality and Other Writings*, ed. Keith Ansell-Pearson, trans. Carol Diethe (Cambridge: Cambridge University Press, 2006).

Norris, Christopher, 'Spinoza and the Conflict of Interpretations', in Dimitris Vardoulakis (ed.), *Spinoza Now* (Minneapolis: University of Minnesota Press, 2011), 3–37.

O'Rourke Boyle, Marjorie, *Christening Pagan Mysteries: Erasmus in Pursuit of Wisdom* (Toronto: University of Toronto Press, 1981).

Oxford Latin Dictionary, ed. P. G. W. Glare (Oxford: Clarendon Press, 1968).

Pascoe, Bruce, *Dark Emu: Aboriginal Australia and the Birth of Agriculture* (Broome: Magabala Books, 2014).

Perche, Diana, 'Ten Years On, It's Time we Learned the Lessons from the Failed Northern Territory Intervention', *The Conversation*, 26 June 2017, available at <http://theconversation.com/ten-years-on-its-time-we-learned-the-lessons-from-the-failed-northern-territory-intervention-79198>

Plato, *Republic*, trans. Paul Shorey (Cambridge, MA: Harvard University Press, 2003).

Pocock, J. G. A., *The Machiavellian Moment: Florentine Political Thought and the Atlantic Republican Tradition* (Princeton: Princeton University Press, 1975).

Polios, Michael-Francis, 'Natural Right and the Failure to Calculate: The Paradox of the Slave in Spinoza's *Tractatus-Theologico Politicus*', *Parrhesia* 32 (2020), 233–52.

Polybius, *The Histories*, trans. W. R. Paton (Cambridge, MA: Harvard University Press, 1979).
Preus, Samuel, 'A Hidden Opponent in Spinoza's *Tractatus*', *Harvard Theological Review* 88 (1995), 361–88.
Preus, Samuel, *Spinoza and the Irrelevance of Biblical Authority* (Cambridge: Cambridge University Press, 2001).
Proietti, Omero, '"Adulescens luxu perditus": Classici latini nell'opera di Spinoza', *Rivista di Filosofia Neo-Scolastica* 77.2 (1985), 210–57.
Prokhovnik, Raia, *Spinoza and Republicanism* (Basingstoke: Palgrave Macmillan, 2004).
Raz, Joseph, *The Authority of Law: Essays on Law and Morality* (Oxford: Oxford University Press, 1979).
Read, Jason, *The Politics of Transindividuality* (Leiden: Brill, 2016).
Ricoeur, Paul, 'The Paradox of Authority', in *Reflections on the Just*, trans. David Pellauer (Chicago: Chicago University Press, 2007), 91–105.
Rosenthal, Michael A., 'Why Spinoza Chose the Hebrews: The Exemplary Function of Prophecy in the *Theological-Political Treatise*', in Heidi M. Ravven and Lenn E. Goodman (eds), *Jewish Themes in Spinoza's Philosophy* (Albany: SUNY, 2002), 225–60.
Ryan, Todd, *Pierre Bayle's Cartesian Metaphysics: Rediscovering Early Modern Philosophy* (New York: Routledge, 2009).
Saar, Martin, *Die Immanenz der Macht: Politische Theorie nach Spinoza* (Frankfurt a.M.: Suhrkamp, 2013).
Sabar, Shalom, 'Between Calvinists and Jews: Hebrew Script in Rembrandt's Art', in Mitchell B. Merback (ed.), *Beyond the Yellow Badge: Anti-Judaism and Antisemitism in Medieval and Early Modern Visual Culture* (Leiden: Brill, 2008), 371–404.
Schama, Simon, *The Embarrassment of Riches: An Interpretation of Dutch Culture in the Golden Age* (New York: Vintage, 1987).
Schmitt, Carl, *Political Theology: Four Chapters on the Concept of Sovereignty*, trans. George D. Schwab (Cambridge, MA: MIT, 1985).
Schmitt, Carl, *The Concept of the Political*, trans. George D. Schwab (Chicago: University of Chicago Press, 1996).
Schmitt, Carl, *The Leviathan in the State Theory of Thomas Hobbes: Meaning and Failure of a Political Symbol*, trans. George Schwab and Erna Hilfstein (Westport, CT: Greenwood Press, 1996).
Sennett, Richard, *Authority* (New York: W.W. Norton, 1980).
Segré, Ivan, *Spinoza: The Ethics of an Outlaw*, trans. David Broder (London: Bloomsbury, 2017).

Sharp, Hasana, *Spinoza and the Politics of Renaturalization* (Chicago: University of Chicago Press, 2011).

Sieyès, Emmanuel Joseph, 'What is the Third Estate?', in *Political Writings*, trans. Michael Sonenscher (Indianapolis: Hackett, 2003).

Skeaff, Christopher, *Becoming Political: Spinoza's Vital Republicanism and the Democratic Power of Judgment* (Chicago: University Chicago Press, 2018).

Smith, Adam, *An Inquiry into the Nature and Causes of the Wealth of Nations*, ed. W.P. Todd, 2 vols in *The Glasgow Edition of the Works and Correspondence of Adam Smith*, vol. 2, ed. R. H Campbell and A. S. Skinner (Oxford: Oxford University Press, 1976).

Smith, Steven B., *Spinoza, Literalism, and the Question of Jewish Identity* (New Haven: Yale University Press, 1997).

Spinoza, *Theological-Political Treatise*, ed. Jonathan Israel, trans. Michael Silverthorne and Jonathan Israel (Cambridge: Cambridge University Press, 2007).

Spinoza, *Theological-Political Treatise*, ed. and trans. Edwin Curley, in *The Collected Works of Spinoza*, vol. 2 (Princeton: Princeton University Press, 2016).

Sreedhar, Suzanne, *Hobbes on Resistance: Defying the Leviathan* (Cambridge: Cambridge University Press, 2010).

Stetter, Jack, 'Spinoza and Judaism in the French Context: The Case of Milner's *Le sage trompeur*', *Modern Judaism* (forthcoming).

Strauss, Leo, *Natural Right and History* (Chicago: University of Chicago Press, 1953).

Strauss, Leo, *Spinoza: Seminar on the Theological Political Treatise, University of Chicago 1959*, transcript available at <https://issuu.com/bouvard6/docs/leo_strauss_-_spinoza_1959>

Strauss, Leo, *The Political Philosophy of Hobbes: Its Basis and its Genesis*, trans. Elsa M. Sinclair (Chicago: University of Chicago Press, 1963).

Strauss, Leo, *Spinoza's Critique of Religion* (New York: Schocken, 1965).

Strauss, Leo, 'Notes on Lucretius', in *Liberalism Ancient and Modern* (Chicago: University of Chicago Press, 1967), 76–139.

Strauss, Leo, *Persecution and the Art of Writing* (Chicago: University of Chicago Press, 1988).

Strauss, Leo, *Hobbes' Critique of Religion and Related Writings*, trans Gabriel Bartlett and Svetozar Minkov (Chicago: University of Chicago Press, 2011)

van Bunge, Wiep, *From Stevin to Spinoza: An Essay on Philosophy in the Seventeenth-Century Dutch Republic* (Leiden: Brill, 2001).

Vardoulakis, Dimitris, 'Stasis: Beyond Political Theology?', *Cultural Critique* 73 (2009), 125–47.
Vardoulakis, Dimitris, *The Doppelgänger: Literature's Philosophy* (New York: Fordham University Press, 2010).
Vardoulakis, Dimitris (ed.), *Spinoza Now* (Minneapolis: University of Minnesota Press, 2011).
Vardoulakis, Dimitris, 'Spinoza's Empty Law: The Possibility of Political Theology', in Beth Lord (ed.), *Spinoza Beyond Philosophy* (Edinburgh: Edinburgh University Press, 2012), 135–48.
Vardoulakis, Dimitris, *Sovereignty and its Other: Toward the Dejustification of Violence* (New York: Fordham University Press, 2013).
Vardoulakis, Dimitris, 'The Freedom to Lie', *Philosophy Today* 58.2 (2014), 141–62.
Vardoulakis, Dimitris, 'Was Donald Trump Elected Because He Is Laughable? Reflections on Trump and Sovereignty', *Public Seminar*, 12 December 2016, available at <www.publicseminar.org/2016/12/was-donald-trump-elected-because-he-is-laughable>
Vardoulakis, Dimitris, *Freedom from the Free Will: On Kafka's Laughter* (Albany: SUNY, 2016).
Vardoulakis, Dimitris, 'Stasis: Notes Toward Agonist Democracy', *Theory & Event* 20.3 (2017), 699–725.
Vardoulakis, Dimitris, 'Autoimmunities: Derrida, Democracy and Political Theology', *Research in Phenomenology* 48 (2018), 29–56.
Vardoulakis, Dimitris, 'Conflict as the Quasi-Transcendental: Or, Why Spinoza's *Theological Political Treatise* Matters for Transindividuality', *Australasian Philosophical Review* 2.1 (2018), 107–12.
Vardoulakis, Dimitris, 'Equality and Power: Spinoza's Reformulation of the Aristotelian Tradition of Egalitarianism', in Kiarina Kordela and Dimitris Vardoulakis (eds), *Spinoza's Authority, Volume 1: Resistance and Power in the* Ethics (London: Bloomsbury, 2018), 11–31.
Vardoulakis, Dimitris, *Stasis Before the State: Nine Theses on Agonistic Democracy* (New York: Fordham University Press, 2018).
Vardoulakis, Dimitris, 'Neoepicureanism', *Philosophy Today* 63.4 (2019), 1011–22.
Vardoulakis, Dimitris, *The Ruse of Techne: Heidegger's Metaphysical Materialism* (forthcoming).
Vardoulakis, Dimitris, *Neoepicureanism: Materialism from Antiquity to Neoliberalism* (forthcoming).
Vardoulakis, Dimitris, *Democracy and Violence* (forthcoming).
Vardoulakis, Dimitris, and Kiarina Kordela, 'Introduction', in *Spinoza's*

Authority, Volume 2: Resistance and Power in the Political Treatises (London: Bloomsbury, 2018), 1–6.

Vogl, Josef, *The Specter of Capital*, trans. Joachim Redner and Robert Savage (Stanford: Stanford University Press, 2015).

von Fritz, Kurt, *The Theory of the Mixed Constitution in Antiquity: A Critical Analysis of Polybius' Political Ideas* (New York: Columbia University Press, 1954).

Warren, James, *Facing Death: Epicurus and his Critics* (Oxford: Oxford University Press, 2004).

Weber, Max, *Economy and Society: An Outline of Interpretative Sociology*, ed. Guenther Roth and Claus Wittich (Berkeley: University of California Press, 1978).

Weber, Max, *The Protestant Ethic and the Spirit of Capitalism*, trans. Talcott Parsons (London: Routledge, 2001).

Weber, Max, *The Vocation Lectures*, ed. David Owen and Tracy B. Strong, trans. Rodney Livingstone (Indianapolis: Hackett, 2004).

Wendt, Fabian, 'Political Authority and the Minimal State', *Social Theory and Practice* 42.1 (2016), 97–122.

Wilson, Catherine, *Epicureanism at the Origins of Modernity* (Oxford: Clarendon Press, 2008).

Wilson, Catherine, *The Pleasure Principle: Epicureanism, A Philosophy for Modern Life* (London: Harper Collins, 2019).

Wittgenstein, Ludwig, *Philosophical Investigations*, trans, G. E. M. Anscombe, P. M. S. Hacker and Joachim Schulte, rev. ed. P. M. S. Hacker and Joachim Schulte (Oxford: Blackwell, 2009).

Wolfe, Charles C., *Materialism: A Historico-Philosophical Introduction* (Cham: Springer, 2016).

Wolff, Robert Paul, *In Defence of Anarchism* (Berkeley: University of California Press, 1998).

Zarka, Yves Charles, *Hobbes and Modern Political Thought*, trans. James Griffith (Edinburgh: Edinburgh University Press, 2018).

Žižek, Slavoj, Eric L. Santer and Kenneth Reinhard, *The Neighbor: Three Inquiries in Political Theology* (Chicago: University of Chicago Press, 2005).

Index

Agamben, Giorgio, 28, 118, 119
Althusser, Louis, 21–2, 176–7, 251, 275
Annas, Julia, 63n31
Arendt, Hannah
  Authority, 25, 122–9
  Between Past and Future, 122–3, 132
  On Revolution, 130–1
  On Violence, 131–2, 139n54, 183, 294
  Origins, 129–30
  The Human Condition, 124, 130
  The Origins of Totalitarianism, 41–3
  What is Freedom, 134n48
Aristotle, 6, 14, 32–3, 52–3, 69, 241, 279
Augustine, 134, 137
Averroes, 180–1

Badiou, Alain, 190
Balibar, Étienne
  From Individuality to Transindividuality, 209, 211, 215, 219
  Spinoza and Politics, 15, 148, 196, 208–9, 211, 212, 261
  The Politics of Transindividuality, 210, 211, 219, 221–2
Bayle, Pierre, 32, 159–60, 170
Benjamin, Walter, 84
Bentham, Jeremy, 34
Benveniste, Émile, 26
Bhandar Brenna, 120–1
Bol, Ferdinand, 84–6
Brown, Alison, 23–4, 35n62, 148–9
Brown, Christopher, 86n13
Brown, Wendy, 45

Casarino, Cesare, 242
Cicero
  De Finibus, 5, 55, 199–201
  De Legibus, 26, 126, 259
Clastres, Pierre, 149, 153–4
Cohen, Herman, 98
Constant, Benjamin, 246
Curley, Edwin, 112

DeBrabander, Firmin, 230
del Lucchese, Filippo, 102n39, 230
Deleuze, Gilles, 1, 20–1, 29–30, 91, 93–4, 136, 166, 193, 222n26
Deleuze, Gilles and Guattari, Pierre-Félix, 69, 70
Della Rocca, Michael, 37
Democritus, 17n13
Derrida, Jaques, 191, 223
Doueihi, Milad, 136
Dumézil, Georges, 26

Epicurus, 5, 6, 12–14, 27, 51, 53–7, 100–1, 110–11, 144, 168, 217–18, 247, 305

Foucault, Michel
  Birth of Biopolitics, 275
  Order of Things, 227
  Society Must be Defended, 280, 291
  The Subject and Power, 141–2
  Will to Power, 141, 142, 170
Frankel, Carlos, 180

Gadamer, Hans-Georg, 174n1
Gatens, Moira and Lloyd, Genevieve, 56, 121n25, 227

Gourgouris, Stathis, 272
Guyau, Jean-Marie, 22–3

Hamill, Graham, 87
Hardt, Michael and Negri, Michael, 257
Hart, Herbert Lionel Adolphus, 119
Hegel, Georg Wilhelm Friedrich, 103–4n44, 160–1
Heidegger, Martin, 14, 44, 316n18
Hill, Mike and Montag, Warren, 211n10
Hobbes, Thomas
　De Cive, 236–7, 238, 239, 240–1, 243–51, 252
　Leviathan, 100, 118, 145, 148, 245, 252, 287
Honig, Bonnie, 45

Israel, Jonathan, 112

Jacobi, Friedrich Heinrich, 162
James, Susan, 98n30, 180
Josephus, Flavius, 265, 267, 268, 269

Kant, Immanuel, 44, 191, 228, 229, 246
Kojève, Alexandre, 25

La Boétie, Étienne, 68
Lange, Frederick, 1, 1n2, 2, 236
Levene, Nancy, 136
Levinas, Emmanuel, 5, 98, 160n38, 173, 175, 189, 191–5, 197
Lordon, Frédéric, 69–70
Lucretius, 4, 16, 59–61, 62–5, 66, 89, 100, 149, 176, 179
Luther, Martin, 27

Macherey, Pierre, 161
Machiavelli, Nicollo
　Discourses, 26, 88, 226n28, 259, 266, 303
　The Prince, 83, 102, 105, 151, 287
Maimonides, 180–2
Marcus, Herbert, 184, 227, 228
Martel, James, 254
Marx, Karl, 148
Matheron, Alexandre, 234, 254
Mill, John Stuart, 34, 186
Milner, Jean-Claude, 98

Montag, Warren, 158, 176, 177
Moreau, Pierre-François, 48n2
Morfino, Vittorio, 102n43, 247

Nadler, Steven, 299
Negri, Antonio, 1, 88, 101, 166, 211, 216, 232, 249–50, 257–8
Nelson, Eric, 268, 269
Nietzsche, Friedrich, 65n38, 126n34

Pascoe, Bruce, 121
Plato, 71, 72, 233
Polybius, 266
Preus, Samuel, 180
Proietti, Omero, 265n3

Read, Jason, 215–16
Ricoeur, Paul, 26
Rijn, Rembrandt, 86–8
Roselli, Cosimo, 79–81

Schama, Simon, 97
Schmitt, Carl, 27, 71, 118, 120, 182
Segré, Ivan, 98, 110
Sharp, Hassana, 136, 166
Shirley, Samuel, 112
Sieyès, Abbé Emmanuel Joseph, 123n30
Sigmund, Freud, 190
Skaeff, Christopher, 33n59
Smith, Adam, 147
Smith, Steven, 233
Spinoza, Baruch
　Ethics, 2–3, 14, 27–8, 30–1, 33, 34–5, 36, 50, 51, 54, 55, 82–3, 91, 102, 103, 116–17, 133n47, 134, 178, 179, 197–8, 200–1, 207–8, 218, 219, 220–1, 229, 239, 241, 318
　Letters, 10, 16–17, 25, 37, 94, 134, 253–4, 282
　Political Treatise, 26, 140, 156, 254, 259, 266, 282–3, 310, 326–7
　Principles of Cartesian Philosophy, 299
　Treatise of Emendations, 9
Strauss, Leo
　Natural Right and History, 240
　Persecution and the Art of Writing, 165n52
　Spinoza's Critique of Religion, 19–20, 161–6, 170

van Berkel, Abraham, 235
Vogel, Fritz, 266
von Fritz, Kurt, 266

Weber, Max, 41

Wilson, Catherine, 18n17
Wolf, Robert Paul, 246n24

Žižek, Slavoj, 190–1

EU representative:
Easy Access System Europe
Mustamäe tee 50, 10621 Tallinn, Estonia
Gpsr.requests@easproject.com

www.ingramcontent.com/pod-product-compliance
Lightning Source LLC
Chambersburg PA
CBHW071826230426
43672CB00013B/2774